PRAISE FOR *RECOVER TO LIVE*

"Christopher Lawford's *Recover to Live* is not only a personally revealing bible of hope and an encyclopedia for those struggling with addictions and their families, friends, and colleagues, it is a robust anthem to inspire the recovery community to come together to make our nation and this world a better place for all of us."

JOSEPH A. CALIFANO, JR., Founder and Chair,
The National Center on Addiction and Substance Abuse at Columbia University; Former U.S. Secretary of Health, Education, and Welfare

"This is an important book by a genuine and insightful man. He is articulate on his subject and clearly researched it to within an inch of its life. If you don't read it you should buy it and hit yourself on the head with it. Especially if you're reading it on a computer."

RUSSELL BRAND, Actor/Comedian

"Christopher Kennedy Lawford's new book *Recover to Live* will be a force with the power to educate as well as motivate transformational personal change. *Recover to Live* may alter the way broader society looks at the disease of addiction and those who are suffering from it."

DREW PINSKY, MD, Host, *Dr. Drew*

"There's great wisdom, insight, and knowledge in this book. *Recover to Live* will help ease the suffering of addicts and their families. It will help repair broken lives and save some."

DAVID SHEFF, *New York Times* Bestselling Author,
Beautiful Boy: A Father's Journey Through His Son's Addiction

"Personal, documented, and relevant is Christopher Lawford's strong and clear message on the Seven Toxic Compulsions that devastate many lives throughout the world. His new book, *Recover to Live*, addresses the serious matter of dependency. It's a great book for your medicine cabinet."

BOB MARTINEZ, Former Governor of Florida,
Drug Czar under President George H. W. Bush

"The best way to read Christopher Lawford's *Recover to Live* is with a highlighter. Chris's book is filled with such clinical history. Best of all, this book offers hope. Chris Lawford knows about recovery because he's living it."

CHRIS MATTHEWS, Author, *Jack Kennedy:
Elusive Hero*; Anchor, MSNBC's *Hardball*

"No disease ever got the help it needed until people who knew the problem spoke out. Chris Lawford is one of those people who speaks the truth about addiction. Addiction has many faces, and Chris Lawford unmasks the variety of ways addiction is our number one public health problem."

PATRICK CARNES, PHD, CAS, Psychologist and Former Clinical Director of Sexual Disorders Services, The Meadows, Wickenburg, Arizona; Author, *Out of the Shadows*

"*Recover to Live* will give you the best information available about the illness of addiction."

MARTIN SHEEN, Emmy Award-Winning Actor and Activist

"Far too many families have suffered the devastating impacts of addiction, and far too few people have the tools to deal with this fast-growing epidemic. Christopher Lawford's *Recover to Live* gives hope to those who are seeking answers and effective strategies to overcome this life-threatening disease. His personal experience, empathy, and insight make this an indispensable guide to those yearning to break the chains of addiction. I encourage anyone who seeks a clearer understanding of the dangers of addiction and path to recovery to read this compelling and informative work."

REP. MARY BONO MACK, U.S. Rep. (R-Calif.), 2003–present

"*Recover to Live* is a lifeline for anyone drowning in addition. There is hope and a better life is possible."

LAWRENCE KUDLOW, Host, CNBC's *The Kudlow Report*

"One of the clearest and most eloquent voices of our day is in your hands. With *Recover to Live*, Chris Lawford has provided anyone struggling with his or her own nightmare of addiction an immediate guidepost, a clear and simple starting point from which to gain real and lasting help."

PATRICK J. KENNEDY, U.S. Rep. (D-R.I.), 1995–2011; and JIM RAMSTAD, U.S. Rep. (R-Minn.), 1991–2009

"Leave it to Christopher Kennedy Lawford to turn over the addiction rock to find a diamond: recovery. Recovery is a whole lot more than abstinence from addictive behavior; it is a new and less self-centered life that rises from the suffering of addiction. Recovery is the reward of working the 12-Step programs of Alcoholics Anonymous and Narcotics Anonymous and their endless addiction clones. These unique programs are the secret weapons in the war on addiction, and the stars of this story. Here you will find a road map to recovery in the cacophonous voices of 100 diverse experts filtered through the one real expert in this book, Chris Kennedy Lawford."

ROBERT L. DUPONT, MD, First Director, National Institute on Drug Abuse; President, Institute for Behavior and Health, Inc.; Second White House Drug Chief; Clinical Professor of Psychiatry, Georgetown Medical School; Author, *The Selfish Brain: Learning from Addiction*

"Addiction is one of America's dirtiest little secrets, an epidemic running amok not only among adults but also among our children. *Recover to Live* provides a helping hand to anyone whose life or loved one has been hurt by it."

MARIANNE WILLIAMSON, *New York Times* Bestselling Author, *The Age of Miracles*; Founder, The Peace Alliance

"Mr. Lawford's new book *Recover to Live* has a clear and powerful message: Anyone can step out of the shadows of addiction and have a better life."

JACK CANFIELD, Bestselling Author, *Success Principles*; Co-Creator, *Chicken Soup for the Soul* Book Series

"Christopher Lawford lived through addiction and recovery and now shares his journey so that we can all *Recover to Live*. It is simply the best book on addiction I have ever read. It is a gift to anybody who wants the authentic reality of addiction."

PAT O'BRIEN, Host, Fox Sports Radio; Former Host, *The Insider*

"Chris has done it again! His work has made it possible for those of us with an addiction of any kind to see the possibility of having an outstanding life. His work is worthy of a Nobel Prize."

LOUIS GOSSETT, JR., Academy Award and Emmy Award-winning Actor

"Better self-help books offer personal perspective from an author who has personally overcome an illness or a personal problem, as well as a mastery method used by the author. Chris Lawford's *Recover to Live* has elevated the standard of self-help books in two important ways. First, the moving and very real personal stories in this book are not just his but those of many who have experienced or shared the experience of being addicted. More importantly—there is no hype about a magical new way to overcome addiction. Lawford offers eminently sensible and practical advice—and seven different, well-tested coping methods to choose from. The compelling writing style, the veracity of personal experience, and the practical coping choices make this an excellent book for those who are struggling with substance abuse and for those who struggle with them."

A. THOMAS MCLELLAN, PHD, CEO, Treatment Research Institute—Philadelphia PA; Former Deputy Director, White House Office of National Drug Control Policy

"Recover to Live provides the most up to date information available on addiction, treatment, and recovery today; the tools and strategies are proven to work and easy to understand and to apply. I highly recommend it to anyone wanting to deal with an unhealthy habit."

EVGENY M. KRUPITSKY, MD, PHD, D.MED.SCI.; Chief, Laboratory of Clinical Psychopharmacology of Addictions, St. Petersburg State Pavlov Medical University; Chief, Department of Addictions, Bekhterev Research Psychoneurological Institute

"Christopher Kennedy Lawford has made another important contribution to the addiction self-help toolkit. With *Recover to Live*, he has moved from memoir to ministration. Recovering people can now shop from his extensive collection of tips—obtained from the leading experts—that will guide them toward recovery. In addition to background information, the extensive variety of tips assures that *Recover to Live* has something for everyone. Perhaps most importantly, by juxtaposing drug use, gambling, and other excessive behaviors, this book reflects the most current science showing that addiction is a singular disorder with many and varied expressions. *Recover to Live* is a must read for anyone interested in changing behavior."

> HOWARD J. SHAFFER, PHD, CAS, Associate Professor of Psychology, Harvard Medical School; Director, Division on Addiction, The Cambridge Health Alliance, a Harvard Medical School Teaching Affiliate

"ALL you need to know to overcome the grip of any addiction and find recovery . . ."

> WILLIAM C. MOYERS, Author, *Broken*

"Mr. Lawford is one of our most articulate, passionate, and outspoken recovering addicts. As a woman sober for 34 years, I agree with him that recovery is a life-long process and that the tools I learned about how to live a sober life were not easily available in the larger community when I first got sober. The sheer volume of information and extraordinary light that is shed by Lawford's book makes it vital reading for everyone—in and out of recovery, in pain or remembering how that pain felt. The book forces open the doors not only for those suffering from the illness but also their family members—to take their stories to the street, to let the world at large know we are all in this boat on a perilous journey if we do not wake from our dreams of denial and secrecy. Lawford presents his deep examination of these problems with a brilliance that goes to the heart of the national health crisis which bleeds in the wings of our lack of understanding of these illnesses. Bravo! I am Judy Collins, and I am a recovering alcoholic."

> JUDY COLLINS, Grammy Award Winning Singer

"Our country is on the verge of an awakening. Activists like Christopher Lawford are pushing the message to the forefront of our collective consciousness in regards to the disease of chemical dependence and life after recovery. A must read to understand this country's epidemic disease."

> ROBERT L. SHAPIRO, Attorney and Chairman, The Brent Shapiro Foundation For Alcohol and Drug Awareness

"*Recover to Live* exceeds expectations. It is striking in its accessibility and lets us access our own vulnerability and choose a solution that fits our worldview. Lawford has fixed his gaze on this sorry state and made solutions accessible. If you relish shared intellectual exploration, read this book and traverse the chasm between knowledge and experience. Lawford's life and journey have allowed him reception by almost everyone of import to alcoholism and addiction research and treatment and he shares them with the reader. Amazingly, he avoids the turgid prose of the academics he interviews and writes his scholarly work not for scholars but for those who think they have a problem. Lawford has the eye of the historian, the voice of a scientist, the hand of a novelist, and the heart of a healer. Lawford's importance lies not in the accuracy of his analyses but in his ability to influence thought, which is where he does us a service."

ANDREA G. BARTHWELL, MD, FASAM,
Two Dreams Outer Banks and Former Deputy Director for Demand
Reduction at the Office of National Drug Control Policy
under President George H. W. Bush

"*Recover to Live* is without a doubt the most thorough, captivating, and essential book about recovery I've ever read. We addicts are always looking for loopholes, and Mr. Lawford has cleverly covered every aspect of recovery possible. He does this with great respect to the addict, as so many books do not. I sincerely hope *Recover to Live* will be found at every drug rehab, clinic, and AA meeting in the country—it will help save countless lives."

KRISTEN JOHNSTON, Actress; Author, *Guts*

"There are millions of Americans suffering from the disease of addiction and many millions more around the world. H.L. Mencken noted in 1920, 'There is always a well-known solution to every human problem—neat, plausible, and wrong.' There is no simple solution to addiction. Many have been helped by 12-Step groups; many have not. Many have been helped by medications or psychological approaches; many have not. Addicts and those that suffer and struggle with them will find in Chris Lawford's book how he and many others found solutions that worked for them and ways that they might get help. It combines the wisdom of these individuals as well as professionals who have dedicated their lives to aid them with the hope that those who suffer may find in these pages something that works for them."

HERBERT D. KLEBER, MD, Professor of Psychiatry and Director,
Division on Substance Abuse, Columbia University College of Physicians and Surgeons; Former Deputy Director for Demand Reduction,
White House Office of National Drug Control Policy

"Recovery is everywhere. Chances are someone in your family, your neighbor, or a co-worker is in recovery. In *Recover to Live*, you'll find out how and why they decided to get help, the many options there are to get well, and the choices you can make to live a new life, joining the over 23 million Americans in long-term recovery from addiction to alcohol and other drugs."

PATRICIA TAYLOR, Executive Director, Faces & Voices of Recovery

"Integrating his own personal experience with scientific research, Christopher Kennedy Lawford delivers a powerful and life-changing message for people who are seeking recovery and for those already in recovery. The message that sustained long-term recovery from any addictive behavior requires a total transformation in every area of one's life is a message worth sharing. *Recover to Live* offers a holistic approach to recovery that works in conjunction with a 12-Step program and encourages the embracing of, not only healthy behaviors, but life itself. An approach to recovery of this kind is long overdue and I highly recommend this book to people in recovery, their families, and professionals in the field."

KITTY S. HARRIS, PHD, LMFT, LCDC, Director, Center for the Study of Addiction and Recovery, Texas Tech University; Author, *Women & Recovery: Finding Hope*

"Lawford shows us the potential for practicing the principles of recovery in all of our affairs. Unlike self-help books that promote limited methods and techniques to deal with highly specific conditions, *Recover to Live* challenges us to be radically open-minded about the ubiquity of addictions and compulsions in our lives. . . . Solutions are found in collaboration, and Lawford has elicited remarkable cooperation from a broad range of addiction treatment professionals. He clearly has learned from his own recovery the power of asking for help. He has also synthesized the combination of experience in recovery with the best of professional knowledge. . . . Lawford offers those in recovery access to the best of academia, and he offers those in academia the benefit of his own experience, strength, and hope in recovery."

JEFFREY D. ROTH, MD, FASAM, AGPA; Addiction Psychiatrist; Author; Medical Director, Working Sobriety Chicago; Editor, *Journal of Groups in Addiction Recovery*

"Clear and comprehensive overview of addictions and how to get free and healthy from them. Highly recommended!"

CHARLES WHITFIELD, MD, FASAM, Author, *Not Crazy: You May Not Be Mentally Ill* and *Wisdom to Know the Difference: Core Issues in Relationships, Recovery and Living*

CHRISTOPHER KENNEDY LAWFORD

Recover *to* Live

Kick Any Habit, Manage Any Addiction

Your Self-Treatment Guide to Alcohol, Drugs, Eating Disorders, Gambling, Hoarding, Smoking, Sex and Porn

BenBella

BenBella Books, Inc.
Dallas, Texas

BenBella
BenBella Books, Inc.
10300 N. Central Expressway, Suite 530
Dallas, TX 75231
www.benbellabooks.com
Send feedback to feedback@benbellabooks.com

Printed in the United States of America
10 9 8 7 6 5 4 3 1
ISBN 978-1-939529-88-6

**Library of Congress Cataloging-in-Publication Data has cataloged the hardcover
edition as follows:**
Lawford, Christopher Kennedy, 1955-
  Recover to live : kick any habit, manage any addiction / by Christopher Kennedy Lawford.
    pages cm
  ISBN 978-1-936661-96-1 (hardcover)—ISBN 978-1-936661-97-8 (ebook) 1.
Substance abuse—Treatment. 2. Habit breaking. 3. Addicts—Rehabilitation. 4.
Behavior modification. I. Title.
  HV4998.L39 2013
  616.86'06—dc23

                                                                    2012048842

Editing by Brian Nicol
Copyediting by Eric Wechter
Production editing by Chris Gage
Proofreading by Cape Cod Compositors and Jenny Bridges
Front cover design by Kit Sweene
Full cover design by Sarah Dombrowsky
Cover photo by Gina Conte
Text design and composition by Elyse Strongin, Neuwirth & Associates, Inc.
Printed by Berryville Graphics, Inc.

Distributed by Perseus Distribution
perseusdistribution.com
To place orders through Perseus Distribution:
Tel: 800-343-4499
Fax: 800-351-5073
E-mail: orderentry@perseusbooks.com

**Significant discounts for bulk sales are available. Please contact Glenn Yeffeth
at glenn@benbellabooks.com or 214-750-3628.**

This book is dedicated to the men and women who spend their lives searching for answers to the challenges confronted by those struggling with addiction.

CONTENTS

PREFACE

Most busy people try to reduce things to their simplest terms: yes/no, black/white, etc. When it comes to thinking about whether we have a problem, again it is easiest to think simply—either we do have a problem or we don't. An added benefit is that if our simple calculation reveals that we don't have a problem, then we don't have to do anything about it! See how easy?

But it's rarely that simple, and there are hidden costs to oversimplifying issues that are actually complex. The issue of substance-use disorders is such a case. This is a relatively new construct; a continuum of substance use from none at all, through harmful use, to addiction. It is much more complicated. (Why'd they have to go and spoil what had been so easy?)

For the past several centuries there was only one substance-use disorder and that was addiction. Though there were structured methods for determining whether someone was addicted to alcohol or other drugs, in practice it was pretty easy to tell—and happily, even in your wildest periods you could safely assume that your substance-use behaviors did not match up to those of the identified "drunks" or "addicts." Simple, easy, worry-free—but often wrong.

We now know from brain research, genetics, and the epidemiology of substance-use behaviors that substance-use *behavior patterns* are not either/or, nor black/white. It is clearly *not* the case that a person can drink alcohol, freebase cocaine, or inject opioids with impunity as long as they do not cross some addiction threshold. Science has demonstrated that the effects of alcohol and other drug use are cumulative, that they are most pernicious when done early in life (i.e., adolescence), and that there are significant and sometimes long-lasting effects from even relatively low-level use.

These "harmful use" effects can impair performance at work, affect ability to function as a parent or spouse, and be particularly detrimental to the treatment of health problems. These effects can occur without your knowing it and at use levels well below what would put you in the Betty Ford Center. A good example is a young man who enjoys smoking marijuana but just on weekends. This level of use would never qualify as addiction, but if his use begins to interfere with his relationship with his girlfriend, if he is driving within four hours following smoking, or if he is also being treated for asthma, then this qualifies as "harmful use." Similarly, a young woman who has one or two glasses of wine during an evening should not worry that this is alcoholic drinking—it isn't. But if she is having trouble sleeping, if she is taking pain medication, and/or if she is being treated for breast cancer, even this low level of drinking can be harmful. Medical research has shown that alcohol at any dose before bedtime can reduce sleep quality, alcohol and opioids can produce a serious drug-drug interaction, and alcohol use—in any amount—accelerates breast tumor growth.

Now if you're thinking, "Why hasn't anyone told me about this continuum stuff before?" there are two reasons. First, the research is relatively new in this area, but it is nonetheless compelling. More importantly, there has never been anything available for someone who "drinks a little too often" or "uses a little too much." The good news is that most people who fall into this part of the continuum have the capacity to reduce their use and improve their lives without drastic measures. Most people whose use is a little too much do not need a "program." But they could use some practical advice and some tips for self-management and monitoring—and that is the reason for this book: *Recover to Live.*

No matter where you are on the problem behavior continuum, there's room for improvement. Most people can do it without professional help, and even when that help is needed, most people with more serious problems improve and lead happier lives. Hence, this book's subtitle: *Kick Any Habit, Manage Any Addiction.*

Recover to Live was written to help people reach their full potential, no matter where they are on the problem continuum. It has three objectives:

1. Provide the most current and credible information available on addiction and recovery

2. Empower people to believe they can do something about it
3. Shift the paradigm on how society views this brain illness

Within any general behavior class—drinking, taking drugs, shopping/hoarding, gambling, smoking, sex and porn—a lot more people have a bad habit, something they do to harmful/problematic levels, than have an addictive disorder. It's the difference between the "hard drinker" and the "alcoholic" referred to in *The Big Book* of Alcoholics Anonymous. About 22 million Americans are dependent on drugs and/or alcohol, while more than 60 million Americans drink or use drugs in harmful ways that interfere with many aspects of their lives and the lives of the people around them. Here's the good news: You can kick a bad habit—your behavior patterns can be modified to non-harmful levels.

But what if your bad habit has progressed and gotten much more serious, perhaps to the point of addiction? Up until now the prevailing attitudes have been that an addicted person needs to "hit bottom" before he is able to accept help and even hope for successful treatment. Actually, science has demonstrated that recovery from even serious addictions is not simply possible, it is expectable. But just saying no, or abstaining, is only a small part of the solution. The full solution is recovery. Because addictions are chronic brain disorders, what is required is disease management, an ongoing program or regimen of self-care that maximizes the chances that your symptom (active addiction) will

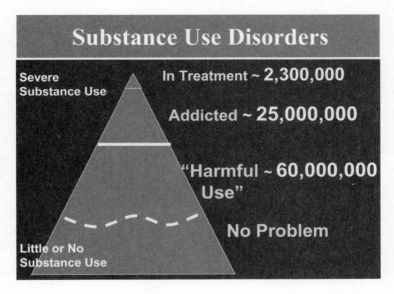

Substance Use Disorders

Severe Substance Use

In Treatment ~ 2,300,000

Addicted ~ 25,000,000

"Harmful ~ 60,000,000 Use"

No Problem

Little or No Substance Use

not recur. Diabetics alter their lifestyles, access professional help, and take insulin if needed to keep their blood sugar in check. The scientifically supported way of dealing with a chronic brain disease is no different than dealing with a chronic physical disease such as diabetes: symptom management through a recovery lifestyle. 12-Step programs, powerlessness notwithstanding, are shining examples of a managed recovery lifestyle.

If any of this rings true for you or for someone you care about, whether you're dealing with a habit or an addiction, then this book may be able to help you. *Recover to Live* not only provides sound recovery tools to *manage* addiction, it also offers sensible strategies to *kick* harmful behavior patterns that have become habits.

Read on.

A. THOMAS MCLELLAN
CEO, Treatment Research Institute, Philadelphia, Pennsylvania

FOREWORD

After many years struggling with addiction, rehab, relapse, and finally recovery, we thought we knew all there was to know about the problem. But we were wrong.

In *Recover to Live*, his latest and best treatise on addiction and recovery, Patrick's cousin, Christopher Kennedy Lawford, has tackled the issue from a kaleidoscope of angles to provide a veritable reference guide, not only for the addicts themselves but also for the families of those battling the disease. The book is a comprehensive source to immediate and sure help.

Through its forthright delivery and clear chapter synopses, *Recover to Live* takes away the mystery, stigma, shame, and marginalization of addiction by providing valuable tools with which to analyze and assess our compulsions. Then it gives expert advice and treatment tools from about 100 of the best and brightest professionals in the field, saving untold time, heartache, and money in the search for answers, guidance, and treatment.

A wise man once said, "At some level we are all addicts." Both of us lived that cruel reality firsthand, and as we read Chris's masterful dismantling and redefining of the disease, we realized the simple truth of those words. We *are* all addicts, and it's often just a matter of degree, self-awareness, and brutal honesty that separates the junkie in the gutter from the functioning alcoholic on Wall Street or in Congress.

We know. We were among them. And because we intimately know this disease, we know the irreplaceable value of early intervention, tough-love support, and compassionate treatment on the long road to recovery.

It took both of us years of roller-coasting through sobriety and relapse to realize that our so-called moral failure was in reality a very physical malady, just as real a malady as cancer, diabetes, or Patrick's asthma. And like asthma or cancer, addiction treatment needs to be focused on healing the brain of its disease, and not merely on "fixing" the addiction.

We in this nation and in many parts of the world are hyperfocused on physical health and fitness, while we ghettoize "mental health" as a separate, but not equal, goal. The two of us have dedicated our professional lives to eradicating that erroneous segregation of the brain from the body.

In 2008 we collaborated on sponsoring the Mental Health Parity and Addiction Equity Act, a bill guaranteeing the dignity of those who struggle with maladies of the mind. Watching the bill pass with bipartisan support was the highlight of our political careers. Eighteen months later, we watched again as President Obama signed health care reform into law—40 years after Patrick's father and Chris's uncle, the late Senator Edward M. Kennedy, first introduced legislation to establish national health care insurance.

And while both bills are law, they are far from reality as various political and corporate entities strive to repeal all forms of government oversight in health care reform. So the fight continues.

Meanwhile, there are millions struggling with the morass of mental illness, from addiction and depression to neurological disorders and traumatic brain injuries, suffering not only from the disease itself, but also from the stigma and stereotype of being labeled with something seen as behavioral, not medical. Society continues to look on mental afflictions as if they were somehow self-inflicted, rather than brutally imposed. It continues to discriminate and disparage, to judge and chastise. "The addict (or the traumatized veteran or the bipolar teenager or the confused elder) is the problem," we are told, ignoring the larger danger of the disease itself.

Thankfully, there are voices of reason in the din. As our population continues to age and decline, as we welcome home hundreds of thousands of war veterans from theaters of indescribable destruction and death with their bodies and brains forever carrying the wounds, and as we see more and more Americans succumb to the ravages of depression and addiction, understanding the brain and its vulnerabilities can't come a moment too soon.

One of the clearest and most eloquent voices of our day is in your hands. With *Recover to Live*, Chris Lawford has provided anyone struggling with his or her own nightmare of addiction an immediate guidepost, a clear and simple starting point from which to gain real and lasting help.

We wish this book had been around when we began our journey to recovery. It would have made the road ahead a hell of a lot less bumpy. But we did eventually find help and got sober, and now can live with a peace and purpose we thought impossible when we were still in the stranglehold of addiction. Unfortunately, many addicts don't have the resources and support that we have to get and stay sober. They each need to find and build their own toolkit of survival.

Recover to Live should be the first tool in that kit.

PATRICK J. KENNEDY   JIM RAMSTAD
U.S. Rep. (D., R.I.), 1995-2011   U.S. Rep. (R., Minn.), 1991-2009

INTRODUCTION
Are We a Culture of Addicts?

The chains of habit are generally too small to be felt until they are too strong to be broken.
—Samuel Johnson

You may have picked up this book out of curiosity. Or maybe you suspect that someone you know, maybe even that someone who stares back at you in the mirror every morning, has a habit that is becoming (or has already become) a serious problem. Perhaps that habit is already showing the symptoms of full-blown dependency.

Whether your interest is in finding out more about an unhealthy habit or an addiction, whether the subject of concern is yourself or someone you care about, this book can help. It draws on the wisdom of about 100 of the world's smartest dependency experts to provide you with the most innovative and useful guidance for diagnosis, treatment, and recovery. But think of this as a GP (general practitioner) book, not a specialist book. And consider their collected wisdom to be signposts along a path toward self-discovery and not just an opportunity for self-help, though it is certainly that, too.

You probably have never heard of these experts because most of them do their magnificent work behind the scenes. They deserve to be recognized and have their findings widely known because they have a lot to offer anyone seeking to improve his or her life. The majority of folks who are suffering, or recovering, from addiction (compulsive dependency) don't know about important developments affecting their treatment and recovery. This book was conceived and executed to help close that knowledge gap.

There is an old saying, "If you think you've got a problem, you probably do." If you're still not sure, ask yourself, or the person you're concerned about, this question: "Do I have control over my habits, or do they dominate my thoughts and unduly influence my behaviors?" By the end of this book, armed with knowledge provided by the experts interviewed for these pages, you should be able to answer that question with confidence.

Unhealthy habits (which experts call nondependent use disorders) can morph into dependencies and become reflected in many different forms of behavior and areas of life. It seems you can be addicted to damn near anything these days, which is to say our culture has stretched the meaning of "addiction" until the word is a generic term for almost any habit. What are you hooked on? Is it the Internet, your cell phone, or the latest techno-whiz gadget? Sound far-fetched? Well, as you may have heard, the revered Diagnostic and Statistical Manual of Mental Disorders (DSM) now includes "Internet Use Disorder" in its pantheon of addictions, although listed in a "for further study" category.

But maybe your addiction is something simpler, such as sugar or caffeine or other relatively harmless attractions. Or have you graduated into more self-destructive habits to "numb out" and try to escape the stress of everyday life? The addiction continuum is broad.

This book will narrow things down and provide guidance for identifying and treating the seven common habits that have the potential to become toxic compulsions. In alphabetical order, they are: alcohol; drugs (both legal and illegal); eating disorders; gambling; hoarding; sex and pornography; and smoking.

You've heard of the Seven Deadly Sins? Let's call these the Seven Toxic Compulsions. When done to excess, each one can have toxic consequences for your mental, physical, and spiritual health, for your relationships, your finances, and your overall experience of life.

Examination of available statistics on the numbers of people with either nondependent use disorders or outright addictions (dependencies) reveals that these habits are the industrialized world's number one emerging health problem. Here are the numbers:

Alcohol abuse: 17 million in the United States can be considered alcoholics; 140 million worldwide. (National Institutes of Health and World Health Organization)

Drugs (illegal): 19.9 million users/abusers in the United States; 208 million users/abusers worldwide. (Substance Abuse and Mental Health Services Administration Data Archive)

Eating disorders: Up to 4 million in the United States have a binge-eating disorder; 1 out of every 100 adolescent girls experience anorexia nervosa; 3 percent of all women are affected by bulimia at some point in their life. (National Eating Disorders Association)

Gambling: 2 to 5 percent of the adult population of the United States—up to 10 million have a problem; world totals are in the same percentage range. (Gamblers Anonymous)

Hoarding: An estimated 1 in 50 adults in the United States and worldwide have this disorder—about 2 million in the United States. (International Obsessive-Compulsive Disorders Foundation)

Sex and Pornography: Up to 8 percent of the adult U.S. population, or about 12 million people, have some form of a sex addiction or compulsive sexual problem. World totals are unknown. (American Association for Marriage and Family Therapy and the Society for the Advancement of Sexual Health)

Smoking: An estimated 1 billion people worldwide have this habit. (World Health Organization)

Only an estimated 1 in 10 persons with an alcohol or drug addiction problem ever receives treatment. This 1 in 10 ratio may also apply to the other five Toxic Compulsions addressed in this book, but may be even lower due to the hidden nature of these problems. As a direct consequence of this lack of treatment, aside from the human cost of deaths and illnesses associated with the undiagnosed and untreated conditions, every nation's health care system is burdened with excessive and rapidly growing costs.

The impact of drug and alcohol abuse and dependency alone on U.S. health care costs can be put into perspective by using statistics for an average year during the first decade of this new century:

Cancer—$96 billion a year in health care spending costs; $338 million a year spent on National Institutes of Health (NIH) research.

Alcoholism—$185 billion a year in health-related costs; $35 million in NIH research support spending annually.

Drug Abuse—$110 billion a year in health-related costs; $63 million in NIH research support spending annually.

(Source: Statistics compiled by Professor Adron Harris, Director, Waggoner Center for Alcohol and Addiction Research, University of Texas at Austin.)

Given that alcoholism is almost twice as costly to the U.S. health care system as cancer, and that drug abuse-related illness is also more expensive than cancer care, why aren't these abuse targets and their potential cost savings the number one health and budgetary issue for all levels of government? I'll get to that question later in this book, when I take a look at the social and political forces that shape public perceptions of whether substance abuse is a mental illness or a moral failing.

Addictions (Dependencies) Come Married to Each Other

Addiction is an old term that comes from the Latin *addictus*, which means a servant or slave, usually to pay off a debt. Later, in the 16th century, it came to mean zealous or compulsive devotion. It's more recently been described in scientific jargon as "instinct gone awry," and a "biological switch" that has been thrown in the brain resulting in a disorder of the brain's reward circuitry.

Over the past decade or so there has been significant debate among experts in the treatment and recovery field about the use of vocabulary and the importance of precision in the way terms are used to describe or stigmatize people. It's important to use language that is both sensitive and clear. With that in mind, I will replace the word *addiction* with the word *dependency* wherever possible in this book, although when some experts are quoted they will sometimes use addiction and dependence or dependency synonymously.

That's also why I use "Toxic Compulsions" as a convenient way to label the seven habits that can become dependencies. Habits can be healthy, or just annoying and worrisome, whereas *toxic* habits have crossed the line to a condition that requires action to keep them from becoming full-blown dependencies.

Dependencies and their subsequent spread within populations are among the principal root causes of illness, disease, and runaway health care costs. They are also contributing factors in crime, incarceration, poverty, homelessness, suicide, and even cultural despair.

Many people struggle with multiple dependency disorders. A smoking habit may pair with alcoholism, or an eating disorder may accompany a hoarding problem. Someone in the throes of an alcohol or drug problem may also have a gambling compulsion combined with an addiction to Internet pornography. These will be referred to as *co-occurring compulsions* (to be distinguished from co-occurring disorders, such as depression or anxiety accompanying drug or alcohol dependence), and they seem to be more prevalent in the 21st century than ever before in recorded history.

"Nobody has ever come into my office without me being able to find the addiction in them and in their family," said Jeffrey Roth, addiction psychiatrist, author, editor of *Journal of Groups in Addiction Recovery*, and medical director, Working Sobriety Chicago. "I've also never met an addict who didn't have addiction in their family. It's not necessarily the alcoholic that comes from an alcoholic. I've seen alcoholics who have a compulsive overeater parent. I've seen compulsive overeaters who've had alcoholic parents. I mean, it's the disease which gets transmitted. It's the disease of addiction and not necessarily the form of the disease that runs in families."

Pamela Hyde, administrator of the Substance Abuse and Mental Health Services Administration (SAMHSA), explained that the general rule of thumb goes like this: Almost half of all people with an identifiable addictive disorder also have an identifiable mental illness or anxiety disorder. And it also works the other way around: 20 percent of people suffering anxiety or mental problems have some sort of addiction. Individuals with more serious mental illnesses have higher levels of co-occurring substance use. "These disorders often go hand in hand," said Hyde. "And concurrent treatment is recommended for persons with addiction who also experience depression, anxiety, or other mental health conditions."

"This shouldn't surprise us. Patients with dual disorders are commonly diagnosed throughout the field of medicine," noted Dr. Thomas McLellan, CEO of the Treatment Research Institute and former deputy director of the White House Office of National Drug Control Policy. "Diabetes and hypertension are a good example," said McLellan. "They co-occur and play off each other. That's what happens in conditions that have similar pathways and similar results. So with addictions, just like the rest of medicine, if you've got two disorders, you've got to treat them both and treat them at the same time because the symptoms of one are going to be important as mediators of recidivism for the other."

Dr. McLellan makes an important point about treating underlying causes of dependency, which I'll explore in more detail later. Because of co-occurring disorders and the ways in which everyone expresses addiction differently, there isn't a single prescription for treatment and recovery that works for everyone. Nor is this a one-size-fits-all sort of book. You will find in these pages a wide net of prescriptions, any one or more of which may be useful in addressing your particular needs and health situation.

What Dependency Is and Isn't

Want to know exactly what distinguishes dependency from an unhealthy habit? You'll find some slight variations in definitions provided by the medical literature. I'll let some of the experts I spoke with contrast these differences.

From Dr. Drew Pinsky, addiction medicine specialist and clinical professor of psychiatry, University of Southern California School of Medicine: Addiction is a biological disorder with a genetic basis. Its hallmark is progressive use in the face of adverse consequences (effects on school or work, health, finances, legal, relationships). There is also a component of denial. Addiction is a biological switch having been thrown in the deep regions of the brain. For the most part, emotional dysregulation is why people go to addictive substances in the first place. They have difficulty regulating feelings, trying to feel better, seeking solutions to emotional states, and inadvertently throwing that switch. You can have bad habits and you can manifest abuse and you can hurt yourself. But you may not have the progressive disorder of addiction.

From Dr. Howard Shaffer, associate professor of psychology, Harvard Medical School, and director, Division on Addictions, the Cambridge Health Alliance: My approach is that gambling or alcohol-related problems or drugs are all expressions of this underlying syndrome that we call "addiction." So the issues for gambling and identifying it are somewhat like the issues for identifying alcohol or drug-related problems. For most people, the movement from recreational or acceptable gambling or drugs or alcohol into problematic use is a very slippery slope. The scientific evidence does not yet indicate with much confidence that addiction is a separate, distinct disorder from the recreational behaviors that people engage in. So it's very hard to know when people cross the line. We have learned that gambling is very similar to substance use. The same or similar kinds of brain activity occur among gamblers as among drug users. So the neurobiology looks more similar for the process addictions [gambling, sex or pornography, etc.—those that don't involve mood- or mind-altering substances] and substance addictions than we ever might have imagined. There's quite a bit of work all around the world showing that these various activities energize the pleasure centers of the brain similar to the way psychoactive drugs energize the pleasure centers of the brain. And that's a very important discovery because it begins to suggest that while drugs can produce physical dependence, drugs don't necessarily produce addiction. They might be correlated and even highly correlated with the presence of addiction, but they're not really a single causal factor because addiction can exist without drugs. The majority of people who use drugs—and that includes cocaine, heroin, and alcohol—don't develop addiction.

From Dr. Nora Volkow, director, National Institute on Drug Abuse: What do I mean by substance-use disorder versus addiction? Addiction I define as the most severe state on the substance-use disorder continuum. Addiction is that state in which a person has actually lost their ability to control their enhanced drive to take the drugs even though they cognitively (by thinking) constantly want to stop it. They just cannot do it. So it's almost like there is a disconnect between your cognitive motivation to stop doing something and your ability to actually enforce that behavior. I would use the metaphor that you're driving a car without brakes, so you cognitively want to stop, you don't want to hurt someone crossing the street, but if you do not have brakes, you're going to be very limited in your ability to stop the car. The research has shown that the areas of the brain that act like our brakes are disrupted by the repeated use of drugs.

From Dr. Patrick Carnes, psychologist, author, and former clinical director of sexual disorders services, The Meadows, Arizona: Addiction is about the reward center of the brain. People ask, "What is addiction?" and I answer, addiction is many things. It's a brain disease. It's a maladaptive response to trauma and stress. It's a deep attachment problem. And the average person says, "Holy moly." I tell them to think in terms of physics. Addiction is like light. You ask a physicist what light is and he'll say, "It all depends on how you're looking at it. If you're looking at it straight on, it comes as a series of waves. If you're looking at it around the corner, it's a bunch of bundles of photons." And so when people ask what addiction is, I say it's a number of things.

It should be noted that some specialists, including Dr. Sally Satel, psychiatrist, Partners in Drug Addiction Counseling and Research and fellow, American Enterprise Institute, prefer to call dependency a "condition" or a "pathological behavior" rather than a brain disease, if only because being stuck with that medical label makes people think they're doomed. Satel believes "that it is far more productive to view addiction as a behavior that operates on several levels, ranging from molecular function and structure to brain physiology to psychology to psychosocial environment and social relations."

What signs or symptoms indicate that you have gone from being a nondependent user to being dependent on a substance or activity? There are some common behaviors. You can pretty much substitute the words *gambling*, *sex*, or any of the other Seven Toxic Compulsions with the word *drug*.

From Dr. Andrea Barthwell, CEO of the North Carolina treatment center Two Dreams Outer Banks: How do I define dependence? Several things. First of all, time lost. The user sets out to use, ends up using for a greater period of time than they expected, and is no longer able to predict what will happen when they start. Time spent, and loss of control. They spend more and more of their time getting the drug, using the drug, and recovering from the use of drug. The drug becomes more important than anything else, so it interferes with other things that are of primary importance to them. A mother's baby is back in the crib and she's in the kitchen cooking freebase on the stove. Or the kid didn't study and has to pull an all-nighter to pass the exam. He's toking on his marijuana pipe; he falls asleep and oversleeps and doesn't go to the exam. And then there are the physical aspects, physical dependence, so when use stops there is withdrawal or adverse consequences, and with repeated use the person has to use more to get the desired effect. That's how I define dependence.

People in the nondependent (unhealthy habit) category of users aren't yet experiencing significant negative consequences from their use of a substance or activity. They remain functional, though they may begin experiencing occasional lapses in judgment or episodes of diminished effectiveness in their work. They may also begin making excuses for their behavior, even lying to themselves or to others.

How do you know for certain if you need treatment for an addiction? The odds are you won't know on your own. Up to 90 percent of people who need treatment don't recognize that they need treatment, according to research data provided by SAMHSA, the Substance Abuse and Mental Health Services Administration.

"There is a good reason for this state of denial," said Dr. Nora Volkow. "The area of the brain that allows you to be aware of your own internal state is disrupted by drugs." This disruption may also create layers of stubborn denial if you have a gambling or other process habit that has become a serious problem.

A Worldwide Health Issue

We in the United States may well possess the gold standard for addiction treatment. After all, we've come a long way from the days when addiction automatically resulted in imprisonment. It's also a good thing we've abandoned the 28-day rehab centers on every street corner, which had been all the rage in the 1980s, until it was discovered that the same addicts had to be readmitted a month later and recycled through the same program again because 28 days wasn't near enough time to address the root causes of their dependence. Such revolving doors were a huge waste of precious resources.

Yet we still have a long way to go before the United States becomes a worthy global model for intervention and long-term recovery, especially when that intervention involves identifying those who have nondependent abuse disorders (unhealthy habits) *before* they erupt into full-blown addiction. The dire situation in much of the rest of the world, however, shows how far the United States has come despite its limitations.

In Russia, addiction psychiatrists commonly practice "scientifically decorated shamanism" rather than evidence-based treatment, according to Dr. Evgeny Krupitsky, chief of the Laboratory of Clinical Psychopharmacology of Addictions at St. Petersburg State Pavlov Medical University. Not only that, but drug-substitution therapy using methadone and buprenorphine is forbidden in Russia, forcing people to undergo nonmedical detox, which is an incredibly arduous and painful way to get clean.

Some parts of Africa fare even worse when it comes to attitudes about the resources needed for treating addictions. "In Kenya, the commonly held idea is that addiction is a matter of personal willpower," said Dr. William Sinkele, founder and executive director of the nonprofit Support for Addictions Prevention and Treatment in Africa, based in Nairobi. "Addiction is not even seen as a disease, but bad character, personal choice (no one is forcing your hand to drink or drug), or a result of witchcraft (someone cursed you)."

In Japanese culture, addiction isn't viewed as an illness. It's considered a stigma that is a disgrace to the family. The burden is placed on family members to shape the addict up using guilt and shame as motivators.

We in the United States have seen wild pendulum swings in both addict and public perceptions of this mind disruption called addiction. These swings go from the more recent user entitlement attitude of "Hey, this is a disease that I have no power over and as a result, I bear no responsibility for my actions or behavior," all the way to the older, more culturally ingrained perception that "Addiction is simply a matter of having no willpower and displaying low morals." The reality of addiction can be found somewhere between these extreme views.

Nobody seems to express much concern about abusers in the nondependent category, even though they number three times the addicted population. Yet, nondependent individuals—in every culture around the world—are the very group on which we need to focus with education campaigns. This population is the breeding ground for future addicts and the health, social, public safety, and economic problems that result.

What we're seeing with virtually all categories of dependency in the United States is the emergence of social movements to normalize use. Medical marijuana is a good example. As more states approve the use of marijuana for medical purposes and the legislated guidelines for what constitutes legitimate medical use get broader and more loosely defined, a perceived social license is issued for unrestricted use and with that, a wider and deepening scale of abuse. (Don't get me started yet on whether marijuana is "harmless" or not. I'll address that health issue in Part One.)

Today, when it comes to alcohol, "the presumption is that it's normal to drink," said Dr. Robert DuPont, President of the Institute for Behavior and Health Inc, first director of the National Institute on Drug Abuse, second White House Drug Chief, and clinical professor of psychiatry at Georgetown Medical School. "If you don't drink, you must be sick. We've even gotten promotional about saying that drinking is not only normal, it's healthy because it improves your heart function.

"The first and most important defensive line in drug abuse prevention is drug *use*," continued DuPont. "It's not *addiction*. It's not a *loss of control*. Those are late consequences of drug use. Once you've crossed that threshold and begun drug use, it becomes difficult to say where the line defining the problem is and what to do about it. When does 'addiction' start and when does 'loss of control' begin? The goal of prevention is best served by focusing first on the decision to use drugs—that line is clear. When drug use is normalized, the result is that the entire population is exposed to the biology of these highly addicting substances, with grim consequences for many. The costs of dealing with the drug problem escalate, including the high costs of treatment when drug use is normalized.

"Everybody is at risk," continued DuPont. "We are all vulnerable because the mammalian brain has a reward system, and these chemicals [drugs and alcohol] produce a reward that is much more intense than any natural reward. Whole populations are being exposed, and we've got a value system encouraging people to try it, to make their own decisions, and to remove the social pressures, whether religion or laws, that keep people from using. This has never happened in the history of the world before."

Addicts Aren't Always Who or What You Think

Here's an inconvenient truth. Addicts in all seven categories of disorders may have been marginalized and stigmatized by our culture as weak-willed, but they bring a lot of value to the table of human experience.

Most of the addiction focus has been on the hellish consequences for addicts and their loved ones when an addiction is out of control. We know the negatives in terms of economic costs, family and relationship disruption, and lives squandered.

But what are the benefits to society of the disease of addiction? That may sound like an absurd question to ask, but bear with me for a moment because it's worth exploration. Often it's the person with a dependency problem who gets other family members into treatment because the sickness in families is there before the symptoms of out-of-control dependency surface.

Put aside moral judgments and consider some other possible values that some high-achieving addicts contribute to society as a result of their affliction. Though it was about mental illness and not about addiction per se, the 2011 book *A First-Rate Madness: Uncovering the Links Between Leadership and Mental Illness* by Dr. Nassir Ghaemi, a professor of psychiatry at Tufts University School of Medicine, made a compelling case that "the very qualities that mark those with mood disorders—realism, empathy, resilience, and creativity—also make for the best leaders in times of crisis."

Think about some of these possible connections. Did Tiger Woods' sex compulsions in some way contribute to his success as a golfer? Why hasn't he been as good a golfer after he was treated for his sexual compulsivity? Would Bill Clinton have been as good a leader without the bad Bill Clinton and Monica Lewinsky in his life? Was sex addiction part of the drive and energy he used to become president? Would Boris Yeltsin have mustered the courage to stand on that tank in 1991 to rally Russians against a Communist coup if he hadn't been drunk at the time? Would Winston Churchill have inspired his country to kick Hitler's butt in World War II if not for his alcoholism, or without it would he have been in the appeasement camp? Did substance abuse help to fuel the musical genius of Janis Joplin, Jimi Hendrix, and Jim Morrison? Would Ernest Hemingway and F. Scott Fitzgerald have been lesser writers without alcohol dependence? How much of the Irish storytelling tradition has been lubricated by alcohol?

The questions go on endlessly, but the addict's value in shaping the events and trends of human history should be acknowledged as something more than an aberration or historical footnote. It should also be noted that if all these "addicts" had been in recovery, they might have, or might not have, taken the same actions, for whatever reason. We'll never know, though it seems reasonable they might have made more of a contribution by having more time and energy at their disposal, rather than spending so much time and energy on their compulsions.

Many of the experts I interviewed made observations about the contributions to society that highly functional addicts have made and continue to make. Dr. Drew Pinsky, addiction medicine specialist and clinical professor at the USC School of Medicine, for example, said it pains him "that addicts are perceived as weak or bad. Because one of the reasons I work with addicts is that they're one of the most powerful, richest, most human groups of people you could ever meet." But as Bill Wilson, cofounder of Alcoholics Anonymous, once said, "If you sober up a horse thief, you've got a sober horse thief."

None of this should imply that these famous people didn't need treatment. Nor should it be interpreted to mean they shouldn't have found their way into a recovery program to deal with their underlying co-occurring disorders, like depression, bipolar disorder, and the like. The point is, you can't take the sex away from Tiger and Bill, the booze away from Winston and Ernest, or the drugs away from Janis and Jimi and be certain they would be the same talented people. Drugs and alcohol tend to make the intolerable more tolerable. These substances take the sharpness off of being human.

These substances do things for people and sometimes—not always, but sometimes—these things can have real benefits to society. It's been my experience that in recovery I am now more productive, imaginative, creative, and human—by far—than I was before, but it took a while. For those of you interested in changing your life into something fuller and more rewarding, you must realize that it will take some time, even though addicts don't do well with delayed gratification.

There is also an undeniable spiritual dimension to recovery from an addiction. You don't have to be in a 12-Step program to experience that, though it certainly helps. After recovering from addiction, you will never see life or its value in quite the same way again. You will take much less for granted. Call it God, a higher power, or just the resilient human spirit, but that journey to reclaim control over your life becomes like Paul on the road to Damascus—simply revelatory.

The addict's contributions to society underscore how addiction seems to serve a cultural and perhaps genetic purpose throughout human history. We know there is a genetic predisposition to alcoholism among certain ethnic groups, the Irish and Native Americans, for example. USC's Pinsky even thinks addiction's genetic heritability may bestow some sort of evolutionary advantage for survival.

"I started thinking, where on the globe do you see this gene?" said Pinsky. "In isolated populations of Ireland, in Northern Europe, in Central Europe, in North American Indians, and in certain parts of Africa. What do those populations have in common? What went on there for millennia that would create a genetic change? It was repeated genocidal military assaults over multiple generations. In these incredibly stressful circumstances, addicts are better fighters and survivors. In peaceful times this trait brought out the potential for addictive disease."

A Few Inconvenient Truths About Dependency

From my many dozens of interviews with addiction experts, some general truths were identified that deserve to be enshrined in public awareness:

- Addiction is a brain illness, not simply a failure of willpower or morals.
- Chronic abuse of both substances and activities such as gambling result in similar changes in the neurotransmitters of the brain.
- Change your behavior and your thinking changes.
- A new "brain model" of addiction is emerging that shows a close link between the symptoms of attention deficit disorder and those of an addicted brain.
- Express self-compassion and you begin to shed feelings of shame, which is at the root of depression and substance abuse.
- The terminology we use regarding addiction is important because it helps to shape public perceptions; these cultural perceptions affect how addicts approach treatment and recovery. (This is one reason why I use "unhealthy" habits in place of the more judgmental "bad" habits.)
- If we can reduce the stigma that society attaches to addiction and the marginalization of addicted people that results from it, we can go a long way toward making treatment and recovery more effective and less costly.
- Even if the underlying cause of addiction turns out to be genetic, people still need to take responsibility for their disease, and for their treatment and recovery.
- There is one widely available and affordable (as in free) form of help in the United States for all addictions—12-Step programs. There are 12-Step programs for just about every form of addictive behavior. They are free. They are easy to join. They offer help in a variety of forms.

But do they work for everyone?

Those who have studied 12-Step programs say that if two addicts walk into a 12-Step meeting, one will never go to another meeting. More than half of those seeking treatment won't even go to meetings or treatment programs that rely on 12-Step programs. And then there are the people who say that the 12-Step process didn't work for them. I would be interested in knowing to what extent they really participated in the program. I also would like to know if they explored alternative mutual aid options such as Smart Recovery (www.smartrecovery.org), Celebrate Recovery (www.celebraterecovery.com.au), or Women for Sobriety (www.womenforsobriety.org).

Later in this book, as one of the Seven Self-Care Tools for recovery described in Part Two, I will use the expert information I have gathered in this book to attempt to demystify and explain the 12-Step programs and related support groups so that more folks might feel comfortable accessing these effective and free help options.

Although this book begins with the experience of dealing with dependency, it becomes a self-help guide for a wide range of human behaviors, from eating and sex to managing money and smoking cigarettes. It builds on the foundation of the 12-Step fellowships to guide you to solutions to the many distortions in human behavior caused by the hijacking of your brain's reward system.

Why Do Habits Become Dependencies?

For many people, abusing something is a way of connecting with other people. They drink or do drugs because they want to be social. They gamble because they want to be social. For others, abusive patterns of use are all about trying to escape the problems in their life by means of a self-medication ritual.

They're not happy. They're struggling with issues they want to escape, so they get over-involved with gambling, drinking, drugs, and so forth—all of those things that help them disassociate from the challenges and frustrations of life. Once they understand why they are abusing that substance or activity, they can begin to make healthier substitutions that deliver the desired brain reward.

We know from cognitive behavioral research, for example, that changing how one thinks about the world and oneself can positively or negatively affect emotional/psychological health and behavior. Both treatment and mutual aid work on this level. Conversely, from emerging research in neurobiology, we see how repeated behavior can help rewire the brain, building new pathways and expanding our capacities in certain functional areas. Both treatment and mutual aid work on this level as well.

Harvard's Prof. Shaffer made the point that "the way to restore control isn't simply to say, 'I won't do it anymore.' Because when you do that, you give the addiction more power. What you need to do is to find out what your addiction means and then substitute new activities that are in conflict with your addiction."

If you're not a dependent user, you might take a hot bath or engage in intense exercise or yoga instead of using alcohol or opiates. Instead of gambling, you might take up group activities that involve competitive (nongambling) games. The possible ranges of healthy substitutions you can use are limited only by your imagination and by your financial resources.

Addiction should also be viewed and treated as a family disease. A strong argument can be made that individual treatment won't work in the long term until the entire family is treated. If you're in a family with an addict, you're part of the problem. The way you help the person you care about is to help yourself first—like putting on your oxygen mask first during an emergency on a plane. It could even mean taking yourself out of the family for a period of time. Each member of an addict's family needs to do an assessment to look at his or her biological, psychological, and social activities to see whether he or she has contributed to this compulsive dependency.

That assessment can help family members determine whether they need to make changes in their own behavior to assist their loved one in recovery. Additionally, each family member can use this assessment to explore how they may have contributed to the broader addiction disease process, which affects the entire family. It's important for them to begin identifying the ways in which they may need to heal from wounds created by the often multigenerational process of addictive disease. Because if they love this person, they should view themselves as throwing a life preserver to save somebody who has gone overboard. However, family members, like the addicted individual, must also first make sure they have their own life jacket by seeking help and support—particularly when the wounds suffered in the family disease process are severe. Otherwise, the tug on the life preserver from the addicted person may only serve to pull them into the water as well.

Can You Recover on Your Own?

From my own experience I can tell you that you can recover from a toxic compulsion on your own. But it took me 10 years to gather the information and accumulate the experience that I needed to break free of my compulsions. So I have good reason for wanting to shorten that process for others by providing them access to the information and guidance in this book.

I started using drugs and alcohol when I was 12 years old. I had a really good time for about eight years. Then one day, I discovered that using was no longer a choice for me. It had become a compulsion. The will to resist its many seductions was no longer there.

When I first did drugs and alcohol, I felt at home. I loved it. It wasn't like, "Oh, I don't know about this." It was, "I like it. Where can I get more of it?" The first four or five times I did heroin, I became violently ill, but what the drug did to the reward center of my brain was so powerful that it never occurred to me not to do it again. That's how potent these substances are for people like me. When you put those substances in my body, something miraculous happens. Not everybody has that experience or the genetic predisposition, but they can develop addiction anyway.

Before I got sober, I had been wrestling with this thing, trying to get better for years. And I tried everything. People had gotten bored with my story. My insurance was gone. I was checking into hospitals with my pillow and my toothbrush and they'd say "Don't bother coming here anymore." That's what a lot of people with substance addictions deal with. So at the end, I was forced to detox on my own.

For a hundred years our culture thought that if you could just get an addict isolated and locked in a room for five days, he would come out and be good as new again. We have learned that just isn't true. You can't treat addiction simply by focusing on the detox. Someone who has done nothing but a detox is likely to use again. Interrupting use and quickly addressing relapse is really what we need to focus on when dealing with this illness. An intervention that follows detox gives the addicted person the tools to prevent relapse and a shot at long-term recovery.

I didn't have this vital information when I was trying to change my life 30 years ago. I thought if I could just create enough physical distance between myself and the drugs I could get well. It never worked. I would go through this 5- to 10-day detox process, depending on what kind of opioid I was taking, and it was horrific, like ants crawling in my bones with a nasty flu chaser. I got through it by lying in bed and watching endless reruns of bad television shows.

You can't normally die from an opiate detox. It will make you feel like you're going to die, but you won't die. That's not the case with other detoxes. You can die from delirium tremors, seizures, and other side effects from alcohol or barbiturates. Anybody who's thinking about a detox on their own must know their medical condition because it can be dangerous depending on the chemicals they're taking.

I've never spoken or written about this part of my experience before because this is a new awareness for me. I thought my addiction was only physical, and that if I could just figure out how to avoid becoming physically dependent on whatever substance I was using, I would be just fine. I could use the drugs and there wouldn't be any of those nasty side effects and consequences. I have since discovered that I wasn't alone in my thinking. It's the preoccupation of most addicts.

I had always thought about the physical piece to recovery, getting healthy and well, but I never really thought about learning how to reprogram my thoughts. I wanted nothing more in my life than to stop using. But once I was let out of that detox room, I was confronted with what many of you reading this book might be confronted with. I would walk out of my apartment after a week of hell—clean and free. I'd take a deep breath, stretch my arms for what felt like the first time in my life, with nothing but promise in front of me, and then I'd take a look down the street and see the entrance to the neighborhood bar, or see the drug dealers on the corner. That's all it took. Just a look. And the game was over. The switch was thrown. The cravings returned.

We addicts are used to immediate gratification. It's difficult to tolerate the feeling of craving for a second because we know there's a solution. All we need is the drug, the drink, the cigarette, the card game, her or him, or whatever it is that makes us think we're okay. The disease lives in the mind. Addicts need to understand that sitting with a craving for five minutes diminishes its hold over their thoughts, and that the longer they sit with it the more it diminishes. They aren't fighting the craving, but waiting for it to pass, as it surely will. Once you know it's the cravings that make you do what you don't want to do, you can no longer be a victim.

There are proven tools such as mindfulness and meditation that can vanquish the cravings and enable those who want to change their lives to make different choices in the moment. I'll discuss all of the different ways to do that later in this book. You have to sit for a short time and be mindful of what is happening within you and to you. It just takes a little bit of time and a lot of strength to sit there for five seconds, five minutes, whatever is necessary, to allow that craving to pass, so you can say to yourself, "Okay, I'm not going to die if I don't walk down to the dealers on the corner or into that bar."

And if you do that practice over a period of time, it's amazing how quickly you can reprogram the circuitry of your mind. It took me years to get there because I didn't yet have the knowledge, mind tools, or techniques to break free of that craving.

There is still another important piece of the recovery puzzle. I went back into a hospital one time and I was convinced to visit a 12-Step recovery meeting, and they basically ruined my drinking and drug using. This disease is so much about feeling isolated and believing that you're the only person with this issue. Because of my family upbringing, I had a lot of rationalizations around being different: *Nobody is like me. I am special. My situation is unique.*

But when you walk into a room full of strangers and open yourself up, just for a little bit, you see that everybody is really just like you. I went into my first meeting and a guy was telling what sounded like my story. I didn't know that guy. I had never seen him before in my life. But he described going through what I was going through, and in that moment of mutual identification our connection obliterated my sense of uniqueness.

It took several years of meetings before I would have my epiphany. I call it my "surrender." But the first time I went to a meeting it ruined my drinking and drug using because once you know you're not that different from all the other folks struggling with addiction, and that there is a solution, you can't pretend otherwise. You can't stay in denial. And that's the beginning of your recovery. That's the first step in putting the drugs and alcohol down and beginning the process of addressing the underlying causes and conditions of your addiction.

I did two things right in the years that I struggled to recover. I didn't die. And I stayed connected to some kind of support, even if it was just calling people up and telling them how my life wasn't working out, or sitting in a shrink's office, still high, making plans about how I might control my drug use tomorrow. I never stopped wanting to get better. If you have a desire to get better, that could be all you need.

Keep in mind that the pathology of addiction manifests in multiple ways. For example, it would not be surprising to find a gambling addict in a casino consorting with a hooker and later doing cocaine with her in the parking lot. Often—perhaps usually—addicted persons have multiple things going on. If you are able to engage in this kind of behavior a few times a year and can afford to do it, it may well not destroy your life. If that's the case—provided you're not hurting yourself or anyone else in the process—I say, "Knock yourself out." This book isn't for you, and I don't want to interfere with whatever it is you believe gives you a good time. I won't burden you with a moral judgment about it. I'm only concerned with folks whose behaviors or activities are killing them or destroying their lives and the lives of those around them, and who have a desire to change.

Trust me, doing it on your own is hard but it's doable. I know thousands of people all over the world who've done it. I did it, so can you!

"A lot of people figure out the relapse prevention strategies on their own," said Sally Satel, psychiatrist, Partners in Drug Addiction Counseling and Research and fellow, American Enterprise Institute. That doesn't mean it's a fast or easy process. And it doesn't mean you won't need support along the way.

But it's important for you to know that according to the U.S. Public Health Service, 90 percent of people who stop smoking cigarettes have done so on their own without entering treatment centers or joining support groups. In my own experience, quitting smoking was more difficult in many ways than getting off heroin. The smoking withdrawal lasts longer and it can make you angry, depressed, and crazy for a while. With heroin, you're sick for a week or 10 days and then you seem better. But with cigarettes, you're crazy with anxiety for a month. It's a tough withdrawal, for a very basic reason: Cigarettes don't have the immediate destructive impact on your life that addiction to alcohol, legal and illegal drugs, sex, or gambling can have. So, it can be more difficult to muster and maintain the work required to free yourself from them.

A lot of the people I've gotten sober with are people who benefitted from hitting bottom. They ended up on the street or in the criminal justice system. They lost their families and their livelihoods. But hitting bottom isn't and shouldn't be the only surefire path to treatment and recovery.

As Dr. Thomas McLellan, CEO of the Treatment Research Institute and former deputy director of the White House Office of National Drug Control Policy, observed, "We believe that one of the reasons there've been such bad results from the treatment of addiction is because we've waited so long to have people bottom out. We need to try and get to people earlier, before they've lost their health. And it's much easier to treat the earlier you intervene."

That's one of the key reasons for the existence of this book. If it can raise somebody's bottom by helping them get there a little quicker, that's a contribution to their recovery and to the greater public good.

We can do something about unhealthy habits and addictions. It's not a hopeless problem. People who have unhealthy habits as well as the disease of addiction can and do get better. Treatment works. Let the experts in this book show you how.

Unhealthy habits and addictions affect our entire society. If we don't act quickly, the problem we as a culture confront will get much worse. There is one certainty when it comes to the disease of addiction: If it goes untreated, it always gets worse for the individual and for society. We've tried locking up addicts, throwing medications at them, or decriminalizing to the point of making some drug use legal. None of these approaches addresses the core issues, which are the causes of addiction and what we can do to address them.

We know that coddling addicts doesn't really work. Just because you have an illness of the mind doesn't mean you don't have responsibility. You may not be responsible for the fact that you have this illness. You can't control which genes you inherited or the circumstances of your life that contributed to your disease. But once you know that you have the disease of addiction, you are responsible for doing something about it. And if you don't address your problem, you can't blame society or anyone in your life for the consequences. Sorry. That's the way it works.

What Responsibilities Should Society Have?

Alcohol and tobacco are both legal, state-sanctioned drugs. And both are dangerous and costly. Tobacco causes the most morbidity and mortality overall and is the larger health care cost. But alcohol and its effects present more imminent danger, especially when public safety and economic productivity costs are taken into account. We know all that, yet both tobacco and alcohol remain regulated and legal. Is there a similar future for marijuana and other drugs that people use for so-called recreation? Will their use be regulated but frowned upon as cigarettes now are? What is the role and responsibility of society when it comes to all forms of addictions or to the availability of disease-causing agents?

Smoking cessation programs have been enormously effective in getting people off cigarettes. Look at how in three decades we have completely changed perceptions about cigarettes and smoking addiction. As Joseph Califano, founder and chair of the National Center on Addiction and Substance Abuse at Columbia University and the former U.S. Secretary of Health, Education, and Welfare, related, only 30 years ago people were smoking in airplanes and in every public building. Doctors were smoking and talking about cigarettes being good for you. Smoking was considered a socially acceptable way to behave.

We've since had a complete sea change in the way we view tobacco. Now you can't smoke much of anywhere in public. And, certainly, a lot of it has to do with overcoming the attitudes that we have about how we look at people who are affected with addiction. We never used to look at a smoker as somebody who was sick. Now we are more likely to. We can do the same thing with other forms of addiction.

We need to make treatments safe again and be more respectful of those seeking help. "We need to invite people as collaborative partners in their own health care to enter the process," said Prof. Shaffer. "And we don't do that with addiction because we believe they can't participate. I've been doing this for almost 40 years, and I tell you they can participate."

Hopefully, the new health care law, if it isn't completely dismantled, will for the first time in history bring addiction into mainstream care through the mandated use of screening for substance-use problems, brief interventions for alcohol and drug use by primary care physicians, and referral to specialty treatment when required. This is one of the most effective ways to make real headway in confronting this problem, both in getting treatment to people sooner, and in medically and socially reducing the stigma and discrimination associated with alcohol and drug problems. Research has demonstrated the effectiveness of brief intervention in reducing problem, nonaddictive substance use and in helping people access treatment sooner.

If you can't access the health care system, if you can't get good care for whatever reason—because you live in the middle of nowhere or you don't have the resources to enter a treatment center—then you may have to do it on your own. It's tricky, and your chances of success are not as good as when you can access good treatment. But you can do it and this book will show you how.

For all of the Seven Toxic Compulsions, it's going to be more or less the same prescription. You need the same support systems. You are going to need to develop techniques like mindfulness, meditation, journaling, cognitive behavioral therapy, exercise and nutrition, and body work to deal with the symptoms. And you are going to need to reach out to find a person or group of people you trust and who will support you in your process of changing your life. There will be craving. There is going to be sleeplessness, but there are techniques you can use to improve your ability to benefit from the sleep you do get. You will doubt yourself and the wisdom of the choice you have made. There will be symptoms of withdrawal. But never let yourself think you don't have the resources you need to do it.

This isn't just a book that contains the most current and credible information in the world about the disease of addiction from some of the most extraordinary people working in the field today. It's also a self-discovery book. It's my hope that after reading it, you will have a better understanding of these substances and behaviors and your relationship to them. What you do then is up to you.

For those folks who are unsure, go ahead, take a look. It may give you information that will ruin the lie you've been telling yourself. You don't have to wait until you're broke or homeless to heal this problem. And once the lie is revealed, you can start getting better because you can start to hear solutions.

A wide variety of people, not just people that truly fit the classic definition of "addict," can benefit from learning the steps involved in the slippery slope from being a so-called "social user" to becoming addicted. As Dr. DuPont says in a later chapter, "If you're having five drinks a day—if there are any days that you have had five or more drinks—you have a problem with alcohol. If you use illicit drugs at all, you have a problem with drugs. If you lie to yourself or others about your gambling or any other addictive activity, you have a problem. It's that simple." Again, as Dr. DuPont has said, "The two most distinctive features of addiction are lying about the addictive behavior and continued addictive behavior after it has caused problems. Addicts lie and they relapse to alcohol and drug use despite their efforts to stop and despite the significant problems that result from their drug use. By the same token, recovery is identified by honesty about the addictive behavior and by abstinence from the addictive behavior."

This book's great information was provided by more than 100 very smart and dedicated experts in brain science, addiction treatment, and recovery. Some of what they say is going to resonate with you; some of it won't. Take what is useful and apply it to your life. The experts speak with a broad range of experience and knowledge, and I have found them to be helpful and wise. I trust that you will, too. I am grateful for their help in creating this book. My goal in featuring them is to enable you to find better ways to deal with some of life's most common and baffling problems, all of which began with behaviors that produced initial pleasure, but which ended up making life miserable and, all too often, short.

For each of the Seven Toxic Compulsions described in Part One you will find a questionnaire, an informal self-diagnosis opportunity, to give you insight into how serious a problem you might have and how deep your denial might be. Part Two gives you simple, yet effective, tools that you can use on your own, or in conjunction with 12-Step and other programs. You will learn about the latest treatment discoveries, the advantages of outpatient or inpatient care, and, most important, the warning signs of when you need to intervene with someone and how to go about it.

You will also learn about the process of recovery from toxic compulsions and how to integrate it into your life as gracefully and naturally as possible. You will be given details about recovery "accelerants" and how they work, along with information about how and why 12-Step programs effectively support recovery. There is also an important chapter about codependency: how to recognize it, and how to break free of it while still giving a recovering addict the support he or she needs.

My hope is that you will find this book to be unique for several reasons. It incorporates the latest American Psychiatric Association diagnostic criteria for dependency, known as DSM-5 (*Diagnostic and Statistical Manual of Mental Disorders, Fifth Edition*), which for the first time addresses gambling and other so-called "process" disorders along with alcohol and drugs. The guiding concept fits the major theme of this book: that dependency of any type is really about biochemical imbalances of a genetic origin in the human brain that, when combined with stress, trigger these various behaviors that are symptoms of addiction.

This book is unique in its approach linking all addictive diseases as one issue that requires a holistic treatment approach. Unlike previous books that only focus on a single dependency, this one links all Seven Toxic Compulsions to what is happening inside the brain with chemicals and genes, and shows how behavior modification practices and therapeutic medicines can counteract these brain imbalances by taking advantage of the brain's natural plasticity, or ability to adapt.

Also, this book is unique because it reveals how "co-occurring disorders" afflict most people who think they have only one toxic compulsion in their life. Most likely they have two or more. A person with an alcohol problem, for example, may also have a smoking problem and a gambling problem. That's why attempting to treat just one disorder without addressing the others, along with their underlying biochemical causes, often results in high relapse rates, or the "whack-a-mole" phenomena of another addiction showing up as soon as one problem is solved. This book brings together the best and most current information from the world's greatest experts—the ones who actually do the science—to give readers an opportunity to understand how all of the major compulsions that are destructive in their life are interconnected.

Always keep in mind that we can manage dependency. It should be our number one public health issue, and we need to think more clearly in terms of management, not cures. In fact, addiction is connected with the top five health disorders tracked by the U.S. Centers for Disease Control and Prevention, yet the agency doesn't study, track, or contribute to eradication efforts for the diseases of addiction.

In a real sense, as Prof. Shaffer said, "Life itself is a disease and we're all going to die eventually. How we live our life really determines what the quality of our life is. If we can make life more worth living, we will reduce the problems of addictive behavior."

If we are lucky this book will help change the field of dependency treatment and recovery so that people with substance and process problems get treated like everybody else who has a health and life problem. It's time to dispense with stigma, discrimination, and outright persecution of those struggling with these health issues. Outdated notions about who is dependent and why no longer serve us, not that they ever really did. Such prejudices only hamper our efforts to tackle these problems.

So think of this book as an intervention for anyone in need of an awakening. Consider it a toolkit of practical techniques for anyone desiring a new vision of hope for reclaiming control over their habits and over their life.

If that person is YOU, then let's get started!

Recover to Live

PART ONE

Is Your Unhealthy Habit Really Dependence?

Your Toxic Compulsion Has "Fellow Travelers"

I f you're old enough you might remember a children's toy consisting of a board with a series of pegs that a young child wielding a mallet attempted to hammer down. The challenge was that each time a peg got hammered down another one popped up elsewhere on the board. I guess this "whack-a-mole" game was supposed to teach the child patience.

For our purposes the toy provides a metaphor for what can happen when we attempt to treat and recover from one compulsion without recognizing and treating other compulsions existing alongside it, and without keeping an eye open for others that may pop up unexpectedly.

Studies show that most gambling addicts also have a problem with alcohol, and most of these folks simultaneously nurse a smoking habit. Many anorexics and bulimics struggle with sexual compulsions.

Or take obesity, which often results from the eating disorder of binge eating. Persons treated for obesity using gastric surgery will often experience other addictive behaviors subsequently, such as gambling or compulsive spending. This tendency toward addiction seems to be "hardwired" into the brain. (*Source: "The obesity epidemic: The role of addiction" Taylor VH, Curtis CM, and Davis C. Can Med Assoc J. 2010 Mar 9;182(4):327–28.*)

Experts I spoke with called this phenomenon either a "transfer of addictions" or "addiction interaction." If you or someone you know is struggling with one of the Seven Toxic Compulsions described in this book, you may see or experience some type of addiction transfer or an intensification of an already existing toxic compulsion.

Most treatment centers don't like to deal with co-occurring compulsions. The reason is straightforwardly financial. For example, to tell someone coming in for alcohol or drug treatment that they must also stop smoking while in treatment might scare people away, and that would affect profits. But the reality is, when left untreated, co-occurring compulsions trigger high relapse rates for the primary compulsion. So my hope is that this book, with its emphasis on education, will help to change attitudes and approaches common in the treatment industry.

Below are the most common co-occurring compulsions, the addictions that often get linked together. Often during treatment when the psychological surface of one toxic compulsion is scratched others are more clearly revealed. Let's call them the "fellow travelers."

FELLOW TRAVELERS

People with	Often also experience
Alcohol Abuse	Eating Disorders, Gambling Compulsion, Smoking Dependence
Drug Abuse	Alcohol Abuse, Eating Disorders, Smoking Dependence
Eating Disorders	Alcohol Abuse, Drug Abuse, Sexual Compulsion, Smoking Dependence
Gambling Compulsion	Alcohol Abuse, Drug Abuse, Eating Disorders, Smoking Dependence
Hoarding Compulsion	Alcohol Abuse, Eating Disorders
Sexual Compulsion	Alcohol Abuse, Drug Abuse, Eating Disorders
Smoking Dependence	Alcohol Abuse, Drug Abuse, Eating Disorders, Gambling Compulsion

To which fellow traveler grouping do you belong?

Even if you think your habit involves just alcohol or some other single compulsion, read through the rest of this book. You may in fact find you've gotten yourself involved with a group of "fellow travelers." You will need to recognize and address all of them eventually if you want a successful long-term recovery.

Just one more thought, one that probably should come with a hazard warning label: It's dangerous for both your thinking and behavior to swing back and forth between abstinence and using—though nearly every addict thinks they can. If you have this illness, trying to control your use rather than ending it could kill you. Never forget that!

If you have a dependency, as opposed to a nondependent use disorder, can you heal yourself and recover on your own? Dr. Howard Shaffer had this answer: "With alcohol, opioids, and gambling, roughly 5 percent to 15 percent of people can do it on their own, which means your chances are really not very good to do it on your own, but the science shows that it is possible. Most people want to think that they can be the one."

I

Toxic Compulsion 1: Alcohol Abuse

It's all right letting yourself go, as long as you can get yourself back.
—Mick Jagger

IN THIS CHAPTER:

- Indicators of an Alcohol Problem
- Time to Get Honest with Yourself
- Percentage of Users Who Become Dependent
- Alcohol Is the Most Dangerous Substance
- Why People Quit Drinking
- Clinical Research Ranks Effective Treatments
- Can You Become a "Moderate" Drinker?
- Who Needs Inpatient Treatment?
- Some Treatment Options
- Your 30-Day Challenge for Alcohol

Hawaii enjoys a well-deserved reputation as the vacation and relaxation capital of the United States. Both visitors and residents commonly seek escape from the pressures and stress of "ordinary" life. And that means they spend plenty of time basking in the sunshine, playing on the beach, or relaxing after rounds of golf or boating. I've seen this firsthand because I own a home in Hawaii and have spent a lot of time there over the years.

That "play" state of mind may be why our slice of paradise has earned the dubious distinction of being the Drinking Problem Capital of America. Both of the top two U.S. cities with the highest percentage of problem drinkers and binge drinkers are in the Aloha State, according to statistics compiled by the U.S. Centers for Disease Control and Prevention (CDC). Hilo on the big island of Hawaii ranks as the drunkest U.S. city, with 30.7 percent of the population meeting the criteria for binge and problem drinking. Close behind in second place is the town of Kapaa on the island of Kauai, with 30.5 percent of its citizenry admitting to excessive alcohol consumption.

What does heavy drinking or binge drinking look like? The CDC in its 2009 nationwide survey defined "heavy drinking" for men as having more than two alcohol beverages a day and for women more than one; binge drinking for men means downing five or more drinks at a time on one or more occasions during a month, and for women it means consuming four or more at least one or more times in a month.

Montana claims two of the other top five drunkest U.S. cities— Butte-Silver Bow at 29.3 percent of the population and Bozeman at 29.2 percent. This could make sense for a couple of reasons: 1) frigid temperatures might keep people indoors longer with more excuses to drink, though by that reasoning Alaska should have been at the top of the list; and, a more likely reason, 2) Montana has one of the nation's highest rates of high school binge drinking. Heavy drinking during the teenage years can influence levels of alcohol abuse later in life.

These days, according to the 2009 National Survey on Drug Use and Health, 86 percent of our kids have used alcohol and half of them are binge drinkers by the time they turn 21. Many of the underage binge drinkers will outgrow the habit, but increasing numbers will continue to succumb to their compulsions. Drinking behavior before the age of 16 is a key indicator of future alcohol use. When kids become heavy drinkers before the age of 15, "they are about six times more likely to end up with alcohol problems," said Peter Delaney, director of the Center for Substance Abuse Treatment at SAMHSA (the Substance Abuse and Mental Health Services Administration).

Pamela Hyde, administrator of SAMHSA, added: "The earlier someone starts using alcohol or drugs, the more likely they are to have an issue in adulthood. And conversely, if you can avoid using alcohol and drugs until you're 25 years old, your chances of getting addicted are greatly lessened."

This brings up an interesting question. Should parents be teaching their teenagers how to drink responsibly, just as we are supposed to teach them how to drive a car safely? Or should we be preaching and enforcing strict abstinence?

Though the minimum drinking age is 21 throughout the United States, 31 states allow parents to furnish alcohol to minors in the home. The statistics on use and abuse that I have seen are revealing. According to a 2004 survey of 6,245 U.S. teens, published in the *Journal of Adolescent Health*, those kids who drank alcohol in moderation with their parents, especially at meals or in religious rituals, were one-third as likely to engage in binge drinking as other teens, and half as likely to become regular drinkers.

There is an additional problem for teen binge drinkers, other than possibly setting a standard for abuse later in life: Alcohol abuse can inflict long-term harm to their developing brains. Using brain scans to study adolescents, university researchers reported in a 2009 issue of the *Journal of Clinical EEG and Neuroscience* that the frontal cortex and hippocampus of adolescents who have 20 or more alcohol drinks a month begin to change. Guess what those brain areas control—our cognitive and executive functions, our memory, our attention, and spatial skills. In other words, judgment becomes warped and impulse control is diminished. Unfortunately, the frontal cortex and the executive functions it coordinates are not fully developed until our early twenties. Alcohol use in adolescence impairs functions that are not yet fully developed.

By now, you should be getting a glimpse of your own pattern of alcohol behaviors, the ones you established early in life. Reflect on that for a few moments.

What kind of drinker were you as a teenager?

Were either of your parents a problem drinker?

How often did you get inebriated?

Was it a pattern that you continued into adulthood?

How often have you tried to stop drinking and failed?

Are you able to be honest with yourself about your drinking habits, or do you sense denial that needs to be penetrated for the truth to be known?

Indicators of an Alcohol Problem

It's not always easy to know if you or someone you love has an alcohol problem and is in need of treatment. There are usually layers of denial—both yours and theirs—which must be penetrated, and then there are the social pressures that must be resisted, pressures that tell us drinking alcohol is a "cool" and socially expected behavior, even though more and more there is a stigma attached to its overuse and abuse. Here are the indicators that a personal alcohol problem may exist:

You carry an alcohol-susceptible gene

From Dr. Drew Pinsky, addiction medicine specialist and clinical professor of psychiatry, University of Southern California School of Medicine: One day we will have a genetic spectrum for the disease of alcoholism. The North American Indian version of the gene that makes them susceptible to alcohol will be different from the Irish-Persian, which can be different from the Northern European, and they are going to have different potentials for the disease. When a person's genetic burden is low, the psychiatric burden or environmental burden has to be high for alcoholism to occur. But fundamentally, in my opinion, the most common issue that precipitates the disease from the genetic potential is something called Emotional Dysregulation. Not just more anxiety, not just more depression, which alcoholics have throughout their history, because they often come from an alcoholic family, but an incapacity to regulate their emotions. So their emotions are too prolonged, too intense, and too negative.

You're anxious or depressed

From Pamela Hyde, administrator of SAMHSA: If you take people who have a mental disorder, who are depressed, 20 percent also have problems with alcohol or drugs. Almost half of all people with an identifiable addictive disorder also have an identifiable mental illness. These disorders often go hand in hand. We have a tendency to say, "Let's take care of the depression and that will make the alcohol go away, or let's take care of the alcohol, and that will take care of the depression." I think the science tells us that integrated treatment, treating both concurrently, is the better way to go.

You're overconfident about handling risks

From Dr. Robert DuPont, President of the Institute for Behavior and Health Inc, first director of the National Institute on Drug Abuse, second White House Drug Chief, and clinical professor of psychiatry at Georgetown Medical School: Is it risky to be a social drinker? My answer is yes. I see lots of people who are social drinkers for many years and then become alcoholics, even later in their lives. The addiction switch gets thrown late for these people. Once that switch is on at any age you don't go back to being a controlled alcohol or drug user.

It's clear that everybody is vulnerable, but some are a lot more vulnerable than others and usually what you find is the people that have a problem really liked alcohol a lot and tolerated it. If you're starting to drink and you don't like it, can't tolerate it, and you feel terrible afterward and that leads you not to use, you're protected from becoming an alcoholic. But if the first time you use you say, "Whoa! That was cool. I can drink and I can hold my drinks," that's a very bad sign.

So what aspects of a person's lifestyle contribute to triggering or exacerbating substance use? Willingness to take risks and self-confidence that you can handle risk are very good predictors.

You exhibit these specific behaviors

From Norman G. Hoffmann, PhD, president of Evince Clinical Assessments: We've been looking at very detailed diagnostic data from over 7,000 people recently. And what we find is that there are certain things that are cardinal measures that you're dependent. If you sacrifice activities in order to use, whether its alcohol or other drugs, or if you've not fulfilled your normal role obligations. You were supposed to do something and didn't because you were preoccupied with drinking. You find yourself thinking a lot of about using when you aren't. That doesn't tend to happen for those who meet either an abuse (nondependent) criteria or the moderate substance-use disorder criteria.

If you set rules and you don't follow them, that's another one that tends to be on the list. If you've not fulfilled your role obligations as a homemaker or as an employee or whatever, if you've been very preoccupied with use, had a compulsion to use where you just felt you couldn't not use. If you regularly experience any of these indicators, then you have a serious issue and you're just not a mild user. If you're one of the many who do experience these issues, then you need to understand that abstinence is probably your only stable out.

You suffer from multiple health problems

Finally, when assessing unhealthy alcohol or drug use, you should look at levels of use that may risk producing health consequences.

Dr. Richard Saitz, professor of medicine and epidemiology and director of the Clinical Addiction Research and Education (CARE) Unit at the Boston University Schools of Medicine and Public Health, proposes asking one single straightforward question to assess risk: How many times in the last year have you had more than five drinks (for men), or four drinks (for women) in a single day? If your answer is one or more times, you have a risk of health consequences from alcohol. It's that simple.

Most people know about some of the obvious health consequences of alcohol abuse, from hangovers to chronic conditions such as liver disease and brain damage (yes, chronic use actually damages and *shrinks* parts of your brain that control judgment, impulses, and memory, along with regulating social and sexual behaviors). But did you also know that the chronic medical condition of alcohol abuse is the third leading cause of death in the United States and has been linked by medical studies to premature aging, high blood pressure, heart attack, stroke, and cancers of the breast, esophagus, stomach, liver, mouth, and throat?

Time to Get Honest with Yourself

We all possess layers of denial and self-deception about aspects of our lives. Whether it's about our vanity ("I look younger than anyone my age.") or about our skill levels ("I'm indispensable in this job.") or our impact on people ("I am universally loved by others."), our minds have a great capacity to trick us and shield us from unpleasant truths.

When it comes to alcohol and drugs and the other Seven Toxic Compulsions, our capacity to fool ourselves, which ordinarily serves to protect us from the wounding of pride, has much broader and deeper repercussions. These can include exclusion, the loss of one's job, family, home, self-respect, and freedom, and even death. Substance abuse is a nasty and devious disorder of the mind that further empowers any natural tendency toward denial so that we end up playing complicated games with our thoughts and our rationalizations in ways that smother the truth and inflict harm on ourselves and others.

That's one reason why it sometimes takes a life trauma such as a spouse leaving or bankruptcy or an unpleasant encounter with the criminal justice system for the layers of denial and the mind games finally to be punctured so that the light of honest self-reflection can shine through.

What sort of denial are you engaging in? What does the echo chamber inside your head sound like? Does any of this feel and sound familiar?

I don't have a problem.

I've never had a problem.

I will never have a problem.

I can always control my drinking.

Okay, occasionally I slip up.

But I can always stop drinking if I really want to.

I enjoy drinking too much to ever stop.

If other people have a problem with my drinking, that's their problem.

Okay, getting drunk and crashing my car into that tree was a slip up.

It will never happen again. I promise.

I know I can control my drinking.

And the mind games and the endless chatter of delusional thoughts go on and on and on.

It's time to get real with yourself, and if you're playing dangerous mind games, it's time to stop. The following two questionnaires are useful screening tools to help you gauge the severity of your drinking. It's an opportunity to shed some light on the matter and help you avoid inflicting unnecessary harm to yourself in the future.

The CAGE Alcohol Addiction Test

This simple test may open your eyes about the true extent of your use of alcohol. Answer yes or no to each question.

1. Have you ever felt you should Cut down on your drinking?

(continued on next page)

(continued from previous page)

2. Have you ever been Annoyed when people have commented on your drinking?

3. Have you ever felt Guilty or badly about your drinking?

4. Have you ever had an Eye-opener first thing in the morning to steady your nerves or get rid of a hangover?

If you answered yes to two or more questions, there is a good chance you have a problem with alcohol and should continue your self-analysis and explore treatment resources.

For more about the CAGE test, visit www.AddictionsAndRecovery.org.

Still not convinced you have an accurate insight into your drinking habits? Don't know if you have an addiction or just a festering bad habit? What follows is a more in-depth series of questions that, if you're able to be honest with yourself, should dispel any doubts about your drinking status.

The AUDIT (Alcohol Use Disorders Identification Test)

To correctly answer some of these questions you need to know the definition of a drink. For this test one drink is:

one can of beer (12 oz or approx 330 ml of 5 percent or less alcohol), or
one glass of wine (5 oz or approx 140 ml of 12 percent alcohol), or
one shot of liquor (1.5 oz or approx 40 ml of 40 percent alcohol).

1. How often do you have a drink containing alcohol?
   Never (score 0)
   Monthly or less (score 1)
   2–4 times a month (score 2)
   2–3 times a week (score 3)
   4 or more times a week (score 4)

2. How many alcoholic drinks do you have on a typical day when you are drinking?

    1 or 2 (0)

    3 or 4 (1)

    5 or 6 (2)

    7–9 (3)

    10 or more (4)

3. How often do you have 6 or more drinks on one occasion?

    Never (0)

    Less than monthly (1)

    Monthly (2)

    Weekly (3)

    Daily or almost daily (4)

4. How often during the past year have you found that you drank more or for a longer time than you intended?

    Never (0)

    Less than monthly (1)

    Monthly (2)

    Weekly (3)

    Daily or almost daily (4)

5. How often during the past year have you failed to do what was normally expected of you because of your drinking?

    Never (0)

    Less than monthly (1)

    Monthly (2)

    Weekly (3)

    Daily or almost daily (4)

6. How often during the past year have you had a drink in the morning to get yourself going after a heavy drinking session?

    Never (0)

    Less than monthly (1)

    Monthly (2)

    Weekly (3)

    Daily or almost daily (4)

(continued on next page)

(continued from previous page)

7. How often during the past year have you felt guilty or remorseful after drinking?
   Never (0)
   Less than monthly (1)
   Monthly (2)
   Weekly (3)
   Daily or almost daily (4)

8. How often during the past year have you been unable to remember what happened the night before because of your drinking?
   Never (0)
   Less than monthly (1)
   Monthly (2)
   Weekly (3)
   Daily or almost daily (4)

9. Have you or anyone else been injured as a result of your drinking?
   No (0)
   Yes, but not in the past year (2)
   Yes, during the past year (4)

10. Has a relative, friend, doctor, or health care worker been concerned about your drinking or suggested that you cut down?
    No (0)
    Yes, but not in the past year (2)
    Yes, during the past year (4)

Your score: _____

AUDIT scores in the 8–15 range represent a medium level of alcohol problems, whereas scores of 16 and above represent a high level of alcohol problems.

The AUDIT (Alcohol-Use Disorders Identification Test) was developed by the World Health Organization (WHO). The test correctly classifies 95 percent of people into either alcoholics or nonalcoholics. It was tested on 2,000 people before being published. The pdf format version of the AUDIT is available through the WHO Web site, where you can also find the Alcohol, Smoking, and Substance Involvement Screening Test (ASSIST): www. who.int/substance_abuse/activities/assist/en/index.html.

Percentage of Users Who Become Dependent

This information comes from the only major study that estimates the percentage of persons using a specific substance who will become dependent on that substance. If you think about the number of people who periodically drink alcohol, the 15.4 percent who become "problem" drinkers translates into tens of millions of users with a habit that may be evolving into a dependency.

Tobacco—31.9 percent
Heroin—23.1 percent
Cocaine—16.7 percent
Alcohol—15.4 percent
Stimulants—11.2 percent
Cannabis—9.1 percent
Psychedelics—4.9 percent
Inhalants—3.7 percent

(Source: "Comparative epidemiology of dependence on tobacco, alcohol, controlled substances, and inhalants: Basic findings from the National Comorbidity Survey." Anthony JC, Warner LA, and Kessler RC. Exp Clin Psychopharmacol. *1994 Aug;2(3):244–68. doi: 10.1037 /1064-1297. 2.3.244.)*

Alcohol Is the Most Dangerous Substance

Here is another collection of comparisons for you to keep in mind. The authors of this study evaluated the relative harm that alcohol, tobacco, and other drugs cause to users and others, whether they be friends, family members, coworkers, the local community, or the broader society. The authors assigned each a harm score on a 100-point scale. The higher the score, the greater the overall harm associated with the substance.

Here is the ranking:

Alcohol—72
Heroin—55
Crack cocaine—54
Methamphetamine—more than 30
Cocaine—less than 30
Tobacco—less than 30
Amphetamine—more than 20
Cannabis—20
GHB—less than 20
Benzodiazepines—15
Ketamine—14
Methadone—13
Butane—12
Anabolic steroids—9
Khat—8
Ecstasy—8
LSD—less than 10
Buprenorphine—less than 10
Mushrooms—less than 10

(*Source: "Drug harms in the UK: A multicriteria decision analysis." Nutt DJ, King LA, and Phillips LD. Lancet. 2010 Nov 6;376(9752):1558–65.*)

Myth buster: alcoholism is a moral weakness

Public opinion polls conducted in the United States throughout the first decade of the 21st century consistently showed that more than half of all people surveyed consider alcohol abuse and alcoholism to be caused by a "moral weakness" or a "character flaw" that can be cured merely by exercising willpower. Poll results for drug abuse and addiction provide similar results about public attitudes.

Although there is no doubt that willpower is important in any person's decision to quit drinking and to remain in recovery, the root cause of alcoholism can be found in a person's genetic predisposition, family history of substance abuse, and underlying psychological triggers such as anxiety and depression. In addition, environment is important. Poverty, social norms, easy access to substances, natural and man-made-disasters—all can contribute to the problem. These are all factors that must be taken into consideration for long-term sobriety to occur.

"There have been about 25 different genes found that are associated with how you respond to alcohol, determining such things as whether you have a tolerance," pointed out clinical psychologist Norman G. Hoffmann, president of Evince Clinical Assessments, a pioneer in the study of treatments for addictions. That shows how complicated the genetic picture of addiction can be. By contrast, research by the National Institutes of Health determined that mutations in just one gene, the LCT gene, determine whether you have lactose intolerance, a painful digestive condition.

As for alcoholism being a disease process, Pamela Hyde, administrator of the federal government's Substance Abuse and Mental Health Services Administration (SAMHSA) program, said, "There is no question that [alcohol is] a disease process. There's also no question that there are some behaviors associated with getting started that tend to be voluntary in the beginning, but very quickly can become the disease process. There are also some behavioral and willpower things associated with remaining in recovery, yet we have to make sure that we stay focused on the disease process of alcoholism, which is not unlike any other disease—diabetes, for example—and it needs to be treated in that way."

WHAT LURKS BENEATH ALCOHOLISM— AN EXPERT'S SUCCESS STORY

From Alan Marlatt, PhD, the late director of the Addictive Behavior Research Center, University of Washington: I got a call from a psychiatrist in the University of Washington Medical School who treats people with depression problems and he said, "Alan, I'm seeing this woman and I have been treating her for depression. I got her on depression meds and am doing therapy with her. Today she said she has this drinking issue. I don't really deal with alcohol treatment, so I referred her to an alcoholism treatment center in Seattle. Well, I'd like you also to meet with her and do an assessment."

By the time this woman came to see me, she'd already been through the alcoholism treatment center folks. And I said, "How is it going?" She said,

(continued on next page)

(continued from previous page)

"Everybody is telling me something different. The psychiatrist said, 'You're probably drinking to self-medicate your depression. And your depression is really causing the drinking.' And then I went to the alcoholism treatment center and they said, 'No, it's the opposite. Your alcoholism is causing your depression, so you should quit drinking.'"

And she said, "I can't do it. I'm not ready to quit drinking. The only thing that makes me feel better when I'm depressed is drinking sherry wine." That was her favorite beverage. She felt stuck, so I suggested that she consider harm reduction therapy, which is basically designed for people who are unwilling or unable to make a commitment to abstinence. For someone like her, it's trying to understand the relationship between her drinking and her depression. Can she learn skills to moderate her drinking that might help to get her back on track, especially if she wasn't willing to go on an abstinence-based program?

She said, "Gosh, I'd be very interested in that." So I met with her on an outpatient basis. I saw her once a week or occasionally twice a week and got her into a standard moderation management kind of program where someone like her keeps track of her drinking, tries to see what the relationship is between her mood and how much she drinks, and, also, what is happening with her life that makes her want to drink more, what triggers her depression. And basically, what emerged was there were a lot of problems going on in her marriage. Her husband was going to Al-Anon, that 12-Step group for family members, and he said, "I'm convinced you're an alcoholic, so unless you completely quit drinking and go to AA, you're in denial."

And when he would say things like that, it just made her angrier and she started to drink more. Eventually, she got a DUI (driving under the influence) and the husband said, "That's it. We're sending you to inpatient treatment. You're endangering our kids." So she agreed to a 30-day detox and residential treatment program. And then she stopped drinking. At the end of this particular program, they have a family weekend. Her husband refused to go. He said, "Look, she has a biological disease. I don't have anything to do with it."

She came back from the program and wasn't drinking. And about two weeks later, she was shopping near where they lived and she saw her husband in a car nearby embracing another woman. She headed to the liquor store and just got totally drunk. Then a woman friend of hers said, "You know, you started learning that meditation practice when you were in treatment?" Her friend really liked meditation and said, "This is a time for us to go on a retreat." And so she agreed and they went on a meditation retreat.

She said, "I was quitting alcohol not just for the retreat, but for the rest of my life." She gave it up altogether. And she is still doing great and I asked her, "Do you sometimes feel like drinking when you're feeling a little depressed?" She replied, "Oh yeah, thoughts come into my mind, but I no longer have to be dictated by my thoughts."

Her success was about finding the right choice. I think that's a virtue of addiction recovery. There are still many people saying, "We'll do an assessment and we'll know what treatment is best for you." No, it doesn't work that way. It's more the patient's choice. You've got to have lots of options so that people can see that there are more ways than one to initiate change, that there are many pathways to recovery.

Inconvenient truth—some teenagers can drink like alcoholics

From Dr. Thomas McLellan, CEO of the Treatment Research Institute and former deputy director of the White House Office of National Drug Control Policy: It turns out that some young people, 18 to 25, can drink alcoholically. Go to any college campus, go to any Army base, and you will see regular use that meets any diagnostic criterion for alcoholics. Now if I said these people were 40 years old—and the science supports me on this—they'll never drink normally again. They won't be able to.

But it is a fact that some people in that range up to 25, or maybe even a little older, can meet the criteria for alcoholism and later age out of the problem. They can meet criteria for marijuana dependence. And they get out of college, go to work in the financial industry, and can use alcohol only on Friday and Saturday night and stop or greatly reduce marijuana use. Many others in this age group, however, don't and probably can't age out of their problem. So, you can't assume that if you're under the age of 25 and have an alcohol or drug problem, it will simply go away as you mature or your life circumstances change. We don't understand what happens between the ages of 25 and 40. But by time you're 40, your chances of aging out of an alcohol or drug problem are slim to none. You can't have been drinking alcohol weekly and then suddenly say, "I guess I'll just start drinking less now."

A colleague of mine looked at a Drexel University's freshman class about 10 years ago. He was very concerned about males who had either a father or an uncle with an alcohol problem. So he measured alcohol consumption in groups who didn't have that first-degree relative and age-matched them with boys going to the same school who did. They were all drinking like fish. They were just drinking way in excess of what was good for them and they were drinking in dangerous fashions.

Here is what he found: Four years after college was over, the sons of the alcoholics were still drinking that way, but the sons of the non-alcoholics had reduced their use substantially.

Why People Quit Drinking

There are myriad reasons why a problem drinker may choose to quit or be pressured into quitting, or at least cutting back on use. Here are six reasons cited by some prominent experts interviewed for this book.

Family health history

From Dr. Leonard Weiss, psychiatrist and "addictionologist," Atlanta Behavioral Care: There is always that person who wanders in and they're just getting to be a bit on the abuse side of things and they just actually stop, it's like a miracle. The main reason they give me is they say, "You know my father, my mother, whoever—they were alcoholic and they died of cirrhosis of the liver and I just—I don't want to go that way." That's the main reason. Usually they somehow get in touch with the fact that they have a genetic proclivity.

Health concerns for the unborn

From Carlton Erickson, Director, Addiction Science Research and Education Center and distinguished professor of pharmacy/toxicology, University of Texas at Austin: Which drugs produce the worst fetal syndrome when the mother uses them during pregnancy? Alcohol by far is the worst drug. It produces the permanent effects: abnormal facial characteristics, and organ developmental defects, including brain underdevelopment. All other recreational drugs (legal or illegal) produce marked, but temporary, effects on the fetus. But the effects of alcohol on the fetus can be lifelong.

Legal consequences

From Pamela Hyde, administrator of SAMHSA: When a person with an alcohol problem is in a criminal situation, such as driving under the influence or something more serious where a person is hurt or dies because of an addiction, sometimes it's the courts that have to say, "You're going to suffer the consequences if you don't get treatment." Of course, if that person with the alcohol caused something more serious such as another's injury or death, the courts will lower the boom. Treatment, if any, will occur behind bars. Some people need these kinds of punitive consequences to change. For others, an intervention by family and friends who say, "You have an issue, we love you, and we want to help you change," is enough. So for some people who need the consequences, try to be supportive. For some people who need the support, the possibility of consequences may be an important part of starting the treatment and recovery process.

Fear of losing something

From Dr. Andrea Barthwell, CEO of the North Carolina treatment center Two Dreams Outer Banks: Some people can make a decision to quit by saying, "I don't like the way my life is going." It is really sort of decade driven. If by the end of your 20s, if you haven't been able to create or maintain healthy relationships, the longing to be connected drives people to seek help. In their 30s, the reality of life sets in. Everything in their 20s is full of promise. And in the 30s, reality sets in and people experience dissatisfaction with where they've gotten in life. Sometimes that dissatisfaction accelerates the process of addiction, or sometimes it sets it off.

In their 40s, it's generally a loss that motivates change. Your parents die, your marriage breaks up, your kids go off to college, you're not performing well at work. Your health goes and you're dealing with that. And in the 50s, if you've survived to that point, it's generally about a rebirth, and a lot of the recovery that I see during the 50s is spontaneous. It's like all the stuff that used to drag me down in a negative way, I don't tolerate anymore. Then, if you haven't left something significant or contributed in some way by your 60s, you start longing for that. You start trying to get busy because you know you don't have much time left and you can't have substance dependence getting in the way.

A desire to achieve something

From Thomas McLellan, PhD, CEO of the Treatment Research Institute and former deputy director of the White House Office of National Drug Control Policy: Quitting can start with asking, "What do you want in your life? Do you want to graduate? Do you want to get that new job, or meet that new girl? How is alcohol helping? How's your drinking helping you to achieve what you want?" If it's not, and usually it isn't, that's a sign, and yet, you're still doing it. Sometimes asking these kinds of questions can bring the person to the point where they're thinking about their behavior in relation to their own goals and that leads them to say, "It's not working for me, actually. I need to change."

When a therapist does this, it's called a motivational intervention and that enables the individual to see that their own life goals are not being met by their substance use. Next they have an opportunity to try different ways of reducing their use. For people who have lost control over alcohol, they need to have something that's important to their lives. Without it, without a goal, without a good job, a good religion, a good woman or a good man, it's very difficult to give up their love affair with that substance.

To end depression

From Dr. Jeffrey D. Roth, addiction psychiatrist, author, editor of Journal of Groups in Addiction Recovery, *and medical director, Working Sobriety Chicago*: I've never had anybody come to talk to me where we didn't find an addiction or compulsive behavior. If somebody comes in and says they're depressed, okay, I say, "You're depressed, are you engaged in any behavior that would be depressing?" And if the answer is, "What do you mean by that?" I say, "Well, for instance, alcohol is a central nervous system depressant. Are you using alcohol?" And the person will say, "Well, I drink recreationally." And my next question is, "Is there a connection between drinking and getting depressed?"

And in general, if the person is using alcohol and they are depressed, there's a connection between their use of alcohol and depression. So I'll say, "Okay, the first thing you might want to consider is, what is your investment in staying depressed based on your continued drinking?" If you continue drinking, you're taking in a depressant and you're likely to be depressed. If being depressed is worth continuing to use alcohol, then I guess you're telling me it's not a problem.

If being depressed is something you'd like to do something about, you have a few choices. If you want to continue drinking a little bit, my question is, "What is your investment in being a little bit depressed?" So it becomes a question of what are you accomplishing by ingesting alcohol. Sometimes people are tired of being depressed and they come in ready to change their life. So they quit drinking.

QUITTING ON YOUR OWN—AN EXPERT'S EXPERIENCE

From Dr. Richard Rawson, associate director, UCLA Integrated Substances Abuse Programs: When I was working as an addictions expert in 1984, I was also drinking four or five beers a night and smoking joints and recreationally doing lots of things. I certainly would not have thought of myself as meeting the criteria for dependence, but I was smart enough to go to a doctor and get annual physicals. He said, "Your cholesterol is too high, your blood pressure is too high, your weight is too high." He would run through a list of things and one question would be: "How's your drinking, how much are you drinking?" And I would always lie and say, "Well, I drink two beers every couple of days."

But eventually, after like the second or third time, he said, "You know I don't understand this; let's talk more about your drinking." And so, "Yeah, okay, all right. So yes, I do drink four or five beers every day and other things." You know this is before screening and brief interventions came along. He said, "Well look, why don't we do an experiment? Why don't you try for a month to reduce your alcohol use and, if you can, down to zero, and come back in a month? Let me draw your lipids and check your blood pressure and see what happens." I just couldn't resist the idea of making a decision with data, so I said yes.

So I did it and it was harder than hell to give up my four beers, but I did it. I found my weight dropped by seven pounds and my lipids were down

(continued on next page)

(continued from previous page)

and my blood pressure was down. My doctor said, "What about doing it for another month?" So, I said, "Okay, you know I'm not an alcoholic, I'm not addicted, but listen, I'll do this other experiment."

I haven't had a drink now in 25 years, and this doctor did it without beating me over the head with a big book, without chastising me, or doing an intervention. What he did was a brief intervention. Health professionals giving clear information and feedback about risk and about possible benefits can make a huge difference. A brief intervention might not work the first time. It might take a couple of visits. But we need more doctors who know what the symptoms of alcohol dependence are and know what questions to ask.

Clinical Research Ranks Effective Treatments

Below are the top 20 alcohol treatment approaches based on the cumulative evidence of effectiveness compiled from the results of 381 clinical trial studies. These characterize what has come to be known as medical science's "evidence-based" treatment options, all of which are available for you to choose if they suit your own treatment needs.

1. Brief intervention
2. Motivational enhancement
3. Acamprosate (a GABA agonist)
4. Community reinforcement
5. Self-change manual
6. Naltrexone (an opiate antagonist)
7. Behavioral self-control training
8. Behavior contracting
9. Social skills training
10. Marital therapy (behavioral)
11. Aversion therapy (nausea)
12. Case management
13. Cognitive therapy
14. Aversion therapy (covert sensitization and apneic)
15. Family therapy

16. Acupuncture
17. Client-centered counseling
18. Aversion therapy (electrical)
19. Exercise
20. Stress management

(Source: Handbook of Alcoholism Treatment Approaches: Effective Alternatives, 3rd ed. *Hester RK and Miller WR, eds. [Boston: Allyn & Bacon, 2003], p. 19.)*

Top 10 treatments are all relatively brief and can be delivered in an outpatient setting

None of the 10 most effective treatment approaches in the list above requires inpatient care, and most revolve around brief interactions with treatment providers and taking responsibility for the course of your own treatment trajectory. A few, of course, can be applied over extended periods of time and gradually have their effect. Even if the recovery pathway only involves taking one of the two medications, you still have control over your path to recovery. Among these top 10 treatments there is an approach "designed for people all along the continuum of severity, from problem drinkers to severely dependent individuals," according to Hester and Miller's *Handbook of Alcoholism.* Remember, too, for many people a formal treatment plan is not always the pathway to recovery. Community-based not-for-profit organizations and other recovery community organizations—all run by people in recovery—can provide a wide variety of support services that supplement and sometimes even replace treatment.

Some treatments don't rank because of too few studies

A number of possibly effective treatment approaches for alcohol-use disorders don't appear in the top 20 list because just two or fewer studies evaluating them had been finished by the time the Hester and Miller handbook was published.

Under-studied treatments include:

- Biofeedback
- Mindfulness
- Transcendental meditation

In the years since the handbook was released, however, numerous studies have been conducted demonstrating the effectiveness of all three of these treatment "tools." I will discuss those results in Part Two of this book. In Appendix Two various mutual-aid recovery resource options are listed, many of them on the Faces and Voices of Recovery Web site, www.facesandvoicesofrecovery.org.html. And with the explosive growth in new technologies comes additional recovery options, including interactive text-messaging platforms and smart phone GPS apps to map high-risk geographic areas.

Also, as of the handbook's 2002 release, only four studies had examined hypnosis as a treatment for alcohol problems, and all four reported no long-term positive effect on the drinking behaviors of study subjects.

What is the verdict on medications as treatment?

From the Miller/Hester handbook: "Many medications designed for the treatment of psychological disorders (e.g., anxiety, depression, psychosis) have been tested, and although these can be useful in treating concomitant disorders, they typically have very little direct effect on drinking. There are, however, two medications that now appear to be quite effective aids in the treatment of alcohol dependence: naltrexone and acamprosate."

Since those comments were published, two more medications have been championed by some treatment centers and addiction experts: Vivitrol and Campral. Vivitrol, is a long-acting (or depot) formulation of naltrexone given by monthly injection. Naltrexone, both in its original pill form and in its newer long-lasting form, blocks the high that alcoholics and persons addicted to opiates such as heroin or oxycodone normally feel. Campral is taken orally and is intended to restore the balance in the brain's neurotransmitter pathways harmed by alcohol abuse, which also helps to reduce cravings.

Although these medications are an improvement over Antabuse (disulfram), the medicine that has been in use for decades and makes a user sick when alcohol is consumed, there is an inherent limitation in relying upon medications for long-term recovery. They may be helpful in reducing urges so the person can get through the early months of recovery, but they don't treat the underlying psychological causes for the disorder, teach the skills needed to achieve sustained recovery, or substitute for the necessary lifestyle changes and family and peer group support necessary for successful long-term recovery.

Taking naltrexone, for example, is a bit of a crap shoot. You just don't know what the response will be. Dr. Thomas McLellan explained why: "If you give naltrexone to alcoholics, you get a pretty modest response. But it turns out if you give naltrexone to those alcoholics who have a particular genetic heritability, you get a really dramatic, almost curative response. If alcoholics don't have that specific genetic combination, you get very little response."

Are there more natural ways to reduce cravings?

To successfully stop drinking and remain sober it's important to limit exposure to the triggers that produce the thoughts that, in turn, release the cravings for alcohol. These triggers can include people, places, memories, emotions, activities—just about anything that connects you to thoughts about alcohol and drinking. Controlling these triggers can be a difficult challenge for anyone. But it's not impossible and the better you get at it, the less "charge" these triggers will carry for you over time.

"You may not be able to completely eliminate your exposure to triggers, but you always have control over your thoughts," observed Dr. Harold C. Urschel, CEO of Urschel Recovery Science Institute, chief of medical strategy for www.enterhealth.com, and author of *Healing the Addicted Brain* (2009, Sourcebooks). "Cravings are common in the recovery process. They are not a sign of weakness or failure. Cravings are like waves in the ocean: They may come in big and strong, but they go out with no strength at all. The startling fact is, people in recovery typically give in to only about 5 percent of their cravings! That means 95 percent of the time, you will not drink or use in response to a craving. That means that you can already resist just about all of your cravings—and with work and time, you can learn to resist the rest and, eventually, they will go away."

In his book and on his Web site, www.EnterHealth.com/HealingtheAddictedBrain, Urschel described five "craving crusher" techniques that anyone can learn to use:

- Distract yourself. Whether by using a meditation practice, doing yoga or exercise, or listening to music, you can distract yourself from cravings when they arise.
- Use flash cards. By writing a list of the positive benefits of resisting cravings and the negative effects of embracing them—and referring to the cards when cravings arise—you can train your brain to stay focused on sobriety.

- Talk it out. This one is commonly used in 12-Step programs. When you feel a craving, contact someone sober by phone or in person to talk about what you're feeling in the moment.
- Stress management. Again, whether it's meditation, yoga, or other stress-managing techniques, or acupuncture, massage, or reflexology performed on you by someone else, it's important to keep your stress levels low to keep triggers at bay.
- Visualization. A variety of sensory awareness techniques fall under the heading of visualization exercises. What they generally have in common is they distract you from the cravings by keeping your attention focused on a serene, positive, and happy place that you create within your mind's eye.

For more detailed information about the above techniques and other ways to reduce alcohol cravings, refer to Part Two of this book for a how-to course on a range of effective and easy-to-learn techniques.

What makes brief interventions effective?

It's important to emphasize that dozens of clinical studies show a significant beneficial effect on a problem drinker can occur when contact with a physician, social worker, or addictions counselor is relatively brief but impactful. Three types of brief interventions rank among the top five most effective evidence-supported treatment approaches.

These approaches contrast sharply with confrontational counseling styles, which, whether delivered in an individual or group setting, "have one of the most dismal track records in outcome research with not a single positive study," concluded the authors of the handbook's chapter on treatment research.

One of those authors, William R. Miller, the distinguished professor of psychology and psychiatry at the University of New Mexico, explained his analysis of findings from 30 studies that identified the six important reasons, or elements, that make these brief conversations so effective:

1. Feedback. People get personal information about themselves and their drinking practices. This isn't a lecture, because lectures have little impact on drinking problems. The information could be the results of a liver function test, showing them where those results put them in relation to the general

population; such results usually surprise them because they think their drinking is quite normal.

2. Responsibility. These interventions tell people it is up to them; no one can make the change for them. Their autonomy is being acknowledged.

3. Advice. The advice-giver shows compassion in expressing concern and suggests a change in the drinking behavior.

4. Menu of options. The drinkers are told there is a range of different approaches, if they want help, so the key is to find what works for them. That is empowering.

5. Empathy. The counselor's style is a listening, compassionate one, rather than an in-your-face authoritarian "I know best" approach.

6. Self-efficacy. Instill optimism: People can and do make changes in their drinking habits.

All of those were mixed together in these 15-minute interventions in the studies analyzed by Prof. Miller. The interventions occurred in a variety of settings, even in places like an emergency room where the alcohol abuser was being stitched up from an injury.

More study results support my optimism. In 2007, British researchers assessed the effectiveness of brief interventions in reducing alcohol consumption by doing a "meta-analysis" of 21 randomized controlled trials involving 7,286 patients in primary care settings. Meta-analysis means statistically comparing the results of multiple studies that address a particular question.

On average, patients who received brief interventions reduced their alcohol consumption by 41 grams a week compared to patients with similar drinking habits who didn't receive intervention. "Brief interventions consistently produced reductions in alcohol consumption," wrote the nine University of Newcastle authors of the study. The effect was clearer and more pronounced in male patients than in women after a follow-up one year later. (*Source: "Effectiveness of brief alcohol interventions in primary care populations." Eileen F. Kaner et al.* Cochrane Database Syst Rev. *2007 Apr 18;(2):CD004148.*)

"Motivational interviewing" inspires drinking habit changes

Motivational interviewing is an effective type of brief intervention pioneered by Prof. Miller. It involves a way of talking to people to encourage the emergence of their own internal motivation for change. He explained it this way:

"There is no formula for the questions that can be asked. I would first ask about your drinking habits. I might ask, 'Tell me about what's been happening in your life that is negative. What is the downside of your drinking? What would be some advantages about changing your drinking? How would you do it? How would you go about that to succeed? How important do you think it is to be drinking?'

"I listen and ask them to give me their own experience. You get the person talking about their own motivations. They begin to see that the cost of their drinking has gotten to the point where it isn't worth it anymore. They begin to desire change."

Can you do a brief intervention on yourself?

Sometimes it's possible, though admittedly it's rare, for someone to ask themselves three or so questions, all brief intervention questions that shake loose not only their realization of their alcohol problem, but also lead to a commitment to addressing the problem. Psychiatrist Leonard Weiss provided three questions that might be used by someone attempting a brief self-intervention:

1. What is my potential in the major areas of my life, and how much is my addiction affecting that potential?
2. What do my family and friends think? (Since none of these decisions is made in a vacuum.)
3. What are my options (practically and financially) for treatment if I make a decision to receive treatment?

(To learn more about interventions and how to conduct them, refer to Part Two of this book and the section "I Love an Addict, How Can I Help Myself?")

Why don't 12-Step programs appear in the top 20 ranking?

You won't find Alcoholics Anonymous and the 12-Step structure in the Hester/Miller handbook's top 20 ranked treatment approaches for three very good reasons: 1) nearly all of the studies done simply tested *coerced attendance* (court orders or employee assistance mandates by employers) at AA meetings, and it's common knowledge that the AA program works most effectively for people who are committed to it by choice; 2) 95 percent of the people who attend their first AA meeting end up dropping out and not staying in the program long enough to experience beneficial results, so few studies have focused on or have followed long-term attendees at AA meetings; and 3) AA and other 12-Step programs are not forms of treatment (i.e., they are not clinical services provided by professional practitioners). *(See Part Two of this book for more information about 12-Step programs and their effectiveness.)*

Can You Become a "Moderate" Drinker?

Between the extremes of uncontrolled problem drinking on the one hand and total abstinence on the other is a type of compromise or middle ground of use called the Moderate Drinking program that seems to work for some people.

For college binge drinkers and adults who feel capable of continuing to drink responsibly but want to reduce their consumption levels, and for people who need to experience an intervention but fear the stigma and shame of doing so with family or friends, computerized and Internet-delivered interventions and drinking-control techniques may be the answer to a prayer.

This evidence-based approach using computers and the Internet has been pioneered by Dr. Reid Hester and his team of clinical researchers at Behavior Therapy Associates in Albuquerque, NM. It involves a cleverly designed series of interlocking components:

- A Drinker's Check-up, a computer-based motivational intervention, available as both an Internet or Windows application, which gives an assessment of drinking habits. The Drinker's Check-up has been included in SAMHSA's National Register of Evidence-based Programs based on clinical study results and the finding that college students reduced their drinking by up to 55 percent in the months following a session.
- For an annual fee of just $59, an interactive Web site, www. moderatedrinking.com, guides alcohol users through steps to control their drinking based on the principles of Behavioral Self-Control Training. Dr. Hester conducted a randomized clinical trial with users of the program and found that their

alcohol consumption was cut nearly in half. There is even a
Facebook page and evidence-based Web apps for people with
alcohol and drug problems.

- To further address the needs of early-stage problem drinkers
  who do not want to abstain, Moderation Management (MM)
  can be joined online (www.moderation.org) or by meeting in
  person at sites around the country. The organization's goal
  is management and control of alcohol consumption rather
  than complete abstinence. About 30 percent of MM members eventually do decide to enter abstinence-based programs after testing whether they could adhere to MM values
  and goals. One key MM assumption is that alcohol abuse,
  in contrast to dependence, is a learned habit and not a disease; and that problem drinkers should take responsibility
  for their own recovery by being offered a choice of behavioral change goals. Dr. Hester is on the board of directors of
  this program.

A 2006 study of the Moderation Management program in the *International Journal of Drug Policy* found that the dropout rate for new
MM members was 61 percent, compared to 81 percent within one
month for Alcoholics Anonymous members. Another interesting difference between the two programs was in the proportion of women
in attendance—66 percent of MM members were women compared
to AA's female membership of just 33 percent. This difference may
reflect the fear of stigma, a particular barrier to women's help-seeking.
The MM online format combined with the use of pseudonyms, and
the fact that MM also encourages a discussion of life problems and
emotional issues other than drinking seems to account for the gender
disparity between MM and AA.

Study author Ana Kosok of Columbia University reached this conclusion: "Women may have needs unmet by AA, which focuses primarily on alcohol cessation . . . MM emphasizes balance in all areas of
life . . . MM may be particularly attractive to women because they need
not leave home or disclose their help-seeking to family and friends,
and because MM may offer more opportunities for attention to personal issues."

In 2011 Dutch researchers studied Web-based program treatments
for problem drinkers and concluded that "Web-based interventions
for problem drinkers improve the availability of alcohol treatment

services and reach a more diverse segment of the population of problem drinkers . . . evidence supports the clinical effectiveness of a diversity of Web-based interventions . . . it seems that the best results are achieved with interventions that use personalized feedback." *(Source: "Attrition in web-based treatment for problem drinkers." Marloes G. Postel et al.* J Med Internet Res. *2011, Dec. 27;13(4):e117.)*

Dr. Hester further observed: "When you're undecided about whether you have a drinking problem and need to change, a 12-Step program or other abstinence-only program may not work at first. Nobody likes to be told what to do. Our Drinker's Check-up online program helps people answer the questions, 'Should I be concerned about my drinking, what risks are there, and how bad are my consequences?' It helps them resolve these questions. There is a lot of data indicating that people are more willing to disclose information about their drug or alcohol use to a computer program than to a person. Anonymity helps to initiate the process of change for many people."

Here are some links to check out for more information:

www.behaviortherapy.com
www.collegedrinkerscheckup.com
www.drinkerscheckup.com
www.moderatedrinking.com
www.moderation.org

CAN "PROBLEM" DRINKERS BE "CONTROL" DRINKERS?
AN EXPERT'S STORY

From Dr. Leonard Weiss, psychiatrist and addictions specialist: I traveled to a Texas city and attended 12-Step meetings with a psychotherapist I'll call Judy. She could be described as your typical AA person. She had a sponsor. I think she had been a heroin, cocaine, and alcohol user. And the bottom line is she was clean and sober for I think at least 10 years when I met her.

Some time went by and she contacted me again to say she hadn't been going to meetings for two years and she was seeing a therapist. She said, "I talked it over with the therapist, I planned this out and I just decided I'm going to do controlled drinking."

(continued on next page)

(continued from previous page)

She goes to yoga and church and she's always experimenting with things and taking on the spiritual things. And she just puts her nose to the grindstone and does things like that. She had just totally divorced herself from AA.

And now the bottom line is again, she hasn't been to meetings in several years and I've actually been with her in a restaurant and it's kind of freaky, when you've known somebody as an AA person, and she's like, "What kind of wine do you have on the menu or what kind of beer." I'm sitting and the hairs of my neck are standing, but she's able to do it. She said the only time she has a problem is when she's home alone and she'll think about maybe having a beer. She said then it just takes a ton of willpower.

But again, she is the only documented case that I know of where an abuser became a controlled user successfully. Now, five years later, she is able to drink in a controlled manner both inside and outside the home, although she has to constantly work at it using therapy, frequent church and yoga meetings, exercise, and diet.

Who Needs Inpatient Treatment?

Before you jump to the conclusion that you or someone you care about needs to enter an inpatient treatment facility, which, needless to say, can be very expensive, carefully consider all of the options and what the following two experts have to say.

From Norman G. Hoffman, clinical psychologist and president of Evince Clinical Assessments: Whether you should be in an inpatient or outpatient program needs to be dictated by whether or not your life is stable enough to benefit from the outpatient program, or whether you need some kind of a controlled, safe environment in which treatment can begin its process. So the issue of who needs a residential placement is really more a function of do you have either a chaotic home life, an environment that's not conducive to recovery, like there's nobody in the family that's supportive, or half of the family members are also addicted? Or has your functioning deteriorated to the point where you really should have some kind of a structured environment for a period of time?

We actually did a study and found that people who appeared to be overtreated, who would've qualified for an outpatient program but for some reason went to inpatient, actually did worse as inpatient. And I think part of the reason for that was—this was in Minnesota in the 1980s—that the person who was less affected being placed in such a program with people having more serious problems, would look around and say, "Well, I haven't lost my job yet, and I haven't lost my spouse yet, and I haven't been in jail yet, so I don't have this problem." And so I think for some of them that would lead to denial and a more serious drinking problem when they left the facility.

From William White, senior research consultant, Chestnut Health Systems: Inpatient and outpatient treatment cannot be adequately compared because they are designed to respond to different levels of problem severity and potentially to different stages of recovery. I would estimate that not more than 20 percent of those meeting diagnostic criteria for a substance-use disorder require inpatient or residential treatment. Inpatient and residential care should be restricted to those with the greatest problem severity and the lowest natural recovery support resources. Inpatient and residential care is particularly appropriate for persons with acute medical/psychological problems who require close monitoring or care during detoxification and early recovery, persons living in a family or social environment that inhibits the initiation of sobriety, and persons for whom past outpatient treatments and community supports have not provided a sufficient framework for achieving recovery stability.

Some Treatment Options

For more information about the self-help oriented treatments mentioned most frequently by the experts interviewed for this book, along with valuable tips about how to utilize these methods and tools, consult the following:

- Acupuncture, Seven Self-Care Tools, p. 264
- Cognitive Behavioral Therapy, Seven Self-Care Tools, p. 235
- Exercise, Seven Self-Care Tools, p. 261
- Group Therapy, Seven Self-Care Tools, p. 240
- Nutrition, Seven Self-Care Tools, p. 256

Your 30-Day Challenge for Alcohol
(developed by Andrea G. Barthwell, MD, FASAM)

Do you have a bad habit or a dependency? Here is another chance to find out.

You've answered the questionnaires for this toxic compulsion. You've read through what the experts have to say and thought about the extent to which you exhibit the behaviors associated with either a nondependent use disorder or a dependency.

Do you still have any doubt about whether you have just a bad habit, or whether your behavior meets the criteria for a dependency?

Create a 30-day challenge for yourself.

Your challenge is to have two drinks every day for a solid month, whether you want to or not. But no more than two drinks a day!

That means either:

- two 12-ounce beers a day;
- or two 6-ounce glasses of wine;
- or two 1-ounce shots of hard liquor.

If you're a nondependent user, you will find it difficult to actually complete a month of daily drinking. Someone with a drinking problem will not only meet the challenge but may well drink more than the two-drink-a-day quota.

Meeting this challenge of drinking every day doesn't mean that you do or don't have a problem, but it's safe to say that if you are unable to drink every day, you probably don't qualify as a problem drinker.

If at the end of this challenge you sense that you really do have a problem, the next step is up to you. Treatment is probably something you need to consider.

II

Toxic Compulsion 2: Drug Abuse

I don't do drugs. I am drugs.
—Salvador Dali

Every time Charlie Sheen or Lindsay Lohan or any of the other troubled celebrities with drug problems make "news" with their latest antics, I usually receive requests from news media outlets to

appear on television or be quoted in print condemning their behavior.
I refuse to participate in these sideshows. For me to get involved would
be a little like a cancer survivor being called on to offer opinions on a
stranger's battle with the disease—it's inappropriate, and the fixation
with whether the patient will survive or not is usually voyeurism, not
compassion.

What the news media and the nondrug-dependent public needs
to realize about celebrity train wrecks is that these self-hatred behaviors on display probably began early in their lives and the seeds of the
compulsion that drive them to engage in these behaviors may have
been sown even before they were born. They may be among the millions of people who carry this drug-abuse vulnerability in their genes.
But most of the media and the viewing public simply look at Sheen or
Lohan and resent what they've achieved and how much they're paid,
and resent them even more for squandering it all away.

Drug-use behavior is about seeking relief from whatever is toxic
inside of the mind. Abusers can't engage the world without substances
because life to them is too painful and overwhelming. When the drugs
and alcohol no longer work as a way to engage life, the use kills slowly
by robbing them of everything that matters, which for celebrities usually comes in the form of a public meltdown spectacle that robs them
of privacy and dignity.

People who successfully engage the world every day and do so with
far fewer gifts than a celebrity may respond with, "Are you kidding
me!" They can't begin to understand the misery inside these addicts.
Until you've walked in the shoes of somebody who needs these substances, you can't possibly understand the tremendous gravitational
pull of the compulsion to use. The best you can hope for from most
"normies" (what those in recovery call "normal" people) is that they'll
summon some compassion or blind faith that it's an illness.

It's easy for folks to fixate on celebrity screw-ups because they're
good theater and they make people feel good about their bias. That
bias is often a reaction to how difficult this illness is to treat. There
is a lot of anger around this illness. People are mad at addiction and
with good reason. It's insidious. It destroys families. It takes away trust,
undermines love. It can turn the most loving and nurturing home into
a prison of anger and fear because there is no easy fix for the problem,
and that infuriates many people.

When I started using drugs at age 12, I was reacting to life changes
that included the divorce of my parents and the murders of two family

members. I was angry and terrified and didn't know it. I was in search of something that would relieve the pain of my life, and I thought I had found it in drugs. It took me 17 years to get clean and sober. So I know how difficult it is to achieve the first step on the road to recovery and healing.

The underlying causes and conditions of drug abuse have to be treated, not only within the user, but within the entire family, if there is to be successful long-term recovery. That's also part of the stigma surrounding this illness. No one likes to think of it as a family or social disease. No one likes to believe that any one of us can become vulnerable to the ravages of its influence. Many people would rather not accept that the true measure of society and its values is how we treat our weakest links.

An estimated 23 million people in the United States have a substance abuse problem and less than 10 percent of them are receiving treatment, according to Dr. Nora Volkow, director of the National Institute on Drug Abuse. "The big glacier in front of us is the lack of recognition that drug addiction is a disease," said Volkow. "You don't choose your genes, nor do you choose the circumstances in which you were born, which will either protect you or make you more vulnerable to drug addiction. You must still take responsibility if you have the disease of addiction. You must take responsibility for your treatment."

The fastest growing drug dependency problem in the United States, and maybe the world, involves legal drugs prescribed by physicians for pain and depression. For details about how this epidemic is affecting people, I encourage you to read Appendix One and the section describing the social and health effects of overprescribing OxyContin pain pills.

My friend the actor Richard Dreyfuss once said that addicts are trying to touch the hand of God. It's certainly been my experience that many of the folks I've met in recovery are searchers. They were searching for something, and substances seemed to provide them with gateways to that something.

Wanting an altered state of consciousness or a mood enhancement is not unusual in this culture, or in the history of human experience, pointed out Dr. Andrea Barthwell, CEO of the North Carolina treatment center Two Dreams Outer Banks. Many cultures continue to seek an altered state of consciousness, but they generally don't do it out of hedonism. In tribal societies the medicine man sits around the campfire and facilitates the elders in sharing an altered state of consciousness that's intended to benefit relationships within the tribe, and there are rules, traditions, and rituals that they respect and follow. When you step outside of those boundaries, as most drug users in Western cultures do, you're doing so for hedonistic or uncontrollable addiction reasons that ultimately destroy the very relationships in your life that ordinarily provide meaning and a sense of purpose.

I can understand why people in our culture would want to engage in escapism. Whether drug use is a first or last resort as a mood elevator or self-medicating ritual, whether it's a quick fix in the struggle with financial hardship and poverty, whether it's to fend off feelings of depression and too much stress, it's no wonder that substantial portions of the population are trying to change their perceptions of reality. But when I see somebody who looks for that kind of escapism on a regular basis and organizes his or her life around it, I have to question whether the self-destructive path they are sliding down is really going to provide them with any meaningful life experience other than an intimate relationship with suffering.

One worthwhile result I see from people who have been enslaved by a drug and broken free is their potential for accelerated character development. Folks who enter prolonged recovery are often wiser and richer in personal resources for having survived the ordeal. Of course, the same could be said for many military veterans who survived combat in a war, or for cancer survivors who successfully battled a disease that severely tested their mind, body, and spirit.

This disease of dependency is cunning, baffling, and powerful, especially when you identify it and challenge its hold over your life. I truly believe that people who struggle with this disease and survive it are remarkable. If you're one of those survivors reading this book, you have a story to tell and wisdom to impart to others.

If you're someone about to embark on this disease-fighting journey based on what you identify about yourself in this chapter, rest assured that you can create a new, more positive life story that will bring you gifts far beyond what you may currently imagine.

Time to Get Honest with Yourself

Do you have a drug-use problem? Is it a habit, or a dependency?

If you don't already know the answer, or even if you think you do, it's worth taking the time to find out. Complete the following quiz, based upon the American Psychiatric Association's definition of dependency and prepared by Dr. Nora Volkow to learn the extent to which your drug of choice has compromised your life.

1. Does your recurrent substance use result in a failure to fulfill major role obligations at work, school, or home?
2. Has your recurrent substance use put you in physically hazardous situations?
3. Have you continued substance use despite having persistent or recurrent social or interpersonal problems caused or exacerbated by the effects of the substance?
4. Are you experiencing a tolerance for the substance, defined by either a need for increased dosing to achieve a desired effect or markedly diminished effect with continued use of the same amount of the substance?
5. Do you experience withdrawal symptoms if you try to stop using?
6. Have you found that you often take in more of the substance or use it over a longer period than you intended?
7. Do you frequently desire to control your substance abuse or have you made unsuccessful efforts to do so?
8. Do you spend a great deal of time in activities necessary to obtain the substance and use the substance or recover from its effects?
9. Have you given up important social, occupational, or recreational activities, or reduced them, because of substance use?
10. Has your substance use continued despite a persistent or recurrent physical or psychological problem that is likely to have been caused or exacerbated by the substance?
11. Do you experience craving or a strong desire or urge to use a specific substance every day?

You likely have a substance-use disorder if you answered yes to two or more of the questions. Answering yes to two or three questions indicates moderate problem severity, and four or more yes answers indicates that you have a high-substance-use disorder.

A Drug-Specific Test: Marijuana

Do you have a problem with marijuana? These 12 questions modified from the 12 questions of Marijuana Anonymous may help you evaluate your relationship with the drug, especially if you answer yes to any of the questions.

1. Has smoking stopped being enjoyable, at least some of the time?
2. Do you smoke alone?
3. Do you find it hard to imagine living without marijuana?
4. Do you choose friends who also smoke?
5. Do you smoke to avoid really confronting your feelings?
6. Do you smoke marijuana when you get upset, as a way of coping?
7. Do you live in a self-defined world outside of regular society, because of your marijuana use?
8. Have you ever promised someone you would quit or cut down (including yourself) and failed to do so?
9. Do you notice that you are not as sharp as you were, or that your memory is worse because of your marijuana habit?
10. When you are nearly out of marijuana, do you start to feel anxious about getting more?
11. Does your life revolve around your use of marijuana?
12. Have friends or family ever told you that your marijuana habit has had a negative effect on your relationship?

If you answered yes to even a single question, you may have a problem with marijuana, and you may want to re-evaluate whether marijuana should be playing the role in your life that it does.

Six Categories of Commonly Abused Drugs (alphabetical)

Here in alphabetical order are the generally accepted categories of abused drugs that I will be using as reference points throughout this book:

Cannabinoids: hashish, marijuana
Depressants: barbiturates (Mebaral, Nembutal, Seconal)
Hallucinogens: ketamine, LSD, peyote, PCP
Inhalants: paint solvent, cooking sprays, correction fluid, marking pens, etc.

Opioids: heroin, opium, OxyContin, morphine, methadone
Stimulants: amphetamine, methamphetamine, cocaine, ecstasy

Percentage of Users Who Become Dependent

The list below estimates your chances of becoming dependent on a drug you choose. Consider these percentages to be your risk factor for developing dependency if you are a regular user. More research needs to be done to determine the dependency risk for methamphetamine, as well as some of the newer painkillers being sold by prescription.

Tobacco—31.9 percent
Heroin—23.1 percent
Cocaine—16.7 percent
Alcohol—15.4 percent
Stimulants—11.2 percent
Cannabis—9.1 percent
Psychedelics—4.9 percent
Inhalants—3.7 percent

(Source: Comparative epidemiology of dependence on tobacco, alcohol, controlled substances, and inhalants: Basic findings from the National Comorbidity Survey. Anthony JC, Warner LA, and Kessler RC. Exp Clin Psychopharmacol. Aug 1994;2(3):244–68. doi: 10.1037/1064-1297.2.3.244.)

Ranking the Most Dangerous Drugs

Danger is a relative term when we talk about the various drugs and their potential for harm to human health and the welfare of others. Where do we start to possibly assess all of the harm inflicted by the misuse of drugs? It turns out in Britain they've come up with an assessment process that makes sense.

In 2010 members of the Independent Scientific Committee on Drugs, led by Prof. David Nutt, Britain's former chief drugs adviser to the government, evaluated 20 drugs based on 16 criteria: nine related to the various harm the drug produces in an individual user and seven related to the harm inflicted on others by the user's drug dependence.

These criteria included mental and physical damage, crime, and costs to health care, to the economy, and to communities.

Which of the 20 harmful substances topped the list? Alcohol "won" hands down, scoring 72 out of a possible 100 points, followed by heroin, crack cocaine, and methamphetamine.

Here are the ranking scores from the study, combining harm to users with harm to others:

Alcohol—72
Heroin—55
Crack cocaine—54
Methamphetamine—just over 30
Cocaine—just under 30
Tobacco—just under 30
Amphetamine—just over 20
Cannabis—20
GHB—just under 20
Benzodiazepines—15
Ketamine—14
Methadone—13
Butane—12
LSD—just under 10
Buprenorphine—just under 10
Mushrooms—just under 10
Anabolic steroids—9
Khat—8
Ecstasy—8

(Source: "Drugs harms in the UK: A multicriteria decision analysis." Nutt DJ, King LA, and Phillips LD. Lancet. 2010 Nov 6;376(9752):1558–65.)

You may be unfamiliar with several of the drugs in this list. Some have been around for centuries; others are recent additions to the lineup of toxic distractions. We probably will never see the end of new designer drugs developed in clandestine labs to profit from the human compulsion for sensory alteration. Periodic casualty lists publicized by the media may be our only signal of a new drug's emergence and a measure of its short-term health consequences.

To illustrate what I mean, one Minnesota teenager died and 10 other teens were hospitalized with serious respiratory problems after a house party in March 2011 when they overdosed on a hallucinogen called "Europa," or "2C-E," which can be purchased legally over the Internet. Its effects are said to resemble those produced by ecstasy or mescaline. A few weeks after the Minnesota incident, a 22-year-old Oklahoma woman also died and two of her friends were hospitalized in critical condition after ingesting Europa at a party.

Many of these new compounds are "cousin drugs," just a molecule different from banned drug relatives, ecstasy, for example. That one molecule can be the difference between whether a drug is technically legal or illegal in a particular state, although federal law does allow prosecution for the sale of so-called "analogue" drugs. It's a constant challenge to enforce federal guidelines, however, because new variations of old drugs or entirely new ones appear so rapidly and the Internet makes distribution so quick and easy.

For our purposes, only the older and better-known drugs with proven physical and/or psychological dependence potential will be discussed and their impacts on health assessed. See Appendix One for detailed descriptions of these drugs.

Your Brain on Drugs

In talking about how our brains react on drugs, Dr. Herbert Kleber, director of the Division on Substance Abuse at the Columbia University College of Physicians and Surgeons and former deputy director for demand reduction in the White House Office of National Drug Control Policy, described how he asks people about the last time they gave up something pleasant, something pleasurable.

"For most people," said Dr. Kleber, "the answer is not very often. Drugs are very pleasurable. We are wired to enjoy these drugs. We have in the brain these receptors and neurotransmitters that are directly activated, slowed, shut down, or otherwise affected by drugs. When this happens, the brain says, 'That was good. Do it again.' In the outside world, there are various plants that produce chemicals that mimic those neurotransmitters in the brain and when you take them, the brain says, 'That was good. Do it again.' So we are wired to enjoy this, and if you have a family history of addiction, you have a much greater likelihood—a four or five times greater chance—of becoming addicted if you try a substance."

Prof. Carlton Erickson, director of the Addiction Science Research and Education Center and distinguished professor of pharmacy/ toxicology at the University of Texas at Austin, described how drugs affect the brain: "All drugs that affect the brain act at the cellular (that is, the nerve cell) level. Nerve cells talk to one another through chemicals called neurotransmitters. Neurotransmitters are made, destroyed, and cause a 'connection' between nerve cells through their release during electrical firing of individual nerve cells. Most drugs that affect the brain (to cause either unwanted or therapeutic effects) act by changing the neurotransmitters' actions.

"There are receptors for drugs in the brain—for opioids (such as morphine), for marijuana (called the 'cannabinoid' receptor), for nicotine (called the 'nicotinic' receptor), and others. Receptors are specialized proteins or enzymes that are the 'lock' in the 'lock and key' concept of receptor activation. A drug actually attaches (or binds) to its specific receptor, which creates a change in the receptor shape or activity. The final result of this activation is increased or decreased firing of the nerve cell.

"Why are these receptors in the brain? Are they there because nature prepared us for the possibility of using drugs? No, the real answer is that drugs activate receptors that are used by naturally occurring chemicals in the brain. Thus, endorphins (naturally occurring morphine-like substances) are released during stress or pain, activate the opioid receptors, and affect stress and pain thresholds during daily life events."

Said Dr. Nora Volkow, director of the National Institute on Drug Abuse: "Psychoactive drugs have the ability to induce changes in the brain that start with the very first use. These changes reflect the attempts that the brain makes to adapt to the abnormally large and/or abrupt changes in the levels of key neurotransmitters. As the use becomes chronic and/or heavier, these adaptive changes become more pronounced, more long lasting, and involve more areas (functions) of the brain. The specific nature and consequences of these cumulative brain changes really depend not only on the type of drug(s) and the manner in which they are abused, but also on a host of other biological and environmental factors that differ widely from person to person. Thus, people reach the point of having a clinically distinct substance-use disorder (i.e., losing control over their use, experiencing cravings or withdrawal when use is stopped) largely based on individual factors. The ability of a person to quit on his or her own is also quite variable and likely depends on how severe the disorder is, whether there are other comorbidities (especially other mental illnesses, which are common), the person's biology (e.g., genes), age, personal history, and social supports."

In their 1999 book *Coming Clean: Overcoming Addiction Without Treatment*, Robert Granfield and William Cloud introduced the concept of "recovery capital," the sum of all the internal and external assets that can be brought to bear to initiate and sustain recovery from alcohol and other drug problems. Recovery capital differs from individual to individual and differs within the same individual at multiple points in time. High recovery capital—i.e., many different assets both internal and external—is crucial to reducing the severity and duration of the substance problem.

Dr. Michael M. Miller, past president of the American Society of Addiction Medicine, provided this perspective about your brain on drugs: "Addiction is not about drugs, it's about your brain. The brains of people who have addictions function differently than the brains of people without addictions. The brains of people with addiction are structurally somewhat different, generally on a molecular or receptor level, or the cellular level. We now know that healing for this disease comes through AA and professional counseling and various psychotherapies. We know that the brain changes in response to psychotherapy, mindfulness, and meditation. A major path we can take is to use medications that help. No medication works perfectly; not every medication for blood pressure works for every patient. But some medications for addiction help somewhat, and some help a lot. We need more medicines and we need more doctors who are trained in how to prescribe them."

Three types of neurotransmitter chemicals in our brains are known to play direct roles in the onset and severity of drug dependence: serotonin, a master mood regulator; dopamine, a pleasure and reward chemical; and noradrenalin, known as the alert and readiness-response chemical. When these brain chemicals are out of balance, either in too much or too little supply, people who expose their brains to drugs and other dependence-reinforcing behaviors (such as gambling) may find the use behavior extremely reinforcing.

"Addiction originates in brain chemistry, is determined by genetics, and is triggered by stress," wrote Dr. David Kipper, Beverly Hills addictive disorders treatment expert, in his 2010 book *The Addiction Solution*, an excellent, easy-to-understand overview of drug dependence as a neurochemical disease. "We don't choose the drugs we abuse. They choose us .... Show me your drug and I'll show you the neurotransmitter that needs balancing .... In addiction terms, self-medication is merely a personal search to gratify the specific biochemical need of a neurotransmitter imbalance."

Probe beneath a person's drug dependency and a psychological cause related to this neurotransmitter imbalance usually emerges. Here is how the three neurotransmitters play out their role in dependence:

Serotonin imbalances (low levels) can produce depression and obsessive thoughts and behaviors; alcohol and opiates (heroin and OxyContin) are the preferred self-medications.

Dopamine imbalances are in the reward and pleasure centers of the brain; a dopamine excess produces hyperactivity. This neurotransmitter is mimicked by the actions of cocaine, methamphetamine, and other stimulants.

Noradrenalin imbalances can generate anxiety or panic attacks in response to stress; an excess of it plays a role in sleep disorders; a self-medicating response is to take one of the 15 or so brand-name medications in the benzodiazepine category, such as Xanax, Valium, and Ativan.

Some drugs act on multiple neurotransmitters. Marijuana affects noradrenalin receptors to reduce anxiety and its use is connected to your dopamine levels. Ecstasy releases a flood of dopamine and serotonin into the brain.

In his private drug-dependency treatment practice, Dr. Kipper prescribes a range of detoxification and stabilizing medications to treat the neurotransmitter imbalances that underlie each particular type of drug dependency. Some of the medications mimic the abused drug at the receptor level of the brain, some are anticraving agents or antianxiety agents, while others are antidepressants or stimulating agents that target dopamine receptors.

Nondependent drug use is a preventable behavior, whereas addiction is a treatable disease of the brain. Although you aren't responsible for your genetic predisposition to this disease or the family, community, social, and cultural environments in which you were raised, you can protect your brain from developing an active disease by not consuming these substances. If you fail to heed the risks and develop the disease— again, that may not be your fault—*treatment is your responsibility.*

Nine Subtle Signs of Addiction

Addicts are usually in a state of denial about all nine of these subtle signs. You ask them if they exhibit any of these behaviors and they'll probably deny it. The drug dependence and its effect on their brain ensures that they can't see themselves or their behaviors clearly enough to have self-awareness about them.

You might have noticed some puzzling behaviors on the part of someone you know and have been unable to interpret what you have seen. Maybe some of these behaviors are your own. Which of these signs are familiar?

Things around the house disappear. If you begin to notice items stored in your living space have been mysteriously disappearing, do a reality check. Could the responsible party be your intimate partner, your child, or another relative? Or could it be someone who visits your home frequently? Addiction to drugs can create financial desperation and that may result in theft to support the habit.

A usually reliable person becomes less so. If a person in your life is no longer dependable—forgetting appointments, being late to work, disappearing without explanation, becoming secretive—this could be a symptom of a drug or alcohol problem, rather than an early stage of dementia or an illicit affair with another person.

Interests dramatically narrow or change. We all undergo periodic changes in what gives us pleasure, but usually these aren't rapid and dramatic alterations in our behavior patterns. If someone loses interest in social activities and in spending time with friends, it could be a sign of depression, but it could also be a symptom of a growing preoccupation with drugs that crowds out the other functions of life.

Unexplained weight and appetite loss. These days we usually celebrate someone's weight loss as a healthy development. Yet, if dramatic weight loss occurs in a matter of weeks, accompanied by a greatly reduced appetite and no increase in exercise habits, it might be worth investigating whether the person is using the stimulants cocaine or crystal methamphetamine. Another symptom of chronic meth use is rapid tooth loss and gum disease.

Dramatic mood swings. A person who used to display balanced or controlled moods may display wild mood swings and unpredictable emotions after chronic drug use. With teenagers this moodiness may be complicated by, or dismissed as, natural hormone changes, though certain drugs can trigger behaviors that go far beyond what is natural. Methamphetamine use can create hair-trigger tempers and volcanic aggressiveness. Marijuana use can sap energy and ambition so that a previously straight-A student one semester becomes a C student or worse the next semester.

Sleeping habits undergo a noticeable change. Drug binges disrupt normal sleep patterns. Many "downer" drugs sedate the user so that the person sleeps longer than what was previously normal, or falls asleep at inappropriate times or inappropriate settings. Using meth or cocaine over time can induce extreme sleep deprivation that can be coupled with sleep binges lasting several days. Heroin or other opioid use can lead to nodding naps alternating with waking states.

Anxiety, paranoia, or panic attacks appear. Excessive stress can trigger anxiety in just about anyone, but if panic attacks and paranoia follow, then the effects of a drug may be at work. Marijuana use generates paranoia in some people, while stimulants can cause panic attacks. Underlying psychological disorders are often exaggerated by chronic use of some drugs. Social anxiety disorders can appear in persons previously comfortable in social situations, until they feel so nervous about interacting with other people that they avoid social situations altogether.

Complaints about a vague illness become more frequent. Chronic drug use results in the user feeling bad much of the time. The symptoms they complain about are often vague and difficult to connect with any specific illness. They use this general malaise as an excuse to miss work and appointments with greater frequency, and they react irritably, or with anger, if the seriousness or true nature of their condition is questioned.

A previously honest person becomes a liar. Over time, drug use can sap a person's shame and warp their conscience so that lying can be rationalized as just a necessary manipulation to facilitate drug use. These lies become stories that the addict tells himself and others. If the drug habit involves a prescription for OxyContin or other painkillers, an addict might lie to a physician by saying an aging parent or child who needs the prescription for pain is embarrassed to ask a physician for help. For teenagers the pattern of lying often involves misleading parents about whom they are hanging out with and what they do in their spare time.

Underlying Problems Can Masquerade as Drug Abuse

From Dr. Stanley Evans, medical director and addictions medicine specialist with Caron Renaissance in Florida: One of the things I have been struck by in my practice is how often people who have underlying addictions, either themselves or in a close family member, present with some kind of dysfunction in their lives, which is readily identified as a drug or alcohol problem. But when you start digging around under-neath, you find these problems masquerade. They have many faces.

I don't go asking a client, "What are you drinking or what drugs are you doing?" I ask them first, "How are you doing? How is your life going? Tell me about yourself. When did you grow up? What was growing up like?" They'll say, "Oh, growing up was fine."

"Oh, really," I'll say. "Well, tell me about Mom and Dad."

"Well Dad was so and so, Mom was so and so."

"What was Dad like?"

Now he begins to give a little hesitation. "What do you mean, what was he like?"

"Oh, what was Dad like?"

And then he begins to tell you and then sometimes it just slips out. "You know Dad didn't have—I didn't know Dad too much."

The point of the matter is after a while you begin to get a flavor of dysfunction. You get a flavor of a not-so-healthy environment for this person as they were growing up. What we know from the science is that as this brain is developing, its interaction with the environment shapes its formation.

And then you go to the laboratory and you see the work that's being done, particularly with epigenetics, showing how the genes change based on the environment that they're exposed to. This epigenome acts like a radio signal, changing how the genes function in response to inputs from the environment. And so people change based on their environment. One way this can be seen is in the case of identical twins. As years pass, minor differences begin to become perceptible and, over time, more pronounced. This is especially true if the twins live for an extended period of time in environments that differ substantially. Free will or choice can also have a significant impact. For example, one twin might choose to be a vegetarian and another might smoke and consume a lot of animal fat.

So this is a world in which most people who end up addicted come from. Epigenetic changes have led them to discover drinks and drugs, and they have a genetic predisposition to get into all kinds of trouble in their reward pathway. So they end up with a problem. For years we've been simplistic in thinking, well, you just stop drinking and you stop drugging and you're going to be fine. Well, that's not the case. Underneath there is a mess that they have to begin to deal with before going forward in life.

Look at our prison system. We have more people incarcerated than any society in the history of man, and at least 60 percent of those people are in there because of addiction and coappearing disorders. Our prisons and jails are the largest mental health institution in the world. The same kind of underlying disorders that put those people in the prisons affect their families. So the tragedy of how we deal with drug use is that we lose an opportunity to really understand what is going on with people before they got caught up with drugs and all kinds of crazy behaviors.

Treatment Success and Remission— What Studies Say

Researchers have examined just about every angle imaginable comparing treatment and remission rates and "polydrug"-use combinations, to give you a sense of what you might expect with trying to control your behavior relative to your drug of choice. Let's take a look at what they found.

Comparing heroin, cocaine, and methamphetamine use over 10 years

Based on an analysis of 1,797 users of the three drugs, five UCLA researchers reported in the journal *Addictive Behaviors* the following results:

Average use levels: Heroin had the highest use at 13 to 18 days per month; meth was used an average of 12 days per month, and cocaine 8 to 11 days.

Age of first use: Heroin use first occurred at an average of 15 years, meth at 19 years, and cocaine at 20 years of age. (These are also the ages of a first arrest for people in each drug category.)

Total months in treatment over 10 years: Meth users spent an average of 4.9 months undergoing treatment for their addiction, compared to 4.8 months for heroin and 3.9 for cocaine.

The demographics of users in the West Coast study population provide some interesting details. Most primary heroin users were male Hispanics or whites, and most cocaine users were male African-Americans, whereas nearly half of meth users were white women.

For heroin use, an early age onset of use and being under supervision of the criminal justice system decreased their likelihood of quitting the drug.

Being under legal-system supervision for cocaine addicts also reduced their likelihood of quitting.

Persons addicted to cocaine who were under legal supervision were also less likely to quit than peers who were not under legal supervision. Meth users who started their habit before the age of 15 and were under legal supervision were less likely to have success in treatment and achieve recovery than those who did not meet both of these criteria. *(Source: "Comparing the dynamic course of heroin, cocaine, and methamphetamine use over 10 years." Hser H, Evans E, Huang D, Brecht ML, and Li L. Addict Behav. 2008 Dec; 33(12):1581–89.)*

Remission rates for methamphetamine, cannabis, and opioid users

A team of researchers from the United States and Australia reviewed worldwide studies done on drug-remission rates between 1990 and 2009 and released their findings in a 2010 issue of *Addictive Behaviors*. Remission was defined as either being abstinent from drug use or meeting diagnostic criteria for no longer being drug dependent over a three-year follow-up period.

Meth: 74 percent of 1,016 users studied were in remission.
Cannabis: 36 percent to 82 percent of users from three different studies were no longer dependent.
Opioids (cocaine and heroin): 23 percent to 93 percent of heroin users from eight studies and 39 percent to 58 percent of cocaine users from four studies were in remission.

Here's how the researchers summarized their findings: "Remission from amphetamine (methamphetamine) dependence was highest overall, with almost one in two persons remitting during a given year; the conservative estimate of remission from cannabis dependence was one in six annually; remission from heroin ranged from one to two in 10 each year; and remission from cocaine dependence ranged from one in twenty to one in eight." The research team added that unfortunately "one issue that cannot be addressed in this review is the rate of relapse after remission." *(Source: "Systematic review of prospective studies investigating 'remission' from amphetamine, cannabis, cocaine or opioid dependence." Calabria B, Degenhardt L, Briegleb C, Vos T, Hall W,*

Lynskey M, Callaghan B, Rana U, and McLaren J. Addict Behav. *2010 Aug;35(8):741–9.)*

Multiple drug use involving heroin, cocaine, methamphetamine, and alcohol

Two separate studies by UCLA Integrated Substance Abuse Program researchers examined the overlap of use between various drugs and, in turn, those same drugs with co-occurring alcohol abuse. It should come as no surprise that polydrug consumption can result in multiple simultaneous dependencies that complicate attempts to treat and recover from addiction.

Among findings from the first study:

- One-third to over half of substance abusers from treatment samples (primarily cocaine or heroin) also reported misuse of other substances. Primary heroin users, for example, used an average of five other substances in the six months prior to admission for treatment.
- Among meth users, secondary use of cocaine or heroin was a good predictor that the person wouldn't complete treatment for meth dependence.
- Polydrug-use treatment outcomes depend on the combination of drugs involved. There was little evidence, for example, that heroin users who also used cannabis had poorer treatment outcomes.
- For those whose primary dependence was cocaine, their alcohol use was "actually higher than their primary cocaine use for most of the 10-year period; and marijuana usage, while less than that of cocaine for most of the observation period, was still at moderate levels of 7 to 11 days per month."
- Primary meth users, on average, used alcohol and marijuana about 6 to 11 days per month.

The study authors concluded: "Treatment for cocaine and meth users should also consider addressing alcohol and marijuana use, particularly among those with higher usage levels of the primary drug." *(Source: "Polydrug use and implications for longitudinal research: Ten-year trajectories for heroin, cocaine, and methamphetamine users." Brecht ML,*

Huang D, Evans E, and Hser YI. Drug Alcohol Depend. *2008 Aug 1;96(3):193–201.)*

In the second UCLA study, researchers found that persons seeking treatment for drug dependence who had a co-occurring alcohol problem had a worse prognosis than those with a drug problem alone. Here are the chief findings:

- Cannabis use significantly reduces "the likelihood of sustained remission from alcohol and cocaine."
- "Population estimates indicate that more than 50 percent of individuals with a drug-use disorder also meet criteria for an alcohol-use disorder."
- "Given these high rates of co-occurrence between alcohol- and drug-use disorders, data on rates of remission from single substances may not accurately reflect remission when viewed broadly in terms of all substances used by an individual."
- A sample of 12,297 persons with a substance-use disorder revealed a remission rate of 67.1 percent if the problem was alcohol only, 70.3 percent remission rate if the problem was a drug only, but just a 58.5 percent remission rate if the problem involved both alcohol and a drug.

(Source: "Do substance type and diagnosis make a difference? A study of remission from alcohol- versus drug-use disorders using the national epidemiologic survey on alcohol and related conditions." Karno MP, Grella CE, Niv N, Warda U, and Moore AA. JSAD. 2008 July;69(4):491–95.)

Based on all of the study research findings above, it should be clear that if you have a real problem with one substance, you should stop using all substances. It's that simple!

Dependency Usually Starts in Adolescence

Most research on toxic compulsions shows that the childhood and teenage years are when the seeds of dependence are sown, seeds that spring forth later to produce the life and health problems we typically see in persons with substance-use disorders.

Changing a kid's drug-use trajectory

Let me introduce you to a European expert on the impact of adolescent drug use on the brain and behavior.

From Gilberto Gerra, Chief of the Drug Prevention and Health Branch of the United Nations Office on Drugs and Crime, based in Vienna, Austria: There's always something at the core, either biologically or environmentally, that pushes a person into abusing drugs. The last six or so of my studies defined all of the environmental influences such as neglect, not being in a good condition with your family, and how all of this affects the brain. You can have biological things coming from the genes you inherited from your parents, and biological influences coming from your environment in the family. All of this can change the brain. We have evidence that the hippocampus area of the brain can be larger or smaller because of neglect and long-term abuse. And if you give intensive and warm care to this child, you can restore the appropriate dimension of the hippocampus; so it's reversible.

An adolescent crisis can be due to conflict with parents or an impulsive temperament. Youth often experiment with drugs because of a small, transitory crisis related to their situation, such as rejection at school or by their peers and the like, or because of temperament. They try to self-medicate to relieve their anxiety, and over time they become slave to the self-medication. You can change the trajectory of children at risk. If you don't change the trajectory, you can predict what happens. You can predict their final destination will be a mental health disorder, substance abuse, prison, even loss of life. But we now know that by working on their resilience and protective factors, we can really change the trajectory of at-risk children. And it's not just done by investing in psychologists, a big intervention, or very expensive specialized care.

Parents don't need a degree in rocket science to change a child's trajectory. It can start with something as simple as "dinner with Daddy." It just involves communication. It means you have to devote undivided time to your children every evening for at least 15 minutes. I say to parents, you start with 15 minutes, then 20 minutes, then half an hour. Undivided time. Stay with them, talk with them, take care of them, ask what they've done at school, share information. The other very important thing is monitoring. If the child says, "Oh Mommy, I'm going out to see a movie or going to a disco club," you say, "Tell me exactly the address of the place, the exact time you will be back, and take this cell phone so I can call you if I need to." This is called monitoring. There's a study from the European Monitoring Center for Drug Abuse in

Lisbon that shows that parents who do active monitoring have 30 percent less substance abuse among their children.

Even when the kid might be sending you to hell in a dark corner of his brain, he still says, "I am of value to my father and mother because they are very much interested in my life. They want to know where I go and what time and with whom and what I do with them." If the parents don't have the courage to monitor the kid, they abandon their responsibility as parents. The message that the child gets is that no one really cares. "I can go rob a bank, kick someone, or kill myself, and no one cares." This is the message they take from it.

You have to set rules for the child: rules about when to take a shower, when to get the bedroom in order, when to contribute to cooking or cleaning, when to do homework. You set rules because you are a good parent. There must be rules for family life and rewards for good behavior. The reward can be money for cutting the lawn or for getting good grades in school. Reward the child and show appreciation when they follow the rules. Don't allow bad behavior, and be very rigorous in applying the rules. Tell the child, "When you decide to stop the bad behavior, you won't find me angry, you won't find me cold, you won't find me upset or irritated with you. You will see the core of unchanging love I have for you." A core of unconditional love and rigorous parenting is the mix that can change the trajectory. For children, the family can play the role a 12-Step program plays for adults.

Should you let a kid hit bottom?

From Dr. Nora Volkow, director of the National Institute on Drug Abuse: The process of addiction starts in adolescence. Adolescence is a period of your life where you are much more willing to take risks and where you have a much greater sense of invincibility. So, when adolescents start taking drugs, it's much harder for them than for adults to realize that they may lose control. Not only are they unaware of the neuroplastic changes occurring in their brains as a result of addiction, they also never really have a complete awareness of the addiction process that has begun. Adolescents become addicted faster. They escalate very, very rapidly.

There's a point, which is not infrequent, when parents throw their children out of the house. Actually, there are certain therapeutic programs that say, "You should throw your child out of the house so that they can hit bottom." The problem is that in the process of hitting bottom, some of these kids die of overdoses. That's hitting the bottom very, very hard. I'm sure that in one case or another this strategy may work, but it has probably more negative consequences than not, because by doing so, you remove the kid's social support. The family has to be educated to recognize that when that kid is stealing from them, it's really a distortion of the kid's personality. It's not a fundamental characteristic of his or her person. It's a hijack—that's really what drugs do.

One of my close friends is dealing with that with one of her sons and she is completely distressed. She said, "This is not his personality and he never used to be like this, how can it be?" And still, even with that knowledge, she had an emotional reaction because we as human beings react emotionally to others. So we have to hold ourselves and say, "Wait a second. This person is suffering from a disease that is leading them to act that way." Otherwise, we get very angry or offended and we disconnect from that person. That's what commonly happens with families who have adolescent users.

A strategy for youth drug prevention

From Gen. Arthur T. Dean, chairman and CEO of the Community Anti-Drug Coalitions of America: At Community Anti-Drug Coalitions of America (CADCA), we believe that by helping young people build self-respect and then teaching them leadership skills, we can prepare them to use their skills and abilities to positively impact their communities. It's a way of giving them ownership of their communities and the opportunity to feel that they are making a difference. We believe that when a young person is equipped and empowered to make a difference and accept ownership they self-actualize.

They see that they are critical to the success of their communities. And that, in effect, is their high. They don't need a false high. They get the high through helping and impacting others through their discipline and their skills.

We teach youth to take responsibility for their actions. The CADCA program teaches them how to be honest and forthright. It builds a sense of community by teaching them integrity, a commitment to service, and loyalty to their community and others.

We believe we've created an extremely effective strategy. It is evidence-based. Coalition-building is a strategy. It is a way to prevent substance abuse through a multisector approach at the community level.

Now, let me better define that. It's all of the stakeholders in the community and we all know what they are. It's law enforcement, health care, education, faith communities, parent groups, youth groups, local government, private business. I could go on and on and on. If those sectors are individually trying to prevent drug use, they're not going to be as effective as when they all come together to do an assessment and begin sharing ideas and resources. When this happens, young people receive the same message from these diverse community stakeholders.

If they are at school and in sports, you ask the coaches to help you implement the message. If they're in a youth program and a faith service, then they're going to get the same message. If they're in the classroom, the same message; if they go to see their doctor, they'll get the same message. If unfortunately they have to see a counselor—or a law enforcement officer—they'll get the same message. If the young people are hearing these positive messages across community sectors, they're going to be effective.

So the coalition is a part of the community. It is a permanent part of the community and it has to implement these strategies on a yearly basis to impact each youth cohort as they move through from 6th grade to 12th grade and on into college. People say that the years between the ages of 10 and 20 are probably the decade that has the most impact on our future development. Think of how many things go on in your life from age 10 to 20. That's when your brain is still growing. That's when you're developing your social skills. That's when you're developing your resiliency skills. That's when you're learning a whole lot of stuff. And if you interfere with those 10 years by putting substances into your brain at the age of 12 or 13, it can change your life trajectory in a permanent way. So if we can keep kids substance-free until they are around 21 or 22, chances are they are going to be okay for the rest of their lives.

What can families do to help keep their kids drug free? It sounds simple, but spending time with them is one of the most important things you can do to keep them from getting into drugs. Involve yourself in the life of your kid from their earliest years. I know it's difficult, and I've had the challenge of being a senior military officer and a very busy executive, but I'll tell you, I've found the time to be an assistant coach and have brought my kids to ballet and soccer when they were five and six. From church programs to the PTA, involve yourself in your kids' lives. Get them involved in activities. It doesn't matter whether they go to music lessons, the math club, or soccer. Occupy them and their energy with something creative. It's just so critical, and all of the research says that if parents involve themselves with kids in these kinds of activities, the kids are about 50 percent less likely to get involved in drugs.

Spend some time with your family at the dinner table. Have three or four meals a week with your family. It's not the fact you're eating with them; it's the fact that you're sitting down and talking to them about their life. As they get older, you want to help them pick good friends. Help them make good decisions about who their friends are. Educate yourself. Don't be naïve about what's happening in your kid's life. Don't be afraid to talk to them about the hard subjects; they'll have those conversations with someone else if you don't.

How to intervene with an adolescent drug abuser

From Dr. Marla Kushner, medical director, Mercy-Dunbar and Mercy-Phillips Health Centers and a clinical professor at Midwestern University, Chicago: When an adolescent shows up in my office, I kick the parents out of the room and begin with their general history. We'll start talking about family history. Do they have a family history of alcoholism or drug dependency? That's the key to understanding, especially with teenagers.

Then I start talking to them in general. We start with cigarettes. If they ever smoked cigarettes or if any of their friends are smoking—we start with that. Then we go to alcohol and move into marijuana, pills, steroids—everything. We start talking about all that stuff. I try to get to all of that the first time, but if not, I always have them come back and there's another opportunity.

And they know when they come to see Dr. Kushner, I'm going to ask them this stuff. So it's a comfortable place, parents aren't in the room, and I always let them know the confidentiality laws. You know if you tell me this stuff, I can't tell your parents. I'm going to help you and I'm going to want you to get support, and family is a good place to do it, but you can tell me stuff so I can help you—even without them.

The younger they start, like 13 or 14, if they're drinking every day, if they're using marijuana before school every day, if they're taking pills, even if it's small use, we're going to start talking about consequences. I really think that consequences define the change between abuse and addiction and whether somebody has a problem or not.

And sometimes they don't think there's a problem. I smoke

marijuana every day, they say, but I don't have a problem. So you have to start helping them figure out what the problem is. Are you getting up in the morning? Well, I miss school every once in a while, they say. How's your relationship with your family? Well, I don't really talk to my family, they say. Those are the types of things you start getting into.

So I'm trying to get them to figure out and identify their own consequences. Because again, if I come in and say, "Oh, yeah, you have a problem, you know," they're not going to listen. But getting *them* to see it's a problem—that's very critical. We start asking some of the CAGE questions. There are specific ones for adolescents. I don't write them down; they're just in my head. I started asking them questions and the more passive they are, the more I know they may be heading down the wrong road.

I'll talk to them about things like, "Hey you know Grandpa is an alcoholic, but did you know that's something that can be passed on genetically?" If they really have a problem, I'll talk about what some of the choices are. I think consequences will get through to them more than anything. They begin to see the school consequences. The family consequences. Not-being-able-to-get-a-job consequences. The consequences with friends and relationships. I kind of lead them to name the consequences on their own.

I also talk all the time to the parents. They're often afraid to talk to their kids if they have drug experiences of their own. But I say, start with that, look at your own stuff. What are you role modeling? Don't lie to your kids about your own experiences because you're going to get caught up in one of those lies. If you say, "Oh, well I never did anything," at some point your college roommate is going to come and talk about the good old days and you'll get caught.

So be honest with them; don't glamorize your use. Tell them the consequences that happened to you. "Oh, yeah I did do this in college and my grades suffered," or "I had a bad relationship with my parents and I just wouldn't recommend that you do this because of A, B, and C." I think it's very important that parents set that tone in the house.

If you set that example and standard at home and you let them know the reasons why, it is going to make a difference. You can't just say, "Don't do drugs." Say, "Don't do drugs and here is why. This is what can happen; we do have family history."

You can only give them so much information they're actually going to take in and accept, but it's almost like the kids who think everybody's having sex. Everybody is not having sex. They're just telling each other they are.

So I talk to kids all the time and say, "Are any of your other friends *not* into drugs or alcohol?" And they'll say, "Well yeah, I've got few." I tell them, "Then you guys have to create the standard." Figure out what's going to be fun. Is it really cool when the ambulance comes at the end of the party and has to take a kid to the emergency room? When you talk to them one-on-one like this, they don't think that's cool. They think it's scary and they don't want that.

Intervention, Treatment, and Recovery at Any Age

You will find a lot of useful information and tips for success in the following pages as experts share what they have seen work in practice.

What can help you quit using heroin or cocaine?

From Dr. Dora Dixie, owner of Day by Day Health Consultants in Chicago, Illinois, medical director of the Women's Treatment Center, and regional director of the American Society of Addiction Medicine: It's the consequences that drive people into treatment. It's never the patient saying, "I'm tired of getting high." Nobody is ever tired of feeling the way they want to feel. You may be tired of hustling, you may be tired of running the streets, you may be tired of prostituting—you may be tired of all the consequences that go with this out-of-control life, but you're not tired of feeling the way you want to feel, because everybody who does cocaine likes the way it makes them feel. So if you're not tired of that, what is it that you're tired of? One thing is you no longer feel the desired effect. That's why you keep doing more and more. Remember that song by Sade, "Never as Good as the First Time"? Now, what do you think she was talking about? Not sex, because it's not that good the first time, so it had to be cocaine. Never as good as the first time, with cocaine, everybody will tell you they're still chasing that, trying to get back that euphoria like with the first high.

Somebody has to believe that they can get well. I tell them the truth about what is going to happen to their body. You are not going to abuse your body with drugs without consequences. It's just not going to happen. And some of them come in because, "Oh, I'm feeling sick" or "I got this" or "I got that." If I had a dollar for every time I say, "You've got a lump on your breast" when I do a physical exam. Or somebody says, "I don't want to die. I don't want to go through that breast cancer process." It's a horrible disease. You can also have a heart attack, stroke, legs cut off, be paralyzed. A lot of bad stuff happens with drugs, especially for the men. This truth really works for the men. You're a big guy. You're going to be lying in your excrement. You're 250 pounds. Who's going to roll you over and change your diaper? You're going to be in a nursing home. You're going to rot. Now I've got your attention. "Okay, what do I need to do?" they finally ask.

Now they're ready for treatment because this is real. And you may forever want heroin or whatever your drug of choice is, but just because you want it, it doesn't mean you have to have it. We've almost made this addiction thing like it's somehow different from many other compulsions, but it isn't. I believe that people can change, but they have to want it.

What can help you quit abusing any drug?

From Dr. Herbert Kleber, director, Division on Substance Abuse, Columbia University College of Physicians and Surgeons and former deputy director for demand reduction in the White House Office of National Drug Control Policy: Can someone who is a recreational user who begins to develop compulsivity avert full-blown addiction? Usually, it takes some outside pressure. There are people who are just able to stop on their own. A person who wakes up in the morning and says, "I'm not going to use anymore," and doesn't. They are the exception rather than a rule. Usually, it takes some sort of outside pressure, whether from a spouse who says, "I'm going to leave you if you don't get help," or the spouse who says, "I'm only going to stay with you if you don't need help." There are people who can do it on their own, but most people require pressure either from a family member or an employer.

I think convincing someone to quit has to be a combination of sticks and carrots. If it's just carrots, you're competing with something that's awfully reinforcing, so just carrots probably isn't going to be enough. Just sticks is often not enough. If there is no love there, if there is no real compassion, no real care, then all the sticks aren't going to matter because the person inside feels like hell.

So it needs to be some combination. I think part of the reason why interventions have gotten a bad rap is, most of the time, the intervention is for people to go to these 30-day rehab facilities. And rehabs are overvalued. Some celebrities have been in and out of rehab a dozen times. I think that ultimately the battle has to be fought on an outpatient basis. It may not be a bad idea to go to a rehab at least once to learn something about the nature of the disease, to see what the possibilities are, to get yourself cleaned for a period of time. You may not have been clean for at least 30 days for a long time, but to keep going in and out, in and out, just makes a mockery of everything. At that point, the rehab has very little to offer you.

Have meaningful treatment that will meet what the person needs. If you take away what little they have, it's probably not going to change very much. So, you have to tailor what it is you're trying to do to the individual. Many of the people I have seen have been very well-to-do individuals. For them, loss of money is not a big threat, but there may be other things, such as loss of custody of their children, that are very important. The reason they're affluent and have more resources may be because of intelligence, or it may be willpower, whatever, but they have certain strengths that the guy who dropped out of high school in tenth grade just doesn't have. So it's not simply the money, it's how they got the money in the first place. Probably the hardest people to treat are the affluent who inherited their wealth. They don't have the character traits that enable them to cope.

One such trait is the presence of the co-occurring disorder, the anxiety, the depression. You can treat addiction without treating those disorders, but the likelihood of relapses is great. And you can treat the psychological disorders without treating the addiction, but you won't get very far. So ideally, if you can find the right setting, the right practitioner, you want to try to do both, treat the addiction and at the same time treat the comorbidity disorder.

Said Dr. Christopher Emerson, a Los Angeles-based psychologist and addiction specialist: "When someone comes into my office with an issue that's drug- or alcohol-related, I immediately assume there's a co-occurring disorder: anxiety, depression, a history of trauma—something that results in emotional dysregulation. The trick is to *find* it, to accurately diagnose and treat it. That doesn't usually happen until someone is clean and sober for at least 90 days. Only then can you begin to clearly see the emotional and psychological conditions under-neath the chemical dependency."

The most promising treatment right now is the treatment for opiate addiction. We have drugs like buprenorphine, which is an excellent drug, and there are now promising new ways of giving it to last six months. And there's a patch that will last for a week. So again, so you don't have to take it every day. Ideally, you don't want the patient to have to take the medication every day.

So, I am optimistic. We have a blocker for opiates that will last 30 days, and my guess is that we will have other forms of that within three to four years that may last up to six months. Those are already being studied in a number of places. So if someone is depressed, I have 15 or 20 antidepressants to choose from. I want as many treatment arrows in my quiver as possible.

More advice on how to quit drugs

From Dr. Sally Satel, psychiatrist, Partners in Drug Addiction Counseling and Research and fellow, American Enterprise Institute: A lot of people figure out relapse-prevention strategies on their own. They might just stop. You stop going to the neighborhood where you got drugs. You change your friends. You change the way you walk home. You get di-rect deposit for your paycheck so you don't have it—or you give it to your wife. One person I know of became a truck driver solely so he could get his urine tested because he knew they tested it.

People use drugs for reasons. I happen to be a big subscriber to the self-medication hypothesis. Happy people may experiment and happy people may even control their drug use, and you must know people who can do that. But in the clinic we only see people who can't control. We only see the folks who need us. Some people, they feel themselves sliding down and they think, "This is not who I am, this is not who I want to be," and all they need is that little push from a session with a shrink.

Addiction can be wholly modified by the things you do consciously. The same is true with something like type 2 diabetes. You just don't eat this or that. It can be something you control. People who have drug problems can and do pull themselves back. With a program like Phoenix House, a nonprofit drug and alcohol rehabilitation program operating in 10 states, they're remaking people, especially younger kids. A person has to have small successes and then the successes accumulate over time to change one's view of self. It might be a "fake it until you make it" approach, and even that can lead to profound insights.

Interventions must involve real consequences

From Dr. Mitch Rosenthal, child psychiatrist and addictions expert; founder and executive director, Rosenthal Center for Clinical and Policy Studies: Most people with drug and alcohol addiction get coerced into treatment. Or they end up scared because of things that happened to them medically. They black out, they have convulsions, they get very sick, and they're afraid they're going to die.

But most people, at least in the Phoenix House experience with more than 140,000 admissions over 43 years, are forced or coerced to treatment by parents, by a husband or wife, by employers, by judges, by probation offices. It's the rare person who wakes up and says, "My life is out of control. I can't stop using drugs. I can't stop doing other hideous things I'm doing." And says, "Mom, take me to treatment," or comes knocking, on their own, at our door.

Once confronted, kids will sometimes say, "What are you talking about, Mom? I'm a drug addict? I'm no different than Billy and Jimmy and all these kids who come over to the house, kids you admire." It's the rare kid who does say, "You know, I think I screwed up. I don't want to be like this anymore; I am uncomfortable with who I am."

But sometimes when you love someone, it's easy for them to deceive you. So sometimes parents are very foggy about whether the kid has really got a problem or not, when they're coming home late, when their friendships are changing, when they're starting to screw up in school. The parents know something's wrong but it's explained away as evolvement to adolescence. There is the danger a parent will want to say, "Well, they may grow out of it." It's denial on the part of parents. And many times those parents will have to get a little clarifying help from someone outside the family, someone who'll say, "No, this is a problem."

I don't think you have to threaten. The statement isn't so much "I'm going to throw you out. You're acting like a shit. I'm throwing you out of here." It's much more like "I really care about you and I am so worried; I can't stand that you're lying like this; I can't stand that you're in such danger. It just fills me with dread, and I will support your health. I want you to get help, but I'm not going to support your illness."

You can do a nonformal intervention. You can do it effectively, but there are times when people have to toughen up. A wife, for example, has to say, "You know, unless you get this straight, I'm going to divorce you." Or parents need to say, "You know, I've gotten you out of jail four times, so I'm not bailing you out one more time. You go into treatment and I'll support your health, I'll support your future. I love you, but I'm not going to support your addiction."

The parent may have to come in and say, "You're going to have to pack up and move out of here. You call me if you want help; otherwise don't call." You have to be brave enough as a parent to do that. Most kids are going to respond to that. But thinking that you're going to love your way out of this and reward them and tell them, "Stop using drugs and I'll buy you a convertible; stop using drugs and I'll give you your own room," it's delusional. The person has to experience real consequences for their actions.

Coercive interventions can be lifesaving. Some people may be able to swim out of a rip tide, but most are going to need a lifeguard to get them out.

How to intervene with someone who has a drug problem

From Dr. Andrea Barthwell, CEO, Two Dreams Outer Banks: Young people who have nondependent use problems have big systems that they create to justify and rationalize what they're doing because they are generally engaging in an illegal behavior and they have to create a cult-like involvement in the activity, steeped in secrecy. They seek to surround themselves with people who either support or condone the drug use. They seek to norm their behavior to their peers. These groups are very prone to stunted emotional growth and lack maturity.

As for intervention, I can tell you what not to do more easily than what to do. You don't engage in "thump therapy" where you pound your fist down on the table and tell people about themselves. You don't go with education alone. If someone is still engaging in a behavior that is destructive in their life, and they've been asked about it, told about it, educated about it once, you don't need to do that again because they're not able to stop using by means of education alone. They need something more. And what do people respond to? They respond to being joined in the process. And you can't join with someone if you're judging them. People cannot begin to make a decision to change their lives until they accept their circumstances.

We spent a lot of time in treatment trying to get people to admit that they have a problem of understanding. We beat them up; we confront them with their issues; we have other people confront them. I have learned that a person can't truly have knowledge of themselves until they feel safe. So I like to approach people in a sort of a three-stage process: coming in, looking in, and looking outward.

Coming in, I like to keep things at a wholly intellectual level. You can talk about stuff that you're not feeling because it doesn't require trust to talk about some things and it's a less risky activity. You meet somebody in a bar, for instance, you can talk about the weather. You're not going to meet somebody and start talking about how you were hurt as a child because your mother was not emotionally available. We know that we can deal on an intellectual level with people. And so what I ask people is to just do a time line. Tell me why they got to me. Just how you got here and then after that, tell me a time line from the first time you used up until now.

And I only want specific instances. I don't want feelings attached to that at all. As they begin to work, they create a verbal history of their addiction and they see how I'm responding to what they're saying. And I'm responding to what they're saying not by being judgmental, not by forcing them to go somewhere they don't want to go, but by being a listener to this history. We start to develop a relationship. They start to understand that there are some consistencies on how I'm dealing with them. They're testing the relationship to see if I'll not be consistent and if maybe I've just been faking and I'm going to start judging them.

But it is real work for the professional or someone's loved one to keep them engaged at the thinking level because at any point when they are testing the relationship that's building around this material, they can run away. It'll blow up and they can run away. And you know, that's what elopements are made of. Really good programs focus on an anti-elopement strategy, not a treatment strategy. It's an anti-elopement strategy in the early period right after arrival.

Keeping you there long enough so you get to a point where you want to get from thinking to feeling is key. When you start dealing with feeling content, then you can go back to the time line and you can say, "These things you've figured were important." Now, what were the feelings associated with these instances that you've told me about? How are you feeling? How are people around you feeling? And we can start having a different kind of conversation. The healing begins inside.

Using an intervention to break through denial

From Dr. Jon Morgenstern, vice president and director of Health and Treatment Research and Analysis of the National Center on Addiction and Substance Abuse at Columbia University: One of the things that we have a stereotype about is if somebody is in denial there really is no talking to them. And I think that is not always the case. Sometimes it's the case, but even among people who look like they're not listening, I think at some level they do listen. And so to me, getting people to a point where they're ready to recognize the problem is a process. It's not something that is a single conversation necessarily, where you talk to somebody and then they wake up and say, "Oh yeah, I agree with you. I think I have a problem."

Those people probably would have recognized the problem themselves anyway. But I advise families that the conversation has to be done with love rather than anger. It has to be done with concern. You have to express, "I love you. I'm concerned about you. I'm worried about you." Don't say, "I'm angry with you; you're fucking up your life." It has to be done from love.

I help families prepare this. Rather than getting very emotional and exaggerating, you need to think to yourself what are the things that you observed about somebody that really worry you? And then convey that information in a clear way.

Then the other thing I say to people is this: "Don't get into an argument." Because one of the things about people who are in denial or people who have a problem is this: They are incredibly good at distraction. They want to get people distracted so they don't have to look at their own behavior. And the best way to distract—the thing that happens most in families—is "Let's get into a fight." If I get into a fight, I can blame you and I can discount your message. So I always say to families, "Don't fight." Don't fight, just say, "I love you; I'm worried about you; here's what I'm observing; I think you need help."

The other thing I say to families is, "Don't accept 'no' as an answer." I say, "Don't fight," but if you get a "no" just say, "Look, I love you ..."

If the person continues to say, "I don't have a problem; I don't really want to talk about this," you just say, "I really love you. I'm not going to drop this."

Two factors are really important in either triggering or exacerbating an addiction. The first is attachment to family and friends. Attachment is a very critical issue. If families have a strong bond, that's really

important. Bond, attachment, is important later on in life. It's fundamental to any recovery.

The second factor is social norms and monitoring. To the extent
that families set clear social norms, that they monitor their children's
behavior and say, "Hey look, here's the norm that we expect from your
behavior and we'll pay attention to that. Who are your friends? What's
your social environment?" That's very, very important and that's true in
recovery, too.

I look at people's social networks—who do you hang out with? If
you're hanging out predominantly with other people who are using
alcohol and drugs, I'm not going to treat you for moderation. I'm going
to say to you, "You need to go to a rehab," because your social environment doesn't have a set of controls that helps you—even if you have
an internalized desire to control your behavior. But just think about
how we respond, how in the world people respond. If you are in an
environment, you take on the characteristics of that social environment. Environment is hugely powerful. So when someone with a drug
problem says, "Well, I don't have to give up my drug-using friends," it's
not true. It's just not true.

*(Note: For more information about interventions and the role of fami-
lies, see Part Two of this book and the section "I Love an Addict, How Can
I Help Myself.")*

Five strategies for reaching someone in active addiction

From William White, senior research consultant, Chestnut Health Systems:

1. Convey your feelings about their drug use and your concerns
   about its effect on them as a person and on your relationship.
2. Refuse to protect them from the consequences of their drug
   use.
3. Convey the link between the growing problems in their life
   and their drug use.
4. Help the person find resources for professional treatment and
   ongoing recovery support.
5. Provide continuity of contact, caring, and support through
   the stages of addiction, recovery initiation, and the transition
   to stable recovery maintenance. Continuity of care over time,
   honest communication of your concern, and willingness to

support recovery but refusal to cosponsor their addiction are all critical.

QUITTING HEROIN—AN EXPERT'S EXPERIENCE

From George Williams, vice president, Community and Government Affairs, Treatment Alternatives for Safe Communities: You have what you call the "functional" addict—folks who have been using heroin for 50 years. They've never stopped working: They go to work every day. You would never know it. They can be functional. They can use once or twice a week. They say, "I'm just out with the chipping man." And their wives or their girlfriends don't know it. They have been able to disguise that they're users over a period of years. When I was in my addiction, my girlfriend didn't know it. So you've got some folks who are functional when using, and then you've got some folks who become very dysfunctional. But usually at some point in time, all of them escalate their use.

Then you've got folks who are right in the middle. They go up and down and then they get back together. They may stop and they may use periodically, every other day. The addicting thing has its own different markers and is determined by the addict's own personality and behavior and friends and social environment.

I've been in recovery since 1984. I had spent about 25 years out there. I became a full-blown addict while in the military. What was it that finally got my attention? My family members, my mother in particular. She would look at me sometimes and say, "Boy, what you're doing? You need some help. You've got to stop it." She would see it, smell it. She could tell. I'm still her son, it's our bloodline. My life got so traumatized I went to the penitentiary. The final mark for me was that.

Firemen, police officers, street guys, women, and so forth, everybody has a different marker that usually gets their attention and says, "Hey this is it." Usually it's their job, family, community, friends, or somebody or something that really matters. And for me, I kept hearing my mother's voice and seeing her face. She was in pain after she found out I'm an addict. And that kept staying in the back of my mind that my mom, she noticed it. She knows what I'm doing. I heard that story a lot when I was doing counseling with folks and we talked about how they came to hit their bottom. There

(continued on next page)

(continued from previous page)

are different kinds of bottoms. There are social bottoms, spiritual bottoms, family bottoms, a professional bottom, and so forth. Sometimes it is a combination of these things where they say, "Hey, enough is enough."

I haven't used since March 15th of 1984. And I would bet if I picked up a drug at any point in my life right now, I'm going to be back to where I was at in a short period of time. I would think that everything starts kicking in. If I use it again, if I relapse, if I go back into that world, I think right then and there things would just start kicking in. My biological, my psychological, my philosophical, my sociological, my spiritual stuff just kicks right back in into that state I left in '84. I think the disease is just dormant, like how a virus goes into remission. And at the point of using again, it kicks up with that full force. There are certain triggers from certain thoughts. You'd be around people and places sometimes and think to yourself, "Damn, could I?" No. The answer always has to be no.

A DRUG ADVOCATE LOSES CONTROL OVER HIS USE

From Matthew Southwell, managing director, Traffasi; founder, UK Harm Reduction Alliance; and chairman, National Drug Users Develoment Agency:
I've been a drug user since I was 16 years old. I'm now 44. I started as a cannabis user and then was part of the Acid House generation. Then I started freebasing cocaine and smoking heroin as well. I was always a polydrug user. I wanted drugs to be nourishing in my life. I enjoy the drugs.

In 1999, I went public as a drug user and did a TV documentary telling people. I was general manager in a hospital at the time. I never believed that I had a problem with drugs. It was always a choice. I didn't believe in the addiction model. I accept it for some people, but not for me. After I came out publicly in 1999, I lost my job. I was sacked because they said they couldn't have the head of a hospital being a public drug user. I faced public stigma as a drug user for the first time in my life.

So I started to organize the UK drug users movement and I was going around the country meeting with other drug users. Then my drug use started to move from being a weekend thing into being more frequent. Because I was a crack user, I was taking heroin to calm down. Ridiculously, I ended up with a habit. For a year I thought I was having regular bouts of flu. But it was the immunosuppressive qualities of crack. Even though I had worked in methadone clinics and I knew it all intellectually, at a personal level it crept up on me and I had a heroin habit. I was using crack and heroin every day, spending 500 pounds a day on it.

My self-esteem was demolished during this period because I had been known as Mr. Control Drug User of the UK. And suddenly I messed up very, very publicly. I was having anxiety attacks and sweating and all that stuff. I did several naltrexone detoxes on my own because I got so desperate to get off. I decided that heroin and crack were not drugs that were useful in my life.

When I was using heroin and crack, I wasn't as effective as a parent as I wanted to be. That was a really big issue for me. I also upset my mom. These were big drivers for me because I'm very family-centered. So family was the big driver for me to stop using heroin and crack. I obviously had some bad effects in my life from using that. It was difficult to manage them, particularly cocaine, which is a very compulsive drug.

Toward the end, when things started to drift, that was one of the early signs that I had a problem. I turned to my peer group and suddenly I saw the expertise that existed among people who stopped using drugs. They could teach me stuff I didn't know. I needed to learn a whole lot of new skills about how to stop using.

Women experience more severe drug-related problems

For a worldwide snapshot of the gender imbalance when it comes to the impact of drug abuse on psychological and physical health, University of Barcelona addictions expert Marta Torrens pored over dozens of country by country substance-use studies, and, in a March 23, 2011, presentation in Vienna before the UN Commission on Narcotic Drugs, revealed these findings:

- Up to 70 percent of all substance abusers also have other psychiatric disorders, the most prevalent being depression, anxiety disorders, and antisocial personality disorder. These mental disorders affect more females than males, with nearly twice as many women than men experiencing depression and mood swings.
- Up to 70 percent of individuals with a combination of

substance-use disorder and mental health disorders don't receive any treatment for their conditions.

- Women are more likely than men to:
  - come from families having other addicted members
  - have experienced more family disruption
  - be in relationships with drug-abusing partners
  - support their substance use through prostitution
  - suffer a high prevalence of violence from intimate partners
  - get sicker more quickly and suffer higher rates of medical problems, especially liver problems, hypertension, anemia, lung cancer, heart failure, HIV, infection, and infertility
- Less than 16 percent of nondrug-using women will experience violence from their intimate partner in a lifetime, whereas up to 57 percent of all drug-abusing women will experience violence in a relationship.

Learn to separate guilt from shame

From Dr. Sarz Maxwell, medical director, Chicago Recovery Alliance: I had a conversation with a patient talking about how he had slipped and used meth for a couple days and then went home. He was talking about how his shame about the slip was very focused on how his six-year-old son was hurt by it.

He was talking about the shame—that he just knew he was an awful person. I then compared it with a situation he had had a couple of weeks earlier while having a snowball fight with his son. He'd thrown a snowball at the house and the kid turned around and the snowball hit him in the face. My patient felt so guilty. The child cried of course, and the father had the same feeling he felt about the drug-use slip.

So it's really important to differentiate guilt and shame. And when he did that, he was able to recognize that the shame, the "I'm a shit" feeling, was a separate entity. It was something inside him that was different from him. That's a key thing when people can stop identifying with the disease. "I'm an addict. I'm a shit. I'm worthless. I have an addiction. It makes me act like a shit and it's worthless."

Addicts emanate shame and the natural, almost neurological, response of people to that shame is contempt. If only people could learn to step back and recognize, "Wow, that's how bad they feel about themselves, and I can respond in a way that is in service to the addict rather than in service to the disease."

Treatment should show addicts their "truth center"

From George Williams, vice president, Community and Government Affairs, Treatment Alternatives for Safe Communities: Anyone I counsel, I try to figure out what is their gatekeeper. What is the one drug that leads them to the other drugs? That's your gatekeeper. Once they realize what the gatekeeper is, then that's the one we want to change their relationship with.

Let's think about how you could change your relationship to drugs. I use the analogy of how, if you've got a girlfriend, or a wife, or loved one, at some point in time you might know that the relationship is not working. And then you start taking the inventory about that relationship and start thinking about it. And then you start thinking about how do you change—how do you get out of the relationship?

You've got to get out of that relationship because it's bad, and that means you've got to stop. You're not talking about the drug thing per se. You try to get them to think about it on their own terms, and in a normal kind of context. They can hear that. Everybody has a "truth center." I don't care who you are, you have what I call the truth center within you somewhere that tells you what you're doing and what you're doing that is not right, and you know it. You wake up knowing it, you go to bed knowing it, and when you do it, you know it.

So I try to get them to get in touch with their truth center, their only truth center, not the 12-Step truth center, not the stages of addiction truth center. But within their own truth center where we can begin to lay the foundation they need within themselves. So go talk to somebody. It could be a friend, it could be a preacher. I don't care if you live in the poorest neighborhood, there are some folks in that neighborhood who have been through what you've been through and came out healthy. Every environment has a source of some kind of protective factors. So find that protective factor and get it connected to you. Confession is good for the soul. You've got to start getting that out.

When I was in my own recovery, I made a change in my diet. I made a decision to become a vegetarian, to stop eating meat. I think some of the cravings came from my diet. I made a decision to stop smoking, because I saw that that's a part of my addiction as well. I started engaging in physical exercise. You see what I'm saying? So, you start to get those revelations to come—this all comes out of your truth center. Willpower is the source of your power. If you change your thoughts using willpower, you can change your world.

How drugs trick the brain so people relapse

From Adron Harris, director, Waggoner Center for Alcohol and Addiction Research, University of Texas: What the science evidence says is that there are three things that can prompt someone to take a drug again. One is stress. A second is the cue from stimuli associated with the drug-taking environment. And a third is the drug itself. Brain-imaging studies show that being exposed again to even a small amount of the drug can promote relapse and craving in humans. So the science argues for abstinence.

In my view, the drug tricks the brain into thinking it's important. It's not actually important. It's something the brain should ignore. But the brain remembers the drug and learns something that's important in our environment. The drug hijacks the machinery of learning and memory. That's one reason why the earlier in life a person begins using a drug, the more likely they are to advance to dependence. Early use is a big risk factor.

Emergency room screening for drug use is being done because something like a quarter to a half of the people who come into an emergency room with a broken bone have a drug problem. It's almost diagnostic that if a person shows up at the ER there is a high chance of drug abuse.

Calling addiction a disease doesn't reduce treatment responsibility

From Dr. Andrea Barthwell, CEO, Two Dreams Outer Banks: Calling dependence a disease can create a dilemma for family members because it's true that addicts act in a way that is beyond their control. So when they hurt people it wasn't that they wanted to hurt people; their brain sent out a primitive response to the executive control center saying, "If you stop doing what you're doing, you're going to die." So their choice is to either use or die, and so they have no other choice but to use.

Family members get upset when they hear that dependency is a disease, because they feel as if we let the user off the hook. Sometimes the patient says, "I didn't mean to hurt you and I should be forgiven for everything." But that's not taking responsibility for the disease.

I refer to addiction as a catastrophic illness in the same way that I view cancer. There are some cancers that if detected early, the chance of full recovery is going to be greater. But with a stage-four cancer, you may not expect such a good outcome. So leaving addiction undiagnosed means that we're going to have more morbidity and mortality. Like other catastrophic diseases, it requires mobilizing some resources at the point of the diagnosis and then developing an individualized treatment plan. Some people are going to need more than other people because there's not a one-size-fits-all treatment.

Seeing addiction as disease should change our drug policies

From Melody Heaps, founder of TASC (Treatment Alternatives for Safe Communities), and chair of the steering committee for HHS/SAMHSA's Partners for Recovery Initiative: I am the head of an agency I founded to change the way we do things, which is arresting and incarcerating people because of their addiction. We have personalized addiction; we have sensationalized it. But we haven't made it a public health initiative.

We haven't done for drug addiction what we've done for smoking. If we did that, then people would begin to understand they don't need to be ashamed because it's a brain disease like any other. As with other diseases, it would be part of the public dialogue about what the signs are and how we look for them. It would get the focus off that personal "It's only me" into "No, it's not just me. It's a condition. It's a part of the diseases that we all deal with. It's not any worse, it's not any better. It's a public health matter."

I think that would help the individual addict begin to take a look at him- or herself with regard to how they fit into this culture with less shame and less stigma, so they don't have to move to a state of denial. It's a disease just like every other disease. It needs to be treated, and it needs information about management and prevention. This is an addiction, this is a brain disease, treatment works, and this is how the drug affects the brain. That's the educational message.

There is no benign drug. Marijuana is not a benign drug, and we don't have to get into legalization; we don't have to get into medical marijuana. That distracts us. We need to show that this is what marijuana does to the juvenile brain. Put the information out there in media ads so that it's equal to other public health issues we as a society have tackled. That's also how we get away from the stigma.

Some politicians think that diverting money from incarceration for drug offenses to treatment for drug abuse makes them appear soft on crime. This idea that you can't be a proponent for treatment without looking like you're soft on crime is a political reality for a lot of politicians. All of the research is coming out showing that if you can offer treatment, particularly in the community to people who are involved in the criminal justice system, you will see crime reduced. That's number one. Number two, the corrections system is costing too much money. What can we do? Let's put some money into alternatives to incarceration.

So the idea that people will see me as soft on crime—we have crossed the political divide on that. We are beyond that right now, because one, budgets are too tight and we can't afford to incarcerate people; and two, because the research has shown that drug treatment does work.

In terms of race, in terms of poverty, there just doesn't seem to be any science that says black people or Hispanic people, because they're poor, have a greater incidence of addiction than white folks. The science isn't there. Poverty makes you vulnerable—let's put it that way— it makes you vulnerable to addiction

The War on Drugs did not reduce drug use in America. It just didn't. There are episodic ups and downs, but the crack-cocaine thing took off in our urban centers and among minority populations just like methamphetamine is taking off in some of our rural and suburban areas.

The other thing that we do as a country is we follow the drug. The latest drug excites us. It really does. Methamphetamine is the worst drug we've ever had, except the last time I heard it was crack cocaine, except the last time I heard it was amphetamines, and then well, it was heroin. We get excited about the drug and we legislate according to the drug, which is insane. I mean, it's just crazy. And again, if people understood the science, if science were driving it, it would change the way we do business.

Most of the 600,000 people coming out of prisons in this country have addiction problems. Legislating against the drug means that we have crack-cocaine laws that still are more severe than regular cocaine laws. We have at least one in three African-American males under the jurisdiction of the criminal justice system. What do you do with that? What does that say about this country? What does that say to a family? What does that say about young people in our schools? But we're not dealing with that because we are still not dealing with addiction as a public health issue, even though the science is there.

Meet the Drug Myth Busters

Five myths about drug dependence

1. Drug abuse leads to dependence. A better phrase is "drug abuse precedes dependence." The myth suggests that drug abuse causes drug dependence, when in reality they are two different drug-use conditions. In many people, dependence is preceded by abuse, but some people develop dependence without going through the progression of drug use, abuse, and dependence. In addition, many people abuse drugs for many years without developing the disease of chemical dependence. It now appears that a person must "have what it takes" to become dependent on drugs. In many cases, genetics is the main risk factor for determining who develops the disease.

2. Drugs cause addiction. An interesting scientific question is, "If drugs cause addiction, then why doesn't everyone who uses drugs too much, too often, become dependent (addicted)?" Scientists are looking into genetic and other factors that cause some people to become dependent while sparing others this brain pathology. As is the case with most chronic conditions, addiction emerges from the interplay of genetic and environmental factors.

3. It takes years for someone to become dependent on a drug. There are anecdotal reports that some people become "instantly dependent" on drugs like alcohol and cocaine, after only a single or just a few exposures to the drug. These people might be genetically loaded for the disease. There are also research studies showing that most people who will become dependent on cocaine do so within three years of starting cocaine use. Most people who become dependent on marijuana are identifiable as such within 12 months of initiating use.

4. All drugs damage brain cells. Actually, relatively few have

been shown to damage brain cells through a toxic effect. These include alcohol (high doses over a long time); inhalants, including paint thinner, airplane glue, correction fluid, and hair sprays (all of these are organ-toxic and highly damaging to all internal organs); methamphetamine; and ecstasy/ MDMA. However, the damage those drugs do should not be discounted. Functional MRI research does show long-lasting impairment from the use of cocaine, methamphetamine, and alcohol. But in general, the brain is marvelously resilient and able to fend off the dangerous effects of most drugs. And damage is not always permanent.

5. Addiction is treated behaviorally, so it must be a behavioral problem. New brain-scan studies are showing that behavioral treatments (e.g., psychotherapy) and medications change brain function similarly. Chemical dependence is a brain disease that can be treated by changing brain function through several different types of treatments. It is not simply a form of bad behavior.

(Source: Carlton Erickson, Director of the Addiction Science Research and Education Center and distinguished professor of pharmacy/toxicology at the University of Texas at Austin. www.utexas.edu/research/asrec/myths.html.)

Mythbuster—only ugly and weak-willed people do drugs

From Dr. Dora Dixie, owner of Day by Day Health Consultants in Chicago, Illinois, medical director of the Women's Treatment Center, and regional director of the American Society of Addiction Medicine: I had my own myths coming into the field of addiction medicine. I used to think that only ugly people would ever do drugs, that there were no pretty people—aesthetically pretty as the world counts beauty—who would ever do drugs because you must be ugly on the outside, therefore you feel ugly and worse on the inside. So you're doing the drugs to hide or to make yourself not feel so ugly or whatever. That was my myth. "Gosh, she's so pretty. He's so handsome. He's so intelligent." It doesn't have anything to do with that.

Weak will—you could quit if you wanted to—or, "If he loved me, he wouldn't do heroin." "If she loved me, she wouldn't be prostituting to get drugs." "If Mama loved me, she wouldn't get drunk every weekend," or whatever. With these myths the person who is not the addict takes the addict's behavior personally, especially if it starts when you're a child because children think the whole world revolves around them.

Another myth I hear is you can't quit drugs because you're possessed by the devil. You're out of grace with God. God has removed himself from you.

Mythbuster—only humans are susceptible to dependency

From Alexandre Laudet, PhD, director of the Center for Study of Addictions and Recovery, National Development and Research Institutes Inc: Animals demonstrate cravings in drug studies, but animals have no moral upbringing. In studies of rats and monkeys, dogs and guinea pigs, they all get addicted to drugs and do so without much trouble. It's a basic physiological process that has nothing to do with being immoral or weak-willed.

Dr. Nora Volkow's four biggest addiction myths

First: The notion that addiction is the result of a personal choice, a sign of a character flaw, or moral weakness. This strong and widespread belief continues to sustain the social stigma that makes life doubly miserable for those battling addiction. But science has completely debunked this myth by showing that, while initial experimentation with a psychoactive substance is often a voluntary choice, the processes that are put in motion by that initial exposure, in vulnerable individuals, can lead to physical and functional changes in the brain, which can, in effect, reprogram behaviors and erode the very ability of that person to exert free will. This is why addiction is not a moral weakness but a bona fide disease of the brain.

Second: In order for treatment to be effective, a person must first hit "rock bottom." Science has shown that the broad array of pharmaceutical, behavioral, and combination therapies that we have available can help many individuals break free from the cycle of addiction at any point in their disease trajectory, particularly if the treatment is sustained.

Third: The fact that addicted individuals often and repeatedly fail in their efforts to remain abstinent for a significant period of time demonstrates that addiction treatment doesn't work. In fact, treatment (at least, evidence-based treatment) does work, although it must be comprehensive and tailored to the individual's specific and often complex problems. Addiction is like many chronic conditions, in which symptoms (in this case, drug use) re-emerge when patients stop their treatment (e.g., medication for blood pressure) or fail to maintain a specific set of behaviors needed to keep them healthy (e.g., diet and exercise for diabetes, heart disease, etc.). In those cases, we recognize that the patient needs to adhere to their treatment or modify it as appropriate in order to maintain their long-term health goals. Addiction, for most affected individuals, is a chronic, relapsing disease, and its treatment may need to continue at some level throughout the patient's life. Thus, relapse should be considered a pre-dictable setback and not a failure of the treatment. This, by the way, also explains why the best treatment outcomes are reported by programs that offer continuity of care for a five-year period.

Fourth: The brain is a static, fully formed entity, at least in adults. The science of the past 20 or so years has painted a dramatically different picture, one in which the brain is being continuously molded and re-shaped by experience (good and bad). It is important to understand that this "plastic" (malleable) nature of the brain is a double-edged sword. On one hand, plasticity allows the extreme stress of combat to induce a disabling PTSD (post-traumatic stress disorder) or addictive drugs to cause long-lasting deficits in brain performance. On the other hand, plasticity also enables lifelong learning and supports the thera-peutic potential of any treatment (behavioral and/or pharmacological) for mental illnesses, including addiction.

Contrasting Drugs and Alcohol Worldwide

From Professor Alejandro Vassilaqui, executive director, Center of Informa-tion and Education for Drug Abuse Prevention (CEDRO, Peru): CE-DRO is an institution that was created about 25 years ago to fight drug consumption. We are the institution that has created the con-science against drugs in Peru and other parts of Central and South America. We have about 400 centers that provide counseling to young people so they won't be involved in any part of the drug cycle.

Our problems are with alcohol first, then marijuana, followed by cocaine. Our biggest problem is there aren't enough treatment centers, particularly for women. Women have been sort of ignored. We need to convince the family that it is up to them to try to convince the members of that family who are drug users to go into treatment. That is the most effective motivator.

One of the big problems with the families and couples is they have the belief that the problem will go away by itself. They think that drug use among children is just a passing fad. People in the upper classes try to hide the problem. But in the middle classes and the lower classes, there is a much better attitude and I believe a much better understanding of the drug problem. People aren't imprisoned here in Peru for using any of the illegal drugs, unless they commit a crime such as selling drugs. We do have 12-Step programs here in big cities and they are very effective.

From Gino Vumbaca, executive director, Australian National Council on Drugs: Australia has developed a good reputation in the region for its approach to drug use. Our response is a mix of law enforcement, prevention, treatment, and harm reduction. The mix may vary at times, but the overwhelming majority of people in these sectors support the continuation of this balanced approach. The most recent survey of Australian attitudes to drug policy and programs shows only 13 percent favoring prison or weekend detention for cannabis possession and 87 percent wanting a referral to treatment, fine, warning, or no action.

The opportunities for Australia's development agenda to take a role in advising, assisting, and supporting countries and people in our region addressing drug use are critical. The evidence is quite clear that drug use creates poorer health, poverty, discrimination, and hardship for communities.

Treating individual drug use as predominantly a health issue, limiting the consequences for people caught up in drug use, working with the countries of our region to develop more humane and effective responses to drug use, and exporting the sophisticated models of drug prevention, treatment, and harm reduction we have developed in Australia are all options that should be considered by governments.

From David Templeman, chief executive officer, Alcohol and Other Drugs Council of Australia: We practice harm reduction in Australia regarding drugs. Addicts can exchange needles in a range of settings, whether it might be done in a pharmacy or in other environments or in a treatment service facility. So there's no stigma attached to that in terms of someone getting and exchanging needles. We have medically certified injecting centers so addicts come into a sterile clean environment and will have access to exchanging needles. The centers were set up to ensure that somebody doesn't die. There have been no deaths in 10 years of operating.

This arrangement also provides a treatment opportunity. Having someone come into that sort of secure environment enables a conversation to happen, an opportunity to actually talk to those people about what they're using, how they're using it. We have the realization here that the idea of developing a drug-free society is living in fantasy land. We're always going to have drugs.

Our biggest problem in Australia is with alcohol. It's the biggest single problem that we have. Australians almost pride themselves internationally on how much they can drink and where they can drink and how they'll drink. You can buy alcohol 24 hours a day, seven days a week. A bottle of wine here is cheaper than a bottle of water. And that's unbelievably ridiculous.

From Dr. William Sinkele, founder and executive director, Support for Addictions Prevention and Treatment in Africa: My experience in Kenya is that poverty is a source of the addiction problem. In Kenya's slums (one-third to one-half of the people of Nairobi live in slums), the stress of growing up in that environment, the easy availability of cheap alcohol and drugs, the ubiquitous presence of bars, lack of employment, idleness, high rate of youth (especially males) who did not finish high school, a macho drinking culture and a culture of binge drinking, and trauma issues (half of the girls/women experience violence or see violence) all contribute to a vulnerability to alcohol and drug abuse and addiction.

I think one of the new frontiers for treatment, even for Africa, is addiction e-counseling and computer-assisted programs using cognitive behavioral approaches. My young adults and children love sending e-mails and being on Facebook. So this happens even in some parts of Africa, especially around the countries bordering the coast.

I am advocating as part of our community-based treatment approach the setting up of recovery centers. We need, after primary care treatment, these day-care-like centers where those in early recovery or right after treatment can learn and get more: relapse prevention, literacy skills, life skills, business skills, a safe place to hang out, etc. I am also advocating a manualized approach to treatment. We have few addiction counselors in Kenya and very few or no treatment centers (other than in South Africa and Egypt), so we need a basic manualized approach using evidence-based modalities (e.g., motivational interviewing, cognitive behavioral interventions, and 12-Step facilitation) adapted to our African situation.

From Gilberto Gerra, chief of the Drug Prevention and Health Branch, United Nations Office on Drugs and Crime, Vienna, Austria: In every

European country, from those with the most right-wing and those with the most left-wing policies on illegal drugs, policymakers share a misleading concept. The most conservative say, "Punish them; these people made a decision to take drugs and we have to punish them until they stop. The leftists say, "These people decided to take drugs and we have to permit them." Is there a right? Is there a right to take drugs if they want? I can't imagine there is one.

In front of you is a 15-year-old, neglected, profoundly traumatized child with no family bond and no engagement in school. On what foundation do they rely when deciding whether to say no or say yes to drugs? There's always something at the core, either biologically or environmentally, that pushes people toward drug use. The biological can also come from the genetic, what you inherited from your parents. We know that brain changes occur as a consequence of drug and alcohol use. So this is a disease. It's not about making a decision for good or bad behavior. To frame drug use in terms of having made a decision, as both the right and left sometimes do, is totally the wrong way to frame the problem.

From Dr. Vladimir Poznyak, coordinator, Management of Substance Abuse unit at the Dept. of Mental Health and Substance Abuse, World Health Organization: The scale of the impact of alcohol and other drug use on global health is not always appreciated. Illicit drugs cause significant mortality. For example, in the Russian Federation, tens of thousands of people die each year from drug use. According to the latest World Health Organization estimates, 2.3 million people die of alcohol-related causes every year.

This is a huge burden. But the nature of alcohol- and drug-use disorders is that the demand for treatment often doesn't correspond to the real prevalence of use disorders in a population. There are many factors accounting for that, including stigma and the availability of services. This underestimate of the true prevalence of the disorders definitely influences the positioning of treatment of alcohol- and drug-use disorders on the national and international agendas.

Some Treatment Options

For more information about the self-help oriented treatments mentioned most frequently by the experts interviewed for this book, along with valuable tips about how to utilize these methods and tools, consult the following:

- Acupuncture, Seven Self-Care Tools, p. 264
- Cognitive Behavioral Therapy, Seven Self-Care Tools, p. 235
- 12-Step Programs, Seven Self-Care Tools, p. 240
- Secular and Faith-based Mutual Aid Groups, Faces and Voices of Recovery, Appendix Two, p. 337
- Medications (for dependence on heroin, opium, and oxycodone)
  - Methadone
  - Buprenorphine
  - Naltrexone
- Mindfulness, Seven Self-Care Tools, p. 249
- Nutrition, Seven Self-Care Tools, p. 256

Your 30-Day Challenge for Drugs

Do you have a bad habit or a dependency? Here is another chance to find out.

You have answered the questionnaires for this toxic compulsion. You have read through what the experts have to say. You have thought about the extent to which you exhibit the behaviors associated with either a nondependent use disorder or a dependency.

Do you still have any doubt about whether you have just a bad habit, or whether your behavior meets the criteria for a dependency?

If so, create a 30-day challenge for yourself.

Our intention isn't to encourage the use of illicit drugs. Ideally, if you're a nondependent drug user, you can stop using for 30 days without any problem. So you could set that as your challenge. But let's make the challenge more interesting. Continue using your drug of choice for a month, but do so with rules and boundaries.

Let's use marijuana as an example. If you use marijuana daily, set a time frame that you will use only after 6 p.m. each day, or you will use only between the hours of 6 p.m. and 7 p.m. This is a control check. Can you control your usage, or does the drug control you?

You must set the goal for 30 days and make a commitment about how often and how much you will use each day. If you alter or in any way break your commitment to the plan, you probably have a problem with that drug. It's that simple.

III

Toxic Compulsion 3: Eating Disorders

Food is an important part of a balanced diet.
—Fran Lebowitz

My first drug was sugar. I was in the fifth or sixth grade in a New York City parochial school on the Upper East Side. We had to wear a jacket and a tie and these little gray pants, and I remember getting bigger and bigger, not being able to fit into my clothes because of the candy I ate to satisfy my craving for sugar.

I was getting fat eating "Sugar Babies"—caramel nuggets that were like pure sugar. I would put three bags in my mouth at a time and suck the juice down. It was just like getting high.

As a child, prior to moving from California to the East Coast when my parents divorced, and before my Uncle Bobby was killed while campaigning for the Democratic nomination for president, I did not have a problem with weight gain. Today, I know that my subsequent sugar fixation was rooted in the trauma I experienced around my parents' divorce and the assassination of my uncle.

I started using drugs in the eighth grade. However, this did not replace or diminish my obsession with and craving for sugar, which remains a challenge for me. Later in life when I enrolled in an inner-city methadone maintenance program to get off heroin, and, at the same time, was going to law school, I practically lived off of Reggie bars and Brussels cookies. I would eat bags of them and would scout stores within a 10-square-block radius of the west side New York City neighborhood where I lived. One day I remember canvassing all those stores and discovering that every one of them was out of my favorites. I realized I'd eaten the stock of every store in my neighborhood.

While I was in early recovery my weight continued to fluctuate greatly. The drugs I had taken all affected my weight one way or the other. Opiates would make me gain weight because I would eat lots of sugar when taking them, and the other drugs would make me thinner because I would not eat as much. At that time I didn't understand that certain food groups, such as bread and pasta, break down into sugar in the body. I craved bread and pasta and I ate them like an addict. I just didn't see the connections, and that's what really matters. Until you see the connections and can relate them to your life, you're not going to change; you'll just figure, well, this is the way I am.

Many addicts—especially those having a problem with food—don't understand that they can actually take steps to reduce their cravings. I don't know whether or not I have a genetic predisposition to sugar addiction. However, I don't recall having problems before the traumas that started with my parents' divorce. If you go to most any 12-Step meeting anywhere in the world, you will find people in recovery who have similar struggles with sugar. Cookies, brownies, and other sweets are almost always available along with the ubiquitous pot or urn of coffee. In locales with refrigerators, you'll generally find lots of ice cream.

When I interviewed Dr. Kelly Brownell, Yale University professor of psychology and public health director of the Rudd Center for Food Policy & Obesity, I was curious about what this expert on nutrition and obesity thinks about the connection between food and addiction. The first point he made is a distinction. Obesity is not always part of addiction or an eating disorder. There are certain environmental circumstances that make unhealthy food behaviors—and the resulting excess weight—more likely, such as junk food in public schools, increasingly large portions served by restaurants, and the endless marketing of unhealthy foods directed at everyone, but particularly children.

"There are some people, probably the extreme cases, whom you might possibly describe with a term like 'food addict,'" Dr. Brownell explained. "Or use the word 'food-addiction' to describe how they interact with food. It's not possible to know how many such people there are, but when you talk to some of these people who classify themselves as food addicts, a lot of the criteria for addiction seem to apply. They overuse the substance. They use it in the face of adverse consequences. They report things like tolerance and withdrawal and they basically say that they're powerless over the food.

"There's very compelling scientific work now suggesting that sugar in particular works on the brain very much like traditional substances of abuse. Now it may not be as strong an effect, but there is such an effect—and it could be enough to adversely affect the diets of millions of people. Some people try to dismiss the concept by saying that it's silly to use the word addiction with something you need to survive. It would be like saying you have an addiction to air. But a large body of science suggests that not all foods are alike. You don't find people with unhealthy compulsions to eat vegetables, but you do find many who have problems with sugar. Certain groups of foods with high levels of refined sugar, white flour, saturated fat, and sodium are commonly sold at a lot of schools. These foods, which usually have highly recognizable brand names, tend to cause problems. The foods most likely to lead to compulsive use are the ones pushed most aggressively by the mainstream food industry. Sugar beverages such as Coke are sold in every corner of the world, and fast food restaurants, such as McDonald's, are nearly as ubiquitous. So, we've created a world that encourages behaviors that can lead to a harmful pattern of interaction between the human brain and the environment."

One of Dr. Brownell's colleagues at Yale, Ashley Gearhardt, co-authored a 2011 study showing that addictive eating behaviors activate the same areas of the brain as dependent use of alcohol or other drugs. Functional magnetic resonance imaging (FMRI) studies were conducted on a group of 48 young women with overeating problems. When these women were shown pictures of a chocolate milk shake, the patterns of brain activation mirrored those of persons with substance-use disorders who were shown pictures of their drug of choice. Women without addictive food behaviors registered far less activity in this reward circuitry of their brains when shown the milk shakes. Once the women with eating disorders actually tasted a milk shake, they recorded much less activity in those brain areas than the "normal" eaters. This is a phenomenon that also occurs with drug and alcohol dependence. The brain begins to adjust to the presence of excess dopamine from substance use and, eventually, the individual must use not to feel high, but rather to simply feel normal or to avoid becoming sick. This leads to cravings for even greater amounts of the abused substance.

Lead study author Gearhardt noted how the brain chemistry involved in chronic overeating produces a vicious cycle of dependence. "At first you want it because it tastes good," wrote Gearhardt, "but as you go from use to abuse to dependence, you begin to crave it, and liking it doesn't play as much of a role. Kids are in an especially dangerous position. From an early age, they are exposed to addictive food." *(Source: "Neural correlates of food addiction." Gearhardt AN, Yokum S, Orr PT, Stice E, Corbin WR, and Brownell KD. Arch Gen Psychiatry. 2011 Aug;68(8):808–16. Epub 2011 Apr 4.)*

Additionally, young people's brains are not fully developed. In particular, the prefrontal cortex is still being wired. This area is responsible for judgment, perspective, and impulse control. No wonder adolescents tend to be lacking in all of these areas. Substance use further impairs prefrontal cortex functioning while supercharging and hijacking the limbic system, which is responsible for feelings of pleasure and drives. An addicted person can irrationally put substance use before health, happiness, family, friends, career, and so forth. The brain is subconsciously driving the individual toward drugs as though his or her life depended on their use.

Other studies have identified specific types of foods as having addictive properties that stimulate binge eating, which in turn can produce obesity. These types of foods include sweets, carbohydrates, fats, sweet/fat combinations, and highly processed or high-salt foods.

Food addiction treatment specialist and author Kay Sheppard, herself in recovery from eating problems since 1977, called food addiction "a physiological, biochemical condition of the body that creates craving for refined carbohydrates. This craving and its underlying biochemistry is comparable to the alcoholic's craving for alcohol . . . Researchers have identified the same gene mutation in a high percentage of individuals who are addicted to alcohol, food, cocaine, and nicotine . . . Refined, processed foods trigger the addictive response in people who are genetically predisposed to the disease of addiction."

Through her work with food addiction clients, chronicled in several of her books, including *From the First Bite: A Complete Guide to Recovery from Food Addiction*, Sheppard has identified a pattern of denial in food addicts that is very similar to what is experienced by all of the other toxic compulsions discussed in these pages. Denial has many faces, each a psychological defense against the fear of confronting a realization of being out of control. Those faces of denial:

- Simple denial: The food addict maintains that something is true when it isn't. "I don't have a problem."
- Minimizing: The addict attempts to make the problem seem insignificant. "I just need to find the right diet."
- Blaming: The addict not only denies responsibility for eating behaviors, but shifts the blame. "My job stress makes me overeat."
- Rationalizing: The addict makes endless illogical excuses for the eating behavior. "I overeat to feel better about life."

Other common defense mechanisms Sheppard has seen in her clients include judging, analyzing, arguing, evading, defiance, withdrawal, joking, and aggression. Until they are overcome, these defense mechanisms can prevent or undermine recovery.

Do you or someone you know exhibit denial or other defense mechanisms when confronted about eating habits? If so, read on. There is much more to having a problem with food than just overeating.

Three Primary Eating Disorders

It's open to debate how many people actually have unhealthy eating habits that qualify as a disorder. Surveys cited by the National Eating Disorders Association estimate that up to 10 million females and 1 million males in the United States have struggled with anorexia or bulimia. Millions more have binge-eating disorders. These are just informed guesses because the stigma and secretiveness associated with these disorders discourage many from seeking medical or psychiatric treatment, much less acknowledging a problem, when surveyed.

The boundaries for what constitutes an eating disorder are periodically stretched by newly invented terms that attempt to categorize newly recognized obsessive-compulsive behaviors involving food. For example, have you ever heard of orthorexia? The National Eating Disorders Association defines it as an obsession with healthy eating in which "food choices become so restrictive, with both variety and calories, that health suffers." It seems ironic, even bizarre, that you could be so health conscious that your health suffers. For such people, their self-esteem becomes linked to a diet purity that's based on overly strict criteria regarding which foods are healthy and which are not. Though it's not yet listed by specialists as an official eating disorder, it's described as similar to other recognized disorders in some of the underlying motivations, such as a compulsion for control and a fear-based desire to improve self-esteem.

Our concern here will be with the three primary eating disorders—anorexia, bulimia, and binge eating. These are the extremes of food obsession, from eating too little to eating too much, which may look different in terms of the behaviors and rituals involved, but share some triggers and brain chemistry.

Obesity is a condition that now defines about one-third of all adults in the United States, a statistic that increased by 50 percent per decade for the past three decades. That is a period in which, not coincidentally, the consumption of addictive foods also grew steadily in popular consumption. In a 2007 medical journal article, Dr. Nora D. Volkow and Dr. Charles P. O'Brien made the case that obesity should be treated as "a brain disorder" to be ranked alongside anorexia and bulimia as a serious addictive condition "with severe impairments and serious adverse outcomes." They went on to say, "We postulate that the underlying brain mechanisms [for obesity] are similar to those that ultimately result in the compulsive drug consumption in addiction . . . both food consumption and drug use are driven by their rewarding properties, which have been linked to increases in dopaminergic [dopamine-related] activity in brain reward circuits . . . ." *(Source: "Issues for DSM-V: Should obesity be included as a brain disorder?" Volkow ND and O'Brien CP. Am J Psychiatry. 2007 May;164:708–10.)*

"The definition for substance addiction definitely applies to eating disorders," said Dr. Kimberly Dennis, medical director of the Timberline Knolls Residential Treatment Center in Illinois. "Denial. Minimization. Powerlessness. Unmanageability. Preoccupation with using, or with the activity. It's because of the stigma associated with addiction that it's controversial to think of eating disorders as being along the addiction spectrum."

Eating-disorder researchers writing in the *Canadian Medical Association Journal* (March 9, 2010) elaborated on the parallels between eating and substance-use disorders. "The process involves a compulsive pattern of use, even in the face of negative health and social consequences . . . both food and drugs induce tolerance over time . . . withdrawal symptoms often occur upon discontinuation of the drug or during dieting . . . there is also a high incidence of relapse with both types of behavior."

Whether eating too much or consuming too little food, the symptoms of addiction are similar. "Getting obsessive with food can take many forms and is a sign that food is being used to medicate one's feelings and emotions, rather than being used in response to physical hunger," observed Donald Altman, a psychotherapist, professor, and eating disorders expert in Portland, Oregon, who is national vice president of The Center for Mindful Eating. "Generally, when it comes to abusing food, I often say that it's not what you're eating, but what's eating at you. If the feeling you have in the body (or mind) can be satisfied by anything other than food, then it is not a physical hunger you are experiencing."

To help determine whether you've gone past typical or normal eating behaviors and strayed into extreme, risky, or dangerous eating behaviors, Altman suggests that you compare yourself and your habits around food to these four signs of "normal," or healthy, eating:

1. Healthy eaters tend to notice their hunger signals and then act on them in a reasonable amount of time. The key idea here is that most people know their hunger signals. If someone asks them, "Rate your hunger on a 1 to 10 scale, with 10 being extreme hunger and 1 being no hunger," they would be able to do that. They would likely be able to describe what hunger in the high 7 to 10 range feels like for them, from a pounding headache to grouchiness or anything in between. Once normal eaters recognize their body's hunger signals, they respond to them. They don't ignore these feelings or experience them in a fearful way.

2. Healthy eaters seek out a variety of food to fulfill their hunger. Normal eaters are not rigid about food and they are not hung up on avoiding certain foods. Normal eaters tend to seek out foods that will satisfy the hunger they are feeling in this moment. In addition, normal eaters enjoy the food they are eating. They allow themselves to taste and savor the food. Even if they may eat quickly, they try to choose food that is pleasing to the taste buds.

3. Healthy eaters tend to enjoy eating in general. The reason that diets often fail is that they limit food variety and that takes away the variety that people like when eating. Savoring food can take many forms. For one thing, food is a social event, and normal eaters often enjoy getting together with friends and family. Sharing food is highly valued and practiced in all cultures as well as religious traditions, and it is a powerful way of cultivating closeness and building trust. If you only eat alone or worry what others will think about the way that you eat, then you may be crossing over from normal or recreational eating into unbalanced eating behavior.

4. Healthy eaters tend to stop eating after they are full. In other words, they pay attention to their hunger and their satiety level. Many people are cued only visually by food—such as, stopping only when all of the food is gone from the plate or by looking at a portion size and thinking it is appropriate. This is very different from normal eaters who notice their hunger level and stop because they are no longer hungry or because they experience a feeling of fullness in the stomach or body. The speed with which one eats can make a difference in overeating. Eating more slowly gives you a more accurate reading of how full you are. If you have time but always eat quickly and then overeat as a result and feel overstuffed or uncomfortable after eating, then you may need to find more balance in your eating.

Are You a Mindful Eater? A Quiz

There are no right or wrong answers in this quiz. This is not a scientific study, but a way to help you determine whether you have mindful eating habits.

Circle "true" or "false" for each answer

1. When I'm at a party or a family function I am usually able to eat just what I want without overeating.
   T   F

2. At work, I am usually able to control myself when people bring cookies and other tempting snacks in.
   T   F

3. I consciously take the time to take a breath or two between bites while I am eating.
   T   F

4. I am very aware of my body's hunger signals, and I know when I am just a little bit hungry.
   T   F

5. I pay attention to my body posture while eating.
   T   F

6. I choose foods because they offer me the energy that I sense my body needs at the moment when I feel hunger.
   T   F

7. Typically, I seek out a wide variety of foods and don't eat the same foods day after day.
   T   F

8. I do not believe that certain foods are "good" and other foods are "bad" and need to always be avoided.
   T   F

9. I almost always stop eating after my body's hunger has been satisfied.
   T   F

10. I almost never feel a sense of guilt and shame about food and eating.
    T   F

11. I rarely think about food throughout the day, except when I am hungry or need to buy food from the store.
    T   F

(continued on next page)

(continued from previous page)

12. I am usually aware of my feelings and emotions before I order, prepare, or eat food.

    T   F

13. When I finish eating, I usually make a conscious decision about how to transition—with a walk, a cup of tea, etc.—before returning to my next activity.

    T   F

14. Even when I am feeling upset, lonely, angry or sad, I do not usually over- or undereat.

    T   F

15. Most of the time, I pace myself while eating so that I can savor and enjoy the taste and texture of my meal for at least 20 minutes.

    T   F

16. I am usually aware of how many times I chew each bite before swallowing.

    T   F

17. Normally, I pause before a meal or snack to say a blessing, have a moment of silence, or to notice my appreciation for the food on my plate.

    T   F

18. I am aware of my surroundings while eating, and usually choose a location where I can eat in a relaxed and unrushed manner.

    T   F

19. As a general rule, my meals at home are eaten without watching the TV, without distraction, and without other activities.

    T   F

20. I have a good idea of where the flavors of saltiness and bitterness are most intensely sensed on my tongue.

    T   F

21. When bored in the evening, I normally find other things to do than eat.

    T   F

22. Those times that I eat too much, or when I eat food that is not the healthiest, I can typically accept this without blaming or shaming myself.

    T   F

23. A trip to the grocery store or a retail super store does not trigger either binge eating or anxiety for me.

    T   F

24. I rarely think about dieting, counting calories on labels, or counting calories while eating meals.

    T   F

25. I am generally accepting of my body at its present weight and shape—even if there are a few things that I would like to change.

    T   F

26. I realize that eating has consequences to my health, and I am pretty good at making food choices based on this awareness.

    T   F

27. Generally, I accept that my eating experiences are unique, and that there is no one right or wrong way to eat.

    T   F

28. I sometimes think about the impact of my food choices on the Earth, society, and other beings.

    T   F

29. I can usually tell the difference between my body's physical and emotional feelings of hunger.

    T   F

30. I do not judge other people's choice of foods or their eating habits.

    T   F

SCORING: To get your mindful eating rating, count up the number of "true" answers. The higher your number, the higher your mindful eating skills. Use the scale below to see where your rating fits in.

1–5 Mindless Eater (food choices could be negatively affecting health)

6–10 Less Skillful Mindful Eater (some awareness, but struggling with food)

11–15 Moderate Mindful Eater Skills (using skills about half the time, needs to intensify practice)

(continued on next page)

(continued from previous page)

16–20 Practicing Mindful Eater (above average mindful eating skills; on the path to moderate and conscious eating)

21–25 Very Skillful Mindful Eater (engages mindful eating skills much of the time)

26–30 Enlightened Eater (extremely skillful at mindful eating and centering and enjoying meals)

Quiz used with permission from Donald Altman, www.mindfulpractices.com

Time to Get Honest with Yourself

This is a self-administered test for eating disorders. Answer "yes" or "no" to these questions (compiled from various eating-disorder groups and Web sites):

Do you feel fat even when other people comment that you are thin?
Do you regularly worry about what you eat?
Have you avoided people who bother you about your eating habits?
Have you often wanted to eat alone rather than with friends or family?
Is it difficult for you to go a day without exercising?
If you're female, have your periods changed significantly or stopped altogether?
If you're male, has your sex drive weakened?
Do you feel depressed when you gain any weight?
Do you cook for other people and refuse to eat what you've prepared?
Do you hide food so others won't see what you're eating?
Do you have problems stopping when you start eating?
Do you lie to others about your eating habits?
Do you feel you would like yourself better if you were thin?
Do you read a lot of books about diet and exercise?
Has your preoccupation with your weight caused you to miss work or school?
Does eating make you feel guilty?
Do you binge on certain foods?
Does eating make you feel bloated and fat?
Do you do things with your food that other people don't do?
Is your fear of eating interfering with your social or family life?
Do you feel anxious when friends or strangers watch you eat?

Do you throw up and take laxatives to control your weight?
Do you have any of these symptoms: dry skin, dry nails, hair is falling out, cavities, weakness, cold hands and feet, fainting, irregular heartbeat, rapid heartbeat, swollen glands?

How many "yes" answers do you think it would take before you have a serious problem?

The answer is one.

Kay Sheppard's quiz: Are you a food addict?

Your answers to the following questions may help you identify whether you have a food addiction problem:

1. Has anyone ever told you that you have a problem with food?
2. Do you think food is a problem for you?
3. Do you eat large amounts of high-calorie food in short amounts of time?
4. Do you eat over feelings?
5. Can you stop eating whenever you wish?
6. Has your eating or weight ever interfered with your jobs, relationships, or finances?
7. How often do you weigh yourself?
8. Do you ever judge yourself by the number on your scale?
9. Do you often eat more than you planned to eat?
10. Have you hidden food or eaten in secret?
11. Have you become angry when someone eats food you have put aside for yourself?
12. Have you ever been anxious about your size, shape, or weight?
13. How many weight-loss programs have you tried?

(continued on next page)

(continued from previous page)

14. List all of the ways you have attempted to lose weight.

15. Do you manipulate ways to be alone so that you can eat privately?

16. Do your friends and companions overeat or binge eat?

17. How often do you overeat?

If your answers to these questions concern you, it's probably time to seek guidance and treatment.

(Source: All contents © Kay Sheppard, www.kaysheppard.com. Used with permission.)

Facts About the Three Primary Eating Disorders

Read over these eating-disorder symptoms, along with descriptions of the triggers and co-occurring compulsions, to help identify whether you or someone you know meets the criteria for a disorder.

Anorexia nervosa

Usual Symptoms: Most anorexics are female and

- have low body weight for their height
- display an intense fear of weight gain
- miss three menstrual periods in a row
- eat only small amounts of a few foods
- exercise even when tired, hurt, or in bad weather

Genetic Link: Genes, hormones, and brain chemicals are factors in the disorder.

Co-Occurring Compulsions: Both alcohol and drugs are often abused; sexual compulsions commonly develop if sexual trauma occurred during adolescence.

Primary Triggers: Stress and depression

Health Effects: Anorexia can kill, as evidenced by what happened to the singer Karen Carpenter. It's difficult for a woman with anorexia to become pregnant. If she does, she is more likely to lose the baby, or it will be born prematurely and with a lower-than-normal birth weight.

Treatment: Psychotherapy that includes family therapy and the Maudsley Approach, cognitive behavioral therapy, dialectical behavior therapy, and certain medications.

Binge eating

Usual Symptoms: The person is often overweight or obese and

- eats even when not really hungry
- often eats alone due to embarrassment
- feels guilty, depressed, or disgusted after overeating
- may voice a desire to be in control of eating habits, but fails to control

Genetic Link: Genes may be involved because hereditary patterns occur in families; brain chemicals also play a role.

Co-Occurring Compulsions: Alcohol abuse is common among binge eaters.

Primary Triggers: Stress, depression, boredom

Health Effects: Weight gains associated with binges can raise the risk for diabetes, hypertension, gallbladder and heart disease, and some types of cancers.

Treatment: Cognitive behavioral therapy (CBT) and mindfulness-based meditations are effective, as are some prescribed appetite suppressants and the antidepressant Prozac.

Bulimia nervosa

Usual Symptoms: Nine out of every 10 are women and

- frequently use diet pills or laxatives
- usually go to bathroom after eating to throw up
- have swollen cheeks or jaw from throwing up frequently
- voice chronic unhappiness with their body size and shape
- voice a fear of gaining weight

Genetic Link: As many as 83 percent of cases are hereditary; if you have a mother or sister with bulimia, you are more likely to develop it yourself.

Co-Occurring Compulsions: The risk for drug and alcohol dependence doubles for people with this disorder; sexual compulsions are common for those who experienced sexual trauma early in life.

Primary Triggers: Stress, depression, and traumatic events

Health Effects: Some of the most severe repercussions for health can happen if a woman with bulimia gets pregnant. These problems include miscarriage and diabetes and high blood pressure in the mother; and in the baby, premature birth, low birth weight, and birth defects such as mental retardation.

Treatment: Cognitive behavioral therapy enables 60 percent of patients to become symptom-free; dialectical behavior therapy and mindfulness-based meditation can be used; family therapy is important; and Prozac has been approved by the U.S. Food and Drug Administration as a medication for bulimia.

(Source: U.S. Department of Health and Human Services, Office on Women's Health, www.womenshealth.gov.)

How the Eating Disorders Are Similar . . . and Not

From Dr. Kimberly Dennis, medical director, Timberline Knolls Residential Treatment Center, Illinois, which specializes in treating eating disorders: In my experience, eating disorders generally have their origins in early developmental trauma. These can be the big "T" traumas such as sexual abuse, or the little "t" traumas such as parents sick with their own addictions or not being able to show up emotionally for their children.

With both anorexia and bulimia, we see a lot of co-occurring disorders—drugs, alcohol, sexual compulsions—and a lot of co-occurring depression. Among our adolescents, girls with sexual trauma often become promiscuous and also develop eating disorders.

Something else I find in common among anorexics and bulimics is a huge problem with authority. Our first conceptions of a loving, higher power really are our parents. If that relationship was rotten and the kid got hurt or wasn't being protected, the authority figure really didn't show up for the kid, then that's going to significantly impair their trust and their ability to have a secure world view. So they feel like they have to control everything.

There is no one body type or body size where you can say, "Okay, you have an eating disorder." There are criteria that we psychiatrists use. To be diagnosed with anorexia nervosa, your body mass index (BMI) needs to be below 18.5, and the definitions we use for being overweight and obese are also based on the BMI.

It's not just that some people are in denial about having an eating disorder. There are plenty of people with eating disorders who have absolutely no desire to get treatment for it. Most people who are bulimic know that there is something very screwed up going on in their relationship with food. But with anorexia, there are people who would fly under the radar of a noneating-disorder specialist. Anorexia is more like a process addiction, such as gambling, than a substance addiction, because anorexia usually involves ritualized behaviors around the eating. The chemical milieu in the bodies of anorexics that's associated with the starving state really fires up their reward system. Normal people, when they're not eating, feel irritable, lethargic, and just don't feel well. People with anorexia, when their body is in a starving state, feel powerful, invincible, and have tons of energy.

Most people with bulimia don't really want to be doing that every day in the grand scheme of things. So bulimia is easier to treat than anorexia because of that. People are much more willing to let go of throwing up every day. The same is true with binge eaters. It doesn't really feed their ego to be a binge eater and be overweight or obese. But people who are anorexic, it really feeds their ego like, "This is what makes me special."

If you have an eating disorder, one of the first things you can do for yourself is attend an Overeaters Anonymous meeting, an Eating Disorders Anonymous meeting, or Anorexics Anonymous and Bulimics Anonymous. When people are told to go to a 12-Step meeting, they say all of the time, "No way . . . you're crazy if you think I'm going to one of those." It's a lot easier if somebody's already in the treatment center and there are 25 other people who can support them in going. It's the group work that makes the treatment tremendously easier. Because they can hear it from other people and see their own lives in other people's experiences. But it takes some of these kids four of five times coming back here before they really bottom out and go forth to live a life in recovery.

Ideally, eating-disorder treatment should probably start with three to six months of residential treatment, followed by a step-down to intensive outpatient care. There should be a high level of care for at least one year. If you can't afford that, then go to as many meetings as you possibly can. Meetings are free.

Hidden forces drive emotional eaters

From Tricia Greaves, president, the Nelson Center for Emotional Healing in Brentwood, California: People who struggle chronically with their weight may be emotional eaters who are using food as a way to soothe pain and manage stress. Despite appearances to the contrary, the unhealthy choices these overeaters make aren't necessarily motivated by sloth or foolishness, but instead are driven by deeper emotional reasons.

Overeating is an easily accessible and socially acceptable activity that can begin as a pleasurable way to take the edge off and can develop into a pernicious addiction. Similar to an alcoholic who has lost the ability to moderate his drinking, so, too, the food addict can't moderate or control his food choices or quantities. On the other hand, the treatment for most substance-based addictions is complete abstinence from the substance, yet a food addict can't ever stop eating altogether.

Unlike the alcoholic who usually starts drinking in early adolescence, the emotional eater typically begins self-medicating with food much earlier in life, thus making the addiction even more primal than the alcoholic's. Buried childhood trauma, loneliness, sexual desire and confusion, and anxiety are many of the hidden forces that drive the overeater to seek the safety and sedation of food.

It is very common for people who have come to the Nelson Center for help with their binge eating and obesity issues to have once been hospitalized for anorexia in their teen years. Their eating disorder simply changed faces: from anorexia early on when they had more self-control and could restrict their eating, to bulimia when they began to lose control of their eating and would suffer horrible food binges and then need to control the effect of their consumption by vomiting or abusing laxatives, to all-out binge eating where they no longer purged and simply suffered the consequences of their binges with weight gain. Those who have experienced this progression are all, at their core, food addicts who have simply passed through various stages of their ability to control their eating. Of course, this is not the case for all who have eating disorders, but it is certainly more common than one might think.

Psychiatrist Dr. Kimberly Dennis's three eating-disorder myths

1. It's just a phase of life and not really a disease.

Eating disorders are a progressive disease, just like substance-use disorders. Without treatment, they get worse over time, not better. A lot of neurobiological, genetic, and research evidence supports this view. I've seen powerful clinical evidence in the experiences of my patients. There's a physical component to this disease and we're powerless over that.

2. People can control it.

People who are caught early and have had the disease for a very short period of time, like some of the adolescents we treat, typically have a lot better prognosis. There are adolescents who have purged a couple of times, and it doesn't really stick with them. They can get on a meal plan and, as long as whatever else is going on with them is treated, it goes away. But I've had many older women, mothers who either have kids or whose kids just moved out of the house, who had issues with food as adolescents that were never treated and who, in these major life transitions, develop eating disorders. I've also seen women in recovery for 20 years from alcoholism who experience some sort of life stressor and develop a full-blown eating disorder.

3. It doesn't really kill people.

Anorexia has the highest mortality rate of any of the psychiatric illnesses.

Myth Buster: Chronic Dieting Isn't an Eating Disorder

Are you a compulsive and chronic dieter who has tried every new weight-loss plan, from WeightWatchers to the Atkins Diet to the South Beach Diet, but you still gain back those pounds you lost within a few months, sending you in search of still another plan? Your compulsion to diet may have become a fourth type of eating disorder after anorexia, bulimia, and binge eating.

Linda Bacon, a nutrition professor in the biology department at City College of San Francisco and associate nutritionist and the University of California, Davis, provided a compelling case that the drive to diet can itself become a disordered eating pattern that requires behavior modification. Prof. Bacon came to this conclusion from her unique blending of two fields of research—she earned a master's degree in contemplative psychotherapy with a specialty in eating disorders and body image, and she received a doctorate in physiology with a focus in nutrition and weight regulation.

"The whole concept of dieting is you are supposed to be restricting yourself and not listening to what your body needs for nourishment," said Bacon. "When people get on the cycle of dieting, they may initially lose weight, but then when the body's compensatory mechanism kicks in, they find they can't maintain the diet anymore and they regain the weight. Then they see themselves as failures. But they still see the idea of dieting as something that works. So they tell themselves, 'I am the problem. Next time I can do it differently.' But, of course, that never happens."

Chronic dieting, in Prof. Bacon's view, increases unhealthy weight-loss behaviors, distracts from other personal health goals, creates a painful food and weight preoccupation, reduces self-esteem, and results in a damaging cycle of weight loss and weight regain that stresses the body by producing inflammation, which raises the risk for many diseases.

Like what happens with bulimia and anorexia, compulsive dieting is rooted in a fear of body acceptance. "It's a fear of fat," said Prof. Bacon. "Most people in the fat category have the perception there is something wrong with their bodies. Most anorexics see themselves as fat, although others see them as thin. It's part of our inability to see and accept ourselves. When we look into the mirror, it isn't something objective we see. It's an image loaded with all these cultural perceptions and colorations.

"One of the most difficult myths in our culture is that we are in control of our weight. If we believe that, we also believe there is something wrong with a fat person. Therefore, they deserve having a stigma for not taking care of themselves. But we don't have the control over our weight that we are led to believe. Some bodies are genetically predisposed to store fat more readily. From an evolutionary perspective, we learned the ability to store fat readily was because we had a lot of famines, and food wasn't consistent during the history of our species. So it's easy for us to get more calories today than our bodies need, and many people are genetically programmed to store those calories. Two people eating the same diet will react differently. Because we believe that weight is usually controllable, then we can blame fat people for their circumstances, and therefore many people feel they have a right to stigmatize them and discriminate against them."

If we think about human obesity at the cellular level, as some scientists have done experimentally, we find that our genes determine our natural or optimal weight in remarkable detail, right down to and including our predilection for craving certain foods. With this realization about the role of genetics in mind, it makes about as much sense to be preoccupied with why someone gets fat as it is to be preoccupied with why someone grows taller than average.

But your genetics aren't necessarily your destiny when it comes to eating disorders, or with any other kinds of compulsive behaviors, points out Prof. Bacon. "Genetics isn't 100 percent of the picture. Behaviors and attitudes and lifestyle habits can help to counteract the influence of genetics. That's where mindfulness practices can be very powerful."

Being fat doesn't necessarily translate into having poor health any more than your being thin automatically translates into you having good health. In a January 2011 article in *Nutrition Journal,* Prof. Bacon and British coauthor Lucy Aphramor summarized the evidence for shifting our attention from weight loss and management to health promotion at any body size. "Randomized controlled clinical trials indicate that a HAES [Health at Every Size] approach is associated with statistically and clinically relevant improvements in physiological measures (e.g., blood pressure, blood lipids), health behaviors (e.g., eating and activity habits, dietary quality), and psychosocial outcomes (such as self-esteem and body image), and that HAES achieves these health outcomes more successfully than weight-loss treatment and without the contraindications associated with a weight focus."

These two study authors listed a series of epidemiological studies that identified an "obesity paradox"—with many diseases, a person's obesity seems to ensure a longer survival rate. For example, "Obese persons with type 2 diabetes, hypertension, cardiovascular disease, and chronic kidney disease all have greater longevity than thinner people with these conditions. Also, obese people who have had heart attacks, coronary bypass, angioplasty, or hemodialysis live longer than thinner people with these histories. In addition, obese senior citizens live longer than thinner senior citizens."

Yes, you're probably rolling your eyes right now after reading those words, as I did, because the findings contradict so much of what we have been led to believe about being fat and being healthy. It all seems so counterintuitive, and yet maybe the prevailing dogma is still another example of the pernicious effects of stigma.

Also known as "intuitive eating" or "fat acceptance," the Health at Every Size approach pioneered by Prof. Bacon and outlined in her book of the same name emphasizes nutrition and exercise, along with developing a positive body image, over the goal of weight loss. You listen to your hunger signals, make connections between what you eat and how you feel, eat only when you're hungry, choose nutritious foods over junk foods, and engage in exercise not to lose weight, but to benefit from its physical and emotional rewards. Discard your bathroom scale and love your body no matter how much you weigh—these are among the guiding principles of this approach to weight and health. In many ways "intuitive" eating is "mindful" eating, and these skills can be learned and practiced for improved nutrient intake and to manage the entire spectrum of eating disorders.

Three studies in particular lent "weight" to this HAES approach. In August 2008, *The Archives of Internal Medicine* published a study reporting that one-third of obese people and half of all overweight adults had normal blood pressure, cholesterol, triglycerides, and blood sugar levels. This finding flew in the face of mainstream medicine's belief that excess weight usually is a primary risk factor for diabetes and heart disease.

A second study, this one federally financed, was conducted by Bacon herself and published by the *Journal of the American Dietetic Association* in 2005. It compared 78 obese women who either adopted the HAES approach or engaged in a diet program. Neither of the two study groups lost any appreciable weight, but the HAES participants showed overall better measurements of health, physical activity, and self-esteem compared to the dieters. Not only that, these healthier behaviors associated with the HAES approach were associated with lower blood pressure and cholesterol readings for the HAES group at follow-up testing two years later.

Finally, a third study, this one from 2009 and published in the *American Journal of Public Health,* demonstrated the importance of the human mind's role in determining health outcomes, regardless of body size. Bacon summarizes the findings: "Results indicated that body image had a much bigger impact on health than body size. In other words, two equally fat women would have very different health outcomes, depending on how they felt about their bodies. Likewise, two women with similar body insecurities would have similar health outcomes, even if one were fat and the other thin. These results suggest that the stigma associated with being fat is a major contributor to obesity-associated disease. Body mass index and health are only weakly related in cultures where obesity is not stigmatized, such as in the South Pacific."

It's your fitness level, not your weight level, which determines how healthy you are and how long you will live. That little known fact about health and mortality emerged from scientific studies conducted over the past decade. "If you want to know who's going to die," Steven Blair, University of South Carolina exercise science professor, told *The New York Times* in 2009, "know their fitness level. Obese individuals who are fit have a death rate one half that of normal-weight people who are not fit."

The lesson to be learned from this research is pretty straightforward: If you're overweight or obese and lead a sedentary lifestyle, if you overindulge in fast food and fats and sweets, if you experience low self-esteem or self-loathing, and you have inadequate access to health care, you're more likely to develop diabetes, heart disease, cancer, and as a result, greatly shorten your lifespan. Avoid all of these pitfalls, and you may escape with your health intact no matter how many pounds over the "norm" you might be.

How Mindfulness-Based Eating Therapy Works

Psychotherapist Donald Altman shares an excerpt from his book The Mindfulness Code *(2010, New World Library) that describes a powerful mindfulness experience, in a group setting, at Providence St. Vincent Hospital in Portland, Oregon, where he once worked as a senior mental health therapist in the eating-disorder clinic:*

Today I am facilitating a group of nine patients with eating disorders. These are mostly adolescent girls and young women diagnosed with anorexia nervosa or bulimia nervosa, conditions so dangerous that the National Institute of Mental Health reports anorexics as having a mortality rate "12 times higher than the annual death rate due to all causes of death among females ages 15–24 in the general population."

After only a few minutes, it is evident that my group is distracted and struggling. When I ask what's going on, they report feeling miserable because they are "stuck in eating-disorder thoughts." So I suggest that we do something different: experience the group room in an entirely new way. Many protest that they already know the room inside out (or at least, they *think* they do). After a short discussion, they finally agree to give this a chance and to approach the experience with an open and curious mind. What they don't know is that they are about to try a mindfulness exercise that's designed to anchor them in the present moment.

We start by taking a few calm breaths together. Then for the next 15 minutes, I guide them around the room. My instructions include having them pay extremely close attention to every little detail—such as the hairline cracks on the floor, the shapes of chair and table legs, and little variations of color on walls, doors, and notebooks. I ask them to notice each movement of their feet and arms as they walk. They listen to the moment-by-moment sounds occurring inside and outside the room, as well as the sounds of their own breathing, movements, and footsteps. At one point, I have them shut their eyes as they hand a familiar object (such as a key, a pen, a notebook, or a purse) to another person who will sense its weight, its coolness or warmth, and its hardness or softness. The room is steeped in quiet as they move about in this deliberately stealthy and purposeful manner.

When I finally ask them to return to their seats, the first thing that surprises them is how much time has passed. After we've settled in, I ask them a deceptively simple question: Where were your eating-disorder thoughts during the last 15 minutes? Silence and an expression of shock and amazement on many of the girls' faces is the answer. Not one person fiddles with a notebook or doodles on a piece of paper—a common occurrence. Their sense of awareness and presence is so strong that it seems to me as if the entire group has awakened from a trance.

After a few moments, one young girl raises her hand with an epiphany of sorts. "For the first time, I feel like my eating-disorder thoughts are a dream world or a fantasy. I feel like for a while I left that world for the real one," she said. Another girl raises her hand and comments, "I suddenly realize that I've been living in the dream world of my eating disorder and that I don't like when it gets interrupted." Others echo a similar story of irritation and unease when the fantasy is interrupted.

For a brief moment, this represents a victory for these girls—many of whom live in a world where distorted thoughts and emotions regarding their body image and rigid beliefs about food and eating steal away the precious hours and days of their lives. Anorexic and bulimic fantasies are difficult to pierce, but today's group exercise brings the hope that anyone can break free of debilitating automatic behaviors, thoughts, and addictions even for a few moments. Today, these girls have directly experienced that possibility.

Some Treatment Options

Some of the treatments listed below, such as cognitive behavioral therapy, work effectively for multiple disorders among the Seven Toxic Compulsions in this book. For eating disorders in particular, there is emerging research evidence that dialectical behavior therapy, originally developed to treat borderline personality disorder, can simultaneously address both disordered eating and substance abuse in many cases. For example, a 2011 study conducted among outpatients at the Concurrent Disorders Clinic at the Centre for Addiction and Mental Health in Toronto, Canada, concluded: "Results from the dialectical behavior therapy revealed that the intervention had a significant positive effect on behavioral and attitudinal features of disordered eating, substance-use severity and use, negative mood regulation, and depressive symptoms." *(Source: "Outcome of dialectical behaviour therapy for concurrent eating and substance use disorders." Courbasson C, Nishikawa Y, and Dixon L. Clin Psychol Psychother. 2011 Mar 17. doi: 10.1002/cpp.748.)*

Anorexia

The Maudsley Approach. Developed by a team of child and adolescent psychiatrists and psychologists at Maudsley Hospital in London, this family-centered outpatient approach to treating anorexics provides an effective alternative to expensive inpatient and day hospital programs. The treatment involves an average of 20 sessions over a 6- to 12-month period during which the parents are coached on playing an active and positive role in the adolescent's treatment regimen with an emphasis on helping the child to take more control over his or her eating habits. Studies of this approach have found two-thirds of adolescents recover from the disorder at the end of the program and up to 90 percent are fully weight-recovered at a five-year follow-up. Outside of Britain, this approach is being used by eating disorder clinics in Sydney and Melbourne, Australia; in Ottawa and Toronto, Canada; and by U.S. programs at Columbia University and Mt. Sinai School of Medicine, New York; at Duke University in Durham, N.C.; The University of

Chicago; Stanford University; and the University of California at San Diego. *(Source: "Manualized family-based treatment for anorexia nervosa: A case series." Le Grange D, Binford R, and Loeb KL.* J Am Acad Child Adolesc Psychiatry. *2005 Jan;44(1):41–6.) (Also see "A comparison of short- and long-term family therapy for adolescent anorexia nervosa." Lock J, Agras WS, Bryson S, and Karemer H.* J Am Acad Child Adolesc Psychiatry. *2005 Jul;44(7):632–39. /www.maudsleyparents.org.)*

For more information, consult the following:

- Dialectical Behavior Therapy, Seven Self-Care Tools, p. 239
- Mindfulness, Seven Self-Care Tools, p. 249
- Psychotherapy (individual and/or group), Seven Self-CareTools, p. 241
- 12-Step Programs, Seven Self-Care Tools, p. 240

Bulimia

The Maudsley Approach. Though not extensively studied for use with bulimics, a 2005 study published in the *International Journal of Eating Disorders* found evidence that this family-based treatment approach is appropriate for adolescents with the disorder. *(Source: "Family-based treatment of eating disorders." Lock J and le Grange D.* Int J Eat Disord. *2005;37, Suppl: S64-7.)*

For more information, consult the following:

- Cognitive Behavioral Therapy, Seven Self-Care Tools, p. 235
- Dialectical Behavior Therapy, Seven Self-Care Tools, p. 239
- Mindfulness, Seven Self-Care Tools, p. 249
- Psychotherapy (individual and/or group), Seven Self-Care Tools, p. 241
- 12-Step Programs, Seven Self-Care Tools, p. 240

Binge eating

Dr. Frank Lawlis, director of Psychological Services, Origins Recovery Center, created a useful audio CD that provides information on how to curb emotional eating and achieve weight loss, which can be found at: www.mindbodyseries.com.

For more information, consult the following:

- Cognitive Behavioral Therapy, Seven Self-Care Tools, p. 235
- Dialectical Behavior Therapy, Seven Self-Care Tools, p. 239
- Mindfulness, Seven Self-Care Tools, p. 249
- Psychotherapy (individual and/or group), Seven Self-Care Tools, p. 241
- 12-Step Programs, Seven Self-Care Tools, p. 240

Your 30-Day Challenge for Eating Disorders

Do you have a bad habit or a dependency? Here is another chance to find out.

You have answered the questionnaires for this toxic compulsion. You have read through what the experts have to say. You have thought about the extent to which you exhibit the behaviors associated with either a nondependent use disorder or a dependency.

Do you still have any doubt about whether you have just a bad habit, or whether your behavior meets the criteria for a dependency?

Create a 30-day challenge for yourself.

Write up a 30-day menu and food plan. This might include the commitment not to eat any sugar for 30 days. It might be a commitment to eat only healthy food such as fruits and vegetables every day. It could be a daily calorie intake limit. Whatever plan you choose, you must stick to it. People who don't have a problem in their relationship with food won't have a problem following their plan. But if you deviate at all from the plan you create, you may have a problem and should seek professional assistance.

IV

Toxic Compulsion 4: Gambling Dependence

The urge to gamble is so universal and its practice is so pleasurable, that I assume it must be evil.
—Heywood Broun

IN THIS CHAPTER:

My problem with gambling is the losing part. I hate to lose money. Losing to me is so unpleasant that I would rather not even play. If it wasn't for that, my risk-taking nature might well make me a candidate to become a problem gambler.

Like most addicts, I like the easy fix, the thing that just drops into your lap for no apparent reason, the thing that just changes your life. This is the kind of magical thinking that leads one to think he is going to find a treasure chest or win the lottery. For me, fortunately, gambling was not a viable pathway for addiction because of my distaste for losing money. I could never get over the fact that those big buildings in Las Vegas didn't get built because there were a lot of people winning.

So it was a bit of a surprise to me when I discovered just how widespread the gambling compulsion has become. A common assumption has been that people with alcohol problems are twice as numerous in the United States as people with gambling problems. When researchers at the University of Buffalo's Research Institute on Addictions reported survey results in 2011 showing that the number of problem gamblers now exceeds the number of persons with alcohol dependence, skepticism was initially expressed by longtime addiction specialists.

Combining data from two U.S. national surveys in which a total of about 5,000 people were interviewed, age patterns for gambling and alcohol involvement were compared. What emerged was the finding that after 21 years of age, alcohol abuse dropped off and gambling problems multiplied until, from ages 31 through 40, gambling was a bigger problem than alcohol abuse. "I didn't expect problem gambling to be more common than alcohol dependence for such a wide age range," commented John Welte, the institute's chief investigator of the study, which was published in the *Journal of Gambling Studies* (March 2011).

Despite the skepticism voiced by some in the treatment field regarding the survey results, other indicators support the view that gambling and the social ills generated by it may be a toxic trend we will have to reckon with for decades to come.

States, churches, synagogues, charities, they've all gotten into the gambling business and helped to make it socially acceptable and available virtually everywhere in this country. So it's not just the huge proliferation in the number of casinos in the United States occurring over the last two decades that characterizes the growing potential for compulsive gambling. All forms of risk taking with money are now readily accessible and everywhere to be found, whether it's lotteries, horse and dog tracks, church bingo games, office betting pools, charity raffles, home poker games, or Internet gaming. (To me, having governments use lottery gambling as a way to support public education seems particularly warped and absurd.) Even chronic betting on stocks and commodities futures in volatile markets can be considered a form of problem gambling with many of the same symptoms of abuse evident.

"Pathological" gamblers—the severely addicted who experience withdrawal symptoms similar to drug dependency—constitute only about 1 percent of adults. But the other category of abusers, "problem" gamblers—people with money woes, strained marriages, and other problems associated with their compulsion to gamble—is a fast-growing segment of the population. There may be 11 million or more problem gamblers in the United States and less than one in 10 of them ever seeks treatment, probably because of the shame, guilt, and stigma associated with being identified as having this disorder.

For simplicity's sake, here is the scale used by Nancy M. Petry, professor of psychiatry at the University of Connecticut Health Center, to identify the types of gamblers and the severity of associated problems:

Level-one gambling—social or recreational with no significant problems. It's fun entertainment for them and they know that losing is part of the game. There is no long-lasting damage in their lives.

Level two—in which gambling-related problems have developed. They pile up bigger debts, maybe some arguments occur at home, maybe they skip out of work once or twice a year, but it's not yet creating full, permanent damage, though early treatment might prevent more serious compulsions later on.

Level three—compulsive gambling with significant gambling-related problems that interfere with daily functioning, also called pathological gambling. These people continue to gamble despite significant harm being inflicted on their lives. They just keep on going and going like Energizer Bunnies.

Dr. Timothy Fong, codirector of the UCLA Gambling Studies Program and associate professor of psychiatry at the Semel Institute at UCLA, likened the levels of gambling compulsion to the "beginning signs of cancer—full-blown pathological gambling is like full-blown cancer that spreads throughout your body and mind."

Key Facts About Gambling Addiction

Professor Nancy Petry's book, *Pathological Gambling* (2005, American Psychological Association), gives us a deeper insight into how problem gambling touches many more lives—and in many more ways—than just that of the gambler. From Petry's book:

- By some estimates, each pathological gambler "directly affects the lives of 8 to 10 other people . . . ranging from spouses to other immediate family members (children, parents, and siblings) to employers and coworkers."
- Helpline statistics from the United States, the United Kingdom, and New Zealand indicate that "over 40 percent of calls [for help] are from partners of gamblers rather than from gamblers themselves."
- Based on the results of 14 studies of people with gambling problems, "young people suffer from disordered gambling at about two to three times the rates of adults."
- Less than 8 percent of pathological gamblers (Level 3) seek treatment (National Research Council, 1999.) Among problem gamblers (Level 2), "virtually none seek or receive assistance."

Is Compulsive Gambling a Genetic Disease?

Treatment expert Arnie Wexler called compulsive gambling "a progressive disease, much like an addiction to alcohol or drugs. In many cases, the gambling addiction is hidden until the gambler becomes unable to function without gambling. Lying becomes a way of life. They will try to convince others and themselves that their lies are truths and they will believe their own lies. Inability to stop gambling often results in financial devastation, broken homes, employment problems, criminal acts and suicide attempts."

Is pathological gambling really a brain disease? Prof. Timothy

Fong has studied the question by conducting neuroscience and brain-imaging studies as an associate professor of psychiatry at UCLA and codirector of the UCLA Gambling Studies Program. "The brains of pathological gamblers are very different than those who do not have a gambling addiction," said Fong. "One of our first research papers showed that gambling addiction caused brain damage similar to that caused by methamphetamine abuse. That raised a question: is gambling somehow neurotoxic just like drugs of abuse?"

Prof. Fong's definition of gambling is broad, including all forms of risk taking. "I'm talking about stocks and investments, the risk-taking behaviors. One reason our economy got into such a mess is that we've become almost a nation of people taking risks well beyond what we could actually afford, and taking those risks repeatedly. That's a form of gambling.

"We know gambling is a genetic disease. There are biological factors passed on from father to son and mother to son that create vulnerabilities. It's a disease that starts early in life. We know that the brains of people with gambling addiction are functioning differently and are built differently from those who don't have gambling addiction."

Dr. Howard Shaffer, associate professor of psychiatry at Harvard Medical School, and director, Division on Addictions, the Cambridge Health Alliance, agrees with Fong: "There's quite a bit of work all around the world showing that various activities like gambling energize the pleasure centers of the brain similarly to the way that psychoactive drugs energize the pleasure centers of the brain. It doesn't matter whether it's a process addiction like gambling or a drug addiction. All will affect the brain and change the way we feel and our subjective state."

To underscore the contention of these experts about the genetic factor, research on twins published in the *Journal of Abnormal Psychology* (March 28, 2011) showed that gambling problems "run in families" and half of the vulnerability to gambling addiction "comes from shared genetic rather than shared environmental influences."

What also fascinates Prof. Fong, and supports a theme of this book, is why "one person falls into gambling addiction, and another person falls into drugs, and another into sexual compulsions. And why, in recovery, they switch addictions."

Gambling Problems Come Linked to Other Disorders

If you've ever been in a casino, you know how common it is for people to be gambling with an alcoholic drink in one hand and a cigarette dangling from a corner of their mouth. It's no secret that the free or low-priced liquor being dispensed so copiously by casino employees is designed to "loosen" gamblers up so they will spend more money than they might normally.

For several decades research evidence has mounted that alcohol and gambling are the proverbial two peas in a pod. A 1998 National Opinion Research Center study found that pathological or problem gamblers had about *seven times* the rate of alcohol dependence as non-gamblers or nonproblem casual gamblers.

Marijuana abuse or dependence is now threatening alcohol abuse and dependence's position as the number one co-occurring disorder with gambling. A 2002 study, cited by the book *Pathological Gambling*, found that in some parts of the United States "patients with marijuana use disorders were more likely to suffer from gambling problems than patients with any other substance-use disorder."

Alcohol- and marijuana-use problems represent just one of a whole list of compulsions associated with problem gambling. Based on a survey of 43,093 people conducted by University of Connecticut Health Center researchers, estimates of the prevalence of co-occurring substance use, mood, and personality disorders among pathological gamblers were developed. Women respondents with likely gambling disorders had co-occurring disorders that were, on average, more severe than those of participating men with likely gambling disorders.

- 73.2 percent of pathological gamblers had an alcohol-use disorder
- 60.8 percent had a personality disorder
- 60.4 percent had nicotine dependence
- 49.6 percent had a mood disorder
- 41.3 percent had an anxiety disorder
- 38.1 percent had a drug-use problem

(Source: "Comorbidity of DSM-IV pathological gambling and other

psychiatric disorders: Results from the National Epidemiologic Survey on Alcohol and Related Conditions." Petry NM, Stinson FS, and Grant BF. J Clin Psychiatry. 2005 May;66(5):564–74.)

For many people problem gambling is also linked to eating disorders, sexual compulsive disorders, and chronic or binge shopping problems.

Professor Nancy Petry of the University of Connecticut Health Center determined in a 2000 study that "severity of gambling problems in substance abusers was significantly and independently predictive of engaging in risky sexual activities that spread infectious diseases." In her seminal book, *Pathological Gambling*, Petry cited studies indicating that among one group of female Gamblers Anonymous members, 20 percent were "compulsive overeaters." Research shows that pathological gamblers also have "increased rates of compulsive buying and [compulsive] sexual behaviors."

Depression and thoughts of suicide shadow pathological gamblers like birds of prey. A Canadian survey of 1,471 college students found that nearly 27 percent of the pathological gamblers among them didn't just fantasize about killing themselves, but had actually attempted suicide.

Harvard's Prof. Howard Shaffer urged anyone seeking help for a gambling problem to also address the underlying disorders that trigger out-of-control gambling. "Gambling often serves—for many, not all—as a self-medication or a treatment, if you will, for these underlying disorders which people are not always aware of. Mood disorders, anxiety, some personality disorders, post-traumatic stress disorders, all are very common among gamblers. There are all kinds of self-help interventions available to get screened for those disorders. My experience is that when we start to pay attention to these associated disorders, people feel much better and are much more in control of their addictive behavior."

Time to Get Honest with Yourself

These questionnaires won't be the first or last word on whether you have a gambling problem, but your answers will, if you are honest with yourself, illuminate the extent to which your gambling behaviors *may* be more than just a controllable habit.

Do you need help? Questions for self-evaluation

- Do you gamble when you are feeling lonely, depressed, angry, or under stress?
- Do you gamble as a way of coping with loss or grief?
- Do you have trouble setting and staying within limits on time and money spent gambling?
- Do you spend money on gambling that you need for essential expenses (rent/mortgage, utilities, etc.)?
- Do people close to you criticize or complain about your gambling?
- Do you gamble to the exclusion of other recreational or social activities?
- Do you borrow money to gamble or to cover expenses due to gambling losses?
- Do you gamble at times when you should be taking care of responsibilities such as work, family, or school?
- Do you return to gambling to try to win back money you have lost?
- Do you find yourself thinking more and more about gambling or getting money for gambling?

(Sources: State of Connecticut, Department of Mental Health and Addiction Services. National Council on Problem Gambling, www.ncpgambling.org.)

Answer yes or no to these statements about your gambling behavior

1. You have often gambled longer than you had planned.
2. You have often gambled until your last dollar was gone.
3. Thoughts of gambling have caused you to lose sleep.
4. You have used your income or savings to gamble while letting bills go unpaid.
5. You have made repeated, unsuccessful attempts to stop gambling.
6. You have broken the law or considered breaking the law to finance your gambling.
7. You have borrowed money to finance your gambling.
8. You have felt depressed or suicidal because of your gambling losses.
9. You have been remorseful after gambling.

10. You have gambled to get money to meet your financial obligations.

If you (or someone you know) answer yes to any of these statements, you may have a gambling problem and should seek professional help and group support. *(Source: The National Problem Gambling HelpLine Network [800-522-4700]).*

Separating "pathological" from "problem" or "social" gamblers

Treatment specialists rely on the American Psychiatric Association's *Diagnostic and Statistical Manual of Mental Disorders* to make determinations about the severity of gambling problems experienced by clients. To receive a diagnosis of pathological gambling, you must be experiencing five or more of the following conditions in your life:

1. You are preoccupied with gambling, meaning you are preoccupied with reliving past gambling experiences, planning the next venture, or thinking of ways to obtain money with which to gamble.
2. You feel the need to gamble with increasing amounts of money to achieve a desired level of excitement.
3. You experience repeated unsuccessful efforts to control, cut back, or stop gambling.
4. You feel restless or irritable when you attempt to cut down or stop gambling.
5. You gamble as a way of escaping problems in your life, or to relieve feelings of helplessness, guilt, anxiety, or depression.
6. After losing money gambling, you often return another day to regain your losses.
7. You lie to family members, therapists, or others to conceal the extent of your involvement with gambling.
8. You have committed illegal acts such as forgery, fraud, theft, or embezzlement to finance your gambling.
9. You have jeopardized or lost a significant relationship, a job, or an educational or career opportunity because of your gambling.
10. You rely on others to provide money to relieve a desperate financial situation caused by your gambling.

Three questions from the brief biosocial gambling screen

For a really short but meaningful assessment of your gambling habits, answer these three questions:

1. During the past year, have you become restless, irritable, or anxious when you have tried to stop or cut back on the time and money spent gambling?
2. During the past year, have you tried to keep your family or friends from knowing how much money and time you spend gambling?
3. During the past year, did you have financial trouble as a result of gambling and did you seek help with living expenses from family, friends, or welfare programs?

Answering yes to any of the three questions indicates you should seek an evaluation from a mental health professional to determine how serious your gambling problem may have become.

Four Clues to Identify Internet Gambling Addiction

One of the fastest growing ways to access games of chance is through the Internet, and it's also about the quickest path to addiction and financial ruin.

While sitting at your computer, you can play electronic slot machines or bet on sporting events as they are being played. The betting has become so sophisticated, accessible, and speedy that you can actually place wagers on whether the next batter in a live major league baseball game will strike out.

Using a credit or debit card, you can almost instantaneously pull out money from your accounts to feed your gambling online. It's easy and it's dangerous. You can go broke without ever leaving your home or standing up to stretch your legs.

Prof. Howard Shaffer of Harvard Medical School and addictions specialist Julia Braverman of Cambridge Health Alliance published a 2010 study in the *European Journal of Public Health* in which they identified behavioral markers for high-risk Internet gambling problems using information about 48,114 people who had opened Internet betting service accounts. Nine out of every 10 were men, with an average age of 28, and they were residents of 21 countries, Germany being the most frequent country of origin.

"It is essential to identify gamblers at higher risk of developing gambling-related problems as early as possible," wrote the study's two authors, explaining why they conducted this analysis of Internet gambling.

They found that within the first month of a person engaging in live-action Internet gambling, four behaviors can help to identify who will be at risk for developing serious gambling problems.

1. Gambling frequency. If an escalating pattern of days spent gambling emerges, that is a warning sign.
2. Gambling intensity. A higher than average number of bets placed per day is another benchmark for trouble.
3. Gambling variability. Normal gamblers exhibit a uniform, stable, and consistent pattern of gambling wagers, whereas high-risk gamblers deviate from this norm by constantly experimenting.
4. Gambling trajectory. If gamblers continually increase the amount of money wagered during the first month, they may be at risk for problems because most studies have shown that nonaddicted gamblers tend to decrease the amount of money they wager after the first eight-day period of gambling.

A GAMBLING TREATMENT EXPERT CONQUERS HIS OWN ADDICTION

From Arnie Wexler, compulsive gambling expert and counselor: My first big win was Memorial Day, 1951. I'm at Roosevelt Raceway in New York. I'm making 50 cents an hour after school in the garment center carrying boxes. And I go to the racetrack and it's a Friday night and I come out of the track with $54 and I'm 14 years old. And I say to myself, "Wow! I could be a millionaire from gambling. Why am I wasting my time working for 50 cents an hour?"

I became the plant manager working in a company supervising 400 to

(continued on next page)

(continued from previous page)

500 people. It was the biggest dress company in America at the time. And I'm stealing every day to support my gambling addiction. The only things I didn't do were to get a gun, mess around with counterfeit money, or mess around with illegal drugs—only because I didn't know where to get them. That's what this addiction does to you. But problem gamblers never believe they're stealing. You believe you're borrowing it, and you're going to put it back when you have the big win.

I would bet thousands of dollars in my early years of gambling when Sheila and I first got married. I'm betting thousands of dollars on baseball games. And then I'm sitting in a poker game with little old ladies and Sheila and me, and the most you could win is $2. Two dollars per game and you know what, I got almost everybody's money and I'm as excited with that game as I am with the thousand dollars that I bet on the baseball game. So I know the disease is not about winning money. It's not always about money. It's not about losing or winning. It's about action.

Once I got a call from a bookmaker on a Monday: "You can't bet tonight because you owe me $500." So I take my car and I sell it to a neighbor for $500 and paid the bookmaker and left Sheila without a car for a few years. And then I decide we're going to move near my father-in-law because he works and doesn't have a car that he takes to work. So she uses his car. That's what gambling does to you. That's all that matters. I couldn't care about my family, my wife, and my kids. A family will never ever again be the same once they have a gambler. There is damage to the family.

On February 2, 1968, Sheila was having a miscarriage. I called my boss at nine o'clock in the morning and said, "I can't come to work. My wife's in the hospital. She's sick." Then I went to a racetrack for the day. At five o'clock I came to visit her in the hospital.

My boss came to me and said, "Arnie, we know you're stealing from the company." He told me I was going to be arrested if I didn't get help. So I walked into a Gamblers Anonymous meeting.

When I finally stopped gambling, I owed 32 people money. They were relatives, friends, ex-bosses, companies I worked for. Today I can't even watch a horserace on the news at night. You got to respect the power of the disease. That's important.

How Does Gambling Resemble Other Addictions?

There are some clear and significant differences between the compulsion to gamble and its attendant problems compared to alcohol and drug abuse, or the other Seven Toxic Compulsions. Compulsive gambling creates a unique set of treatment and recovery challenges.

From Howard J. Shaffer, associate professor of psychology, Harvard Medical School, and director, Division on Addictions, the Cambridge Health Alliance: I don't thinking gambling is very different from substance-use disorders. You may have a more rapid loss of money with gambling than with drug use. But I don't see a difference genetically, biochemically, or neurobiologically. Each expression of addiction brings unique problems. Gambling brings all kinds of money and debt problems with it, usually family problems as well, and then the emotional problems. Now among pathological gamblers, the treatment seekers, they're fairly quick to say that they like the action. It's not the winning or the losing; it's the action. Gamblers like the rush of the action. But no one really needs to drink alcohol, use psychoactive drugs, or gamble. It's not a requirement of life. So if you're struggling with any of those, if you're insisting on continuing your relationship with any of those addictions, it's important to ask yourself the same questions: What does it do for me? What do I need from this? Are there other substitutes that would be less problematic for me in my life? Why do I want to keep struggling with this? What does this struggle do for me? Do I just want to be sort of uncomfortable all the time?

From Arnie Wexler, compulsive gambling expert and counselor: This addiction is a little different than alcohol and drugs. There's no track marks, no dilated pupils, no smell. It's invisible. If I came here and told you I was an alcoholic and hadn't had a drink in 43 years, but then I had a drink, you'd know it right away. You smell it, you see it. But if I just came from the casino, or called my bookmaker, or bought a hundred lottery tickets 10 minutes ago, you wouldn't know. Problem gamblers have shame and guilt. Unlike alcoholics who might go around saying, "I'm an alcoholic," it's very rare to get gamblers to admit they have a problem. They're embarrassed. They're afraid. Your drug dealer is not sending a limo for you. A casino is sending a limo. They're giving you free rooms and meals. They're giving you a feeling, a fantasy. That doesn't happen in other addictions.

From Sheila Wexler, compulsive gambling expert and counselor: Gamblers go further, longer, and they don't pass out. So they usually don't get intervened upon as soon as someone with a drug or an alcohol problem. And the more you can bet, the more excitement you have. But when you can't make that bet, any level of bet will do. With alcoholism, there's a point where reverse tolerance takes place, where the little amount kills you or certainly makes you pass out. With gambling, you could go out there forever and ever. There's no change. There may be more excitement if you could bet more money. They put everything in jeopardy. It doesn't matter. Your wife doesn't matter. The kids don't matter. The job doesn't matter.

From Dr. Timothy Fong, codirector of the UCLA Gambling Studies Program and associate professor of psychiatry at the Semel Institute at UCLA: A lot of gamblers say, "My problem isn't that I gamble too much. My problem is that I don't have enough money or time to gamble with." And those same people will say, "If I just keep on playing, eventually I'm going to win." You don't get that from drug addicts or alcoholics. They don't say, "If I just got the perfect hit of cocaine, my life would be perfect." There are some similarities between gambling and other types of addiction recovery. When we focus on our treatment for gambling, it's very much like what we do for drugs and alcohol. It's about learning to tolerate negative feelings. It's about learning to let go of past traumas. It's about dealing with yourself in the moment from liking who you are. It's about tolerating shades of gray and not living in black or white. It's about living in the moment and not living in a fantasy world.

Nine gambling myths

From Arnie and Sheila Wexler, who present workshops and seminars on compulsive gambling addiction and run a national hotline for problem gamblers: 888-LAST BET:

1. The big win is just around the corner with the next bet I make.
2. I can get even again, and then I will stop gambling.
3. I am not like drug addicts or alcoholics.
4. I can stop anytime I want. I just don't want to stop.
5. I am too young to be a gambling addict.
6. If I had more money I know I could win.
7. I am smarter than the rest of the gamblers.
8. The losses are not my fault right now because I'm having bad luck.
9. I know I can beat this game.

Top 10 reasons why compulsive gamblers quit

A 2002 study in the journal *Addiction Research and Theory* surveyed problem gamblers who had successfully terminated their gambling dependence. Here are their reasons, along with the percentage of survey respondents who cited that reason for quitting:

1. Financial concerns—96 percent
2. Emotional factors—92 percent
3. Concern about family/children—69 percent
4. Hitting "rock bottom"—61 percent
5. Pros and cons evaluated—54 percent
6. Humiliating event happened—50 percent
7. Physical health concerns—48 percent
8. Work problems—43 percent
9. Confrontation with loved one—43 percent
10. Major lifestyle change—43 percent

After four decades of working with problem gamblers, Arnie Wexler evolved his own unique take on what motivates people to quit: "What gets a gambling addict into treatment? Pain. They lose everything. And intervention. The wife has to say something like 'I'm putting the house in my name, or I'm leaving.' The gambler must understand he has an addiction. He must be willing to attend Gamblers Anonymous and seek professional help. By the time a gambler is ready to get help, he has no more money, for the most part. And his family is sick and tired of bailing him out."

Sometimes pathological gamblers quit only when they are seized by despair after a lifetime of denying the problem. They even attempt suicide. Dr. Timothy Fong, codirector of the UCLA Gambling Studies Program and associate professor of psychiatry at the Semel Institute at UCLA, relates one such case from among his patient files: "We saw a gentleman in our psychiatric hospital, he was 80 years old, had been gambling for 60 years. He's gambled incredible amounts of money away as a pathological gambler for 60 years. Never wanted to seek help, never wanted his family to seek help for him. They were basically living in pain and suffering for 60 years as a family. And that finally ended when he jumped off a building and broke both of his legs and his pelvis. It's just an awful tragedy. The family had supported him in his addiction for years. It's an example where harm and suffering can go on for decades and no one will notice. And we're really trying to bring that out of the shadows and really tell folks, you know, these signs and symptoms are not just somebody's personality. They are, in fact, signs of a disease."

Some Pathological Gamblers "Recover" Without Quitting

It's an inconvenient truth, but there is study evidence that some gamblers with a pathological habit can undergo cognitive behavioral treatments and, with more healthy thinking patterns in place, can control their gambling behaviors until they no longer have a "problem" as defined by diagnostic manual criteria.

Australian researchers divided up a group of female pathological gamblers into two groups—one that underwent cognitive behavior treatment to control their gambling until it was no longer a problem, and another that experienced the same treatment regimen but with the goal of complete abstinence from gambling. The study authors concluded that "pathological gamblers selecting controlled gambling displayed comparable levels of improvement to those displayed by gamblers selecting abstinence ... 89 percent of the gamblers selecting abstinence compared with 82 percent selecting controlled gambling no longer satisfied the diagnostic criteria for pathological gambling by the completion of the six-month follow-up period." *(Source: "A preliminary investigation of abstinence and controlled gambling as self-selected goals of treatment for female pathological gambling." Dowling N, Smith D, and Thomas T. J. Gambl Stud. 2009 Jun;25 (2):201–14.)*

A second study a year later, also from Australia and published in the journal *Addiction,* came to a similar conclusion after surveying 4,764 adults to identify gamblers who met the criteria for pathological gaming. Just 104 of those surveyed, about 2 percent, screened positive for a lifetime history of pathological gambling, and of those, 44 had severely cut back gambling until it was no longer a problem affecting their lives. This "controlled gambling" was mostly achieved without resort to any formal intervention therapy. *(Source: "Pathological gambling recovery in the absence of abstinence." Slutske WS, Piasecki TM, Blaszczynski A, and Martin NG. Addiction. 2010 Dec;105(12):2169–75.)*

"The findings are in line with what has been seen in the treatment of alcohol abuse," the Reuters news agency commented on the study.

"That is, some people in recovery cut back on drinking rather than abstaining completely. This approach is sometimes referred to as 'harm reduction.' And the results suggest that problem gamblers, too, can recover even if they do not quit altogether."

Dr. Timothy Fong, codirector of the UCLA Gambling Studies Program and associate professor of psychiatry at the Semel Institute at UCLA, added this perspective: "There probably is a significant percentage of gamblers who can do it on a controlled basis. The problem is we don't know who they are and what they're capable of when they show up in our office. A lot of times gamblers will come in and if I say to them, 'You can never ever place a bet the rest of your natural life,' that's someone who's never going to come back to our office. Whereas if I say, 'Listen, my goal is to eliminate pain and suffering from your life and if that means getting rid of your gambling, fine, if that means controlling your gambling, great. If that means limiting your gambling, that's fine, too. Then they are more likely to come back. I don't care whether they stop gambling or not, as long as they get rid of the damage in their life."

Some Pathological Gamblers "Recover" Without Treatment

A study appearing in a 2006 issue of *The American Journal of Psychiatry* evaluated two surveys involving more than 45,000 pathological gamblers in the United States. Only about 12 percent had ever sought individual or group treatment or attended meetings of Gamblers Anonymous.

"About one-third of the individuals with pathological gambling disorder in these two nationally representative U.S. samples were characterized by natural recovery," observed the study author. Recovery could be defined as either total abstinence, or some level of controlled gambling that reduces the level of harm previously associated with compulsive gaming. *(Source: "Natural recovery and treatment-seeking in pathological gambling: results of two U.S. national surveys." Slutske WS. Am J Psychiatry. 2006 Feb;163(2):297–301.)*

Natural recovery can result either from pressure exerted by friends and family members to change gambling behaviors or from an exercise of willpower and impulse control techniques learned and practiced by the gambler on his or her own.

"It is possible for people to recover from addiction on their own without treatment," observed Harvard's Prof. Howard Shaffer. "The way to restore control isn't simply to say, 'I won't do it anymore.' Because when you do that, you give the addiction more power. What you need to do is to find out what your addiction means, why you have it, and then substitute new activities that are in conflict with your addiction."

Dependence Often Begins Early in Life

Gambling behavior conditioning usually starts in childhood. Whether the first exposure was raffles and prizes at a kid's restaurant, or watching the *Wheel of Fortune* game show on television, kids get a steady diet of cultural messaging that many of the rewards in life come from taking risks that challenge luck and chance.

By the time these kids become teenagers, gambling behaviors take root alongside drug and alcohol abuse to form what psychologists call "conduct disorders." A 2011 study published in the *American Journal of Addiction*, for example, surveyed 2,274 youth 14 to 21 years of age and found a pattern in which "problem gambling occurs within a problem-behavior syndrome with other substance-use behaviors."

Being male, black or Hispanic, were found to be significant predictors of who would become a problem gambler at this age. "Clinical interventions for one specific problem behavior in youth," concluded the researchers at the University at Buffalo Research Institute on Addictions, "should consider assessing the other problem behaviors as well." *(Source: "The co-occurrence of gambling with substance use and conduct disorder among youth in the United States." Barnes GM, Welte JW, Hoffman JH, and Tidwell MC. Am J Addict. 2011 Mar–Apr;20(2):166–73.)*

Women and Adolescents Are the Fastest Growing Groups of Addicts

It's definitely a stereotype, though still a common one, that men are the most likely candidates to become problem gamblers. Whatever the source of the myth, adult men today are no longer the primary pool from which new gamblers are drawn. Women and adolescents can now claim that dubious distinction.

From Sheila Wexler, compulsive gambling expert and counselor: More than 50 percent of the people we see for treatment are women. A large percentage of them play slot machines. They got addicted later in life. They don't have this pumped-up ego thing that male gamblers have. They're kind of meek and maybe uncomfortable with themselves and something happens in their life—a divorce, the children leave home, they're lonely—and they become escape gamblers. With slot machines you don't have to be educated in gambling, unlike with blackjack and other card games. You just stick your money in the machine and you have this oblivion for whatever length of time you can sit at that machine. I had a lady that came to me for help, a 73-year-old woman, who lost a quarter of a million dollars in slot machines. I have female clients who have embezzled money to support their gambling habit. One African-American lady, 42 years old, a very religious lady who went to church every Sunday, got hooked on slot machines and embezzled a million and a half dollars from the county she worked for. She lost it all in slot machines. She got a 17-year jail sentence.

From Arnie Wexler, compulsive gambling expert and counselor: We run this gambling hotline and in the last three years, one third of all the calls coming in are coming in are from poker players between the ages of 12 and 30, young kids, or parents of these kids. I see these kids all the time who don't want to go to college. They're going to be professional poker players.

From Prof. Timothy Fong, codirector of the UCLA Gambling Studies Program and associate professor of psychiatry at the Semel Institute at UCLA: We know gambling as a disease starts very early in life. We're talking kindergarten years, if not earlier, when people are exposed to rewards and games and money. Think about how Chuck E. Cheese restaurants have raffles and prizes. It is part of our culture but it taps into the biological underpinnings of those who are genetically vulnerable. We know this generation of kids is growing up in a culture that promotes and celebrates gambling. You think of a poker player as a sports figure, a role model. This culture is very much of an impulse-driven, immediate reward-driven culture. We see a lot of very smart, young kids who decide to become professional poker players instead of going to graduate school and getting PhDs and real jobs. So what we're seeing is that gambling throughout America is probably having a much more subtle impact on our culture than we ever thought.

If you're in a relationship with a problem gambler

There are general do and don't lists for those of you who have a pathological or problem gambler in your life. Whether the person is a relative or a friend, these pieces of advice are offered to help you cope with the impact of their often unpredictable and disturbing behaviors.

Do the following:

- Continue to recognize your partner or friend's good qualities.
- Always remain calm when speaking to your partner or friend about their gambling and its consequences.
- Explain the gambling problem to your children if you are the spouse of a problem gambler.
- Seek the support of others dealing with similar problems. This could take the form of attending Gam-Anon, a self-help group for the families of problem gamblers. Let your partner know that you are seeking help for your own sake because of the way gambling affects you and the family.
- Make a commitment to allot time for the treatment of problem gambling.
- Take control of family finances and continually review bank and credit card statements to monitor the gambler's behavior and protect the family.

Don't do the following:

- Get angry, preach, or lecture.
- Make threats or issue ultimatums unless you intend to carry them out.
- Exclude the problem gambler from family life and activities.
- Bail out the gambler.
- Cover-up or deny the existence of the problem to yourself, your family, or other people in your life.
- Expect immediate recovery, or that all problems will be resolved once the gambling stops.

(Source: Connecticut Department of Mental Health and Addiction Services, www.ct.gov/dmhas.)

Tips on How to Keep Your Gambling Recreational

Gambling always needs to be viewed as a periodic form of entertainment, not as a way for you to make money or relieve stress and boredom. When you lose money, as you inevitably will, the loss should be viewed as the cost of entertainment for the day no different than tickets to a movie or play.

The California Office of Problem Gambling, part of that state's Department of Alcohol and Drug Programs, provides these guidelines to moderate your play and help prevent gambling from undermining your life. I have taken the liberty of expanding their tip advice and adding a few more of my own:

- Never borrow money to gamble.
- Never gamble with money needed for everyday expenses or for your mortgage, rent, or monthly expenses.
- Set a dollar limit for the day and stick to it, which means leave your debit and credit cards at home or in the car.
- Set a time limit for gambling and stick to it. Whether you're winning or losing, leave the casino or stop your play when you reach that time limit.
- Take frequent breaks from your gambling. This means breaks of days and weeks between gambling episodes, and frequent breaks while you are gambling. Most casinos have restaurants or even live music and other forms of entertainment to distract you. Take advantage of these distractions as a reminder that compulsive gambling is a trap that should be avoided.
- Never chase your losses. Trying to win back what you have lost is usually a recipe for losing even more money and, as a result, feeling bad about yourself.
- Never let your gambling become a substitute for your family and friends, and never let it interfere with your relationship obligations.
- Never use gambling as a way to cope with any emotional or physical pain that you might be feeling. That means never gamble when you feel stressed, depressed, or troubled.
- If you feel compelled to gamble and don't trust yourself to keep promises about the amount spent or the time spent,

bring a trustworthy friend or nongambling friend along and ask him to remind you that you have promises to keep.

- If you don't trust yourself to keep any of these promises you make to yourself, you have just triggered one of the warning signs for problem gambling. That means it's time to seek help.

Behavior Substitution Can Be an Effective Treatment

To complete treatment and maintain recovery from pathological or problem gambling, one must address the underlying issues or disorders—whether it's boredom, depression, or loneliness—that trigger and prolong the gambling fixation. One strategy involves substituting healthier alternative behaviors and activities when the urge to gamble surfaces.

Examples of substitution include:

GAMBLING REASON	ACTIVITY SUBSTITUTE
Excitement	Ride a roller coaster; go rock climbing, mountain biking, or go-kart racing.
Boredom, loneliness	Seek out people or groups who share your passion for music, sports, art, books, or stimulating conversation.
Stress relief	Engage in daily exercise (especially with groups of people), learn meditation or deep-breathing exercises, or book massages.

(Source: Adapted from Helpguide.org.)

Two Experts on Their Treatment Approaches

Every treatment specialist has a slightly different approach to pathological gambling depending on the gambler and the severity of the problem. Here are two of the leading U.S. experts on their treatment priorities.

From Prof. Timothy Fong, codirector of the UCLA Gambling Studies Program and associate professor of psychiatry at the Semel Institute at UCLA: What's undeniable is that when people come into our office now, compared to 10 or 15 years ago, their problems are much more severe. That's because of the ability for people to get more money through running a credit card. And then online gambling, just being able to tap into your bank account so easily, it creates problems at a much quicker rate than it ever did before.

We use biological approaches, psychological approaches, and then social approaches to treatment. Our psychological treatments are really geared at helping people develop ways to control their behavior. And that might be something as simple as having people identify high-risk situations when they're likely to gamble, such as when they have money in their hands or when they have an argument with their wife. We give them tools on how to say no to the urges.

We use a lot of psychological therapy to get people more motivated to look at how to build a life with lots of things other than just gambling. With many of our gamblers, you'd ask, "What else do you enjoy in life?" And they'd say, "Nothing, it's just gambling." And so psychological treatments look at why they don't do other things, like exercise, spending time with their family, working on their jobs, or going back to school.

And then we have social treatments really geared at making it harder for them to gamble. So things like limited access to cash and credit, or surrounding themselves with people who are committed to recovery from gambling, like Gamblers Anonymous. As an example, I had a guy I had tried everything with, but it wasn't until we took away his car that he was able to finally get four or five months of freedom from gambling.

I know the person who's going to get better is the one who has the ability to be honest with themselves and the people around them. It's critical to also treat the family of problem gamblers because that is often times where most of the damage has occurred.

(For more information on these treatment approaches, go to trans-formgambling.ca.gov., or to uclagamblingprogram.org.)

From Prof. Howard Shaffer, associate professor of psychology, Harvard Medical School, and director, Division on Addictions, the Cambridge Health Alliance: Loved ones need to have a candid conversation with the gambler because the limiting factor for gamblers, unfortunately, is personal wealth—gambling ends when there's no more money. They need to have this candid conversation early on because you don't want it to get to that point where all the doors are closed for the gambling family member because there's no money left.

The idea is to protect this person early on the same way we would protect the person with substance-use or alcohol-related problems. We'd cut off their access to money. Other people might have to take over by power of attorney; banks need to be notified; credit cards need to be cancelled; and all of the financial limitations need to be imposed. Hopefully, that would happen after a candid conversation. But it might have to be imposed with the coordination of the whole family.

Consequences and monitoring are keys, but I think for the vast majority of people who've struggled with this issue, the loss of their family, the fear of losing their family, or the fear of loss of a job will go a very long way to helping them regain control.

When people come to me, I don't expect them to want to change. I expect them to wish that they would want to change. My job is to motivate them. I think ambivalence is the heart of addiction. Exorcising that ambivalence, helping people see what they get from addiction, as well as how it hurts them, is essential to recovery. The "just say no" attitude, the "just don't do it" attitude is not going to work.

What About Medication as a Treatment?

Abnormalities in serotonin, norephinephrine, dopamine, and opioid systems have been noted in gamblers, making these systems targets for pharmacotherapy (drug therapy), according to Prof. Nancy Petry.

Three types of medications have been used to treat pathological gamblers: serotonin reuptake inhibitors, mood stabilizers, and opioid antagonists. Although some positive effects have been noted, "the results are far from conclusive," said Petry. Patients who have alcohol dependence accompanying their pathological gambling sometimes respond favorably to treatment by the drug naltrexone, which has been approved for diminishing the urges for alcohol.

Dr. Timothy Fong, codirector of the UCLA Gambling Studies Program and associate professor of psychiatry at the Semel Institute at UCLA, is more optimistic about the effectiveness of medications to treat gambling control issues. "The biological treatments we use are essentially medications to help take away urges and cravings," said Fong. "None of them is FDA approved. We also have a variety of other things like lithium or other antidepressants. There's another one called N-acetyl, or NAC, which is one that we have used to take away the urges. We now have a toolbox of about six or seven meds that we know can effectively dent the urges and cravings for gambling."

Effective Treatment Combinations

Cognitive behavioral therapy, a talking process designed to resolve dysfunctional emotions, has a proven record of benefits in treating problem gamblers. Studies showing its effectiveness are numerous.

For example, a study by Canadian researchers applied cognitive correction techniques in a group setting to target pathological gamblers' erroneous assumptions and perceptions about randomness and chance, then used the therapeutic process to address issues of relapse prevention. Post-treatment results showed that 88 percent of those treated with cognitive therapy no longer met diagnostic criteria for pathological gambling, compared to only 20 percent in a control group that didn't use cognitive therapy. When those using the cognitive approach were evaluated in 6-, 12-, and 24-month follow-up visits, they had maintained their improvement in self-control. *(Source: "Group therapy for pathological gamblers: A cognitive approach." Ladouceur R, Sylvain C, Boutin C, Lachance S, Doucet C, and Leblond J. Behav Res Ther. 2003 May;41(5):587–96.)*

As further insurance for treatment success and relapse prevention, cognitive therapy, either in a group or one-on-one therapeutic setting, can be combined with attendance at Gamblers Anonymous meetings. The evidence from studies strongly suggests that "a combined intervention may enhance therapy engagement and reduce relapse rates." *(Source: "Gamblers anonymous and cognitive-behavioral therapies for pathological gamblers." Petry NM. J Gambl Stud. 2005 Spring;21(1):27–33.)*

Some Treatment Options

For more information about the self-help-oriented treatments mentioned most frequently by the experts interviewed for this book, along with valuable tips about how to utilize these methods and tools, consult the following:

- Brief and motivational interviewing, Seven Self-Care Tools, p. 238
- Cognitive Behavioral Therapy, Seven Self-Care Tools, p. 235
- 12-Step Programs, Seven Self-Care Tools, p. 240

Your 30-Day Challenge for Gambling

Do you have a bad habit or a dependency? Here is another chance to find out.

You have answered the questionnaires for this toxic compulsion. You have read through what the experts have to say. You have thought about the extent to which you exhibit the behaviors associated with either a nondependent use disorder or a dependency.

Do you still have any doubt about whether you have just a bad habit, or whether your behavior meets the criteria for a dependency?

Create a 30-day challenge for yourself. Every time you gamble for 30 days, do three things before you play:

- Set a money-loss amount limit.
- Set a money-winnings amount limit.
- Set a time limit, such as "I will not gamble for more than one hour."

When any one of these three limits is achieved, you leave and stop playing for that day. If you can't stop, if you can't leave, you probably have a gambling problem and should seek professional assistance.

V

Toxic Compulsion 5: Hoarding

We are not cisterns made for hoarding, we are channels made for sharing.
—Billy Graham

IN THIS CHAPTER:

- Who Are the Hoarders?
- Is It Really Just Obsessive-Compulsive Disorder?
- 10 Signs and Symptoms of Hoarding
- Some Inconvenient Truths About Hoarding
- Time to Get Honest with Yourself
- Proposed Diagnostic Criteria for Hoarding
- Five Warning Signs That a "Hobby" Has Become Hoarding
- Animal Collecting May Not Be Compassion
- Hoarding and Compulsive Shopping Are Related
- Hoarding Symptoms Often Appear in Childhood
- An Effective Hoarding Treatment Approach
- Some Treatment Options
- Your 30-Day Challenge for Hoarding

D o you remember when saving things, or even being a pack rat, was considered a sign of frugality? Maybe that attitude was a holdover from the Depression-era generation that went through such privation during hard economic times that "saving for a rainy day" became an expression of their survival instinct.

Over the years I've been in homes that were so stuffed with belongings that I thought to myself, "There's a problem here." At the time, I just considered the chaos to be something temporary that I shouldn't worry about. I didn't have any knowledge that there might be a disease condition involved. I didn't even know about the word *hoarding* until just before starting the research for this book. This is how far and how fast we've come in terms of identifying these brain compulsions.

Maybe you've seen one of the "reality" television shows about hoarders and their hoarding habits. These stories can be as riveting and gut-wrenching as watching a slow-motion train wreck. In the United States, both The Learning Channel (TLC) and the Arts & Entertainment (A&E) network feature dramatic and widely watched shows about the compulsion some people have to hoard consumer items and even animals, and the heartbreaking attempts of family and friends to intervene, with assistance from addiction treatment experts.

Compulsive hoarding has also been labeled "disposophobia" because the person with this disorder feels a real and palpable fear of throwing or giving anything away, even if the items are essentially worthless. If you've ever had the experience of throwing something away and then a few days later realizing you really needed that item and wishing you hadn't discarded it, you have a small glimpse at what motivates some hoarders to keep everything they acquire. It's a pathological fear that, to the hoarder, is intense and is fortified by endless rationalizations. You just never know when something that seems worthless today will prove to be useful or valuable tomorrow!

As the acquired items pile up over time, every square foot of living space becomes storage space. That includes the kitchen and bathroom. Eventually, cooking and cleaning and showering and sleeping are encumbered by the mess, a process that whittles away at the hoarder's dietary health, bodily cleanliness, and self-respect. Some hoarders use their bathtubs and refrigerators to store items. Hoarding experts described for me studies in which 45 percent of hoarders were unable to use their refrigerators, 42 percent couldn't use their kitchen sinks, and 42 percent couldn't use their bathtubs, all because the clutter was so thick in their houses or apartments that these important parts of functional and healthy living had been hidden until the hoarder no longer made use of them.

Other hoarders allow uneaten or unopened food months past their expiration dates to accumulate in their refrigerators or on kitchen countertops until it becomes moldy and a magnet for mice, rats, and ants. If animals are kept around as pets, their urine and feces get buried under the accumulating piles of clutter. The stench can be unbearable for visitors, but the hoarder may slowly get used to it as a "normal" state of living.

Hoarding can take many forms. It might start out as collecting and evolve into cluttering. Many hoarders truly believe they are just messy collectors. Remember Imelda Marcos, wife of the late President of the Phillippines Ferdinand Marcos? When he was deposed in a pro-democracy coup a few decades ago it was found that Imelda kept a collection of several thousand pairs of shoes in her many closets. What reasonable person would have a need for several thousand pairs of shoes, most of which had never been worn? Her obsession with footwear bears a classic hallmark symptom of hoarders—their fixation with acquiring but never discarding.

Dr. Charles L. Whitfield, a psychotherapist and trauma recovery expert, noted that hoarding is one of those disorders that can rapidly go from a harmless habit into an unhealthy fixation. It's not always easy to tell where a person is on the continuum from habit to fixation. "A library is a place of hoarding for books, for instance, but they are very well organized," said Whitfield. "With the typical hoarder, the one where you can't get through their house because there is no path, even that type of hoarder may know a path for how to get through it all. So there may be some semblance of organization to them that isn't apparent to outsiders. *Herb & Dorothy* is a film out on DVD about a librarian and postal clerk who collected modern art. They were hoarders and took their meager salaries and bought art, about 4,000 pieces, which they had under their beds and on their floors until there was almost no room to walk around in their small home. They donated 1,000 pieces to the National Gallery of Art. They turned hoarding into something positive. So the severity of hoarding can sometimes be related to how disorganized or organized a person is in their categorizing and sorting out of what they hoard."

Some hoarders are prone to anthropomorphizing objects, which means they tend to treat the objects as if they had feelings like human beings. Dr. Gail Steketee, a dean and professor at the Boston University School of Social Work, described one such case: "It was a delightful woman who struggled with hoarding, quite successfully, in fact. But she continued to struggle with anthropomorphizing of objects.

This woman worried that the dishes on the bottom of the dishwasher would be upset that other dishes were put on top of them. In her story is the clear problem of thoughts and beliefs that contribute to hoarding—that objects are given more value than they really have, that people have a strong wish to control their things so no one else can touch them, that they see beauty and opportunity in many things and save them, even if these attributes can never be realized."

Who Are the Hoarders?

Mayo Clinic addictions specialists note that studies show about half of diagnosed hoarders have a history of alcohol dependence. Many experience eating disorders, making them overweight or obese. They are also particularly prone to experiencing major depression, anxiety disorders, and attention deficit hyperactivity disorder (ADHD). All of these maladies may be triggered by early childhood trauma, abuse, unstable upbringing, and parental neglect. This is a history also shared by many people with other types of addictive behaviors, such as drug and alcohol abuse.

A 2010 survey study of 751 adults with self-reported hoarding symptoms discovered that the onset of hoarding symptoms was typically between 11 and 15 years. Late onset of symptoms, after age 40, was rare. Stressful and traumatic events were commonly described by the survey respondents. *(Source: "Course of compulsive hoarding and its relationship to life events." Tolin DF, Meunier SA, Frost RO, and Steketee G. Depress Anxiety. 2010 Sep;27(9):829–38.)*

The potential safety and health pitfalls of hoarding should be obvious. Messy homes become fire hazards and obstacle courses that increase the risks of falls and injury. Clutter creates unsanitary living conditions with insects and rodents proliferating. Financial repercussions might include eviction by landlords, fines from government agencies, and the cost of maintaining storage facilities when the home becomes overburdened. Hoarding often provokes conflicts with family members, creates social isolation, and interferes with a normal, productive life.

Studies have examined the economic and social burden of compulsive hoarding. The disorder is associated with an average of seven work-impairment days a month, which is equivalent to what has been reported by persons with psychotic disorders. Hoarders are "nearly three times as likely to be overweight or obese as family members . . . and 8 to 12 percent [have] been evicted or threatened with eviction due to hoarding," a 2008 study reported. *(Source: "The economic and social burden of compulsive hoarding." Tolin DF, Frost RO, Steketee G, Gray KD, and Fitch KE. Psychiatry Res. 2008 Aug 15;160(2):200–11.)*

If you are getting the impression that hoarding is a uniquely American problem, perhaps owing to our overly materialistic life-styles, you would be mistaken. Few studies of hoarders have been conducted in other countries, but those that have been undertaken show patterns very similar to our own results. In Japan, a group of 186 OCD (obsessive-compulsive disorder) patients were assessed, and 54 were found to be compulsive hoarders, leading the researchers to conclude that hoarding "was similar to [results] reported in Western countries." *(Source: "Clinical features and treatment characteristics of compulsive hoarding in Japanese patients with obsessive-compulsive disorder." Hisato Matsunaga et al. CNS Spectr. 2010 Apr;15(4):258–65.)*

Is It Really Just Obsessive-Compulsive Disorder?

Until a decade or so ago, the prevailing opinion of the psychiatric profession held that hoarding compulsions were a subset of OCD and should be treated the same way. More recent science studies using brain scans have dramatically altered that consensus opinion.

Brain imaging studies using positron-emission tomography (PET) scans have demonstrated that cerebral glucose metabolism patterns in hoarders are quite different from the patterns seen in nonhoarding OCD patients. The most important difference was decreased activity among hoarders in the part of the brain responsible for attention, decision-making, and focus, which can lead to poor judgment and emotional disturbances. Any damage to the right medial prefrontal cortex of the brain can stimulate the compulsion for hoarding. *(Source: "Cerebral glucose metabolism in obsessive-compulsive hoarding." Sanjaya Saxena et al. Am J Psychiatry. 2004 Jun;161(6):1038–48.)*

Writing on behalf of the International OCD Foundation, Dr. Gail Steketee, dean and professor at the Boston University School of Social Work, has made these four behavioral distinctions between OCD and hoarding:

1. Few hoarders experience unwanted thoughts about hoarding, whereas this is a defining feature of OCD sufferers.

2. Hoarders generally feel distress only when they are forced to discard something and it's more grief-like than the anxiety seen with OCD.
3. Hoarding can be experienced as pleasurable when objects are acquired, which almost never happens with OCD people.
4. At least 80 percent of hoarders never exhibit any other OCD behavioral features.

It's now clear that compulsive hoarding is a separate disorder from OCD and needs to be classified by mental health professionals with its own diagnostic criteria, along with separate intervention and treatment approaches.

10 Signs and Symptoms of Hoarding

This summary of hoarding clues was posted by the Mayo Clinic staff (www.mayoclinic.com). A general rule of thumb is that a hoarder will show most if not all of the following tendencies:

1. Living spaces are cluttered far beyond "normal" standards.
2. The person regularly exhibits an inability to discard unneeded items.
3. Stacks of newspapers, magazines, or junk mail are kept.
4. Items are moved from one pile to another, but nothing is discarded.
5. Seemingly useless or unneeded items are acquired, such as other people's trash or even straws and napkins from a restaurant.
6. Difficulty occurs in organizing items that are acquired.
7. The hoarder engages in procrastination and exhibits difficulty managing daily activities or making important decisions.
8. Embarrassment or shame is shown by the hoarder about their living conditions.
9. There may be discomfort in allowing other people to touch or borrow their possessions, which indicates an excessive attachment to these items.
10. Over time the hoarder becomes increasingly isolated from other people.

Some Inconvenient Truths About Hoarding

Some of these pieces of information defining hoarders and hoarding may come as a surprise to you, as they did to me. For example, I certainly had no idea that more males than females meet the criteria for hoarding.

- Hoarding is *more prevalent in older than younger people*, though the initial onset of symptoms usually occurs in childhood.
- With each decade of life, the *severity of hoarding increases*.
- Half of older adults with a hoarding problem *also suffer from major depression and mood and anxiety disorders*.
- Study evidence is mounting that *hoarders' brains have executive functioning deficits that affect judgment*.
- Research has found that *hoarding is genetically influenced* and that up to 80 percent of hoarders had first-degree relatives who were considered "pack rats" or hoarders.
- *Most hoarders live on fixed incomes* and experience financial problems from having to pay for extra storage space, purchasing unneeded consumer items, and being hit with housing fines by landlords or government agencies.
- A persistent public perception of hoarders is that most are women; in fact, according to study surveys done in the United States and Britain, *the numbers of men who hoard outnumber women*.

(Source: International OCD Foundation, www.ocfoundation.org.)

Time to Get Honest with Yourself

Use the following scale of 0 to 8 to answer the five questions, which will help determine whether you have a hoarding problem.

Questions to answer:

1. To what extent is it difficult for you to use the rooms in your home because of the clutter or the number of your possessions?

(continued on next page)

(continued from previous page)

0   1   2   3   4   5   6   7   8
Not difficult   Mild   Moderate   Severe   Extremely Difficult

2. To what extent do you have difficulty discarding (or recycling, selling, or giving away) ordinary things that other people would get rid of?

0   1   2   3   4   5   6   7   8
Not difficult   Mild   Moderate   Severe   Extremely Difficult

3. To what extent do you currently have a problem with collecting free things or buying more things than you need or can use or can afford?

0   1   2   3   4   5   6   7   8
Not difficult   Mild   Moderate   Severe   Extremely Difficult

4. To what extent do you experience emotional distress because of clutter, difficulty discarding, or problems with buying or ac-quiring things?

0   1   2   3   4   5   6   7   8
Not difficult   Mild   Moderate   Severe   Extremely Difficult

5. To what extent do you experience impairment in your life (daily routine, job, school, social activities, family activities, or financial difficulties) because of clutter, difficulty discarding, or problems with buying or acquiring things?

0   1   2   3   4   5   6   7   8
Not difficult   Mild   Moderate   Severe   Extremely Difficult

Scoring Yourself

Four or less is the average score for people without a hoarding problem. Twenty-four or more is the mean average for people with serious hoarding problems.

(Source: "A brief interview for assessing compulsive hoarding: The hoarding rating scale-interview." Tolin, DF, Frost RO, and Steketee G. Psychiatry Res. 2010 Jun 30:178(1); 147–52. doi: 10.1016/j.psychres.2009.05.001.)

Proposed Diagnostic Criteria for Hoarding

Here are the proposed diagnostic criteria for hoarding that will go into the DSM-V (*Diagnostic and Statistical Manual*), the so-called "psychiatric Bible" used by treatment specialists for guidelines on how to diagnose disorders:

A. Persistent difficulty discarding or parting with personal possessions, even those of apparently useless or limited value, due to strong urges to save items, distress, and/or indecision associated with discarding.

B. The symptoms result in the accumulation of a large number of possessions that fill up and clutter the active living areas of the home, workplace, or other personal surroundings (e.g., office, vehicle, yard) and prevent normal use of the space. If all living areas are uncluttered, it is only because of others' efforts (e.g., family members, authorities) to keep these areas free of possessions.

C. The symptoms cause clinically significant distress or impairment in social, occupational, or other important areas of functioning (including maintaining a safe environment for self and others).

D. The hoarding symptoms are not due to a general medical condition (e.g., brain injury, cerebrovascular disease).

E. The hoarding symptoms are not restricted to the symptoms of another mental disorder (e.g., hoarding due to obsessions in obsessive-compulsive disorder, lack of motivation in major depressive disorder, delusions in schizophrenia or another psychotic disorder, cognitive deficits in dementia, restricted interests in autistic disorder, food storing in Prader-Willi syndrome).

Five Warning Signs That a "Hobby" Has Become Hoarding

"It can be difficult to sort out whether someone has a compulsive hoarding problem," said Dr. Daniel K. Hall-Flavin, an addictions psychiatrist and professor at the Mayo Clinic and former medical director for the National Council on Alcoholism and Drug Dependence. "Hoarders typically deny that they have a problem."

What may be obvious to outside observers—that the person has a serious hoarding problem—will be rationalized by the hoarder in numerous ways. For one, many hoarders choose to believe they are just collectors with a clutter problem. But real collectors, whether it's of old newspapers and magazines, model cars, plates, antiques, or any other item, tend to organize, categorize, and carefully display the items as a collection. Hoarders generally don't do that.

Here are Dr. Hall-Flavin's five warning signs you can look for to determine if a "collecting hobby" has become an unhealthy obsession:

1. The person is constantly acquiring things they don't need and doing so by acquiring duplicate items that often lay unopened.
2. The person has piles of clutter everywhere, without organization, making it difficult to move around in the dwelling.
3. The person can no longer sort, organize, or make rational decisions about his or her possessions.
4. The person has tremendous difficulty throwing anything away, so he or she rarely if ever does.
5. You and other visitors are discouraged from entering the person's home, or certain areas of the home have been closed off to hide a clutter problem.

Animal Collecting May Not Be Compassion

At what point does a person's desire to shelter homeless animals and save them from death in municipal animal control facilities become motivated and controlled by something more than human compassion?

It's a tricky question. What feels like genuine, caring concern for animal welfare on the part of pet collectors can appear to be animal hoarding and pet cruelty to outside observers.

Hoarded animals can be of one species—cats or dogs are a common choice—or multiple species living together in the same indoor or outdoor space. One fellow featured on a reality television show kept thousands of rats in his home, all uncaged, until they literally overran the place. His rat hoarding began after his wife died in a car accident. A woman on another reality show kept pet chickens everywhere in and around her home, even after they had died and become mummified.

Studies of pet hoarders indicate that most also live in homes that are "cluttered, disorganized, and dysfunctional," according to the journal *Depression and Anxiety. (Source: "Comparison of object and animal hoarding." Frost RO, Patronek G, and Rosenfield E.* Depress Anxiety. *2011 Oct 3;28(10):885–91. doi: 10.1002/da.20826. Epub 2011 May 23.)*

Pet hoarders meet the same diagnostic criteria that mental health experts apply to object hoarding. Sampling of case reports from animal control agencies in various cities have determined that 76 percent of animal hoarders were female and half of them were 60 years of age or older living in single-person households. The animals were usually cats, dogs, birds, and farm animals, and the median number of animals involved totaled 39, though in some cases more than 100 animals were found densely packed together. In 80 percent of the cases, the animals were either found dead or in poor condition. *(Source: "Hoarding of animals: An under-recognized public health problem in a difficult-to-study population." Patronek GJ.* Public Health Rep. *1999 Jan–Feb;114(1):81–7.)*

In another study of animal hoarding, 16 people who fit the criteria were compared to 11 people who owned large numbers of animals but didn't meet the mental health standards for hoarding. Both groups were mainly middle-aged white women who owned an average of 31 animals. "Themes found significantly more often among animal hoarding participants than controls [the nonhoarding group] included problems with early attachment, chaotic childhood environments, significant mental health concerns, attribution of human characteristics to animals, and the presence of more dysfunctional current relationships." *(Source: "Characteristics and antecedents of people who hoard animals." Steketee G, Gibson A, Frost RO, Alabisco J, Arluke A, and Patronek G.* Rev Gen Psychol. *2011 Jun;15(2):114–24.)*

Pet hoarders are usually deeply attached to the animals they keep. Many hoarders have turned to animals for the loving relationship they have failed to achieve with other humans. Yet they cannot comprehend that having dozens or hundreds of animals around may be doing more harm than good to these creatures. Like hoarders of consumer goods, animal hoarders have lost sight of boundaries.

Failure to provide proper care for animals is a crime in every state of the United States and in many other countries. So there can be definite legal ramifications to the out-of-control hoarding of animals that must be factored into any concerned person's decision to intervene. Public health agencies may also have a role to play in any situations that involve animal crowding and unsanitary conditions.

If you collect large numbers of animals, or know someone who does, ask this series of questions to help you determine whether the situation is a problem that needs addressing:

- Has the number of animals grown beyond an ability to care for them properly?
- Are they being given proper nutrition, veterinary care, and adequate sanitation?
- Does the pet owner fail to act on the deteriorating condition of the animals (starvation, disease, and death)?
- Are the animals crowded together, whether indoors or outdoors, in ways that limit their movements unnaturally? Are they suffering from neglect?
- If other family members live with the pet collector, have their lives been negatively impacted by the numbers of animals present?
- Does the presence of a large number of animals affect neighbors with day and night noise and odor problems?

At www.animalconcerns.org you will find information about the Hoarding of Animals Research Consortium at Tufts University, a group of researchers who have assembled a wealth of information about animal cruelty, the legal issues involved, hoarder intervention and treatment approaches, and general resources about animal hoarding, all under the guidance of veterinary epidemiologist Dr. Gary Patronek and social worker/rehabilitation counselor Jane N. Nathanson.

Hoarding and Compulsive Shopping Are Related

Most of the experts I interviewed for this book drew connections between hoarding and the impulse-control disorder known as compulsive buying. You don't need to be a shopaholic to be a hoarder. Some hoarders collect from trash cans, or they simply can't bring themselves to throw away what they purchase based on otherwise normal buying habits. But a significant number of hoarders support their compulsion with excessive spending on items they may never use or even remove from its packaging.

From psychologist and compulsive buying specialist Dr. April Lane Benson of New York City, author of two authoritative books on this disorder: What shopping addiction looks like is when somebody is spending so much time, energy, and/or money shopping, or even thinking about shopping, that it is impairing their life in some significant way. Financial impairment is the most obvious. But there are people on welfare who are compulsive buyers. What they buy is not very expensive, but they can't stop. There is also all kind of damage done to relationships, to occupational functioning, to their spiritual health. They feel hollow. One-third of the people I work with are not in debt. It's the other consequences that are making them seek treatment.

They use shopping as a quick fix for the blues. In the short-run, that actually works. We have research studies that look at three different time points: before the purchase, at the point of purchase, and after the purchase. And compulsive buyers start out below the normal buyer, but at the point of purchase, their moods shoot way up above the normal buyer. And then after the purchase, it dies down, but it doesn't go down quite as far as it was before the purchase. Whereas the normal buyer starts at a particular point; at the purchase they feel better and after the purchase they feel even better.

There are other addictions that co-occur with shopping. What I see the most are eating disorders along with compulsive buying. There is also panic disorder and major depression. I see less alcoholism and drug addiction, but that may just be my sample. Study results suggest that 5.8 percent of the U.S. population might be compulsive buyers. It's almost evenly distributed between the two genders. It's almost as prevalent as eating disorders and substance abuse.

There are new studies showing what kind of brain function is related to compulsive buying. Some people are just hardwired for this addiction and that makes it much more difficult to treat. It depends on how soon the person gets help and how good the help and support is. I think that people who have this problem, if they do the hard work of really developing the muscles [in the mind] they need to resist the urge to buy, and if they understand what they are really shopping for [to relieve a mood] and the consequences of compulsivity, they can succeed in treatment and regain control over their spending habits and their life.

Are you a chronic spender and shopaholic? Find out!

Though only a trained clinician can diagnose compulsive buying disorder, asking yourself the following questions can provide you with some clues as to whether you have a compulsive buying problem or not.

Choose the response that best describes you.

Add up your score on the six questions. A score of 25 or more is suggestive of compulsive buying disorder.

	STRONGLY DISAGREE					STRONGLY AGREE	
1. My closet has unopened shopping bags in it.	1	2	3	4	5	6	7
2. Others might consider me a shopaholic.	1	2	3	4	5	6	7
3. Much of my life centers around buying things.	1	2	3	4	5	6	7
4. I consider myself an impulse purchaser.	1	2	3	4	5	6	7
	NEVER					VERY OFTEN	
5. I buy things I do not need.	1	2	3	4	5	6	7
6. I buy things I did not plan to buy.	1	2	3	4	5	6	7

(Source: The Richmond Compulsive Buying Scale (assessment tool). "An expanded conceptualization and a new measure of compulsive buying." Ridgway NM, Kukar-Kinney M, and Monroe KB. J Consum Res. *2008 Dec;(35)4: 622–39. doi: 10.1086/591108. Epub 27 August 2008.)*

Hoarding Symptoms Often Appear in Childhood

Stressful life events play a crucial role in triggering the hoarding compulsion. Experts generally agree that hoarding often develops as a result of childhood trauma, the death of a loved one, divorce, or other dramatic and troubling events in a person's life.

Because hoarding often starts in adolescence, perhaps as a seemingly innocuous collecting "hobby" or a preoccupation with saving broken toys, outdated school papers, or other unneeded items, there appears to be an association with having an older family member who has compulsive hoarding tendencies.

"There are genetic and neurological features that seem to mark people with hoarding compared to those who don't hoard," said Dr. Gail Steketee, dean and professor, Boston University School of Social Work. "We do know that hoarding runs in families, but we don't yet know enough about the nature/nurture questions. Geneticists working on this do think that genetic linkages will be identified."

Most of us collected something as kids. Maybe it was baseball cards, dolls, stamps, coins, comic books, or whatever else we placed value on. Our parents probably encouraged the hobby as a harmless way to occupy our time and develop specialized interests.

At what point does such an activity become obsessive-compulsive, one of the first symptoms of a hoarding disorder whose severity can intensify later in life?

Such questions about child hoarders are the career focus of Dr. Lisa Merlo, assistant professor of psychiatry, chief of undergraduate education, and director of Addiction Medicine Public Health Research Group, University of Florida.

"Many kids go through a hoarding phase without developing the full-blown disorder," Dr. Merlo explained. "Often the disorder starts off as something like a rock collection. Then it becomes a string collection, or gum wrappers, and other items of less and less value. Maybe the child keeps old school assignments long after they have lost their learning value. That progression may be a sign that the compulsion to keep things is developing into the disorder."

It's important to detect a hoarding tendency early in life, Dr. Merlo stressed, because early intervention can make treatment much more effective. Hoarding and related obsessive-compulsive disorders often begin as a result of childhood traumas, events which may seem trivial to adults but which may be profound and life-altering for sensitive children.

"Traumas that can cause hoarding for a child include getting a bad grade in school or getting rejected for the cheerleading squad or the basketball team," said Dr. Greene. "The developing brain is more vulnerable to these sorts of experiences. With kids it can be hard to determine whether the hoarding is primary or secondary to obsessive-compulsive disorder. Again, that is why if we can treat it early in childhood, we can prevent the disorder from growing in severity."

An Effective Hoarding Treatment Approach

Experts on hoarding disorders whom I consulted are in agreement that the most effective treatment strategy for hoarding is to combine motivational interviewing with cognitive behavioral therapy (CBT), a combination of therapies that work irrespective of the hoarder's age.

Motivational interviewing is an effective type of brief intervention that involves a way of talking to people to encourage the emergence of their own internal motivation for change. The therapist or counselor asks a series of questions. These might include:

- What is the downside of your hoarding?
- What would be some advantages to changing your behavior?
- How would you go about making these changes?
- What would it take for you to succeed?

Once a person begins talking about their own motivations, they begin to see that the cost of their hoarding behavior has gotten to the point where it isn't worth continuing it anymore. Most hoarders begin to desire change and healing.

As a next step, the hoarder will be given an effective self-help tool known as cognitive behavioral therapy. This exercise enables the person to explore the reasons why hoarding occurs, learn how to improve decision-making skills and then to organize and categorize possessions for disposal, and learn to practice relaxation skills to reinforce healthy habits and decision-making.

In the book *Overcoming Compulsive Hoarding* the authors (Jerome Bubrick, Fugen Neziroglu, Patricia B. Perkins, and Jose Yaryura-Tobias) provide several detailed chapters on CBT, showing with exercises how to use this strategy to identify and change thought patterns that keep people stuck in their hoarding habit. Another excellent book, *Digging Out* by Michael A. Tompkins, PhD, teaches readers how to create a "harm reduction" plan for a hoarder that applies an effective step-by-step process for reducing problems associated with hoarding, though not necessarily "curing" the hoarder. This approach is especially useful if the hoarder is resistant to change.

Once a psychological reconditioning structure is in place, a professional organizer can be brought in to the home to help the hoarder go through the process of de-cluttering the living space.

Hoarders get better quicker when the combination therapy of

motivational interviewing and CBT is used. That was borne out in a 2010 study of such a combination on 16 children who received 14 sessions of 90 minutes each over a three-week period. Children in combination treatment significantly reduced the time needed for treatment compared to a control group of kids. *(Source: "Cognitive behavioral therapy plus motivational interviewing improves outcome for pediatric obsessive-compulsive disorder: A preliminary study." Lisa J. Merlo et al.* Cogn Behav Ther. *2010 Mar;39(1):24–7.)*

Dr. Gail Steketee, dean and professor, Boston University School of Social Work, described her treatment approach this way: "A combination of motivational interviewing whenever the person expresses ambivalence; skills training in organizing, problem solving, and decision-making; cognitive therapy; and behavioral practice to resist acquiring and discarding. We also must go into the home to make sure the treatments are applied regularly, daily, where the hoarding occurs. We need at least 26 sessions and often this will take nine months or more to make a real dent in the clutter if it's severe. The only predictors of better outcomes that we've been able to identify so far are being female, having less severe hoarding, having fewer other symptoms of OCD and social anxiety. If you expected treatment to work, it was more likely to do so."

Beyond identifying and treating hoarders, we have much work to do as a culture educating ourselves about this disorder. "It's difficult for some people to understand how anyone can get to this severe point of hoarding without it being their fault," said the University of Florida's Dr. Lisa Merlo. "As a society we have this immense stigma toward disorders where loss of control is a primary component. People need to have empathy as opposed to blaming the hoarder, because it's not a choice. Hoarders aren't hoarding because it's enjoyable. They are trapped and are prisoners of their own disorder. It has literally taken over their life. We are pulling them out of a prison when we give them treatment. It's never too late to help a hoarder. You should never give up hope on them no matter how severe their disorder."

Some Treatment Options

For more information about the self-help oriented treatments mentioned most frequently by the experts interviewed for this book, along with valuable tips about how to utilize these methods and tools, consult the following:

- Cognitive Behavioral Therapy, Seven Self-Care Tools, p. 235
- Paroxetine: a medication used to treat the symptoms of OCD; in one 2007 study only 28 percent of hoarders given the drug responded favorably.
- Support Groups: Children of Hoarders (www.childrenof-hoarders.com), Clutterers Anonymous (www.cluttersanony-mous.net), Messies Anonymous (www.messies.com)

Your 30-Day Challenge for Hoarding

Do you have a bad habit or a dependency? Here is another chance to find out.

You have answered the questionnaires for this toxic compulsion. You have read through what the experts have to say. You have thought about the extent to which you exhibit the behaviors associated with either a nondependent use disorder or a dependency.

Do you still have any doubt about whether you have just a bad habit, or whether your behavior meets the criteria for a dependency?

Create a 30-day challenge for yourself.

Every day for 30 days, you will sort your mail and immediately discard into the trash anything that isn't a bill or must be quickly responded to.

Once you put something into the garbage, you can't take it out, and you must empty your garbage into outside receptacles for pickup.

You will also go into your pantry and refrigerator and throw out all food that has expired or appears to be uneatable.

If you can stick to this plan for 30 days without cheating, you may not have a hoarding compulsion that is a problem.

VI

Toxic Compulsion 6: Sex and Pornography

The happiness of a man in this life does not consist in the absence but in the mastery of his passions.
—Alfred Lord Tennyson

IN THIS CHAPTER:

- Most Sexual Compulsives Have Other Disorders
- Does Sexual Compulsivity Have a Genetic Cause?
- Childhood Origins of Sexual Compulsions
- Time to Get Honest with Yourself
- Are You a Sex Addict, or Just Shaming Yourself?
- What Separates Male from Female Addicts
- Cybersex Can Be Gasoline on a Sex-Addiction Fire
- Sex and Porn Addiction Among College Students
- Some Myths About Sexual Addiction
- Is Abstinence a Practical Solution?
- There Will Be Withdrawal Symptoms
- Treatment Needs to Be a Holistic Experience
- An Ancient Sexual Practice as Treatment Today
- Some Treatment Options
- Your 30-Day Challenge for Sex and Porn Compulsions

Based on my experience and observation, if a sexual compulsion gets in the way of your ability to connect to another human being, or you have dysfunction in your family around that, it makes overcoming any addiction more difficult because you have no skill set for engaging people. It's that ability to engage people in authentic relationships that is a key to treatment and recovery.

Sex is a huge issue for people who come into recovery. There always seem to be sexual issues that need to be dealt with along with the alcohol and drugs. In 12-Step programs it is even suggested that you don't have a relationship for the first year because most people don't know how, and they make bad choices that complicate the recovery process.

We live in an age when sensory overload and the temptations for overindulgence are constant intrusions into our experience of life. USC's Dr. Drew Pinsky described the onslaught that we and our children face: "The Internet and the sexual content that flows into people's homes is literally a stress on biological systems. And for those with a tendency to sexual addiction or compulsion, it's like having a crack pipe in your house 24/7."

Sexual addiction experts talk in terms of as many as 16 million Americans exhibiting some form of compulsive sexual behavior (also called hypersexual disorder), one-third of them being women. This compulsive behavior could range from repeated affairs outside of marriage and uncontrolled promiscuity to obsessive masturbation, exhibitionism, voyeurism, or a fixation with pornography. What sets apart someone who just likes sex from a sex addict is the extent of abnormal preoccupation with sexuality and the negative consequences this compulsion has in the person's life.

Sex-obsessed people today struggle with their personal obsessions compounded by the influences from our cultural obsession with sex. For decades that cultural obsession has been reflected in the popularity of magazines such as *Playboy,* founded by Hugh Hefner, who probably fits the classic definition of a sex addict. Gay Talese in his book *Thy Neighbor's Wife,* for example, described Hefner as "a sex junkie with an insatiable habit."

Looking for Mr. Goodbar, a 1977 movie, brought the subject of sexual compulsions—and how women engage in them—into public awareness like no other movie or book before it. It starred Diane Keaton as a female teacher of deaf children who had a secret life at night as a sex addict. Perhaps not coincidentally around the time of the movie's release, 12-Step programs, modeled after Alcoholics Anonymous, for people with sexual compulsivity began appearing in cities around the United States.

The conflict and torment that sex addicts experience got even wider public attention starting in the 1980s when the first of many television evangelists had their sex compulsions exposed. Remember Jimmy Swaggert, Jim Bakker, and Ted Haggard, to name just a few from among dozens over the years? Then there were the widely publicized political sex scandals involving out-of-control compulsivity by the likes of President Bill Clinton, U.S. senators John Edwards, Larry Craig, Gary Hart, and U.S. congressmen Anthony Weiner, Chris Lee, Mark Foley, Robert Bauman . . . a casualty list that goes on and on, regardless of political party or ideology.

"Addicts profess extreme sexual propriety, even to the extent of moral self-righteousness about sexual matters," said Dr. Patrick Carnes in his book *Out of the Shadows: Understanding Sexual Addiction.* "Cover-ups, lies, and deceptions are made to conceal personal sexual behavior. The addict's protestations of high sexual morality are like a smoke screen, obscuring the impact of sexual obsession."

Sexual addiction isn't really about sex. "It's really about pain, or escaping, or anxiety reduction," wrote Dr. Carnes. "It's a solution, but it's a solution that doesn't work." Dr. Carnes noted that sexual addiction has been likened "to 'the athlete's foot of the mind.' It never goes away. It is always asking to be scratched, promising relief. To scratch, however, is to cause pain and to intensify the itch."

Dr. Charles L. Whitfield, psychotherapist and trauma recovery expert, took this point of view even deeper: "A sexual compulsion is not just a disorder. It's also a way to help heal from childhood or later traumas. Look at prostitution. What they're doing is turning a curse into a gift, in a way. The curse of sexual abuse is that up to 90 percent of prostitutes or women who work as exotic dancers have a history of childhood sexual abuse. As prostitutes or dancers, they're now being paid for being sexual, and they are also more in control of their situation. They don't realize it, but they are trying to heal from trauma through this repeated sexual behavior."

Being secretive about your actions and feeling shame are two classic markers for having a sexual addiction. But it's important to note that the kind of sex you have doesn't define sex addiction, nor does whom you have sex with define sex addiction, though some people obviously feel shame because of the social stigmas attached to homosexuality or other forms of nonviolent sexual activity between consenting adults. Most sex offenders—such as rapists, child molesters, etc.—don't fit the criteria for sex addiction, unless they are serial offenders.

The three primary criteria for determining whether you've crossed the line from healthy sexuality to some kind of problem sexuality are similar to that for any other addiction:

1. Loss of control. You say to yourself, "I'm not going on that porn site again," or "I'm not going to sleep with that person again," or "I'm not going to call that escort service," yet you find yourself returning to that same behavior.
2. You continue the behavior despite negative consequences. You come close to getting caught; your wife discovers incriminating e-mails or receipts from an escort service, for example, yet you continue the risky behavior.
3. Sexual activity preoccupies your thoughts. It becomes an obsession. If you go to a party you're reflexively scouting out who might prove to be a desirable sex partner. Or when you go on the Internet, your thoughts automatically turn to whether you should check out your favorite porn site and masturbate.

"There are two things that sex addicts don't do well," said addictions expert Robert Weiss, director, Sex and Intimacy Disorder Programs, Elements Behavioral Health. "One is travel, and the other is having unstructured time alone.

"Most sex addicts will get on a plane and get all excited about, 'Wow, who can I hook up with?' They're thinking about bars they can go to, or checking out the next city's personals on Craigslist. Whatever it is. They get aroused by the anticipation of that. Their brains release dopamine and they're having a pleasurable experience of fantasizing. The intense fantasy that they're engaging in creates neurochemical changes that narrow their thinking. They get lost in this neurochemical bath of arousal, not necessarily genital arousal, but emotional arousal. Then they start taking steps toward the fantasy. The closer they get to the behavior, the more dopamine is released and the more emotion that is aroused. They are less able to think clearly because of the narrowing and they go further toward this goal even though intellectually they may be saying to themselves, 'I don't want to do this. I shouldn't do this. This is going to cause problems.' But they're lost in the bubble. It just escalates into a slippery slope. That's why addicts need a lot of structure, stability, and consistency. Send them off on their own and they get anxious and start to feel dysregulated inside."

Other behaviors that set sex addicts apart revolve around a warped perception of reality. As Weiss explained, "Let's say your wife found out that you saw a hooker last weekend. She's furious and wants to leave you and you really love her and want to save your marriage. A healthy person would say, 'There's no way I would do that again.' An addict might say, 'There's no way I will ever let myself get caught again.' A healthy person would not make decisions that clearly will cause them consequences. An addict doesn't learn from their mistakes. They're not guided by what is most important to us in terms of mental health. Addicts ignore reality. The sexually compulsive behavior is more important to them than the healthy realities they see in front of them."

Most Sexual Compulsives Have Other Disorders

Based on study survey results, Dr. Patrick Carnes has listed some of the co-occurring compulsions and disorders documented among identified sex addicts. Interactions between these various disorders tend to reinforce one another, making treatment and recovery more challenging.

- 38 percent of sex addicts also struggle with an eating disorder.
- 42 percent of sex addicts also have a problem with chemical dependency.
- Among cocaine addicts, 50 to 70 percent have a problem with sexual compulsion.
- Gambling and spending sprees are frequent counterparts to sexual addiction.
- Depression affects many people with sex addictions; 17 percent of them have attempted suicide and 72 percent have considered it.

Does Sexual Compulsivity Have a Genetic Cause?

While sex addiction has been theorized to have genetic causes, much like substance addiction, scientific evidence has been lacking until recently.

In 2010 a team of scientists administered an anonymous survey to 181 young adults in New York, asking about their personal history of sexual behavior and intimate relationships. Each person also underwent genetic testing. What emerged was striking.

Those young people who were most likely to report being promiscuous possessed a certain variant in the DRD4 gene, which controls how much dopamine is released during sexual activity. Sex provided those with the aberrant gene a much bigger dopamine high. It was also found that those with the gene variation reported "a more than 50 percent increase in instances of sexual infidelity" over those people without that variant.

Concluded the researchers: "Individual differences in sexual behavior are likely partially mediated by individual genetic variation in genes' coding for motivation and reward in the brain." *(Source: "Associations between dopamine D4 receptor gene variation with both infidelity and sexual promiscuity." Justin R. Garcia et al. PLoS One. 2010 Nov 30;5(11):e14162. doi:10.1371/journal.pone.0014162.)*

Though these findings await replication in larger studies, they do suggest that genetic influences on the course of sex dependency must be factored into treatment programs as future research identifies more specific vulnerabilities.

Childhood Origins of Sexual Compulsions

"I'm not even sure that sex addiction is a disease," said psychotherapist Alexandra Katehakis, clinical director of the Center for Healthy Sex in Los Angeles. "I believe it's a problem of affect dysregulation [mood swings]. It's rooted in the brain and the autonomic nervous system. There is a lot of research showing that childhood trauma is what leads to addiction.

"If you've got an anxious or depressed mother, you're going to have an anxious or depressed infant because she is coregulating and setting up that nervous system. So if you've got somebody who's just not there mentally in early infancy, of course that person's child is going to have problems because the brain and nervous system are not setting up optimally. You're going to get addiction from that.

"We see it a lot in sex addicts. Many are anxious-avoidant or anxious-ambivalent in how they attach in terms of their ability to connect, have intimacy, and get regulation from another person to say, 'You know, I'm really upset, I need a hug.' Instead of saying, 'I'm just upset and anxious. I'm going to take a drink,' or 'I'm going to go jack off to porn.'

"So I'm seeing it more as a problem of autonomic nervous system dysregulation. And that comes from early childhood-attachment patterns, early relational trauma, and the kind of nurturing and attention that we get [or don't get] from infancy up to the time we leave our homes."

By the time someone with this sort of deficit from childhood reaches adulthood, and sexual compulsivity takes over their thoughts and life, they feel empty inside. It's what AA calls a hole in the soul.

Time to Get Honest with Yourself

The following is a series of questions adapted from the Sexual Recovery Anonymous Web site that describe feelings and behaviors around sex. Check "yes" or "no" and then tabulate your answers.

Yes No

___ ___ Do you think about sex much of the time?

___ ___ Do you often feel shame, regret, or remorse after sexual fantasy or behavior?

___ ___ Do you want to stop masturbating but can't?

___ ___ Do you have difficulty staying monogamous in a relationship?

___ ___ Do you break promises to yourself about stopping unwanted sexual behavior?

___ ___ Does your sexual behavior isolate you from friends, family, etc.?

___ ___ Does your obsession with pornography interfere with having real relationships?

___ ___ Do you obsessively sexualize people you see in public?

___ ___ Do you put yourself at risk for sexually transmitted diseases?

___ ___ Are you afraid that your "double life" and sexual secrets will be discovered?

___ ___ Have you spent a great deal of time or money on sex?

___ ___ Has your sexual behavior put you in dangerous situations?

___ ___ Have you hurt yourself or others as a result of your sexual behavior?

___ ___ Have you engaged in any of the following: voyeurism, exhibitionism, anonymous sex, phone sex, trading for sex, paying for or being paid for sex, abusive sex?

___ ___ Are you unable to say no to other people's sexual advances?

___ ___ Have you risked or lost your job because of your sexual behavior?

(continued on next page)

(continued from previous page)

Yes No

___ ___ *Do you feel that sex is your most important need?*

___ ___ *Do you confuse sex with love?*

___ ___ *Has your sexual behavior made your life unmanageable?*

The above questions are intended to help you decide if you have a problem. Though there is no scoring system, the more yes answers you give, the greater the severity of your problem and the more you need treatment.

Are You a Sex Addict, or Just Shaming Yourself?

From certified sexologist and anger management specialist Veronica Monet of Northern California, who works with her addiction clients—60 percent men, 40 percent women—to separate their feelings of shame about their sexual preferences and behaviors from sexual rituals that constitute symptoms of sexual compulsion and addiction: Sex addiction is real and it is real dangerous. But a lot of sex is just that—a lot of sex. If every married person who cheats on their spouse is a sex addict, then about half of America is addicted to sex and that just ain't so. A much more pervasive condition is sexual shame. Most of us *do* suffer from sexual shame, and labeling everything from infidelity to group sex to BDSM (bondage/sadomasochism) as evidence of sex addiction only piles more sexual shame on what should be our God-given right to diversity and choice.

With sex addicts the first thing I have to do is extract them from the shame. There is nothing about shame that I find redeeming. Guilt and remorse have some positives, such as realizing that people have been hurt by your behaviors. But shame is usually about an attack on a person because of their sexual preferences. Sometimes that attack to induce shame comes from the stigmas of society and religion. Sometimes it is just self-inflicted. It's important to dismantle the shame first so the task of treatment and recovery can begin.

The painful truth about sex addiction is that it rarely involves flying to South America to rendezvous with a lover or making it with every porn star, stripper, waitress, model, ad infinitum that catches your eye.

No, most sex addicts are jerking off to online porn while the rest of their life fails to get lived. They go broke paying for porn, prostitutes, and strippers. They are lonely because they cannot form a relationship with a real live human for free. And some sex addicts can't even stop masturbating long enough to hold down a job. Some of my clients have lost several jobs due to masturbating to online porn at work. They're so addicted to porn they become *agirlophobic!* They have intimacy issues and an inability to express feelings. Sex addicts cannot stop. Sex addicts are *not* having fun. Sex addicts feel like dying.

To help you sort out shame from addiction, Monet lists a series of symptoms that differentiate the two:

Sexual Shame Symptoms:
1. You are afraid others will find out.
2. Your wife or husband is threatening to leave you.
3. Your church and/or religious leader (pastor, priest, rabbi, chaplain, etc.) disapproves.
4. Your behavior is against the law.
5. You feel guilty.
6. You worry you are a sex addict.
7. You feel worthless and/or bad and/or defective.

Sex-addiction Symptoms:
1. You would like to enjoy more intimacy but you can't get off unless you do your "ritual."
2. You spend so much time having sex and/or masturbating and/or viewing online porn that you don't have time for other things in life.
3. Your sexual interests and behaviors are costing you more money than you can afford.
4. Your sexual obsessions have caused you to lose one or more jobs.
5. Your sexual obsessions dominate your thoughts so you can't think of much else.
6. You don't enjoy what you are doing anymore but you can't stop.
7. You can't stop!

As a further diagnostic tool, Monet sends her clients to www.sexhelp.com, a site created by Dr. Patrick Carnes, where they can answer his sex-addiction questionnaire.

What Separates Male from Female Addicts

From Robert Weiss, sexual-addiction clinician and expert and director, Sex and Intimacy Disorder Programs, Elements Behavioral Health: I've seen a couple thousand men and I can count on one hand the number who came in and said, "I want to be a better person. I don't want to do this anymore." They all come in because of their wife, their boss, or because of being arrested. They are threatened with losing everything and the consequences jog them out of denial.

The most common client that we see is a 38- to 42-year-old man who has two kids under the age of seven. He's been married for 10 or 12 years and he had some sexual intimacy and romance issues when he was younger. But then he met her, the one, and fell in love. They bonded and started having sex and so he stopped acting up. He stopped seeing hookers and he's thinking, "Well, I get it. I just never met the right person that's why I was doing all that. And so now that I've met the right person, I'm never going to tell her about what I used to do because I don't want her to be disappointed in me."

Then somewhere about 18 months to two years into the relationship, he returns to the pursuit of using sexual images or experiences as a way of self-soothing, self-medicating, or whatever. Why does he turn? Here is an approach that works particularly with the men. It's talking about personal integrity. Most men that I've worked with know that they are not living in integrity and integrity comes with integration—the idea of one. So if I'm doing this over here and I'm doing that over there, that's not integrated. It's very stressful, by the way, to be disintegrated. You live a double life. Most men that I work with, they've split off parts of their lives so profoundly that there's a lot of anxiety and unhappiness with not being the person that they want to be or that they would want their children to know. So without integrity, you can't really be vulnerable, because you can't be known. And the key to intimacy is being vulnerable.

Here is the thing about women. Number one, they don't want to be identified as a sex addict for a number of reasons. It's so shameful for a woman to come forward. A man who has had a lot of sex is perceived as a stud. A woman who is having a lot of sex in our culture is always a slut. So it's very hard for a woman to come to terms with what she's really been doing, even harder for a woman than for a man.

So women will go into therapy or treatment saying they have problems with love, problems with relationships. They may be hooking up four times a week, too, but in their minds, their denial is, "Well, maybe I'll find the right guy." Guys are not thinking that way. We're much more linear and much more visual, much more—like, "I'll get some booty this week." Women are thinking, "Well, maybe I'll meet the right person this time." So a woman will much more readily identify with love addiction and relationship addiction or abused relationships than with sex addiction.

One of the things I observed about the women I've documented is that women who have problems with repetitive patterns of compulsive addictive relationships or compulsive addictive pursuit of sexual behavior have a much harder time getting sober from drugs and alcohol. If a woman has repetitive patterns of being unable to get sober in drugs and alcohol, it's not at all unlikely that she has some problems with sex or relationships.

Another difference between men and women involving sex addiction is that only 15 to 20 percent of the men that I worked with have overt sexual abuse in their history. But with the women, 60 to 70 percent of the sex addicts have overt sexual abuse. Rape, violation, incest, or whatever it is. So if that doesn't get dealt with in treatment, they're going to keep acting it out. They're also more likely to become sex workers as a result.

Said Alexandra Katehakis, clinical director of the Center for Healthy Sex in Los Angeles: "Being labeled with the term 'sex addict' is difficult because nobody wants to be stigmatized and because other people want to make fun of it. We make fun of mental illness in this country. I mean, we've turned the actor Charlie Sheen into a circus act. He's like the village idiot that we are all laughing at. And this is someone who is in a hell of a lot of pain.

"So likewise with sex addicts. If you tell someone 'I'm a recovering alcoholic,' they say 'Congratulations,' and they shake your hand. If you say 'I'm a recovering sex addict,' they're like, 'I don't know if you should be around my kids.'"

Cybersex Can Be Gasoline on a Sex-Addiction Fire

Computers and the Internet are but the latest technologies to magnify and make more accessible some of humankind's oldest obsessions.

Before this technology emerged we had the motion picture industry and its "blue" films portraying sex acts. Before that came the invention of photography and 19th-century French postcards showing nudes and a variety of sexual acts. Before that we had mural art of sex scenes showcased in the homes and public buildings of ancient Rome and Greece.

Anonymity on the Web allows people to be anyone they want in sex chat rooms. We can access images of almost any type of sexual behavior. We can solicit sex services in private, without having to cruise around in public to find them. We can view pornographic movies for free without having to publicly visit porn theaters. The Internet has reduced the risks of punishment for those who engage in exhibitionism and voyeurism. Yet cybersex also creates a real danger of relapse for those in recovery from other types of sex addiction.

Are you one of those people at risk?

The following questions on the Sexaholics Anonymous Web site (www.sa.org) help you identify whether you have a cybersex problem:

- Do you have a problem with viewing pornography on the Internet?
- Has your illicit Internet use put your job at risk?
- Have you lost needed sleep due to obsessive Internet use?
- Have you lied to others to cover your Internet activity?
- Have you missed important events or meetings because you were on the Internet engaged in sexual activity?

With cybersex addiction, tolerances will develop over time for many addicts so they feel compelled to seek out images of sexual acts that are new to them, such as sadism and masochism, or illegal imagery such as child porn. "It goes back to the reward center of the brain," said Alexandra Katehakis, clinical director of the Center for Healthy Sex in Los Angeles. "There's not enough novelty for the dopamine to be released. So they're going to seek images that are going to sometimes simultaneously repulse them, but their bodies get aroused because it's so novel and weird. Going down that road can be dangerous because the minute they download child pornography they're going to have the FBI knocking at their door."

It may surprise you, as it did me, to learn that an estimated 40 percent of the most extreme cybersex users are women. "The anonymity of the Net allows women to ignore the normal inhibitions that keep them safe," said Dr. Patrick Carnes. "Addicts view cybersex use as having no consequences. With this impaired thinking, addicts believe that they can stop whenever they want."

But sex addicts, especially those engaging in cybersex, can't stop whenever they choose. Observed Dr. Carnes: "Cybersex addicts can quickly become focused on new types of behavior in a very short amount of time—what has taken other sex addicts a decade to develop before the advent of the Internet." The trancelike state induced by hours of Internet use, combined with a desire for more intense excitement, can cause some people to cross lines they may never imagine crossing with a real human being. Child porn is an example.

"Sexual activity on the Internet has fundamentally altered our sexuality," said Dr. Carnes. "Barriers and obstacles to sexual exploration were literally obliterated overnight. There are now people struggling with sexual compulsivity who never would have been if not for the Internet." Dr. Carnes cited those surprising statistics showing that about 40 percent of these sex addicts are women.

Abstinence from computer use or Internet use may not be professionally possible for many sex addicts given the nature of their jobs. Thus it might be advisable for them to put a porn filter on their computer to prevent access to Web sites associated with pornography or other sexual activity.

Sex and Porn Addiction Among College Students

Self-professed recovered sex addict Michael Leahy, author of *Porn University* (2009, Northfield Publishing), used a 33-question sexual-addiction screening test developed by Dr. Patrick Carnes to survey 28,798 students at 110 colleges and universities in the United States, Canada, and several other countries from 2006 to 2008. About 59 percent were male, 41 percent female. Here are some of the highlights of Leahy's findings:

- 69 percent of males had their first exposure to pornography between the ages of 10 and 14; 68 percent of females had their first exposure at age 13 and up.
- More women than men (8 percent versus 5 percent) regularly sought sexual pleasure by either sadomasochistically experiencing or inflicting sexual pain.

- 5 percent of women and 13 percent of men admitted having had sexual relations with a minor
- In answer to the question "Do you have trouble stopping your own inappropriate sexual behaviors?" 26 percent of males and 18 percent of females said yes.
- 38 percent of males and 23 percent of females said they made unsuccessful efforts to stop engaging in sexual activities they wanted to stop.

Some Myths About Sexual Addiction

Society has myths that we perpetuate and we each have our own myths that we buy into based on our prejudices and preconceived notions. This expert listed five of the more common myths she commonly hears about sexual compulsions.

From Alexandra Katehakis, clinical director of the Center for Healthy Sex in Los Angeles:

1. If you're a sex addict you're probably also a pedophile.
2. If you're a sex addict you can never get better.
3. If you're a sex addict you love to have sex.
4. All sex addicts were sexually abused as children.
5. Other countries don't have the sex-addiction problems of the United States.

Concerning this latter myth, I had a French camera team from a news channel here to see me after the golfer Tiger Woods went into a sex-addiction treatment clinic, and they were saying to me, "We want to talk to you about sex addiction because we don't have this in France."

I laughed because I thought it was so cute. They said, "We don't get this." I don't think that's true. I think it's just looked at and thought about differently in other cultures. Look at what happened in Italy with the prime minister's affairs with young girls. The women there were up in arms and saying, "We are sick of this double standard. This is not okay for us anymore." So I think sex-addiction problems are just seen differently in other countries.

Is Abstinence a Practical Solution?

For alcohol, drugs, smoking, and gambling compulsions, complete abstinence may be an effective and necessary antidote to dependence and the cravings associated with it. We weren't born to drink alcohol, do drugs, smoke, or gamble. But sex, like eating, is a natural and necessary urge we are born with.

Abstinence from sexual expression may work for a limited period—unlike for eating disorders, where fasting could eventually produce death—but it's a rare person outside of devout celibate monks and nuns who can willfully and completely extinguish the full scope of their sexual appetites. Consequently, the emphasis on treating sexual compulsions must necessarily involve learning self-control to regulate behaviors, rather than treatment to suffocate sexuality.

Here is how the group Sex Addicts Anonymous (SAA) describes the difference between abstinence and celibacy: "In SAA we use the term abstinence. When we admit that we are powerless over our addictive sexual behavior, we accept that we cannot behave in certain ways. These behaviors are very compelling before we do them, but afterward they leave us feeling shameful, remorseful, empty, and craving. We call these behaviors acting out. Abstinence does not mean giving up sex. That is celibacy. We don't give up our healthy sexual expressions; we give up acting-out: compulsive, painful, and destructive behaviors."

Similarly, another 12-Step fellowship group, Sexual Compulsives Anonymous, describes its vision of sexual sobriety this way: "Our primary purpose is to stay sexually sober and to help others to achieve sexual sobriety. Members are encouraged to develop their own sexual recovery plan, and to define sexual sobriety for themselves. We are not here to repress our God-given sexuality, but to learn how to express it in ways that will not make unreasonable demands on our time and energy, place us in legal jeopardy; or endanger our mental, physical, or spiritual health."

There Will Be Withdrawal Symptoms

During the early phase of sobriety from a sexual compulsion you may feel a range of intense and turbulent emotions as if you are on a roller coaster.

Comments from members of the group Sexual Recovery Anonymous produced these withdrawal descriptions: "We were confused and vulnerable. Emotions ranged from feelings of wholeness and wellness to feelings of despair and emptiness. Feelings that were unfamiliar overcame us in ways we didn't understand. Feelings that seemed familiar became deeper and more intense. Many of us were overwhelmed by anger, rage, fear, loneliness, sadness, and depression. Some of us cried for the first time since childhood. In addition to the emotional distress, many of us had physical discomfort such as sleeplessness, exhaustion, hyperactivity, and headaches. Some of us felt as though we were gripping the edge of a cliff, distressed and in pain, barely keeping our sobriety."

Addictions clinician and expert Robert Weiss saw these withdrawal symptoms in his patients firsthand. "There is a withdrawal," said Weiss. "People can expect mood swings, irritability, longing, and the like, for six months minimum, until they have their coping mechanism in place to begin to feel better. Part of withdrawal is they're going to go into an argument with the sick brain: 'Why can't I? What's the big deal?' They're going to hear all of their denials come up. And they have to have someone they can talk about all of this with."

Here is a warning sign of possible relapse Weiss looks for among people in recovery: "When somebody comes into treatment and says, 'Oh, thank God, I went to your program. I'm never going to do that again. I feel so much better.' I really worry about that person. It's the person who comes out of treatment and says, 'I'm going to be vulnerable for this always. I need to have lots of resources. I could do this again at any time.' That person really gets their vulnerability. They get that this is a lifetime deal. The desire to use other people or experiences to self-soothe is a lifetime thing."

Over time, as those in recovery stay with the treatment program, the healing pain of withdrawal symptoms and the feelings of shame begin to dissolve.

Treatment Needs to Be a Holistic Experience

Sexual addiction is also a family illness, and the more family members who are involved in a person's treatment process, the higher the recovery rate for addicts and the more healing that takes place in the family relationships. That is a consensus opinion from all of the sex-addiction experts I interviewed.

Beyond that, the individual treatment tool that every expert mentioned as a "first response" to sexual compulsivity is cognitive behavioral therapy (CBT).

Alexandra Katehakis described her use of CBT in psychotherapy: "The gold standard for treatment for sex addiction right now is a task-centered approach. It's cognitive behavioral treatment protocol that gets people to stop the behavior, look at all their secrets, lies, excuses, problems. Essentially, it's a first step to break through denial and to get people to really look at who they've been hurting, how they've been self-destructing, what they've been doing to their lives. That's the cornerstone of the treatment protocol.

"Then, who the person is will determine on how much childhood trauma work they need. Depending on whether or not they're also using drugs and alcohol, or if they are sex offenders, that will determine whether or not they need to go into an inpatient setting versus an outpatient setting, or whether we can continue to treat them in our office."

In cities such as Los Angeles, many addiction treatment therapists now are trained in EMDR (eye movement desensitization and reprocessing), a form of psychotherapy to resolve the development of trauma-related disorders that trigger sexual and other compulsions. The therapists may also be trained in Somatic Experiencing, which involves a body movement and massage approach to releasing trauma. These and other related natural modalities are designed as a trauma resolution process so the person doesn't need to automatically reach for a drug to make them feel better. Meditation and yoga can also be a tremendous intervention for trauma because you're moving your body and you're focused on your breathing. Mindfulness practices can help CBT to bring about awareness of the choices that a person is making in their life and creates a "power of now" approach to changing those choices and the resulting behaviors.

Another piece of the treatment puzzle recommended by all the experts is the various 12-Step programs for sexual compulsivity. Observed Katehakis: "If people work a program and they come out of isolation and reach toward other human beings, they will get sober and that's the beauty of the 12-Step program. The program is a gigantic coregulatory process. I'm talking about Sex Addicts Anonymous and Love Addicts Anonymous, whatever the 12-Step program is.

"If you have deeper trauma, then you have to do trauma work. You've got to do the kind of work that a therapist would do. Not everybody has the means to go to therapy. But if people work a 12-Step program, which is about human beings helping other human beings, caring about each other, making phone calls, having fellowship, having a sponsor, that is what starts to change the brain and the nervous system. It takes 90 days to build a new character. Well, my understanding is it takes 90 days to grow new dendrites, to build new dendrites, for the brain to start growing again.

"So coming out of isolation, being transparent, being accountable, are some easy things that people can do, and maybe they go see a therapist for six sessions or something to try to get their head on straight about what needs to be done and what other actions they can take depending on exactly what they are up to, and then being socially engaged. Instead of going to see that prostitute, how about you go do something else? Do you have a hobby that you really used to enjoy but you're not doing anymore? Is there a friend you haven't seen for a while? Do you need to do something with your kids?"

Robert Weiss, sexual-addition clinician and expert and director, Sex and Intimacy Disorder Programs, Elements Behavioral Health, added this useful advice about attending 12-Step meetings: "Addicts always go into those 12-Step program rooms at the beginning in fear and separation, and look at the people who are worse than them, and say, 'Oh, I'm not as bad as that one. What am I doing here?' And so we tell people to look for the similarities, not the differences. If you go in there looking for reasons that you don't belong, you're going to find them. You have to look for the reason that you *do* belong. If you stay long enough, at least six meetings, you're going to hear the stories. You're going to get engaged and you're going to identify."

An Ancient Sexual Practice as Treatment Today

You may have heard the terms "tantra" or "tantric" and reactively associated them with something salacious, exotic, or New Age-y that bears little relationship to the practical problems of treating sexual compulsions. How wrong you would be!

Tantra is about adding mindfulness to the sexual act in a way that elevates sex above and beyond mere physical pleasure. Developed in India many hundreds of years ago, tantric sex (known as "left-handed" tantra to distinguish it from a strictly spiritual practice) involves a ritual that includes rhythmic breathing, meditation, visualizations, and other methods to focus and heighten the sexual experience.

Tantric practices can be done on your own, though it's preferable to engage with a partner, preferably an intimate partner you love and want to deepen a relationship with. Keep in mind that tantra isn't about lust. It's about channeling sexual energy to make the sexual act healthier. Sex therapists such as Veronica Monet teach tantra to clients as a tool to control sexual compulsions.

Being open-minded to a practice like tantra provides you with more choices. You don't have to be a slave to your compulsions. Practicing tantric sex is a perfect application of mindfulness, a useful tool mentioned by most every expert on every compulsion that I have interviewed. Mindful sex can deepen your relationship with another person, which is always an important element in recovery from any addiction or compulsion.

There is a lot of information about tantra and how to do it on Web sites and in books out there. A good place to start would be any book by Margot Anand, psychologist, Sorbonne, and the world's leading authority on Tantra.

Some Treatment Options

For more information about the self-help oriented treatments mentioned most frequently by the experts interviewed for this book, along with valuable tips about how to utilize these methods and tools, consult the following:

- Cognitive Behavioral Therapy, Seven Self-Care Tools, p. 235
- Meditation, Seven Self-Care Tools, p. 253
- Mindfulness, Seven Self-Care Tools, p. 249
- Somatics, Seven Self-Care Tools, p. 268
- 12-Step Programs, Seven Self-Care Tools, p. 240

Sex Addicts Anonymous (www.sexaa.org)
Sexaholics Anonymous   (www.sa.org)
Sex and Love Addicts Anonymous FWS (www.slaafws.org)
Sexual Compulsives Anonymous (www.sca-recovery.org)
Sexual Recovery Anonymous   (www.sexualrecovery.org)
Codependents of Sexual Addiction: for families and friends of
     sex addicts (www.cosa-recovery.org)

Your 30-Day Challenge for Sex and Porn Compulsions

Do you have a bad habit or a dependency? Here is another chance to find out.

You have answered the questionnaires for this toxic compulsion. You have read through what the experts have to say. You have thought about the extent to which you exhibit the behaviors associated with either a nondependent use disorder or a dependency.

Do you still have any doubt about whether you have just a bad habit, or whether your behavior meets the criteria for a dependency?

Create a 30-day challenge for yourself.

For sexual compulsions that involve other people, commit to going on three dates in public places with a person before you will have sex with that person.

If your habit or compulsion revolves around pornography and masturbation, commit to remaining abstinent for 30 days. That means avoiding all pornographic literature, Web sites, and movies during that period.

Should you fail to stick to the plan for 30 days, you probably have a problem and should seek professional assistance.

VII

Toxic Compulsion 7: Nicotine Dependence (Smoking)

To cease smoking is the easiest thing I ever did. I ought to know because I've done it a thousand times.
—Mark Twain

IN THIS CHAPTER:

- A Genetic Reason Why Some Get Hooked
- Estimated Percentage of Users Who Become Dependent
- Some Inconvenient Truths About Nicotine
- Smoking Facts from the American Legacy Foundation
- Time to Get Honest with Yourself
- How Smoking Became Socially Unacceptable
- Nicotine Dependence Usually Begins Before Adulthood
- What Parents Can Do to Prevent Children from Smoking
- Break Nicotine and Other Dependencies Simultaneously
- How to Quit Smoking on Your Own
- More on Murray Kelly's Approach to Quitting
- Michael Rabinoff's 10 Tips for Quitting
- What About Acupuncture and Hypnotherapy?
- What About the Effectiveness of New Drugs?
- Do Electronic Cigarettes Reduce Harm?
- Some Treatment Options
- Your 30-Day Challenge for Nicotine Dependence

When I was going through recovery from drug use, one of my mentors said to me, "You are not really sober until you quit smoking." My reaction was immediate: "Screw you!" I didn't buy into that at all.

Now I know it's true. I eventually did quit smoking when I was eight months into recovery, and what my mentor friend had said to me had a lot to do with my decision to quit. This is a message that people in recovery need to start accepting, and it's one of the reasons why I wrote this book. If we are smoking, overeating, gambling problematically, or spending inordinate amounts of time on porn, we will have a shallower recovery from our primary toxic compulsion if we continue to smoke than we would otherwise.

Both my father and mother smoked cigarettes and drank alcohol. My mom didn't smoke that much, but the combination of alcohol and cigarettes caused her tongue cancer, which she battled for seven horrible years before it killed her. My mom's experience had a lot to do with my addressing and ultimately overcoming my nicotine addiction.

I remember going to a workshop for relationships where smoking wasn't allowed. They told us that nicotine is as powerful as heroin when it comes to suppressing feelings. Murray Kelley, executive director of the Tobacco Healing Centre in Canada, agrees: "Tobacco is more powerful than heroin for suppressing feelings."

This was all a big revelation to me. I knew that smoking is bad for your health (and I am including cigarettes, cigars, and chewing tobacco), but I never imagined that it could undermine relationships or recovery from other forms of substance abuse. I didn't know it was also getting in the way of my emotional and psychological growth.

Trying to quit smoking cigarettes was more difficult for me than getting off of heroin. Nicotine is a powerful drug. When I stopped smoking, I was nuts for a month. With heroin, you're sick for a week and then you're better. But with cigarettes, you're crazy with the anxiety and all of the other withdrawal symptoms, and they last for a month. It's a tough withdrawal and I don't envy anyone going through the process. But after having gone through it, I understand why every treatment center for every addiction should have a smoking-cessation program. Getting off nicotine dependence truly does facilitate recovery from other forms of substance abuse.

It shouldn't be surprising that my opinion is shared by millions of people who have tried to quit smoking, although it's not acknowledged by tobacco company executives who peddle and profit from this nicotine drug. One of the most amazingly irresponsible statements I've ever seen a corporate executive make was in May 2011 when the CEO of cigarette maker Philip Morris insisted to a cancer nurse at the company's annual shareholder meeting that "it is not that hard to quit." He had just conceded that his company's product is, and I am quoting, "harmful and addictive," yet he tried to rationalize the continued sale and use of cigarettes based on the habit being easy to give up.

That same week saw the publication of a landmark study in the *Proceedings of the National Academy of Science* demonstrating that genetic factors make it much more difficult for some people to quit smoking. Scientists at the Tobacco Use Research Center at the University of Pennsylvania used PET (positron-emission tomography) scans to capture images of "mu-opioid receptors" in the brains of smokers, receptors that increased their pleasure from nicotine while simultaneously making it more difficult to quit absorbing nicotine.

"The brain's opioid system plays a role in smoking rewards," concluded study coauthor Dr. Caryn Lerman, "and quitting smoking and some of the variability in our ability to quit among smokers is attributable to genetic factors. Genetic variations may make it more difficult to quit than it is for someone else who smokes the same amount for the same amount of time."

U.S Public Health Service statistics indicate that nearly half of all U.S. smokers try to quit at least once each year, yet less than 7 percent are successful. It takes the average person 8 to 11 attempts at quitting before they finally succeed. Now we know another of the many reasons why—they must not only exert sustained willpower to quit, they must overpower their genetic programming.

CEO of North Carolina treatment center Two Dreams Outer Banks Dr. Andrea Barthwell detailed other reasons why nicotine keeps so many people under its powerful influence: "Once you start smoking, if you smoke at a certain level over a certain period of time, you're dependent, there's no question about it. You're not able to stop easily. One reason is that nicotine is unique compared to other drugs because of the nicotine receptors in the human body. It's an amazing drug. Nicotine can relax the muscles of the stomach so you don't feel stuffed after eating, but it can also suppress hunger when you're hungry. It can stimulate you when you're sitting at your desk, but it can also calm you at a party. It delivers precisely what you want it to deliver. And its effect is so subtle that people don't feel impaired from it until they're not smoking and start to feel the withdrawal after 18 hours without cigarettes. If you want to know whether you're dependent on cigarettes or not, just try not to smoke for 18 hours and see how light-headed you get. It's altering your mood, and for most people, it's harder to quit than heroin."

Nicotine dependence experts I spoke with uniformly described tobacco as the most devastating addiction in human history, having killed 10 times more people worldwide than all other addictions combined. An estimated 1.7 billion people on this planet are smokers. China alone has 400 million people with a nicotine problem. The impact on health care costs by tobacco use is a big reason why every major country on record now reports runaway spending on both government and private medical programs.

A Genetic Reason Why Some Get Hooked

If you're a smoker, have you noticed how your negative moods can trigger chronic smoking or even relapses after days and weeks of not smoking? If you've ever wondered why, think in terms of genetic programming.

The first evidence for a genetic association between smoking severity and the onset of negativity or dark moods only surfaced recently, in 2008, from research on a group of test subjects conducted at the University of Pittsburgh's Department of Psychiatry. The triggers were dopamine and opioid gene variants that increased the brain's sensation of a smoking reward to counter the effects of moodiness. *(Source: "Dopamine and opioid gene variants are associated with increased smoking reward and reinforcement owing to negative mood." Kenneth A. Perkins et al. Behav Pharmacol. 2008 Sep;19(5–6):641–9.)*

A second study by the same research team found evidence in test subjects that your genes help to determine your initial sensitivity to nicotine the first time you smoke a cigarette. The genes involved function in the dopamine D4 and D2 receptors in the brain that help determine whether you will develop dependence or not. *(Source: "Gene and gene by sex associations with initial sensitivity to nicotine in nonsmokers." Kenneth A. Perkins et al. Behav Pharmacol. 2008 Sep;19(5–6):630–40.)*

Estimated Percentage of Users Who Become Dependent

Most smokers find themselves surprised by the following statistics, which compare your chances of getting hooked on cigarettes with that of alcohol and various illegal drugs. It may be hard for some folks to believe, but you run more than twice the risk of becoming dependent on nicotine than you do for alcohol.

Tobacco—31.9 percent
Heroin—23.1 percent
Cocaine—16.7 percent
Alcohol—15.4 percent
Stimulants—11.2 percent
Cannabis—9.1 percent
Psychedelics—4.9 percent
Inhalants—3.7 percent

(Source: Comparative epidemiology of dependence on tobacco, alcohol, controlled substances, and inhalants: Basic findings from the National Comorbidity Survey. Anthony JC, Warner LA, and Kessler RC. Exp Clin Psychopharmacol. Aug 1994;2(3):244–68. doi: 10.1037/1064-1297.2.3.244.)

If you're a smoker, you may be wondering if I'm trying to make a case that nicotine is too difficult a dependence to break. Maybe you're even beginning to have doubts whether you should even try. Not so! Think again! Believe me, going through withdrawal is not only something you can accomplish using the advice in this chapter, it's all very much worth it in the end. Think of it as a necessary smoker's rite of passage to better health and a longer life.

Some Inconvenient Truths About Nicotine

From Carlton Erickson, director of the Addiction Science Research and Education Center, and distinguished professor of pharmacy/toxicology at the University of Texas at Austin: Smokers are one of the more accomplished groups of rationalizers among the toxic compulsion groups of people. You have to be good at rationalizing to ignore the steady drumbeat of health industry warnings and continue pretending your nicotine dependency isn't going to eventually damage your health or even kill you. Some of those warnings:

- A Canadian study has suggested that so-called "light" or "mild" cigarettes have all of the nicotine and most of the toxins found in regular cigarettes. Six types of light cigarettes were compared to regular brands and found to have 5 percent more nicotine. Out of 44 toxins measured, the lights contained all but four. One Canadian executive has stated that the terms *mild* and *light* should be banned altogether, since there is no benefit whatsoever of these brands to public health.

- Can nicotine change the genetic susceptibility to disease in children of smokers? One study indicated that women who smoke during pregnancy might produce genetic damage that can cause their grandchildren to develop asthma. The researchers speculated that mothers who smoke might have altered their children's mitochondrial (inside the cell) DNA, which in turn could diminish immune function and raise susceptibility to asthma—traits that they could pass along to their children.

- What ingredients in tobacco are "addictive"? Obviously, nicotine, which is one of the most dependence-producing chemicals in existence. What about tars? Nope. What about other components of smoke? Nope. What about carbon monoxide? Nope. Since nicotine is such an addictive chemical, searching for other substances in tobacco that are dependence-producing is only an academic exercise. So is searching for other "reasons" for tobacco addiction. Yet some tobacco company executives are refusing to state that smoking is addictive, because they are "not sure" that nicotine is the only reason that smokers become addicted!

- Children born of mothers who smoke during pregnancy are more prone to sudden infant death syndrome (SIDS). At least one study puts this risk as second to SIDS caused by placing a sleeping baby on its stomach in a crib.

- Research has shown that newborns go through withdrawal (reduced mental function) when they are born of mothers who smoke during pregnancy. Whether this reduced mental function is temporary or permanent is still to be determined.

- There are reasons that babies born of mothers who smoke

during pregnancy are smaller and lighter than other infants. The main reason is that these babies are deprived of oxygen during their fetal growth period. When a person smokes, they inhale tars and carbon monoxide. Both of these reduce oxygen in the blood, leading to long-term effects on the person. Imagine how sensitive a developing fetus can be to such an effect!

- According to some research, regular exposure to secondhand smoke can double a person's risk of heart disease. Anyone who has been in the house of a smoker can understand the lingering smoke odor that permeates fabrics and hangs on walls, floors, etc. This residue contains tars and remnants of smoked tobacco that can be dangerous. When this material floats in higher concentrations in the air during active smoking, it can be inhaled by others and cause many of the same detrimental effects experienced by the active smoker.

- Nicotine, when given to animals, is extremely toxic. Why can humans smoke nicotine in cigarettes? Well, when cigarettes are smoked, much of the nicotine is "vaporized" (broken down), so the toxic effects are reduced.

- What are the effects of smoking cigarettes? People who smoke report that cigarettes make them more relaxed, or sometimes more energized. Beyond that, there are no beneficial effects of smoking. The detrimental effects of smoking far outweigh the few beneficial effects. The detrimental effects include greatly increased risk of lung cancer and heart disease; increased incidence of other cancers (particularly oral-pharyngeal); halitosis (bad breath); early signs of aging (wrinkled skin, etc.); and side-stream (secondhand) smoke effects on those around the smoker, which can be particularly detrimental to young children. Smoking is the leading cause of lung cancer.

Smoking Facts from the American Legacy Foundation

Finally, here are a few more damning pieces of information for you to weigh if quitting still isn't an option for you:

- 80 percent of all smokers have their first cigarette before age 18.

- One-third of all smokers began before age of 14.
- 21.7 percent of high school students smoke cigarettes.
- There are 63 cancer-causing chemicals in cigarettes, including carbon monoxide, formaldehyde, arsenic, lead, and radon.
- Smokers die an average of 10 to 14 years earlier than nonsmokers.
- 44 percent of all recovering alcoholics die of tobacco addiction.

Time to Get Honest with Yourself

Perhaps the following scoring system to determine your severity of nicotine dependence will also provide you with a standard by which to measure your success at getting yourself off the nicotine treadmill.

The Fagerström Test for Nicotine Dependence

1. How soon after you wake up do you smoke your first cigarette?
   Within 5 minutes (3 points)
   5 to 30 minutes (2 points)
   31 to 60 minutes (1 point)
   After 60 minutes (0 points)

2. Do you find it difficult not to smoke in places where you shouldn't, such as in church or school, in a movie, at the library, on a bus, in court, or in a hospital?
   Yes (1 point)
   No (0 points)

3. Which cigarette would you most hate to give up; which cigarette do you treasure the most?
   The first one in the morning (1 point)
   Any other one (0 points)

4. How many cigarettes do you smoke each day?
   10 or fewer (0 points)
   11 to 20 (1 point)
   21 to 30 (2 points)
   31 or more (3 points)

5. Do you smoke more during the first few hours after waking up than during the rest of the day?

    Yes (1 point)

    No (0 points)

6. Do you still smoke if you are so sick that you are in bed most of the day or if you have a cold or the flu and have trouble breathing?

    Yes (1 point)

    No (0 points)

Scoring: 7 to 10 points = highly dependent; 4 to 6 points = moderately dependent; less than 4 points = minimally dependent.

(Source: Adapted from "The Fagerström test for nicotine dependence: A revision of the Fagerström Tolerance Questionnaire. Heatherton TF, Kozlowski LT, Frecker RC, and Fagerström KO. Br J Addict. 1991 Sep;86(9):1119–27.)

A TREATMENT EXPERT'S EXPERIENCE WITH ADDICTION

From Dr. Cheryl Healton, professor of clinical public health at the Mailman School of Public Health of Columbia University and the president and CEO of the American Legacy Foundation: My mother was a chain-smoker while she was pregnant, so I was already born with nicotine receptors in my brain. I was probably already biologically addicted to nicotine when I was born. I come from a long family line of nicotine addicts.

I became a chain-smoker. I quit one Mother's Day. I had been chewing Nicorette around my kids, but still chain-smoking when I could. And my husband went out in the morning and just as he was leaving I said, "Please make sure you bring my Nicorette prescription. I'm out." I also was out of cigarettes, so I was out of nicotine.

And they came back about an hour later, and they brought flowers and presents and food to make brunch and everything. And I said, "Honey, did you pick up my nicotine prescription?" And he said, "Oh, rats! I forgot." And I felt a total rage. I felt like I could just reach out and wring his neck. I mean I never felt such a rage. I never touched any form of nicotine after that. That was it.

And I had a horrific six months. I couldn't write because I had been taking so much nicotine in between chewing and putting the patch on. It was crazy.

How Smoking Became Socially Unacceptable

From Joseph A. Califano Jr., secretary of the U.S. Department of Health,
Education, and Welfare (1977–1979) and founder and chairman of The
National Center on Addiction and Substance Abuse (CASA) at Columbia
University: My son is a head and neck cancer surgeon. My wife is
on the board of Memorial Sloan-Kettering. You can go to Memorial
Sloan-Kettering and you'll see people sitting in wheelchairs outside
the hospital smoking, and they have just been operated on for lung
cancer. You'll see people with tracheotomies putting the cigarette in
there. My son says, "I operate on people with throat cancer and they
come back a month later and I say, 'Are you smoking?' and they say, 'No
doc, I'm not smoking.'" He can smell the nicotine. So if in that kind of
a situation people are not willing to stop smoking, that tells you how
addictive nicotine is and how hard it is to quit.

I started a National Smoking Campaign in January of 1978. I an-
nounced it. I said that HEW (Health, Education, and Welfare) would
be a smoke-free building. I came to work the next morning and there
were employees outside demonstrating because they couldn't smoke in
their offices. Employees were saying, "We demand the right to smoke
in our office." What happened over time, and the most important
thing that happened, was that smoking became socially unacceptable
and was recognized as a major health problem. Remember, in the beginning the tobacco industry was arguing that smoking didn't cause
cancer, it didn't cause heart disease, it didn't cause emphysema or any
of these things we now know to be true.

But there were a lot of other things going on. Smoking cessation
became very financially helpful to the real estate industry. They recognized it's a hell a lot cheaper to keep a building and maintain it if you
didn't have any smoking in the building. You don't have to change the
drapes as frequently. You don't have to change the carpet, you don't
have burns, you don't have all the other problems. So they jumped on
this smoke-free building thing. Secondly, we discovered that secondhand smoke could affect people, that you could get cancer, lung cancer,
you can get heart problems. If you were a kid in a family where everybody was smoking, that became very important to people. We don't
want to expose our children to this.

Thirdly, what we recognized about smoking is something we can
recognize about almost all these addictions. Nobody starts smoking in
their mid-20s. Everybody who was hooked as an adult, almost without

exception, was hooked while they were teenagers, before they were 21. And then we said, "My God, the tobacco industry is aiming at these kids. That's who they're after." And we had this enormous disclosure of what the tobacco industry was really doing. So they became the bad guys, and all of it became a major social force.

Now, we still have a smoking problem among the poorer communities. That's greater among the uneducated people than it is the educated. I think they haven't really gotten the message, but I do think if you look at New York City, we've made smoking very expensive. A carton of cigarettes in New York City is about $115. And the impact is really showing up in the poorer neighborhoods now. We're seeing sharp declines in smoking. It's just too expensive for kids to initiate. In New York City it's cheaper to buy heroin than a pack of cigarettes.

Nicotine Dependence Usually Begins Before Adulthood

From Dr. Cheryl Healton, professor of clinical public health at the Mailman School of Public Health of Columbia University and president and CEO of the American Legacy Foundation: About 90 percent of smokers start as young people and a lot of it may have to do with the childhood trauma they experienced. With nicotine receptors you're laying down a super highway for other drugs. Ask a thousand kids, "What was the first drug you consumed?" If you exempt caffeine, the answer is going to be nicotine. That's followed by other drugs. I'm not saying that nicotine is a gateway drug in the traditional sense of the term. Though I think it could be. But it definitely alters the mind.

We know that nicotine and alcohol cross the placenta. My mother was a chain-smoker while she was pregnant. So I was already born with nicotine receptors in my brain. I was probably already addicted to nicotine when I was born.

When the kid starts smoking and particularly once they've become addicted, they may want to quit, but they don't yet have enough of a sense that there are going to be any immediate health consequences. So the motivation isn't there. That doesn't mean the teens don't quit smoking. Some do. What happens is that teens fiddle around with tobacco and then they decide to stop before they've actually been smoking frequently enough to be that biologically addicted.

What Parents Can Do to Prevent Children from Smoking

Your children's future health is up to you right now! Your attitudes, behaviors, rules, and standards help to frame how your children will respond to the toxic temptations of life, particularly the decision to smoke or not to smoke. The American Legacy Foundation, www.americanlegacy.org, has compiled this list of what parents can and should do:

1. Be a role model. Children of parents who smoke are more likely to take up smoking themselves, whereas the children of nonsmokers are less likely to smoke.
2. Make your home a smoke-free zone. Secondhand smoke is a big cause of lung cancer and heart disease among nonsmokers.
3. Don't give up trying to quit. It usually takes a half-dozen tries before a smoker successfully stops. When children see how difficult it is for a parent to quit smoking, it provides a deterrent to picking up the habit.
4. Never smoke around your children anywhere. Make your motor vehicle a smoke-free zone just like your home.
5. Educate your children about tobacco marketing. Point out how billions of dollars are spent each year by the tobacco industry in an attempt to influence kids and grab a portion of their money. Especially be vigilant about the portrayal of smoking in movies, which often influence kids to start the habit.
6. Educate your children about the health risks. Give them information showing how smoking severely affects long-term health and appearance in many ways.
7. Get to know your children's friends. Let your children know the importance of resisting peer pressure to smoke. Teach them the importance of being a role model.
8. Keep the lines of communication open with your children. Start a dialogue about tobacco at an early age, five years and up. Continue to provide them with age-appropriate information and conversations as they mature.
9. Encourage their decision-making skills. Show your children how to weigh the consequences of beginning a smoking habit.

10. If they start smoking, encourage them to quit. For helpful tips on how to encourage a child to stop, visit www.becomeanex.org.

Break Nicotine and Other Dependencies Simultaneously

Every type of toxic compulsion treatment center in the world, in my opinion, should have a nicotine-cessation program. Smoking treatment experts I spoke with are in overwhelming agreement that it's important for you to treat your nicotine dependency along with any other dependencies you have all at the same time, whether it's alcohol, drugs, gambling, or the other toxic compulsions in this book. The compelling reason for this "holistic" treatment approach becomes clear from reading the clinical evidence—if you continue to smoke, your likelihood of relapse with the other compulsions is much higher.

To illustrate what I mean, consider the findings from two major studies showing a connection between tobacco use and drug and alcohol abuse. In the first, conducted in 2005, a team of psychiatric researchers examined 1,307 smokers and their alcohol consumption levels. "Most individuals with alcohol-use disorders are dependent on both alcohol and nicotine," the researchers concluded, "and combined use of both substances is more damaging to health than use of either alone."

Those persons who quit smoking "consumed less alcohol than those who continued smoking. In addition, quitters demonstrated a significant reduction in alcohol consumption at the time of smoking cessation, which was sustained for six months post-cessation. These findings suggest that individuals in treatment for alcohol-use disorders who are motivated to stop smoking can safely be encouraged to do so without jeopardizing their sobriety." (*Source: "Smoking cessation and alcohol consumption in individuals in treatment for alcohol-use disorders." Friend KB and Pagano ME.* J Addict Dis. *2005;24(2):61–75.*)

Findings from the second study, conducted in 2009, were even more conclusive and revealing. Here is a summary:

"Numerous investigators have reported high prevalence rates of tobacco use (up to 90 percent) in patients admitted for substance abuse treatment compared to prevalence rates of 20.8 percent in the general population. Ongoing tobacco use has been linked to relapses of drug and alcohol abuse, but when individuals are encouraged to stop using tobacco in treatment, substance abuse recovery rates improve. [Another study] found that recovering alcoholics who were repeatedly encouraged to quit smoking in treatment were almost twice as likely to remain abstinent from alcohol over the one year of follow-up compared to those who received no counseling regarding their tobacco use.

"Tobacco cessation in conjunction with substance abuse treatment is still uncommon in many in- and outpatient programs that treat addiction. In fact, the majority of well-known treatment facilities in the United States providing services to medical professionals allow clients in treatment to continue using tobacco products.

"Ongoing tobacco use may serve as an independent risk factor for relapse to drugs and alcohol use . . .

"Chronic nicotine use can adversely affect plasticity and neurogenesis in the hippocampus and interfere with new learning and memory. This information suggests that tobacco cessation may be an important part of overall treatment, to enhance the patients' ability to master the educational material presented to them and effectively deal with the issues pertinent to successful recovery. New findings indicate that smoking may interfere with an alcoholic's neurocognitive recovery during the first six to nine months of alcohol abstinence." (*Source: "Tobacco use by physicians in a physician health program, implications for treatment and monitoring." Elizabeth B. Stuyt et al.* Am J Addict. *2009 Mar–Apr;18(2):103–8. doi: 10.1080/10550490902773015. Epub 18 Feb 2010.*)

Murray Kelly, executive director of the Tobacco Healing Centre in Canada, added this bit of this advice: "If your treatment center says, 'No, no, don't worry about tobacco, just quit drinking or stop using drugs,' well, keep in mind that 37 percent of the addiction counselors in the United States smoke. So they may have their own denial or agenda.

"So what I would say to any smoker is, first of all, if you have another addiction, don't be afraid of taking tobacco on. Be careful though and keep the alcohol recovery program at the center of your life. And I would recommend you go to more meetings than you would regularly go to for the first phase of your tobacco recovery. If you have other process addiction issues—sexual addiction, Internet porn, compulsive disorders—then you may need an integrated team response.

"Studies here at my center in conjunction with two other recovery centers have had the same results. Over one year, we have five times the rate of continuous sobriety if our clients stop smoking."

For those of you tackling multiple toxic compulsions, the Web site www.becomeanex.org includes chat rooms for people who are breaking alcohol and tobacco dependence at the same time.

How to Quit Smoking on Your Own

Prepared by Professor Murray Kelly, executive director, Tobacco Healing Center, Residential Treatment for Tobacco Addiction, Ottawa, Canada.

A. Know that you are fighting for your life and that you are suffering from a profound and deadly addiction.

B. Prepare yourself well and have a comprehensive recovery plan.

C. Remember, it is your mind that is addicted so it's not much use to you.

D. Build a secure support network, which will stay in place for 180 days.

E. Develop a daily practice. A daily action plan. Map the day. Every day.

F. Join a 12-Step group dedicated to tobacco recovery, such as Nicotine Anonymous. If one does not exist in your area, then start one.

G. Pick a quit day and stick to it.

H. Begin even if you become afraid.

I. Use a nicotine withdrawal strategy (can be nicotine gum or electronic cigarettes)

J. Get a sponsor or very good friend to walk with you on this path for six months.

K. Always remind yourself that you are fighting for your life and the lives of your children and grandchildren. You recover for yourself because you are worth it, but when times get really hard, focus on the idea of helping your descendants. This is what we call the "pull through." It gets us past those black holes of relapse without falling back into our old tobacco-addicted ways.

L. Learn your lesson well, incorporate it into your recovery plan, and proceed with this new information. Relapse is normal, and using this approach ensures you stay in recovery and break free from this most powerful of all addictions.

Commit to this process and dedicate your efforts to your own recovery. If you need assistance or wish to join an online support community come to the www.tobaccohealingcenter.com Web site. Good luck on your journey to freedom.

Prof. Kelly's three questions

To supplement the information provided above, Prof. Kelly designed these questions to provide you or your counselor with enough information to structure a "patch" approach to treatment, which will give you a "steady state" of nicotine levels and keep you out of withdrawal while you learn how to live tobacco-free.

1. **How old where you when you started smoking?**
   If you started before 16, you may have a loss issue in childhood that needs attending to and tobacco is part of your survival strategy.

2. **How long after rising do you need a smoke?**
   If you smoke within 20 minutes after rising, it may be useful to awaken with high nicotine levels so you will not relapse in the morning. Put a patch on about two hours before you rise.

3. **How many cigarettes do you smoke on a bad day?**
   If you smoke 15 or more on tough days, then you may find it helpful to use two patches in rotation. Put one on about two hours before you rise and another at 1 p.m. Then simply rotate through the 24-hour period for as long as it takes to feel free.

Self-dosing

It has proven very useful to have a means of self-dosing with nicotine when under stress to prevent a buildup leading to relapse. We suggest an inhaler, 4 mg. nicotine gum, or the nicotine lozenges. Simply dose until you feel relaxed and the stress buildup has passed.

Together, the patch provides the steady release of nicotine and the self-dosing devices allow for self-regulating under stressful conditions.

More on Murray Kelly's Approach to Quitting

"I'm a big believer in the comprehensive assessment of your own condition," said Prof. Kelly, executive director of the Tobacco Healing Centre in Canada. "If you can get a professional to help you, you're way ahead in the game. And you can design your own recovery plan and you can implement it. You can go to Nicotine Anonymous as your 12-Step grounding.

"Nicotine replacement is a very good strategy. I will recommend it for a hundred days. I recommend that for the first 30 days you self-dose the nicotine and you wear a patch for your steady-state delivery and use a self-dosing mechanism like the inhaler, the lozenge, or the gum.

"The inhaler is very much like a cigarette or a cigar. It allows you to self-dose and self-regulate through stressful times until you learn other ways to cope—meditation, going to meetings, a long walk, fitness, prayer, acupuncture, yoga, whatever the combination of skills, any of the calming ways to relax. Smokeless electronic cigarettes—anything that helps the tobacco-addicted person get that smoke out of their lungs and out of their bloodstream—are recommended.

"Nicotine stimulates the brain's neurotransmitters and dopamine is released. But it also stimulates the panic and anxiety centers causing it to bulk up and then overreact to external stimulation for the rest of your life. And the only way to heal it is to stop smoking, and then it takes about four-and-a-half months for the brain to reset so that a hug, a gesture, or a nice walk releases the same dopamine that we become dependent on to be released through the nicotine gas.

"When the nicotine gas comes into your brain, it crashes in there with a greater force than mainline heroin. That's in fact what we're addicted to. At my center, I measure their blood levels and I put them on nicotine replacement that's close to their blood levels when they smoke and 30 days later they can't even remember they had a patch on. It turns out that it's not about the drug nicotine. It's about the delivery system of the gas going into the lungs, into the bloodstream, and wham, smacking into the brain in seven seconds.

"When you quit smoking, the real challenge is to self-regulate your anxiety and your stress. I have never experienced anything in my own personal life or in my therapeutic instrument offerings that has more benefit over the long term than meditation. And it doesn't have to be where the consciousness of the creator of the universe springs into your soul articulated. In fact, if that happens, you've probably made a mistake. It's just the simple fact of being quiet and accepting that moment as it ends and letting the mind have a rest from speculating about what could be. Meditation is just a calm, loving, relaxing tool.

"The art of meditation is quieting the mind, quieting the heart and soul, and coming into a composed stillness. And in that moment, your mind is at peace; everything is rock solid. And as you do that for 21 days in a row, it changes everything in the way you process information.

"I have my clients do very deep breathing work as well, and I find that just before we do meditation, everybody gets into their grounded feeling and it goes really well. And then we have a break for 20 minutes. We all come back for our post-session briefing. We don't want anybody going back to the room with an issue that's hurting them. We'll have a meditation to end that, and literally after three or four days of that, we look like zombies in a yoga center. It's probably not the best way to put it, but we're in touch finally with something that's bigger and greater than our own single selves.

"You'll notice in 12-Step programs the people who get the higher power thing, whatever that is, you really can't tell anybody what that is. It's like trying to tell somebody what love is. You know what it is, but darn it if you can tell anybody about it. But you can get there, you can get to a higher power plane of existential calm by using meditation, and it gradually becomes an energy that leads you to a higher power."

If you need support in achieving your goal, check out www.healthrally .com.

Michael Rabinoff's 10 Tips for Quitting

From Michael Rabinoff, DO, PhD, author of Ending the Tobacco Holocaust *(2010, Elite Books), and psychiatrist, UCLA research faculty. He also works with clients on ending their smoking dependence. visit www.tobac-cobook.com/tobacco-holocaust-top-ten-tips.html:*

1. **Have a "big enough why."** Spend time thinking about why you want to quit. Then write down the reasons. Post your written reasons on your refrigerator and elsewhere, and let the list remind you every day of these important reasons. It's your life, so be motivated to succeed. Some famous motivational speakers and "gurus" use leverage to give the smoker motivation to quit. Tony Robbins, for example, has charged people $15,000 or more for a one-hour smoking cessation session. If you're willing to pay $15,000 to quit, you're probably motivated, and also more likely to succeed. Other trainers may have the person (besides paying a fair amount of money) do tasks, such as homework exercises, before the person is taken as a client. Doing so ensures that the person is motivated to quit, which helps get better results. My tip is for you to determine the real reasons you want to quit and to internally experience how important it is for you to quit once you know your big enough why. Take time every day to experience the feeling of how important it is for you to quit, once you know your personal reasons ... once you know your big enough "why."

2. **Throw away all cigarettes and related items.** Toss them in the garbage. All cigarettes, matches, ashtrays, lighters, rolling papers, cigars, hookahs, logo clothing, and other items tobacco companies use to brand you as a smoker. Discard anything to do with smoking. Don't allow any of that stuff at home, at work, or in your car. Some say to put away ashtrays and lighters. I say throw them away, so that it will cost you money if you don't stick to your goal of quitting.

3. **Set a quit date.** Determine a definite date when you will quit or will start a gradual scheduled reduction program. For more information on gradual scheduled reduction, see pages 341–343 in *Ending the Tobacco Holocaust*.

4. **Change your identity and self-image to "I am a nonsmoker."** You are no longer a smoker having a problem with quitting. Change your identity to that of a nonsmoker, so that smoking isn't congruent with who you are. In a calm moment, you may want to close your eyes and visualize yourself as smoke-free, happily breathing fresh healthy air into your lungs, and feeling relaxed and refreshed doing so.

5. **Share your goal with friends and family.** Tell them you're quitting and ask for their support in helping you to do so. (Hypnotist Marshall Sylver has people come up on stage and tell the audience that if any one of them ever sees them smoke again, then that person from the audience can collect $1,000 from them. How's that for social and financial motivation?)

6. **Avoid all triggers and learn new replacement behaviors.** Identify your personal triggers for smoking beforehand and write them down. Avoid alcohol, coffee, and other triggers for smoking. If you smoke when you are anxious, replace that behavior with a new one, perhaps simply breathing in fresh air in a relaxing manner. Some possible relaxation methods include progressive muscle relaxation, deep breathing, internal visualization, and meditation. Some people learn yoga, meditation on the breath, and other techniques to quickly relax and to replace the urge to smoke. When's the last time you just took a good ol' deep breath and relaxed? If you've been drawing in cigarette-poisoned air to get that deep breath, skip the poison and just breathe the fresh air. Over the long run, your body will thank you. An excellent book to help you avoid temptation, deal with urges to smoke, and not relapse once you have quit is *Out of the Ashes: Help for People Who Have Stopped Smoking*, by Peter and Peggy Holmes.

7. **Set a no-smoking policy.** Don't allow anyone to smoke in your home or car and avoid other people when they are smoking. Even a few whiffs of smoke have been known to entice people trying to quit back to smoking. According to Laura Juliano, PhD, ". . . the relapse process begins with a single smoking episode, which may appear at the outset to be a *lapse* or a *slip*. Although it is possible that an individual could achieve long-term abstinence despite having had a smoking lapse, this is rarely the case. Rather, 79 to 97 percent of individuals who experience a smoking lapse subsequently return to some pattern of regular smoking (indicated by three or more consecutive days of smoking)." Assert your right to fresh air. Take your efforts seriously and (as much as possible) avoid all tobacco smoke. Those efforts will pay off when you successfully quit.

8. **Get support.** Utilize group counseling, an individual counselor, Nicotine Anonymous, and/or quitlines. For example, the National Cancer Institute Smoking Quitline toll-free number

is 1-877-44U-QUIT. The most recent scientific data show that people who try to quit on their own have less than a 5 percent chance of being smoke-free one year later.

9. **Use scientifically proven methods.** Use methods that have been confirmed to be effective by research. When testing single methods in rigorously designed studies, the best results have been shown in studies using medications, such as with the new Chantix (varenicline), bupropion SR (brand name Zyban or Wellbutrin), or with second-line medications, nortriptyline hydrochloride, or clonidine. Other medications available are supported by less data than those named above, and new medications may be approved in the next few years. Nicotine replacement therapies have helped many people, though the data is less dramatic for them than for medications. These therapies include the nicotine patch, nicotine gum, nicotine nasal spray, and the nicotine inhaler. (Don't smoke when you use these replacement methods.) I believe that gradual, scheduled reduction methods have the potential to be more effective than nicotine replacement therapies (see pages 341–343 in *Ending the Tobacco Holocaust*).

10. **Combine methods and "commit to quit."** Combining methods for quitting seems to be most effective, though there are far fewer studies that have tested the many possible combinations than have tested single methods. At Kaiser Permanente, the best results seem to be obtained when patients take a seven-week class, use the nicotine patch and bupropion SR, talk with a counselor from the smoking cessation department, and also use outside quitting resources, such as books, the Internet, quitlines, and/or Nicotine Anonymous. Your goal isn't to prove one method or the other; it is to quit smoking and live a healthy life. So put in the effort for your own physical and financial well-being, as well as your family's, your friends', and society's.

I may get some flak from colleagues for saying this, but I also think that if the standard methods don't work for you, try any non-harmful method that fits your budget, that you like, and that you think may help you to quit. While methods such as hypnosis haven't been proven effective according to the standards required by the scientific community, many people claim it has helped them (e.g., hypnosis worked for celebrities Matt Damon and Ben Affleck, but not for Robert Downey Jr.). Also, there's no reason why methods such as hypnosis can't be combined with standard scientifically proven methods (such approaches are called complementary medicine). One caution: Herbal supplements may have interactions with medications, so talk with your physician before you try them.

If money and time are big issues, try the scientifically proven methods first. However, we're talking about your life here, so if you're not constrained by money and time limitations, then invest your money and time to be successful at quitting. If using non-harmful complementary methods helps you to achieve success, that's wonderful.

Never give up! The average smoker takes 10 to 11 attempts to finally quit. (Most smokers try repeatedly to quit on their own with no outside help and we know that approach typically gets poor results.) With current methods, as tested in large populations, there still is more than a 50 percent chance of not succeeding for one year. I hope that doesn't happen to you, but if it does, don't give up. More than 50 percent of all smokers have successfully quit. View each attempt as a learning experience on the way to successfully quitting.

On the other hand, if this is your first attempt to quit, I don't want to influence you to believe that you need to attempt quitting many times before you can be successful. Millions of people have been successful at quitting for life with their first attempt to quit. For a first-time attempt it might be helpful to remember the words of the *Star Wars* Jedi master Yoda: "Do, or do not. There is no 'try.'"

What About Acupuncture and Hypnotherapy?

You've probably heard some of the same anecdotes that I have about the usefulness of acupuncture or hypnosis in smoking cessation efforts. Some people swear the procedures helped them quit smoking when all other methods failed.

But are the two techniques "evidence based," which is to say, do peer-reviewed, controlled science studies back up the effectiveness claims? I decided to find out.

The best way to assess the overall effectiveness of any medical procedure is to find a study that evaluates the consensus findings of all the other studies that had previously been done on the subject. Here is what I found concerning acupuncture and hypnotherapy.

"There is no consistent, bias-free evidence that acupuncture [is] effective for smoking cessation," concluded a 2011 survey of 33 studies of acupuncture and smoking. "But lack of evidence and methodological problems mean that no firm conclusions can be drawn." In other words, this procedure may or may not be effective for you, but so far there isn't enough evidence to give it a stamp of approval by medical science. *(Source: "Acupuncture and related interventions for smoking cessation." Adrian R White et al.* Cochrane Database Syst Rev. *doi: 10.1002/14651858.CD000009.pub3. Epub 19 Jan 2011.)*

"We have not shown that hypnotherapy has a greater effect on six-month quit rates than other interventions or no treatment," concluded a 2010 survey of 11 published studies comparing hypnotherapy with other treatment interventions. "There is not enough evidence to show whether hypnotherapy could be as effective as counseling treatment." *(Source: "Hypnotherapy for smoking cessation." Joanne Barnes et al.* Cochrane Database Syst Rev. *2010 Oct 6;(10):CD001008.)*

Don't interpret my mention of these two skeptical study surveys as a personal recommendation against using acupuncture or hypnotherapy to break your smoking habit. Either method might work for you. They just don't work for everyone. It's important to have the available scientific evidence on the record for you to evaluate how best to spend your money and time.

Though it isn't hypnotherapy, there are other ways to "retrain your brain" to stop smoking, such as the CD developed by Dr. Frank Lawlis, director of Psychological Services at Origins Recovery Center, available at www.mindbodyseries.com.

What About the Effectiveness of New Drugs?

Western countries have access to Pfizer Inc.'s pill Chantix to help smokers quit, but a 12-week supply runs about $300 and in the United States, the drug carries a warning label for psychiatric risks.

Eastern Europe and Russia have had access for at least four decades to a Bulgarian antismoking treatment drug called Cytisine, sold as Tabex, made from laburnum seeds, which contain a natural nicotine substitute. The drug has attracted interest here. Generic versions cost $17 or less a month, a price cheap enough for most developing countries, where two-thirds of the world's one billion smokers live. An additional advantage is that Cytisine use shows no signs of any serious side effects.

A September 2011 study in *The New England Journal of Medicine* tested Cytisine on 740 smokers in Poland, comparing them to people who unknowingly took placebo (sugar) pills. After one year, 8.4 percent of those taking Cytisine had stopped smoking compared to 2.4 percent of the dummy pill-takers. That was a much lower success rate than the 15 to 30 percent of people who quit by using Chantix, according to studies done on that drug.

Do Electronic Cigarettes Reduce Harm?

If you want to reduce the negative health consequences of smoking, but you aren't ready for smoking cessation or the use of drugs, then electronic cigarettes may be an option. These can be considered either a smokeless smoking alternative to cigarettes or a tool toward a smoking cessation goal.

These devices are handheld and deliver battery-powered vaporized nicotine without combusting tobacco. The act of "smoking" one of these devices is called "vaping" because the user is inhaling just vapor rather than smoke, which is a good thing since smoke typically contains thousands of different trace amounts of chemicals, many of which are harmful to health. By contrast, the primary components of electronic cigarette cartridges are propylene glycol, glycerin, and nicotine. Neither the tobacco industry nor the pharmaceutical industry manufactures or distributes these devices.

"We conclude that electronic cigarettes show tremendous promise in the fight against tobacco-related morbidity and mortality," wrote the authors of a 2010 study. *(Source: "Electronic cigarettes as a harm reduction strategy for tobacco control: A step forward or a repeat of past mistakes?" Cahn Z and Sigel M. JPHP. 2011 Feb;32(1):16–31. doi:10.1057/ jphp.2010.41. Epub 2010 Dec 9.)*

Details about Virgin Vapor, an electronic device worth recommending, can be found at www.virginvapor.com. What sets Virgin Vapor apart from other electronic cigarettes is the e-liquid formula, which is flavored with a choice of 100 USDA certified organic flavorings ranging from blueberry to banana-nut muffin and chocolate cake espresso. The smokable liquid also doesn't contain unhealthy chemical additives of any sort and is packaged in glass rather than plastic bottles. Flavors can also be customized.

Some Treatment Options

For more information about the self-help oriented treatments mentioned most frequently by the experts interviewed for this book, along with valuable tips about how to utilize these methods and tools, consult the following:

- Acupuncture, Seven Self-Care Tools, p. 264
- 12-Step Programs, Seven Self-Care Tools, p. 240
- Meditation, Seven Self-Care Tools, p. 253
- Mindfulness, Seven Self-Care Tools, p. 249

Your 30-Day Challenge for Nicotine Dependence

Do you have a bad habit or a dependency? Here is another chance to find out.

You have answered the questionnaires for this toxic compulsion. You have read through what the experts have to say. You have thought about the extent to which you exhibit the behaviors associated with either a nondependent use disorder or a dependency.

Do you still have any doubt about whether you have just a bad habit, or whether your behavior meets the criteria for a dependency?

Create a 30-day challenge for yourself.

Don't smoke a single cigarette, cigar, or chew tobacco for 30 days. If you can do that, you don't have a dependency on nicotine.

Unlike the other toxic compulsion challenges, this one is very simple and straightforward. It's all or nothing. If you're smoking, you're addicted, especially if it's cigarettes.

PART TWO

Which Treatment Tools Work Best for You?

VIII

I Love an Addict, How Can I Help Myself?

More than those who hate you, more than all your enemies, an undisciplined mind does greater harm.
   —Buddha, from *The Dhammapada*

If you want to be happy, set a goal that commands your thoughts, liberates your energy and inspires your hopes.
   —Andrew Carnegie

You could say this chapter is about the Eighth Toxic Compulsion—codependency, otherwise known as being "stuck," because the family system you grew up in is altered and dramatically affected by the addictive behaviors of one of its members. If you don't address this collective corrosion, you may not be able to use the self-care tools in this book very effectively or stay in recovery very long.

It was the cofounder of Alcoholics Anonymous, Bill Wilson, who said: "If you sober up a horse thief, you've got a sober horse thief." By the same token, even if you clean up a person with a dependency for any of these toxic compulsions, there is probably a codependent somebody in that person's life who is still stuck in a system of behaviors that can undermine recovery.

This subject is the overlooked holy grail of recovery. It is the issue that needs to be fundamentally addressed, not only by the people who are affected by somebody's addiction disease, but also by the addicts themselves. Even when you take the alcohol and drugs and other compulsions out of their life and out of the family structure, their system is still broken, still corroded by years of neglect. The relational toxicity is like a virus of attitudes and perceptions, affecting how you see the world, how you relate to life.

People come to me all the time and they say, "My daughter has a problem," or "My son has a problem," or "My wife has a problem." And I reply, "Okay, you want to know what to do? You're not going to like it." And they go, "Oh, really?" They are sort of surprised. I tell them, "You go take care of yourself." And usually they react with, "No, you don't get it. My son (or daughter or other loved one) has the problem, not me." They simply don't want to see how they are a part of the problem.

In AA's big book on alcoholism there is the statement "The root cause of our alcoholism is our defective relations with others." That statement applies to all of the toxic compulsions discussed in this book, not just alcoholism. We ruin our relationships, and that makes us so uncomfortable we further engage in the toxic compulsions to distract ourselves. This is at the core of how enabling behaviors evolve.

Most enablers believe they're doing something for somebody who is in trouble and they wrap it up in this idea that "My kid is drowning and I'm going to save them." What kind of monster wouldn't try to save their loved one, right? The problem is they need to realize their family dynamic is probably at the center of why the loved one is drowning in a compulsion. Yes, there is a genetic component, and yes, there is a childhood trauma component, but everything is exacerbated by a toxic family dynamic. If that is unaddressed, it creates an enabling highway, and the enabler has as much invested in that highway as the person suffering with the active addiction.

Both of my parents had a problem with alcohol. My mother was a powerful and amazing woman in so many ways. Yet her life was a mess not just because of her circumstances, which included two brothers who were assassinated and a divorce. I don't diminish the importance of her circumstances. But her alcoholism never allowed her to process these experiences, and to deal with and move on from it. She was stuck, and we children had to stand by and watch this person we loved in unbelievable pain act it out in all sorts of ways. We were powerless to do anything about it. There was nothing I could do that would help her, and that affected me for the rest of my life.

If somebody is engaged in their addiction and they're not dying, and I mean like literally dying on a floor somewhere, the family and loved ones need to establish firm boundaries. There was a time when I was dying on a floor and I couldn't get up. I had pleurisy and pneumonia. I was on the methadone maintenance program. I was shooting cocaine every day, and I was in law school. I was on the floor of my apartment and I couldn't get up. All I could do was dial my mother. I didn't want to dial 911 because I was afraid it might get the media involved. So I called my mother, the last person I wanted to call. She came over and I remember her stepping over my body to get to the phone. I'm crying because I literally can't get up off the floor. My mother called somebody and an ambulance took me to a New York hospital. They saved me and convinced me to go to rehab, and my only question was, "Can I get methadone in rehab?"

At that point, somebody had to save me. Otherwise, I would have died. If my mother had said, "No, you're a drug addict. I'm not coming over there," I might have died. So you first of all have to address the urgent life-and-death stuff. Once that was done, she should have said to me, "Look, these are your options. You go to treatment. If you don't go to treatment, lose my number. There's no money, there's no nothing. I will support you in your recovery for a period of time. Then you're on your own. I really mean it." And if she had done that, my drug addiction probably would have ended that day.

But my mother wasn't healthy enough to do it. All of the stuff she did and who she was—giving up her life for her kids, the family she came from, her disappointments in life, her need to feel like the mother of the year—all made her an enabler. It was all about her. She loved me and cared about me and wanted me to be healthy, but it was really all about her.

So I say to people in a relationship with an addict, go take care of yourself and you will change everything. Most people don't get it, or won't do it. They don't understand the connection. I am hoping this section of the book will help to make those interconnections much clearer and give urgency to the need to break free of them.

You have to focus on yourself. You must take care of yourself. When you do that, everything changes in the family system, because a sick system cannot tolerate somebody who is healthy. Either you leave the system, or the system changes. Many people think that seems too drastic. They don't grasp how they are the product of a system that's brilliant at obscuring reality. They don't see how the attitude of family and friends that says, "Okay, let's just get him clean and sober and we're done," is the real problem.

I am here to tell you there is no immediate gratification in this process. The process is difficult, painful, and it takes courage. The best you can hope for is that you'll stop your enabling. But I can also reassure you that there is freedom at the end of this road no matter who you are, whether you're the toxic compulsion person or the victim of a toxic compulsion person. There is freedom awaiting you, in the way you live your life. That will be the best narcotic you've ever had.

Recovery isn't about just putting down the substances or stopping the compulsion processes. It's about changing the core of who we are, and that's a process that could last a lifetime and probably will.

So be gentle with yourself. But be as honest as you can be. Understand this as a process and your vision will change over time. It will change if you have commitment. Once you see more clearly, you simply can't do it anymore. The clarity will absolutely obliterate your need to engage in these toxic enabling behaviors.

How Stuck Are You?

Are you an enabler? Are you unknowingly helping to perpetuate someone's compulsion problem? If you're not sure, here is a simple litmus test devised by treatment experts Dr. Morteza Kahleghi and Dr. Karen Khaleghi in their book *The Anatomy of Addiction* (2011, Palgrave Macmillan): "Empowering someone is doing something for someone, or helping him to do something that he does not have the capacity to do himself; enabling is doing something for someone that she can do, or very well ought to be doing, for herself."

If you're unsure whether you're contributing to someone's self-destructive behaviors, ask yourself the following series of questions:

Do I make excuses, to myself and others, for the person's bad behaviors and judgment? This might include minimizing the person's compulsion control problem, calling it a "passing phase"; or it might be contacting a teacher or a boss with excuses for the person when he or she fails to show up on time.

Do I remain silent in order to avoid confrontations and arguments? This can be due to a fear of losing the person's love, or a fear of being subjected to verbal abuse or physical reactions when you voice an opinion.

Do I take on responsibilities that should rightfully be the other person's? This might include paying an adult child's bills or keeping their personal affairs in order when they are fully capable of doing so on their own.

Another Way to Know If You're "Stuck"

Miles Adcox, CEO of Onsite Workshops (www.onsiteworkshops. com), uses a 10-point evaluation of "stuckness." His definition was developed in 1989 by 22 treatment experts: Codependency is a pattern of painful dependency on compulsive behaviors and on approval from others in an attempt to find safety, self-worth, and identity.

Answer the following 10 questions as honestly as you can:

- Do you feel responsible for other people's thoughts, actions, feelings, and well being?
- Is it easier for you to feel and express anger toward injustices done to others than about injustices done to you?
- Do you feel best and most comfortable when you are giving to others?
- Do you feel insecure and guilty when someone gives to you?
- Do you feel compelled to help other people resolve their problems? Is that something you live for?
- Do you lose interest in your own life when you are involved with someone?
- Are you often unable to stop talking, thinking, or feeling about someone else?
- Do you stay in relationships that don't work and tolerate abuse to keep people loving you?
- Do you leave bad relationships only to form new ones that turn out just as bad?
- Do you feel empty, bored, or worthless if you don't have someone in your life to take care of, or if you have no problems to solve or crisis to deal with?

The more yes answers you gave to these questions, the deeper into a codependency "stuck" pattern you probably find yourself.

What Family Treatment Experts Advise

In their book *Unchain Your Brain: 10 Steps to Breaking the Addictions That Steal Your Life* (2010, MindWorks Press), Dr. Daniel G. Amen and Dr. David E. Smith described the importance of treating addiction as a family affair and an opportunity to create a brain-healthy family. People who simply drop their child or relative off at a treatment facility and say, "Fix this person," usually are afraid someone will point out their role in contributing to the problem or that they have the problem themselves.

"To heal one person, the whole family must be healed," the two doctors wrote. "Family members have to examine their own behaviors to determine how they might be contributing to the problem and be willing to change their ways. They need to get involved in the addicted person's treatment and recovery by attending family day events at treatment centers, participating in family therapy or couples therapy, and accompanying them to support groups."

Some other perspectives follow below.

Families hold a life preserver

From Prof. Howard Shaffer, associate professor of psychology, Harvard Medical School, and director, Division on Addictions, the Cambridge Health Alliance: Families of people with addiction need to do the same kind of assessment that an addict does. They really have to look at their biological, psychological, and social activities to see whether they've contributed to this addiction unknowingly or knowingly, and whether they have to make changes in order to help their loved ones out of the situation they're in. Even if they find a genetic predisposition from generations past, but no addiction for several generations, it's easy to blame the other person and say, "Hey, they've got the same problem." The family needs to educate itself about the nature of addiction. They need to learn how to minimize relapse opportunities for their loved one. Because if they love this person, they should view themselves as holding a life preserver for somebody who's fallen overboard. They can throw the life preserver in good conscience, but they've got to hold on to the other end.

Are families harder to treat than addicts?

From Miles Adcox, CEO of Onsite Workshops in Tennessee, devoted to therapeutic trauma and compulsivity programs: When you get underneath the codependence, you get a lot of the same compulsive behaviors and a lot of the same symptoms that come from the compulsivity. So you're looking at three categories of symptoms that we see in a lot of codependences: delusion (meaning denial), emotional suppression, and compulsive behaviors. What you see on both sides is chronic low self-worth and relationship problems. Untreated codependency can cause medical problems, and anxiety and stress can get to a point where you can be damaged physically as well. You hear a lot of times from addiction professionals that the family is harder to talk to than the patient. They say, "I'm more frustrated with the family than with the patient." And the reason they say that is because a high percentage of professionals in substance abuse counseling and treatment are recovering addicts and alcoholics themselves. They've done their work to get sober, so there's a level of comfort for them to sit in front of another addict early on in recovery. But a large majority of families have not done their stage-two work. They haven't done their codependency relationship work. So when the family member has the same level of resistance that is seen in the addict, there's a real discomfort . . . and we don't know what to do with them.

What we've found is that almost everybody with addiction has some level of trauma. And in codependency we found the same thing. So you could say that all self-defeating, self-destructive, persistent, resistant-to-change behavior is rooted in trauma—trauma that was most likely born out of a family system. I actually see this a little stronger in the process addictions, such as gambling. It manifests itself a little differently because it wears a different mask. In chemical dependency or alcohol, enabling is real clear. It's because you've got one person who's doing this behavior. And it could kill him at any time. And yet you've got another person who comes in and enables that to continue happening. So most people from afar can sit back and look at that and say, "Okay, that's codependency and that's addiction; that's really clear." I challenge people in our field to have the same level of empathy for the family as they do for the addict, because nobody is really waving the codependency flag or talking about it in treatment much anymore.

Use your leverage to get an addict's attention

From Dr. Drew Pinsky, addiction medicine specialist and clinical professor of psychiatry, University of Southern California School of Medicine: The one thing I tell family members is to use whatever leverage you have. Remember, it's not about you, it's about them. So you have to come from a loving place, but you can come from a very firm place, too. Use law enforcement, use money, use anything you can to get their attention. You may not get their attention until they're sitting in the jail, homeless, and you're saying, "I'm sorry, I'm not going to bail you out." That gets their attention.

You must confront someone with firm caring

From Dr. Herbert Kleber, director of the Division on Substance Abuse at the Columbia University College of Physicians and Surgeons and former deputy director for demand reduction in the White House Office of National Drug Control Policy: When you have someone, either a family member or a friend, who has problems with alcohol or other drugs and you want to help them, nagging them is not going to help. You have to somehow show them that you not only care, but that you're not going to continue to put up with their behavior. So if the two of you go out together and he insists on wanting to drive home and you let him drive, you're not doing a favor for your friend, let alone for yourself. So you want to be supportive, but you don't want to jeopardize your safety or, in a sense, enable that individual by acting as if what he's doing is perfectly fine. You have to carefully confront the individual in a way that comes across as loving, that says you care, but also can't always be covering up or apologizing, doing all those things that mean "enable."

You must learn to "own" the process

From Sid Goodman, director, Caron Renaissance treatment facility, Florida: Families do not cause nor can they hope to cure addiction in their loved ones. Neither can treatment staff. The family contribution to later addictive disease is the failure to allow their children to complete necessary developmental tasks. But, both staff and families can play vital roles in the recovery process. A recognition that the work must be done by the addict is, in fact, crucial to understanding addiction as a biopsychosocial disease. It may take a village to nurture that process, but there is no alternative to the patient working through these defensive structures and owning the process.

You must work the steps with your partner

From Dr. Patrick Carnes, psychologist, author, and former clinical director of sexual disorders services, The Meadows, Arizona: In Recovering Couples Anonymous (RCA), they call it the three-legged stool: my recovery, your recovery, our recovery. In family therapy, to treat somebody individually about something that is a couples or family problem often makes things worse. They get sent off separately to Al-Anon, AA, SA, S-Anon, JA, or J-Anon, and they go to their separate meetings and tell their stories. But it's a sympathetic audience. She's in her group and the women are saying, "You don't have to let him walk all over you." And he's in his group and they say, "You've got system boundaries with her." So they come home and it's like the shootout at the O.K. Corral. The 12 Steps are master works of neuroscience, but you have to do it together with your partner. In RCA, the honesty goes up and, with it, the health of the relationship, because you've got other couples watching. Couples speak to you differently about both sides of the story. So if you're in recovery and are a couple, you've got to realize that you do a dance together and you've got to learn how to use the 12 Steps together as a couple.

Codependency in Asia is about shame

From Billy Pick, regional advisor, Office of HIV/AIDS, Bureau for Global Health, United States Agency for International Development: In Asia the cultures are based on family. They don't view addiction as a disease over there. It's viewed as a kind of moral failing. It's not only seen as a moral failing by you, but it's a moral failing by your entire family. So codependency in Asia is astronomical, particularly concerning the youth, because parents don't want neighbors to know their kid has a problem. That would embarrass the entire family. It's a shame-based culture, and everything is about outward appearances. The first family counseling I ever saw in China was a bunch of guys sitting there with their heads down and a mother yelling at them about how embarrassed the family was and how much shame they had brought on the family. They don't understand the concept of codependence yet. They would say that's how families are supposed to behave.

Say you care, and there are consequences

From Pamela Hyde, administrator, Substance Abuse and Mental Health Services Administration (SAMHSA): Sometimes people wonder, "What can I do? I see my friend who's clearly doing what she shouldn't and how can I deal with that?" It's everything from expressing concern, being open to discussion, trying to not preach, but trying to raise concerns, trying to ask questions about whether or not that person thinks about that as a problem or not; maybe providing information that sometimes adults are drinking at levels they don't realize are problematic. And just letting people know that there's a concern. I think one of the biggest issues is people understanding that somebody else cares about them, and offering to say, "What you're doing is problematic for yourself and for your family and friends." To change their life, some people just need family or friends to say they care, and that if the behavior continues there will be consequences.

Letting a group of people love you

From Dr. Jeffrey D. Roth, addiction psychiatrist, author, editor of Journal of Groups in Addiction Recovery, *and medical director, Working Sobriety Chicago:* "How can I get him to stop?" What I say to that person is, "Who wants to help right now?" If the person says, "I want to help get my husband to stop drinking," I'll say, "If you want your husband to stop drinking, you may need to lead the way into recovery. Are you willing to do that?" If the person says, "I'll do anything that it takes." I'll say, "Really?" And they'll say, "Yes." And I'll say, "Are you willing to go to a meeting?" And they'll say, "You want me to go into an AA meeting?" And I'll say, "No, unless you have a problem with drinking, in which case, yes, you can go to an AA meeting. But since you're concerned about your husband's drinking, have you ever heard of Al-Anon?" Some have, some haven't. Some of them have various different excuses why they don't want to go to Al-Anon: "Oh, I hate those meetings," or, "I went to one five years ago and all that happened was I listened to everybody else's problems and I felt worse than I felt before." I'll say, "Oh, isn't that interesting? You went to the Al-Anon meeting to try and help everybody else, just like you're trying to help your husband, and it didn't work. Well, congratulations. I guess maybe you learned something at that meeting."

"Would you be willing to go to an Al-Anon meeting and consider the possibility that instead of giving all those people help, that you instead take their help?" And the person will say, "Those people were messed up. They could never be of any help to me." And my next response is, "Well I tell you what, how about we do a diagnostic test. This is not going to be therapeutic. You're not going to enjoy this. It's not going to make you feel any better. I'd like to simply do it as a diagnostic test because even if you're not interested in going to Al-Anon, you're saying you're interested in coming to group psychotherapy with me." And my experience is that if you're allergic to any support from any group, in Al-Anon you're probably going to be allergic to the support that you're going to get there.

Let's find out what the allergy is now before you come into a group. There's no point coming into group and then leaving right away and thinking you've had enough failures in your life. You think you're a failure because your husband hasn't stopped drinking. So go to the Al-Anon meeting, sit there, and don't even give them your real name. Don't introduce yourself. After you attend the meeting, I'd like you to make a list of 10 reasons why it was the worst experience in your whole life. Bring it back to me and let's talk about it, because whatever it is you didn't like about the Al-Anon meeting, you're going to find you don't like about what I do. Because even though the structure is very different, it's a group of people. And my speculation is you may need to get used to people loving you in order to take in some love from your husband. What do you have to lose?

Children sense when something is wrong

From Jerry Moe, vice president and national director, Children's Programs for the Betty Ford Center and advisory board member of the National Association for Children of Alcoholics: A woman who was in treatment here at the center had kids who were seven, eight, and nine. I must have met with her four or five times, trying to convince her to let the kids come to the children's program, because what so often happens in treatment is people who go into treatment for their own addiction often grew up in a family where there is addiction. That's generational; it gets passed down. Well, finally she said, "Okay, here is the deal. My kids can come to the children's program provided that"—and she took out a piece of paper. She had, like, six conditions I had to follow: I couldn't talk about this, couldn't do this, you can't mention this. And you know what? I looked at her and said, "Absolutely." And so the kids came into the program.

And what's really different about what we do is that we work with boys and girls for 25 hours over four days. You really begin to see what's going on in their lives. So 45 minutes into the program that day we take a break. We show the kids where the restrooms are, and I'm waiting outside for the seven-year-old boy to come out. He comes out and we're walking back to the group room and he grabs my sleeve and tugs it really hard. He points for me to bend down because he wants to whisper and he says, "Do you want to know a secret?" And I say, "Only if you want to tell me." And he says, "I know where my mom keeps her needles." He went on to tell me her story. I think often we adults don't want to admit that kids know what's going on. Kids know that something is wrong, but nobody really explains it to them, and so many kids say, "It must be me. Maybe I'm doing something wrong." I would say that happens 70 percent of the time. Part of the conspiracy of silence is children are left confused. If kids aren't given an explanation that sounds truthful and that's age-appropriate, they'll make up a story for it all to make sense. So we have to find language to help kids understand what's going on with their parents because addiction is a family disease. It takes everybody hostage.

An effective treatment approach for Hispanic families

From Dr. Jose Szapocznik, professor and chair, University of Miami Miller School of Medicine, Department of Epidemiology and Public Health: We have found in Hispanic families that the members are strongly engaged with each other. Sometimes the passion is negative, but even negative passion is a connection. So that is something we work with very effectively. We developed a treatment approach in which we address the kinds of conflicts that go on in these families when the kids are engaging in drug use and other delinquent behaviors. It's a rebelliousness and rejection of parental authority that brings a lot of kids into treatment.

In family sessions, something as simple as saying to a mother or father, "You feel very, very strongly about your child. You must care about your child an awful a lot. You want your child to succeed. You really love Johnny and you are frustrated, but you really love Johnny and want the best for him." Parents very quickly say yes. And at that point, we might turn to the child and say, "Did you know that your parent is concerned for you, that your parent wants the best for you, that your parent loves you?" Typically, the child will say, "No, I didn't know." And so we transform an interactional pattern from, let's say a father or mother was fighting with the kid and the kid was withdrawing, to an interactional pattern where they can talk about any concerns that the parent has for this child. What are the expectations, the emotions, the ambitions; what are the parent's wishes? And we move from there to Johnny—"What is it that you want, and does your father know what you want?" And then you start to have a conversation at a very different level where they're talking more adult to adult, and where that angry, negative effect really calms down. Family approaches to treatment are really the most effective. And it's much easier for somebody from the outside to do an intervention because the parent is caught up in their own emotions as a family member. The parent must learn to say, "I support you, but not your illness."

Sometimes confrontation is necessary if there is some urgency, if the child is endangering his life. But confrontation is a very inefficient intervention because you get a lot of resistance. Instead of just saying that it's a family issue, you say, "Mom, I can see how worried and how painful this is to you and how sad you are." And all of a sudden you are beginning to identify that there is more than one patient in the family. We can spread the patient input to all family members in a way that they feel they have something to gain without ever having to confront their feelings that this isn't their issue. If you begin to change the environment of the kid, the family and social environment, even if it's just the way they interact with each other, the kid becomes a different person. And often the kid will outgrow the drug use.

Families save the addict to save themselves

From Debra Jay, interventionist, lecturer, and coauthor with her husband, Jeff Jay, of Love First: A Family's Guide to Intervention *(2008, Hazelden)*: We know when we do interventions we're looking at late-stage alcoholics. The family isn't seeing there's a problem, or they're dismissing it as something else, like he's immature, or he's under a lot of stress—all the typical excuses a family makes for the disease.

The onset of the disease does not correspond with the onset of symptoms. As an example, with diabetes, by the time you have symptoms, you've had the disease for a long time. That happens with addiction as well. Once addiction takes hold, it's not easy to just have a conversation with an alcoholic or an addict and get them to change their behavior.

There are so many myths in our field. The first one, which I think is the most pervasive, the most damaging, I call the "action stopping" myth. It says you can't help an alcoholic until he wants help. So that's it for families: Step back and let the addiction run through your family like a freight train. There's nothing you can do. And we hear that all the time. We hear it from doctors; we hear it from people in AA. It just stops people from thinking about it. Well, it's a completely different story when you say, "If you can't help an alcoholic until he wants help, what will get him to want help?" You see, now I'm thinking differently. Now that opens up the door to possibility. Now I can start looking for solutions and answers.

And then there is the myth about "hitting bottom." And this is really important in terms of families, because when a family is told that you have to let your alcoholic hit bottom, what nobody tells the family is, "Guess what, you're going along for the ride." If we say the alcoholic is going to have to hit bottom, even the smallest child is going to have to hit bottom along with them. And that's just not acceptable. The solution for the alcoholic can't be the undoing of the family. We presume in saying that the alcoholic has hit bottom that they go running off to AA or to a treatment center. But the reality is they're proficient at collecting enablers, and alcoholics can bounce along the bottom for a long time and get people to clean up the mess, get people to save them from themselves, save them from their addiction.

This is a family disease, but we do not treat it that way. The way things have been set up, even with AA, is that when a person gets out of treatment, we tell family members their recovery is sort of none your business, so don't ask them what they're doing, don't ask them about their meetings, don't ask them if they have a sponsor. They don't want you staring over their shoulder. And this is the same person who has wreaked havoc on this family forever. When you talk about enabling, we've always focused on the family as if they're madly trying to save the alcoholic. The truth of the matter is they're trying to save themselves. They have to save the alcoholic to save themselves. And what do you say to a mother with three small children who is depending on that alcoholic to bring the money home to pay the mortgage? Just let him go? No! You can't tell her that because she's going to be on the street with three small children. Keep him employed and keep him functioning, because I'm saving myself, I'm saving the family.

Put yourself into a nonshaming environment

From Ann Smith, executive director, Breakthrough at Caron, and a recognized pioneer in helping adults to shift destructive life patterns to improve their relationships: I don't call it codependency anymore. Instead of codependent, I use the word "stuck." So the therapy we do is about getting unstuck. Codependency was a partial explanation. It's really all about attachment. We all have attachment needs. When they're not met, we feel sick. But we are not sick. When your abandonment needs are not met, you are not sick, you are hurting. But there are all these shaming labels of "look how sick we are." I don't look at good people as sick. With positive psychology, we don't attribute blame and shame to people who are doing the best they can do given the circumstances they were in. But we do give them full responsibility for changing it.

Here is our basic premise: All of us are born expecting we will have all of our needs met by one or more people who are designated as ours. And we expect that as our emotional needs are met, the wiring in our brains will be positively affected by that experience, and we are hard-wired to attach to that person in those years between birth and years three and five. We're not taking in information. We are processing experience. So in those experiences, if that attachment, that connection, that love connection, is interrupted or is really inconsistent, then we as individuals have to start working harder at figuring out how we're going to attach to *them*, since they're not coming to us. And so we start to adapt, and we figure out ways to do that.

Everybody who comes here to Caron comes with an attachment problem. Every human being begins with that same need for connection. In a lot of people, it is disrupted in some way. If it's disrupted really early, you're going to have major problems. If it's disrupted early but not in a major way, you're going to limp a little. If you're in a really crazy family but the attachment is secure, you're going to be fine. It doesn't mean you're going to be fine biologically speaking. You could have depression, anxiety, all kinds of things you could have inherited. But you're not going to have the kind of attachment injury that we're talking about. I don't care if they're an addict or whatever they are, it's the same. And their issues are around relationships. So an addict before they became an addict had all these issues, after they got sober they still have all these. It's not really about addiction. An addiction is just a young adult's way or a teenager's way of pushing that pain away for a period of time.

So when we get people in here who are in recovery, especially the ones who are not sober for very long, they still describe themselves as an addict. And they attribute every single thing that's wrong with them to addiction. And honestly, it's got nothing to do with it. Their addiction was a period of time where they found that drugs or alcohol or whatever process was helpful in managing those emotions—until it backfired.

Family provides an environment for recovery

From Dr. Jon Morgenstern, vice president and director of Health and Treatment Research and Analysis at Columbia University's National Center on Addiction and Substance Abuse: Families have to keep in mind that 80 percent of interventions fail. And then what happens after your intervention fails? What is the next step? You can't lock people up. That's what people want to do. But you have to get the person with a problem in a position where they have to do something that's not entirely coerced. Interventions often must wait until the person has become highly motivated for treatment. I'm a very big believer in the effect of environment as a powerful factor in recovery. The family can provide the context of environment.

What does a successful family intervention look like?

From Paul J. Gallant, founder of Gallant & Associates and a board-registered interventionist: The most important part is telling people that their loved one does not have to hit bottom. So raising the bottom is the challenge. I tell folks if one person in the family system has had enough, then intervention is possible. That is the key piece. The second most important part is understanding that this is a family-system problem, and when we approach a family, everyone needs to take action to get into recovery. A lot of families only want to point the finger, saying, "Just fix them."

A lot of times I get a call from a sibling or a father or mother and we begin to address the denial that exists in the family. A good intervention means that people have had enough and are willing to set boundaries and limits. It's really good when there is leverage. If the guy's father has had enough of his son's cocaine use and the son works in the family business, for instance, there is leverage. Another example would be a pilot who might lose his license unless he gets sober.

I did an intervention once with seven family members. The mom was the subject of this intervention. We had her parents present, along with the husband and children. What helped make it effective is that we had seven different viewpoints of this woman's problem with alcohol. Each person wrote a love letter that followed a format. Each told the mom three things: They expressed how they love her; they shared some memories and some of her qualities; and they told her their concerns and gave behavioral examples of how her alcoholism had affected them.

Some family members talked about Christmas dinner, or an afternoon out on a boat. They had specific times and incidents when her alcoholism had caused them shame or embarrassment. All participants at the preintervention meeting had in hand a completed intervention letter. We met that evening and talked about what an intervention is and is not. It's not family therapy. It's not about her bad marriage. We got everybody more comfortable with the process and what would happen the following morning. We talked about the disease of alcoholism and recovery, the family role, and the treatment center.

We met at 7 a.m. and showed up at the mom's home. She was in the kitchen, and I introduced myself. This is the surprise model of intervention, and 85 percent of the time we get our person into treatment the morning of the intervention. She listened to the seven letters being read, and I asked her if she was willing to accept the help that her family offered. She was tearful and said yes, so we took her straight to the treatment center. We got the husband into Al-Anon and got him a counselor; we got the kids into Al-Anon; and every single person in that room except one accepted the help. We helped the mom get sober, but she would return to this home and that's why it's always important for the family to get help, too. The word "intervention" means a change in course, and that's what these families need.

Can family or friends intervene on their own?

From Bill Teuteberg, professional interventionist, Minneapolis, Minnesota: It's not always necessary for family and friends to have an interventionist involved. But it depends on the dynamics of the family. It should be possible for a family to intervene with itself, but it needs to be a care confrontation rather than an intervention. Family or friends need to say, "We love you, but we can't continue to support you in killing yourself. We've made arrangements to help you, and to find help for ourselves." Leverage and consequences are necessary for this to work. Often that involves money. It never happens without the use of leverage and consequences being spelled out. Maybe 25 percent of these types of interventions succeed. The person might walk out of the family system or friendships for a month or so, but they come back if the family system holds itself together and people keep their commitment to boundaries.

I get 300 phone calls a year about interventions, and no two are alike. Before someone calls me, usually the intervention process has already started, but in a haphazard way. Someone may have expressed their concerns to the person with the problem, but maybe that conversation didn't go well. At least 50 percent of the time, in my experience, the rest of the family is sicker than the person they're pointing the finger at. So you double your chances of success in an intervention if you have a professional interventionist involved, because that person can establish who in the family has agendas other than just getting their family member into treatment. If the intervention is set up correctly, it's usually successful.

Recommended Family Self-Help Groups

Here are two particularly effective and ethical groups that can provide support for family members trying to heal the damage caused by an addict in the family:

Recovering Couples Anonymous is a world service organization (existing in eight countries) that describes its mission this way: "Ours is a fellowship of recovering couples. We are committed to restoring healthy communication and caring and, as we do this, we find greater joy and intimacy. Many of us participate in other 12-Step fellowships. We share our experience, strength, and hope with each other that we may solve our common problems and help other recovering couples restore their relationships. The only requirement for RCA membership is a desire to remain in a committed relationship." (www.recovering-couples.org)

Al-Anon Family Groups were established for family and friends of problem drinkers. Alateen is a branch of the program designed for teenagers. The group's Web site hosts a list of questions to ask yourself to help determine whether it's a program that would be helpful to you or someone you care about. The group describes its function this way: "In Al-Anon, members do not give direction or advice to other members. Instead, they share their personal experiences and stories and invite other members to 'take what they like and leave the rest'— that is, to determine for themselves what lesson they could apply to their own lives." (www.al-anon.alateen.org)

IX

Dependency Starts . . . and Ends . . . in Your Brain

Change your thoughts and you change your world.
    —Norman Vincent Peale

What we have learned from medical science studies over the last decade or so is that dependency and unhealthy habits can result from the interaction of two primary factors—your genetics and your environment. Specific genes and various combinations of genes have been identified that make a person more susceptible to toxic compulsions and as a result, can make quitting or controlling those compulsions much more difficult.

In late 2011 the American Society of Addiction Medicine changed its long-held definition of addiction to now call it "a primary, chronic disease of brain reward, motivation, memory, and related circuitry." For the first time, gambling and other "process" compulsions were lumped together with alcoholism and drug dependence as behavioral symptoms of this brain disorder. This recognition came a half-century after the American Medical Association first declared alcoholism a disease.

In my conversations with the experts, they overwhelmingly agreed that toxic compulsions are a very complicated illness. Two kids can grow up in the same family where there's a genetic predisposition toward alcoholism or addiction, yet one of them goes down that road but the other one doesn't. Why? Did the addict tolerate the environmental influences less well than his or her sibling? This is where the illness is individual-specific and gene-specific, not family determined. There are many different environmental impacts, and the way an individual processes those has a lot to do with whether that person will have a problem or not. That's particularly true with the primary triggers of anxiety and depression, which animate all of the Seven Toxic Compulsions. Some people learn to control and process their anxieties and moods more effectively, while others feel compelled to self-medicate with one or more toxic behaviors.

You've already seen in Part One of this book how interconnected all seven of the toxic compulsions can be. If you're a pathological gambler, for example, you probably also have a problem with nicotine dependence, drugs, or alcohol. Now I want to bring you up to speed about the latest findings on the causes of these compulsions. With this understanding as a roadmap, we can devise and recommend treatment strategies that truly address the roots of this brain illness. Keep in mind that what follows are generalizations based on the prevailing scientific evidence about genetic and environmental influences on the developing brain and the impact of chronic compulsive use over time.

The Bad News: You Unknowingly Ran a Gauntlet

There is an entire subterranean origin to toxic compulsion risk levels that you grew up with. These unconsciously acquired risk factors wait in ambush and can eventually emerge to hijack your life. I'll bet you never knew or suspected that you ran a gauntlet of hidden trip wires from the moment you were conceived, through your experience in the womb, and then after birth and into the awkward years of adolescence. If you got through this gauntlet without acquiring a susceptibility to one or more of the Seven Toxic Compulsions, you deserve congratulations. You were blessed with a head start to winning the good health lottery.

Genetic programming: Genes are molecular units of heredity; they are the code for traits and tendencies you received at conception from your parents. As discussed earlier in this book, geneticists continue to discover individual genes and combinations of genes that indicate a heightened susceptibility to developing one or more of the Seven Toxic Compulsions. At least 25 genes that determine your susceptibility to alcoholism have been identified. Other genes are known to dictate your cravings to overindulge in certain foods and sexual behaviors. The first time you smoked a cigarette it was a gene that helped determine your initial sensitivity to nicotine and whether you're a ready candidate for developing dependence.

"About 50 percent of the variation in the risk for developing various addictions can be accounted for by heredity," said David J. Linden, a professor of neuroscience at the Johns Hopkins University School of Medicine, editor-in-chief of *The Journal of Neurophysiology*, and author of *The Compass of Pleasure: How Our Brains Make Fatty Foods, Orgasms, Exercise, Marijuana, Generosity, Vodka, Learning, and Gambling Feel So Good.* "There is no single 'addiction gene,' and it is likely that a large number of genes are involved." Linden pointed out how carriers of an A1 variant gene are "significantly more likely to become addicted to alcohol, cocaine, or nicotine," and carriers of a gene that decreases D2 dopamine receptor function in the brain are "more likely to develop addictions to both substances (such as alcohol, nicotine, opiates, and food) and behaviors (such as compulsive gambling or compulsive sex)."

It's extremely important to state (as I will again later in this book) that your genes are not necessarily your destiny, because it's your environment (including your thoughts and behaviors) that acts to either reinforce or neutralize any genetic predispositions. "Given what we know about the genetic predispositions for and biological substrates of addiction, it's easy to conclude that we're all slaves to our genes and our brain chemistry," observed Prof. Linden. "That's simply not true . . . . Yes, our genes and our neural circuits predispose us to certain behaviors, but our brains are malleable, and we can alter their neural circuits with experience." Such experiences include talk therapy and mindful meditation.

Womb influences: You've probably heard of fetal alcohol syndrome, in which a mother's alcohol consumption affects the fetus and results in the child being born with many of the symptoms of alcoholism. You also probably know that an expectant mother smoking cigarettes raises the risk that her child will be born prematurely, with low birth weight, and with the symptoms of nicotine dependence. These are all well-documented scientific facts. The same pattern holds true for drug abuse by pregnant women. Remember the news headlines a few years ago about the birth of crack-cocaine babies? So if your mother drank alcohol, used drugs, or smoked while you were in the womb, your susceptibility to these habits has been intensified.

Infant trauma: Trauma is an emotional or psychological wound from a stressful event or period in one's life that can be felt at either the conscious or unconscious level of awareness. Up until two years of age, if your mother or other caregiver didn't pay attention to you because she was an alcoholic or you had a sibling to whom she was paying more attention to—or whatever the reason—and you never connected and adequately bonded with her, such neglect has an environmental effect on the right frontal lobe of your brain. This is the area that determines how you connect to people. You will spend the rest of your life trying to connect and if you can't do it with people, you'll try through substances or compulsive behaviors.

There is an old AA saying that the root cause of our alcoholism is our defective relations with others. That is exactly what pioneering clinician scientist Dr. Allan Schore of the Department of Psychiatry and Biobehavioral Sciences at UCLA's Geffen School of Medicine is beginning to prove. His research on "attachment theory" shows the importance of the unconscious forces that drive human thoughts, emotions, and behaviors. In response to a caregiver's neglect, an infant develops one of two response patterns: hyperarousal (from experiencing high levels of anxiety) or dissociation (from feelings of disconnect from self or surroundings). Either of these relational trauma patterns can be associated with the child developing an inability to self-regulate the intensity and duration of emotional states, which results in a compulsion for self-medicating later in life.

Childhood trauma: Trauma during adolescence and the effect of those traumas on the developing brain can compound the harm of infant neglect. Divorce can be trauma for a child. Moving can be trauma. An abusive, alcoholic parent can produce trauma in a child. There are levels of trauma, and some kids have a greater capacity to adapt and tolerate than others. Because the human brain continues to develop until about the age of 21, there are many opportunities for traumatic damage to be inflicted.

Dr. Charles Whitfield, a psychotherapist and trauma recovery expert, observed how "strong to overwhelming" evidence exists to show that problems with alcohol, drugs, smoking, and eating disorders all can be traced to childhood trauma. Though links to gambling, hoarding, and sexual compulsions have yet to be thoroughly documented, Whitfield suspects these compulsions will also eventually be found to have a genesis in childhood traumas.

It wasn't until I was about 17 years into recovery that I started to understand my own post-traumatic stress disorder, which most alcoholics and addicts have. What I went through as a kid—alcoholism in my home, my parents' divorce, the public murder of my two uncles—gave me PTSD, and though it wasn't as severe as what a soldier experiences on a battlefield, it still necessitated my search for treatment.

"Post-traumatic stress disorder is often mistaken as depression," said Dr. Whitfield, "and it's this PTSD from childhood traumas that triggers dependencies, which might start off as bad habits. A complicating factor is that the psychiatric drugs often prescribed for these compulsions are essentially all addicting. Psychiatry doesn't like to talk about that. These drugs (antidepressants, antipsychotics, and mood-stabilizers) have introduced a major wrench into the wheels of recovery from substance abuse and dependence. Well over half the people who take them can't stop without experiencing bothersome to severe withdrawal reactions that resemble various kinds of 'mental illness.' These psychiatric drugs also commonly cause weight gain, anorgasmia [inability to achieve orgasm], oversedation or overstimulation, and a numbing of our minds and emotions. And they don't work well for many people—people who are being prescribed a string of more psychiatric drugs, even while they become less functional overall in their lives."

According to Whitfield, anxiety and depression, the two most common "triggers" said to initiate dependence or a relapse from recovery, are the two most misdiagnosed symptoms of the traumas experienced early in life.

The Good News: You Can Retrain Your Brain

Despite the gauntlet you went through, despite the damage that may have been inflicted on your brain and in your thinking from chemical imbalances and chronic abuse, you still retain the capacity to rehabilitate your mind and your life. Damage can be reversed and dependencies and cravings can be subdued by engaging in practices that manipulate the plasticity of your brain to reshape your thoughts and behaviors.

It almost sounds too good to be true, but believe me, this is all firmly rooted in the latest scientific findings. In just the past five years scientists have made remarkable discoveries indicating that even though after about the age of 21 the adult human has a brain that seems to be fully formed, that brain still malleable. You can still change its structure. It still has the capacity to be altered and changed as a result of our thoughts, behaviors, practices, and rituals.

The term that brain scientists have come up with to describe our innate transformational capacity is *neuroplasticity*. I'll defer here to several experts for a more detailed explanation.

In their book *You Are Not Your Brain: The 4-Step Solution for Changing Bad Habits, Ending Unhealthy Thinking, and Taking Control of Your Life*, Dr. Jeffrey M. Schwartz and Dr. Rebecca Gladding wrote: "Neuroplasticity is the ability of the brain to take on new functions based on a person's changing needs and actions. Neuroplasticity includes any process that results in a change in the brain's structure, circuits, chemical composition, or functions in response to changes in the brain's environment."

Dr. Daniel J. Siegel, codirector, UCLA Mindful Awareness Research Center, further elaborates this in his book *The Mindful Brain*, discussing how you can focus your attention in specific ways to activate your brain's circuitry to change the connectivity of its neurons. One of the tools to address toxic compulsions, which I describe later, is mindful practice of focused attention and awareness. This takes advantage of your brain's neuroplasticity and expands its potential to heal areas of the brain that contribute to your cravings and compulsivity.

"Neuroplastic changes not only reveal structural alterations [in the brain]," wrote Siegel, "but they are accompanied by changes in brain function, mental experience (such as feelings and emotional balance), and bodily states (such as response to stress and immune function)."

We commonly see neuroplasticity at work in a person's ability to recover from a stroke. Blood flow decreases in certain parts of the brain during a stroke, resulting in damage to that area. Damage to the motor cortex, for example, can produce paralysis, whereas damage to the brain's speech area can impair talking. Physical therapy helps the stroke victim to "teach" other brain areas to assume control over walking or talking, giving those brain areas a new function, which is neuroplasticity in action as a natural brain mechanism.

Taking this natural self-healing capacity one step further is the concept of *self-directed neuroplasticity*, or using our willpower to decide how and why our brain will be rewired. Research psychiatrists Schwartz and Gladding defined it this way: "Using the power of focused attention, along with the ability to apply commitment, hard work, and dedication to direct your choices and actions, thereby rewiring your brain to work for you and with your true self."

Warping your brain with chronic abuse of any of the Seven Toxic Compulsions is an example of neuroplasticity being used in a *harmful* way. Conversely, your understanding and subsequent use of self-directed neuroplasticity gives you the opportunity to reverse the damage, and it empowers you to engage in only healthy behaviors.

Throughout the remainder of this book, I'll provide practical "tools" that have been recommended by experts, based on their research and/or clinical practice, to assist you in managing and recovering from the Seven Toxic Compulsions. Many of these tools were designed, or have been accidently discovered, to take advantage of neuroplasticity to retrain your brain so you can live a healthier life.

Welcome to the new frontier!

X

Seven Self-Care Tools with Proven Benefits

What follows are some of the self-care suggestions that came up most often in my interviews with the experts cited in this book. To varying degrees, there is well-documented science to back up these "tools" for use in treatment, continuing recovery, and personal transformation.

When I use the self-care term "tools" to describe these approaches, I don't mean in any way to minimize the seriousness of the compulsions being addressed. These compulsions destroy lives. They are serious business. If you have a chronic dependence problem and you've been chronic for a number of years, you're probably going to need more treatment resources than what these seven tools have to offer, and that means seeking professional help and guidance.

For those of you who have the most severe forms of addiction and dependence, I strongly urge you to get good professional help. You have to be careful because there are people out there who don't know what they're doing. The people I refer to in this book *do*.

You will probably notice that medication isn't one of the tools. That's because medication isn't necessarily beneficial or applicable to all of the Seven Toxic Compulsions. But depending on your compulsion and the severity of it, and your co-occurring underlying disorders, such as depression, you may need an assessment from a doctor as to whether you should be medicated at any stage of your treatment process.

Medication can be a number of things, and there are three different types. The first is substitution therapy. If you've got a heroin or another opiate problem, you may benefit from a substitution or maintenance therapy with buprenorphine or methadone, or go through detoxification and then work a long-term recovery program. The second medication type is drug therapy for cravings and drug effects. Naltrexone is commonly prescribed as a blocking agent for the craving and the "high" of alcohol or opiates. Finally, the third type is a kind of "Band-Aid" medicine, such as antidepressants, that treats the associated symptoms caused by the childhood or later trauma that you've never dealt with.

The seven tools can be used both in treatment and as continuing practices to assist in recovery, which for most of us means use over a lifetime. There is a synergy between all of those tools if you put them into practice together.

Everything presented here, to whatever extent possible, is evidence-based; however, it's important to keep in mind that not all useful strategies and practices can feasibly be subjected to the gold standard determination typically used to assess the effectiveness of medications: the randomized clinical trial. Other research strategies are accepted and used when randomized clinical trials aren't feasible.

Cognitive behavioral therapy can be effective to varying degrees for all seven compulsions. 12-Step programs work for all seven compulsions, though the evidence is currently lacking for hoarding compulsion. Meditation and mindfulness can be useful for all of the compulsions, and potentially so can acupuncture. Nutrition and exercise were also described as important by most of the experts.

Many experts and much of the research I've seen advocate a holistic approach to treating all of the Seven Toxic Compulsions. That means simultaneously using as many combinations of tools as you possibly can. Psychotherapist Dr. Ronald Alexander of Santa Monica, California, puts it this way: "The treatment for any addiction certainly needs to be holistic. That would include cognitive behavioral therapy, group therapy, a 12-Step program, meditation, mindfulness, exercise, yoga, changes in diet and nutrition, even acupuncture and vitamin supplements for some people who have been really deep in the rabbit hole of addiction. It's a model you see practiced at Cottonwood, Sierra Tucson, and a few other treatment centers. You have to remember that treating addiction is like psychological boot camp. You need at least 90 days to go through all of the withdrawal and psychological reconstituting that needs to go on. So you need all of these tools for treatment and a successful long-term recovery."

Another expert, Dr. Charles O'Brien, professor, Department of Psychiatry, the Charles O'Brien Center for Addiction Treatment, University of Pennsylvania, elaborated on how to use the holistic treatment model: "We've actually shown that if you tailor the treatment to the patient, you get a much better outcome than treating everybody the same way. There is no one thing that cures addiction. But you can use medications and behavioral therapies, 12-Step programs, group therapy, individual family therapy, motivational counseling, mindfulness, exercise, and cognitive behavioral therapy. All of these things can be tailored to the individual. There are even some excellent programs that are available now for cognitive behavioral therapy that can be done by computer. It is directed at their mood disorder and it really does work and it's efficient and cost effective."

Anchoring yourself in recovery can be expensive. If you lack the resources to enter a treatment facility or to hire a therapist, these tools may be a lifeline. I've tried to identify useful and effective resources that are available to everyone at little or no cost.

These tools have been likened to arrows in a quiver. All are basically arrows pointing and directing you to create a new life and a new relationship to life. There are things that you can rely on at different times in your early recovery. And then later in your recovery, their use will give you benefits for the rest of your life.

Compulsions and dependency survive in the dark. All of these tools, especially those designed to change behaviors, will shine a light on the bogeyman. Addiction thrives in isolation. The more you look at it, the brighter that light becomes, and the less hold these compulsions will have over your mind and your life.

Tool 1—Cognitive Behavioral Therapy

Over the years, I've done a lot of different kinds of therapy. I was with a very good therapist for many years before I ever got sober. Once I asked him, "Hey, Ed, what good did all that therapy do for me, because I never got sober? But I know it probably built you a new tennis court?" He's a very good, smart guy and he said, "I don't know, Chris. Maybe it kept you alive."

Talk therapy can be a powerful gateway tool. It may not get you where you want to go right away, but it keeps a door open. It provides at least one person in your life with whom you're trying to be truthful, somebody who's more or less unbiased so you can be honest and hear things you might not be able to hear from many of the people close to you.

If you have a compulsion, no matter what the level of severity, you need to find somebody you can trust and confide in. If a therapeutic relationship is too costly, you need to confide in a family member or a trusted friend. This could also be done in a 12-Step program after you've found a sponsor. The important thing is to start the process of revealing yourself to another human being. It's a relational tool and absolutely crucial to recovery.

People with severe compulsions who have never been in a therapeutic relationship have difficulty revealing personal things. It takes a long time to do that. It takes trust, and it takes time to build that trust. Therapy can work—it does work—but it takes commitment.

There are many different forms of therapy. Cognitive behavioral therapy (CBT) is just one of them; but it just happens to be the one recommended most often by the experts I surveyed.

They didn't call it CBT when I was doing it. I've done behavioral therapy, which basically identifies why you do certain things and shows you ways to change those behaviors. That is some of the most effective kind of therapy for people like us, because this is all about changing behaviors and the thoughts that animate our behaviors.

The biggest problem addicts have is that they believe the way they feel. They believe that if they feel bad, they need to do this one thing to feel better. And the critical thing is to get enough space between the feeling and the behavior so you can actually change the behavior. A therapist can help you identify which behaviors result from which feelings. It's a process. It doesn't happen overnight.

Somebody once said to me, "When you do something different, when you behave differently, even if it's the right (normal) behavior, it feels wrong to an addict, because we equate good feeling with good (normal) behavior even though we know it's not." That connection is so strong because we're such slaves to the way we feel. Addicts don't have great tolerance for things that don't feel good because they are addicted to immediate gratification and the immediacy of the feeling.

That's why CBT and mindfulness and meditation all work, but you've got to convince people that they have to take the time to let it work. That's the biggest challenge. You drink alcohol, you smoke a cigarette or stick a needle in your arm, you go to the Internet for some porn, or go to a casino—it's immediate. You get it right away. You get the jolt, and you get the thing right into your brain. These tools don't work right away. It's a whole new skill set people have to learn, yet this CBT technique definitely works.

CBT is based on the idea that your thoughts can both *obstruct* your ability to heal from physical or mental injury and can *enhance* your capacity to heal, depending on whether you are able to identify the negative or irrational beliefs that hold you back, and then are able to reframe those toxic thoughts. When toxic thoughts or reactions emerge and threaten to trigger cravings, CBT enables you to develop coping strategies based on healthier thoughts.

Psychotherapist, professor, eating disorder expert, and national vice president of the Center for Mindful Eating Donald Altman of Portland, Oregon, uses CBT with his eating-disorder patients and has had positive results, even surpassing the 50 percent reduction in compulsive eating behaviors that has been obtained in published studies on CBT. He explained how CBT offers anyone with one of the Seven Toxic Compulsions these skill sets:

1. It challenges distorted thoughts and beliefs. It can alter your beliefs about whatever compulsions hold you hostage.
2. It works to regulate emotions by having patients challenge the basis for their emotional distress—and the underlying behaviors. It helps the patients identify their thinking errors or cognitive distortions. Then, the individual can more easily look for evidence that disproves or discredits these thoughts. In this way, one is able to challenge the thoughts that are the basis for the emotional distress.
3. It increases understanding of the primary emotions and secondary emotions triggered by beliefs that increase distress. It increases an understanding of those underlying core beliefs—such as "I'm worthless" or "I'm unlovable"—that produce distorted thoughts.
4. It supports a person learning how to embrace the adaptive expression of emotion into something more positive. It supports a person learning how to take a broader perspective on any situation. In addition, it promotes the practice of being more realistic about any given situation.
5. It utilizes a psycho-educational component that helps people make the link between triggering events and the thoughts,

emotions, and behavior that follow. In other words, you learn to trace the cause and effect pattern in your mind that contributes to compulsive thoughts and behaviors

Studies examining the impact of CBT on drug and alcohol relapse, along with binge-eating disorders, have been uniformly promising. Here are a couple of examples.

Researchers writing in a 2005 issue of *The American Journal of Psychiatry* reviewed results from dozens of studies on the development of behavioral therapies for drug and alcohol dependency. They had this to say about CBT: "Several studies have demonstrated that cognitive behavioral therapy's effects are durable and that continuing improvement may occur even after the end of treatment." One study found CBT to be "more effective than standard treatment" for methamphetamine-dependent individuals. Another study of 450 marijuana-dependent persons "demonstrated that a nine-session individual approach that integrated CBT and motivational interviewing was more effective than a two-session motivational interviewing approach, which was in turn more effective than a delayed-treatment control condition." *(Source: "Behavioral therapies for drug abuse." Carroll KM and Onken LS.* Am J Psychiatry. *2005 Aug;162(8):1452–60.)*

A Florida study of older military veterans with alcohol- or drug-use problems, many of whom were homeless, also showed CBT's effectiveness. The University of South Florida research team put 49 of the veterans/patients through a 16-week CBT program emphasizing the teaching of coping skills. A follow-up after six months found that those who did the CBT program "demonstrated much higher rates of abstinence" compared to those who didn't complete the program. *(Source: "Cognitive-behavioral treatment of older veterans with substance abuse problems." Lawrence Schonfeld et al.* J Geriatr Psychiatry Neurol. *2000 Fall;13(3):124–9. doi: 10.1177.)*

In another study, researchers at Canada's University of Toronto Centre for Addiction and Mental Health put 38 people diagnosed with binge-eating disorder combined with a substance-use disorder through a 16-week mindfulness-based CBT program. "Participants significantly improved on measures of objective binge-eating episodes, disordered-eating attitudes, alcohol and drug addiction severity, and depression. CBT appears to hold promise in treating individuals with coexisting binge-eating disorder and substance-use disorders." *(Source: "Mindfulness-action based cognitive behavioral therapy for concurrent binge eating disorder and substance use disorders." Christine M. Courbasson et al. Eat Disord. 2011 Jan;19(1):17–33.)*

The latest innovation using CBT for compulsive disorders involves interactive online CBT programs that can be accessed from home. For more information, go to www.recover2live.com.

Several studies have assessed the value of online CBT. At the Yale University School of Medicine, Division of Substance Abuse, Prof. Kathleen Carroll and five other researchers conducted a randomized clinical trial in which 73 persons seeking outpatient treatment for substance dependence were placed in either a treatment-as-usual group or in eight weeks of biweekly access to computer-based CBT training. Participants were interviewed at 1-, 3-, and 6-month intervals after the termination of the two study treatments. Significant differences were found between the two groups. "Those assigned to treatment-as-usual increased their drug use across time, while those assigned to CBT tended to improve slightly . . . computerized CBT appears to have both short-term and enduring effects on drug use." *(Source: "Enduring effects of a computer-assisted training program for cognitive behavioral therapy: A 6-month follow-up of CBT4CBT." Kathleen M. Carroll et al. Drug Alcohol Depend. 2009 Feb 1;100(1–2):178–81.)*

Another potentially useful tool—voice dialogue

Though this process isn't directly connected to CBT, it does involve a type of reprogramming of thoughts that could be useful in treatment and recovery. The principle behind the practice of voice dialogue is that we all have different voices within us attached to recurring thoughts. It's not different personalities, but it is different aspects of self that are embodied in certain voices. For example, we have the voice of hope and the voice of inspiration, the voices of cynicism and doubt. We have our controller voice and multiple other voices we reactively obey or respond to.

For everyone there are certain dominant voices. Control freaks have the controller voice that dominates and influences decisions and perceptions, and this voice tries to censor what is thought or spoken. Or there might be a victim voice of someone who's constantly in despair, or a sort of masochistic voice characterized by diminished self-esteem.

Part of the process of voice dialogue is to determine which are your predominant voices and then to work with those voices to either diminish or enhance them. It's not hypnosis. It's a one-on-one process of being asked a series of questions, doing a short meditation, and going into a place within yourself where you access the particular voice that needs to be worked with.

If you have a bad habit or a compulsion dependency, you try to determine what voices are connected to that. If you have a voice of cravings, for example, when you work with that particular voice, you might ask it a series of questions: "Why are you in control? What role do you serve? What feelings come up whenever this voice is dominant? What are the early warning signs of feelings or sensations you have when that voice is going to make an appearance?"

Sometimes the sessions are recorded, sometimes not, but the person who's being asked the questions begins by feeling and embodying the voice in the moment. Everyone can learn to do this. You begin to sense exactly what is involved in the cravings, how to control the cravings based on the early warning signals, and what counterbalancing voices you need to summon in the moment—counterbalancing voices you can shift into to diminish a voice of neediness or a voice of craving.

No peer-reviewed science studies, at least as far as I know, have been conducted on the voice dialogue technique. I have included it here as a potentially useful tool for recovery in the hope that studies might happen one day. For more information, read *Embracing Ourselves: The Voice Dialogue Manual*, by Hal Stone, Sidra Stone, and Shakti Gawain.

Tool 2—12-Step Programs (and Other Groups)

Each of the various 12-Step programs for the Seven Toxic Compulsions are based on Alcoholics Anonymous, so they're all branches of the same tree, which is about eight decades old. In a very real sense, 12-Step programs are the way of personal transformation.

All of the experts I spoke with say these group programs can be helpful. For some people, being involved in 12-Step meetings can be the difference between life and death. That doesn't necessarily mean if you go to a 12-Step program you're going to like it or that it's going to work quickly for you. But it should be tried. If you don't like it, there are other things to consider, such as group therapy. Having a group dynamic involved in your support system, whatever form that takes, is a critical piece of recovery.

If you're a person who has a bad habit rather than dependency, a 12-Step program most likely isn't for you. That doesn't mean it wouldn't be worth going, but you may benefit more from moderation management meetings or a group with a therapist to talk about your underlying issues.

Some treatment experts urge caution about relying entirely on a 12-Step program during recovery. Dr. Morteza Khaleghi and Dr. Karen Khaleghi, addictions specialists and founders of Creative Care in Southern California, explain in their book *The Anatomy of Addiction* how 12-Step programs "are rarely the answer in and of themselves for most addicts. The problem is—and this problem is made stunningly clear in the indisputably dismal relapse rates—that the examination of a client's emotional history prescribed in the 12 steps does not go deep enough. And, all too frequently, it doesn't even touch upon underlying physiological or psychological issues that, left untreated, will sabotage sobriety as surely as night follows day."

What distinguishes 12-Step programs from group psychotherapy?

Jeffrey Roth, addiction psychiatrist, author, editor of *Journal of Groups in Addiction Recovery*, and medical director, Working Sobriety Chicago, leads group psychotherapy sessions. He describes what separates his process from the 12-Step program structure: "You go to a 12-Step meeting and the boundaries of that meeting are that there's no professional approach in there. And that's according to their traditions. There's no crosstalk. And there's a reason that there's no crosstalk, because that fits the structure of the meeting.

"Group psychotherapy is exactly the opposite. Group psychotherapy is all crosstalk. The 12-Step meeting is an opportunity to share experience, strength, and hope. The group psychotherapy is an opportunity to share your insanity. The more insanity you let go of in the group, the more you can see it, and the more you can accept the help of the group as a higher power in doing your personal inventory."

Scientific studies support 12-Step's effectiveness

Probably no one alive has studied 12-Step programs longer or more intensively than Dr. Scott Tonigan, research professor, Center on Alcoholism, Substance Abuse, and Addictions, University of New Mexico. By his count, he has sat through at least 1,000 different 12-Step meetings, taking notes, interviewing participants, and later conducting studies to determine what factors make the program effective for the recovery of some people but not others.

"The evidence is clear that 12-Step attendance is beneficial for many, but not all, problem drinkers and polysubstance abusers," Dr. Tonigan explained. "Those who continue to attend and work the steps and have a sponsor derive great benefits, including increased abstinence. Meeting attendance and having a sponsor are very important. Other things are less clear, like spiritual growth. We are seeing a number of recent studies that point to the scientific possibility that increased spirituality does predict improvement. Six or seven studies now indicate that changes in spiritual practices partially explain the benefits of 12-Step programs, though the studies also find that atheists or people with social phobias generally don't engage well in these programs.

"The role that spirituality may serve in 12-Step programs is a broad terrain, but what we are seeing is that the practice of prayer and meditation helps explain the success of the program. Mindfulness and meditation do inhibit a drinking response when drinking cues are present, and they put a safety on those triggers. I have no doubt that also occurs (along with consequent brain changes) as a result of 12-Step program social interactions."

Because there is so much variance in how 12-Step programs and the various meetings are practiced and conducted, because there is so much migration between groups—someone attending Narcotics Anonymous one week and Alcoholics Anonymous the next—trying to measure the overall effects of these groups and their various practices on long-term sobriety becomes a unique challenge for researchers like Dr. Tonigan. But he and his colleagues have found that across the various 12-Step programs, the processes involved are much more similar than different. It's usually just a difference based on emphasis, although that emphasis will help to determine whether a person feels like he or she can fit into and feel comfortable sharing with a particular meeting and group.

There is also a research question around whether the principle of "harm reduction," an emphasis on reducing substance use rather than complete abstinence, has any place in the 12-Step program's structure, where abstinence has been one of the guiding mantras for decades. In results that surprised him, Dr. Tonigan found that harm reduction is already being widely practiced, but in virtual secrecy. "Up until recently," noted Dr. Tonigan, "I would have said the harm reduction approach has no place in 12-Step programs because of the programs' emphasis on abstinence. But our research shows that about 20 percent of people we studied in AA who reported complete alcohol abstinence also reported the use of illicit drugs, such as low marijuana use. That made us reevaluate what abstinence really means and what sobriety really means in 12-Step programs and the role of harm reduction."

Here is a summary of 12-Step study findings produced by Dr. Tonigan and other scientists over the past few years:

In a 2010 study of 1,726 people with an alcohol-use disorder, the team of Dr. Tonigan and four other researchers found that "attending AA was associated with increases in spiritual practices, especially for those initially low on this measure at treatment intake" and that "AA leads to better alcohol-use outcomes, in part, by enhancing individuals' spiritual practices." *(Source: "Spirituality in recovery: A lagged mediational analysis of alcoholics anonymous' principal theoretical mechanism of behavior change." John F. Kelly et al. Alcohol Clin Exp Res. 2011 Mar;35(3):454– 63. doi: 10.1111/j.1530-0277.2010.01362.x. Epub 2010 Dec 16.)*

To examine the relationship between relapse and volunteer work in AA, which usually involves serving as a sponsor helping other alcoholics, Dr. Tonigan and three other researchers did an intensive examination in 2004 of AA participants and concluded: "These findings provide compelling evidence that recovering alcoholics who help other alcoholics maintain long-term sobriety following formal treatment are themselves better able to maintain their own sobriety." This finding reinforced the sentiment often heard in AA meetings that "You can't keep it unless you give it away." *(Source: "Helping other alcoholics in Alcoholics Anonymous and drinking outcomes: Findings from project MATCH." Maria E. Pagano et al. J Stud Alcohol. 2004 Nov;65(6):766–73.)*

At four Kaiser Permanente hospital programs in Northern California, researchers monitored 357 adolescents with drug and alcohol disorders to determine the effect that their participation in 12-Step meetings had on long-term recovery. The study concluded: "12-Step attendance at 3 years was associated with both alcohol and drug abstinence at 3 years. Similarly, 12-Step activity involvement was associated significantly with 30-day alcohol and drug abstinence . . . the findings suggest the importance of 12-Step affiliation in maintaining long-term recovery." *(Source: "12-Step affiliation and 3-year substance use outcomes among adolescents: Social support and religious service attendance as potential mediators." Felicia W. Chi et al. Addiction. 2009 Jun;104(6):927–39.)*

An expert's story of recovery using 12-Step meetings

From Dr. Robert DuPont, President of the Institute for Behavior and Health Inc, first director of the National Institute on Drug Abuse, second

White House Drug Chief, and clinical professor of psychiatry at George-town Medical School: When my daughter Caroline was a freshman at Georgetown, she called me the day after Halloween to say that she had a problem and needed help. One of the young men in her dormitory, whom I will call David, the night before had thought Caroline—dressed for Halloween as a black cat—was the devil. He thought he had to kick her. He was obviously psychotic. Their friends had to subdue David before they learned that his disturbed mental state was caused by his use of marijuana and hallucinogens.

On her call the next day, I asked Caroline to tell a bit more about David. She told me that he was a minority student from another city. On a full scholarship, David was the first person in his family to go to college. She emphasized that David was the most popular student in the dormitory. Everyone thought he was the smartest kid in their class. They really wanted to save him.

I suggested that Caroline take David to a meeting of Narcotics Anonymous. She responded, "I don't know where to find a meeting." We talked through how to do that. I suggested that there was sure to be an NA meeting near Georgetown at noon. Caroline took David by the hand and walked him to that meeting. For the next week, each day, Caroline went to the noon meeting with David. She held his hand and sat right next to him. For the rest of that year David went to NA meetings every day and he didn't use drugs. But when he went to his home that summer he relapsed. In distress, he called Caroline asking, "What do I do now?" She responded, "One of the nice things about AA and NA is that there are meetings everywhere you go, including right now in your town. Get a new sponsor and work the program." David did. He never relapsed again.

When they graduated, my wife and I had an informal dinner for Caroline and her friends at a nearby restaurant. David sat next to me. He told me that Caroline had saved his life. "If she had not gone to the meetings with me for a week and sat there holding my hand, I would not have been able to go to the meetings." David told me that his father had been a jazz musician who died at 25 of a heroin overdose. David continued, "If there had been a Caroline in his life, I would have known my father."

Four years later this young man graduated from medical school. Now married with a young daughter, he is practicing medicine. David continues to go to a lot of AA and NA meetings. He tells people how he got into that fellowship and what a difference it made in his life.

David's story made a big impression not only on Caroline and David, but on their whole dormitory—and on me.

The commune that became a treatment community

Communal living is another model for a group recovery setting. For example, a place in Italy called San Patrignano, which has no therapists, is a community where thousands of people have overcome heroin addiction just by coming together and working together in a community.

Monica Luppi, international outreach and relations officer at San Patrignano, described how this program works: "It wasn't started with the idea of being a treatment center for drug addicts. It was founded by a local entrepreneur in the 1970s to help some heroin addicts who were living on the street have a place to stay. The idea was you could come if you were someone who probably needs love, or a good kick in the ass, anything a real good parent would give you. It began as a kind of a hippie commune. It was built by the people who were the first addicts to come here. The founder had no training in treatment. He just had a big heart.

"Now, more than 30 years later, about 1,600 people live here. It's become like a small town, or a very well-oiled machine. It feels like one big family. If you're looking around, you can't tell who has arrived yesterday and who's been here 20 years. There's no hierarchy. It's not like the guy in the white lab coat saying, 'Okay, you're admitted or you're in phase one or whatever.' It's very natural. It's not at all like treatment. We don't even talk about drugs. I went through the program starting in 2000, so I've been here 11 years.

"The treatment here is everyday life. When someone first arrives, they are assigned to a person who will be like a big brother, sister, or sponsor who teaches them the rules. The treatment is you're in a group of people who become like your little kind of related family. You learn your job. It's not busy work; it's always something productive, and it's good training. We take orders and make stuff that's sold all over the world. So the treatment is interaction with people.

"There's no talk of groups and there's no talk of being a patient or being cured or anything like that. I've barely ever heard people talking about drugs. Once you're here it's not an issue anymore because there are no drugs here, so it's about you. The philosophy behind San Patrignano is that drugs are just the last little kind of symptom of what's gnawing at you. So we try to make sure that people come here after they have been thoroughly prepared mentally and are ready and motivated and know what they're up against.

"The program is individual for everyone, but usually it lasts three-and-a-half to four years. The decision to leave, again, is very individualized. It's been built up over relationships all those years where you have very strong ties with the people around you. They know you and you've talked about it, and when the time is getting close and you know you've done certain things inside of yourself, there are conversations you have. It's not like an evaluation process or you decide when you're ready. You know the person so well that you can say, 'Maybe you should go and see what that outside world is like for a week or 10 days and realize what you're going to be up against.'

"We have about 50 volunteer associations in 50 different cities around Italy made up of former San Patrignano residents and parents of residents who wanted to volunteer. These groups hold meetings where people who want to go to San Patrignano can show up and ask for help. These groups prepare the person, which means helping them to detox and to understand what will be expected of them. These associations also become points of reference when people leave San Patrignano, especially if the person doesn't have good family relationships. At the same time, these associations are places for the parents to go while you're in the community, so the family does a parallel path, because obviously you can't just fix just a piece of a car that's broken. The whole car is usually broken, so the parents work on themselves in the association.

"We used to have people coming in who were in their 40s. That was the norm 10 years ago. Now we see many young kids, 17 and 18 years old, coming in. So we focus a lot more now on providing education for people. We've built a huge center for people for formal education. People finish their education, high school, whatever, and we get them to be as independent as possible.

"We don't have state funding. Half of our 23 million euros budget every year comes through our work, our own services, and the other half comes from donations, a couple of patrons, and grants from foundations. That works out to about 35 euros a day for each person at San Patrignano. Our success rate is also quite high. In 2007 two universities did a study sampling of 517 of our former residents and found that 72 percent were drug-free two to three years after leaving.

"The energy of this place pushes people to be good. In my 11 years here I have never seen more than four or five shoving matches. It never goes beyond that. About 30,000 people have come through here. They were all considered the worst addicts, the ones that nothing could be done for, the ones who had been in prison or gone through 20 rehabs. They screwed up everything they could screw up, until they got here."

"Harm reduction" groups and programs

SMART (Self-Management And Recovery Training) Recovery is an alternative to 12-Step programs and covers all types of toxic compulsions, although most members are dealing with drug and alcohol issues. It's a worldwide nonprofit organization of free support groups with an emphasis on self-empowerment and developing self-control.

This approach can involve controlled use, or reduced use, as opposed to an emphasis on enforcing immediate abstinence. It's known as the "harm reduction" model of treatment and gives users various tools, including instructions on behavioral self-control techniques. The SMART Recovery mission statement reads, in part: "To support individuals who have chosen to abstain, or are considering abstinence from any type of addictive behaviors (substances or activities), by teaching how to change self-defeating thinking, emotions, and actions; and to work toward long-term satisfactions and quality of life."

Dr. Thomas Horvath, psychologist, president of SMART Recovery, and president of Pyrysys Psychology Group, Inc. drew several distinctions between SMART and the structure of 12-Step programs: "SMART Recovery meetings are an active discussion with a facilitator, as opposed to the monologues you hear in 12-Step meetings. The majority of SMART Recovery people do believe in God, according to our member surveys, but we don't include the Higher Power angle as the 12-Step programs do. We are available to people at all levels of problems and work with them toward both abstinence and harm reduction. We use eight or so tools in our program. These will look familiar to any cognitive behavioral therapist."

Dr. Horvath's workbook for overcoming addictions, based on SMART Recovery principles, is titled *Sex, Drugs, Gambling & Chocolate*. For more information about the differences between SMART Recovery support meetings and 12-Step approaches to recovery, visit www.smartrecovery.org/

A second group that uses a harm reduction model for problem drinking is the Moderation Management Network Inc. (www.moderation.org). Dr. Thomas Horvath is on its board of directors, along with Dr. Reid Hester and, at one time, the late Dr. Alan Marlatt, all of whom were interviewed for this book.

Moderation Management describes itself on its Web site as "a behavioral change program and national support group network for people concerned about their drinking and who desire to make positive lifestyle changes. MM empowers individuals to accept personal responsibility for choosing and maintaining their own path, whether moderation or abstinence. MM promotes early self-recognition of risky drinking behavior, when moderate drinking is a more easily achievable goal."

MM also provides a "supportive mutual-help environment that encourages people who are concerned about their drinking to take action to cut back or quit drinking before drinking problems become severe. A nine-step professionally reviewed program provides information about alcohol, moderate drinking guidelines and limits, drink monitoring exercises, goal setting techniques, and self-management strategies. As a major part of the program, members also use the nine steps to find balance and moderation in many other areas of their lives, one small step at a time."

Other noteworthy groups

Women For Sobriety (www.womenforsobriety.org). Here is how the group defines itself: "Women for Sobriety (WFS) is an organization whose purpose is to help all women find their individual path to recovery through discovery of self, gained by sharing experiences, hopes, and encouragement with other women in similar circumstances. We are an abstinence-based self-help program for women facing issues of alcohol or drug addiction. Our 'New Life' program acknowledges the very special needs women have in recovery—the need to nurture feelings of self-value and self-worth and the desire to discard feelings of guilt, shame, and humiliation. WFS is unique in that it is an organization of women for women. We are not affiliated with any other recovery organization and stand on our own principles and philosophies. We recognize each woman's necessity for self-discovery. WFS offers a variety of recovery tools to guide a woman in developing coping skills which focus on emotional growth, spiritual growth, self-esteem, and a healthy lifestyle. Our vision is to encourage all women in developing personal growth and continued abstinence through the 'New Life' program."

LifeRing Secular Recovery (www.lifering.org). Established in 2001, this nonprofit abstinence-based support group is operated on the principle that "You can get clean and sober regardless of your belief or disbelief in a 'higher power.' We welcome people regardless of their 'drug of choice.' We encourage crosstalk in meetings. We each build Personal Recovery Programs tailored to our individual makeup."

Nonsecular, faith-based resources include organizations Celebrate Recovery (www.celebraterecovery.com/), Calix Society (www.calixsociety.org/), JACS (Jewish Alcoholics, Chemically Dependent Persons and Significant Others, www.jacsweb.org/), Millati Islami (www.millatiislami.org/), Buddhist Recovery Network (www.buddhistrecovery.org/), and many more. Find additional possibilities in Appendix Two of this book.

Tool 3—Mindfulness

When skeptical people hear the term *mindfulness* they may automatically think it's New Age gibberish or Eastern religious dogma. People need to know there is science behind the technique and that the practice of mindfulness has an effect on the brain, on the way the brain actually changes itself.

Mindfulness is a wonderful tool when you're dealing with cravings or the triggers or the impulses; it can help you become less reactive. I remember a doctor saying to me many years ago, "When you want to use drugs, you should just go sit at the beach and watch the ocean." I guess what he was trying to tell me was that watching the waves coming in and going out is just a way to focus your mind so you don't give in to the cravings. Now with mindfulness we have an actual practice with protocols and a basis in science—you can actually train your mind to lessen its reactivity.

Addiction is all about reactivity. "I feel bad, I have to take this or do that." Addicts are reactionary and undisciplined in their thoughts. Mindfulness teaches mind discipline and creates a structure so we are no longer slaves to our triggers and cravings and desires. We learn to create some distance between the impulse, the craving, and the behavior. If you do that, you have a chance of changing the behavior. It's what spiritual people call "witness consciousness," where you can actually create space between your thoughts.

Mindfulness is understanding that you don't have to be attached to your thoughts. Mindfulness is proactive. It's actually about *doing* something. You're maintaining a space between your thoughts and you're mindful about your behavior. You're mindful about what's happening and what you're going to do (or not do) about it.

"Mindfulness helps individuals *move beyond addiction by actually resetting the brain's neuro networks to produce positive mental states* of optimism, encouragement, openness, and positive thinking (as opposed to negativity, rumination, and reactivity)," observed Donald Altman, a psychotherapist, professor, and eating disorder expert in Portland, Oregon, who is national vice president of the Center for Mindful Eating.

Altman and other therapists associated with the center practice the following principles of mindfulness:

- Mindfulness is deliberately paying attention, nonjudgmentally.
- Mindfulness encompasses both internal processes and external environments.
- Mindfulness is being aware of what is present for you mentally, emotionally, and physically in each moment.
- With practice, mindfulness cultivates the possibility of freeing yourself of reactive, habitual patterns of thinking, feeling, and acting.
- Mindfulness promotes balance, choice, wisdom, and acceptance of what is.

Be mindful of your deceptive brain messages

One reason you may not be able to stop unhealthy behaviors and compulsions is that "You have bought into your deceptive brain messages and assimilated them into your sense of who you are," wrote Dr. Jeffrey Schwartz and Dr. Rebecca Gladding in their book *You Are Not Your Brain: The 4-Step Solution for Changing Bad Habits, Ending Unhealthy Thinking, and Taking Control of Your Life.*

Deceptive thoughts come in multiple ways. You may have bought into the brain message that someone doesn't love you, not because this is reality but because you are feeling your own damaged self-esteem. You might buy into the deceptive brain message that your family approves of your toxic compulsion simply because they remain silent about it, when in reality they are too passive, afraid, or enabling to challenge the damage you are inflicting on yourself and on your relationships.

To counteract these sorts of self-deceptions, the UCLA-based mindfulness experts Schwartz and Gladding developed a four-step approach to evaluating the toxic thoughts that surface, particularly when you're in the throes of a compulsion. Here are the steps:

1. Re-label the thought or uncomfortable sensation. If you're having a recurring "what-if" worry-thought about something, for example, label it for yourself as "Here I am playing the what-if game again." That helps break the thought recurrence cycle.
2. Re-frame the brain message. Ask yourself *why* the thoughts and urges keep bothering you. Repeat to yourself: "This isn't really me; this is just my brain spewing out these false messages."
3. Re-focus your attention. When the false and deceptive thoughts and urges arise, practice shifting your attention toward healthy and productive thoughts and personal goals. Practice until this becomes second nature.
4. Re-value the thoughts and urges. Put them into perspective for what they are—just sensations that flow from deceptive brain messages. They have little or no value and deserve to be dismissed, not dwelled on.

These four steps are designed to help you "wire new, healthy routines into your repertoire and into your brain." This is particularly important to practice when you're feeling stressed because "stress causes your brain to recruit its old, hardwired routines to go into overdrive."

Two mindfulness coping skills

A month before he died in early 2011, Dr. Alan Marlatt, director of the Addictive Behavior Research Center at the University of Washington, described for me the following two mindfulness skills that he and his colleagues taught people battling compulsions:

Urge surfing: "I learned this from a guy who was trying to quit smoking," said Marlatt. "He said to me, 'As soon as I have an urge to smoke, it just gets higher and higher and if I don't have a cigarette, I think I'm going to go crazy.' I explained to him how urges are like conditioned responses. If you don't give in to the response, it will go down. And the guy said, 'Oh, so it's like an ocean wave.' It turned out he was a surfer from San Diego. So he got this idea that if he could ride the wave—that urge—and surf it, using his breath as a kind of surfboard, he could get through it and go down the other side. And it worked. After about two weeks, he was able to quit smoking by just doing this coping skill that resembles surfing."

SOBER space: "This is an acronym to use when you're on the verge of losing your willpower and giving in to an urge. Stop what you're doing, just pause. Observe how you're feeling and what you're thinking in the moment. Breathe. Focus your breath and get it centered. Expand your awareness, observe things beyond the urge. Respond mindfully. You have a choice. You can exercise that choice."

Scientific studies support mindfulness benefits

It makes positive changes in your brain. Harvard Medical School researchers did brain magnetic resonance imaging on 16 participants before and after they did an eight-week program of mindfulness-based stress reduction (MBSR). On average, each participant spent 27 minutes each day practicing the mindfulness exercise. The research team measured the brain's plasticity and concluded, "The results suggest that participation in MBSR is associated with changes in gray matter concentration in brain regions involved in learning and memory processes, emotion regulation, self-referential processing, and perspective taking." An additional benefit was a decrease in gray matter density in the amygdala, that part of the brain involved in heightened anxiety and stress. *(Source: "Mindfulness practice leads to increases in regional brain gray matter density." Britta K. Hölzel et al. Psychiatry Res. 2011 Jan 30;191(1):36–43.)*

It can treat co-occurring disorders. Yale University School of Medicine researchers examined mindfulness study results on both depression and substance-use disorders, which are often co-occurring. They observed: "Mindfulness training has been shown recently to benefit both depression and substance-use disorders, suggesting that this approach may target common behavioral and neurobiological processes." *(Source: "Mindfulness-based treatments for co-occurring depression and substance use disorders: What can we learn from the brain?" Judson A. Brewer et al. Addiction. 2010 Oct;105(10):1698–706.)*

It can be effective for relapse prevention. Mindfulness-based cognitive therapy (MBCT) studies involving 593 participants were analyzed to determine the effectiveness in reducing relapse or recurrence of major depressive disorder. Though the focus was on depression, these results also have application to any relapse from compulsions, particularly substance abuse. The study authors concluded that MBCT reduced the risk of relapse/recurrence by 34 percent compared to treatment-as-usual approaches. In two studies, MBCT was just as effective as the use of antidepressant medications. *(Source: "The effect of mindfulness-based cognitive therapy for prevention of relapse in recurrent major depressive disorder: A systematic review and meta-analysis." Piet J. Hougaard E.* Clin Psychol Rev. *2011 Aug;31(6):1032–40.)*

Relapse prevention for substance use. University of Washington researchers put 168 adults with substance-use disorders through an eight-week outpatient mindfulness-based relapse prevention (MBRP) program. They were assessed at two- and four-month intervals after the intervention. Those in the MBRP program, as opposed to those who had treatment as usual, showed "significantly lower rates of substance use over the four-month post-intervention period. Additionally, MBRP participants demonstrated greater decreases in craving, and increases in acceptance and acting with awareness." *(Source: "Mindfulness-based relapse prevention for substance use disorders: A pilot efficacy trial." Sarah Bowen et al.* Subst Abus. *2009 Oct–Dec;30(4):295–305.)*

Alcohol relapse prevention. In this University of Wisconsin School of Medicine study of alcohol-dependent adults, 15 of them were enrolled in an eight-week mindfulness meditation relapse prevention course. After the course, "Their severity of depression, anxiety, stress and craving, and documented relapse triggers decreased, and the degree of mindfulness increased. Participants rated the meditation course as 'very important' and a 'useful relapse prevention tool.'" *(Source: "Mindfulness meditation for alcohol relapse prevention: A feasibility pilot study." Aleksandra Zgierska et al.* J Addict Med. *2008 Sept;2(3):165–73.)*

Tool 4—Meditation

In 12-Step programs they talk about the 11th-step being prayer and meditation to increase your conscious contact with God, as you understand God. So whatever that means to you, there are two aspects to prayer and meditation. Prayer is talking to God, meditation is listening to God.

Meditation can radically change your life. Anybody who has done it will tell you that. If you meditate at the same time every day and in the same place every day, meditation becomes like an energy that builds up. The more you do it, the more energy you create in that place, and that energy facilitates the act of quieting your mind, of stilling the craziness that's usually going on in the head of an addict.

There are many different traditions of meditation. You don't have to walk into an ashram with yogis and do this in front of a group of strangers. You can do it on your own, when and where you choose.

What do all of the various meditation traditions have in common? In her book *The Blissful Brain* author Shanida Nataraja proposed these four criteria to assess whether a practice amounts to meditation:

1. The specific technique is clearly defined and can be taught.
2. It has to involve the progressive relaxation of muscles.
3. It must involve reducing brain activity, what is known as logical processing functions of the brain.
4. It must be self-induced by the practitioner.

The late Prof. Alan Marlatt, former director of the Addictive Behavior Research Center at the University of Washington, noted how meditation "may serve as a useful alternative to alcohol use and may result in some of the same positive consequences, including tension reduction and relaxation." Not only that, but Marlatt noticed in his patients how "meditation may also provide a useful antidote to the experience of craving, which is often characteristic of addictive behavior and is strongly related to relapse following a period of abstinence. The heightened state of present-focused awareness that is encouraged by meditation may directly counteract the conditioned automatic response to use alcohol in response to cravings and urges."

Marlatt and other treatment experts began utilizing two techniques in particular—transcendental meditation (TM) and Vipassana meditation (VM)—to help people reduce alcohol-related cravings and problems. TM involves the meditator using a mantra (which is a word or phrase that is repeated silently), as you sit with eyes closed, during two 20-minute periods every day. Vipassana meditation doesn't involve a mantra. Instead, the meditator focuses awareness on the breathing process while sitting silently with eyes closed.

At the Chopra Center in Southern California, founded by Dr. Deepak Chopra, meditation is the centerpiece of a treatment regimen for compulsions around alcohol, drugs, smoking, overeating, and gambling. "In our decades of experience working with people attempting to free themselves from addictions, we have found meditation to be the most powerful tool to change negative patterns," wrote Chopra and Dr. David Simon, medical director of the Chopra Center, in their book *Freedom from Addiction*. "In fact we have never witnessed a person relapse when they are meditating regularly."

That makes perfect sense to me. Compulsions create turbulent thoughts and stress in the body. Meditation helps to quiet the mind and relax the body. If you're meditating every day, you have less free attention for generating or responding to compulsive cravings. As an example, a Danish study did brain scans on meditators and discovered a significant increase in the release of dopamine during the act of meditating, which means the brain's pleasure circuit is activated, the same part of the brain that gets activated by compulsive cravings. *(Source: "Increased dopamine tone during meditation-induced change of consciousness." Troels W. Kjaer et al. Cogn Brain Res. 2002 Apr;13(2):255–9.)*

Dr. Ronald Alexander, a psychotherapist and executive director of OpenMind Training Institute, uses a variety of meditation techniques in working with his clients. "Mindfulness practice helps us to develop the capacity to see clearly what we're attached to so we can let go of it and end our suffering," he explained. "There is a great meditation that you use when treating addicts that's called the 'death meditation.' You actually take somebody through their own death and then take them to the body decay process. You also take them to the kind of death they would have if they were to continue drinking or using drugs. It's heavy stuff. I learned it in Sri Lanka. And they use it in Thailand at some of the monasteries where they send people to cure addiction. They make the person do the death meditation every day. And sometimes two or three times a day, so they see their body system shutting down, what it's like to have liver failure and cirrhosis. What it's like to experience their heart stop, or not being able to eat solid food anymore. The meditation is motivating. I don't think you have to have a soft approach when you're dealing with addicts and addiction. This is a meditation that motivates people to really live in the moment."

A high percentage of prison inmates enter prison facilities with a substance-abuse problem and once released, many relapse, resulting in more criminal behavior and more prison time. To test whether Vipassana meditation might be useful in lowering the relapse rate, Prof. Alan Marlatt and a team of nine researchers from the University of Washington put a group of inmates through a meditation course. "Results indicate that after release from jail, participants in the VM course, as compared with those in a treatment-as-usual control condition, showed significant reductions in alcohol, marijuana, and crack-cocaine use. VM participants showed decreases in alcohol-related problems and psychiatric symptoms as well as increases in positive psychosocial outcomes." *(Source: "Mindfulness meditation and substance use in an incarcerated population." Sarah W. Bowen et al.* Psychol Addict Behav. *2006 Sep;20(3):343–7.)*

A second study of inmates a year later yielded similar results for Vipassana meditation, showing that the emphasis of Vipassana on acceptance rather than suppression of unwanted thoughts (cravings) helped to reduce substance abuse. In this experiment, 173 inmates at a Seattle jail were divided into two groups—a treatment-as-usual control group and a group who completed a meditation course over 10 days of intensive training. Participants ranged in age from 19 to 58 years, and 79 percent were male. From the study findings: "Individuals who participated in the 10-day Vipassana meditation course reported greater decreases in their attempts to avoid unwanted thoughts than individuals who did not take the course. Change in levels of avoidance partially mediated the relationship between Vipassana course participation and alcohol use and consequences three months following release from jail. These results provide support for the hypothesis that avoidance of unwanted thoughts may be an important component in the relationship between meditation and alcohol use." *(Source: "The role of thought suppression in the relation between mindfulness meditation and alcohol use." Sarah W. Bowen et al.* Addict Behav. *2007 Oct;32(10):2324–28. doi: 10.1016. Epub 2007 January 23.)*

For more information on how mindfulness meditation has been shown to dramatically change criminal and addictive behaviors in various prisons, visit Vipassana (Insight) Meditation Prison Trust at www.prison.dhamma.org.

Tool 5—Nutrition and Exercise

Let's start with nutrition, because without having proper levels of nutrients in your body, you won't be able to summon the energy to exercise at an optimal level, and you certainly can't remain physically or mentally healthy in the long term. There is even a case to be made that eating the "wrong" foods and not enough of the "good" foods can trigger or worsen many of the Seven Toxic Compulsions.

During the 1980s one of the pioneer investigators into the role that nutrients play in behaviors and the mind was Stephen J. Schoenthaler, a professor of criminal justice and sociology at California State

University. He and a team of colleagues examined the interaction between nutrient intake and crime, antisocial behaviors, and educational performance of schoolchildren. Since four out of every five prison inmates have a problem with alcohol or illegal drug use at the time they are incarcerated, according to research from the National Center on Addiction and Substance Abuse, the effect of nutrition on the brain could offer a cost-effective treatment approach.

Kathleen DesMaisons, PhD, conducted a nutrition-based program to treat alcoholics in San Mateo County, California, for three and a half years, through 1997. DesMaisons focused on diet and nutrition to reduce the sugar cravings that prompted DUI offenders with flawed carbohydrate metabolisms to crave the sugar in alcohol. A control group that didn't receive the nutrition education re-offended with alcohol-related crimes at four times the rate of those who were in the nutrition program.

More clinical evidence for the key role that brain neurotransmitter deficiencies play in drug, alcohol, and toxic foods abuse came from studies by pharmacogeneticist Kenneth Blum at the University of Texas at San Antonio. His research with both animal and human test subjects during the 1990s confirmed that malnourished brains seek comfort from the abuse of substances.

Dr. Charles Gant successfully used a nutrition-based medicine approach to treating substance abuse when he served as medical director of Tully Hill Hospital, a rehabilitation facility in Syracuse, New York. His emphasis then and since has been on the use of nutritional supplements to treat biochemical imbalances in the brain that contribute to substance abuse and subsequent relapses from that abuse.

In his book *End Your Addiction Now*, Dr. Gant made a case that compulsive substance use usually results from biochemical imbalances caused by one or more of four risk factors:

1. Poor nutrition
2. Exposure to toxins, including chemicals in the foods we eat
3. Stress
4. Genetic vulnerabilities

Based on questionnaire results from patients and readers of the book, Gant recommends nutritional supplements that include amino acids, vitamins, and minerals to boost neurotransmitter production to help "reduce or eliminate your substance urges, mood swings, irritability, difficulty in concentrating, sleep problems, and other symptoms."

For example, if you complete the serotonin deficiency questionnaire and discover that you have a deficit in this critical neurotransmitter, which could be a cause of your substance urges, Gant proposes taking a nutrient regimen of 5HTP (up to 300 mg three times a day), L-glutamine (up to 1,000 mg four times a day), B-complex vitamin (one capsule three times a day), vitamin C (at least 500 mg three times daily), and a multimineral supplement of calcium, magnesium, potassium, iron, zinc, manganese, chromium, selenium, and molybdenum.

(For more information on Gant's nutritional approach to compulsions, go to Connected Pathways LLC's Web site: www.connectedpathways.com.)

Another nutritional medicine expert, Dr. Hyla Cass, a professor at the UCLA School of Medicine, coauthored a book with the British nutritionist Patrick Holford titled *Natural Highs*, in which they provided a nutritional and exercise-centered program for counteracting substance addiction caused by brain-chemical imbalances. "Since neurotransmitters are literally made from nutrients—amino acids, vitamins, and minerals," they wrote, "we can formulate the perfect 'brain food' to improve how we feel and think."

(For more information see: www.cassmd.com *or* www.naturalhighs-book.com)

Substance treatment specialist Dr. Kenneth W. Thompson, medical director of Caron, cautions: "There is currently insufficient science to support the use of nutritional supplements for the treatment of addiction. There are many gimmicks and pseudoscience surrounding justification of various supplements. Chemicals and supplements advertised as precursors to vital brain neurotransmitters required to feel good do not necessarily result in improvement in the brain's chemistry when taken orally. But I'm a big believer in regular exercise, healthy diets with good nutrition, watching your intake of concentrated sweets and white flour, etcetera."

So be careful about what you choose to try, but also be willing to experiment a little to see what works for you. Consider getting a checkup first, and consult with a physician to determine whether any of these supplements may interact with any prescribed medications.

As Dr. Frank Lawlis and Dr. Maggie Greenwood-Robinson pointed out in their book *The Brain Power Cookbook,* "Food is an unsung hero when it comes to addictions," and while "eating healthy foods won't necessarily break the hold of an addiction, it will help rebuild a body nutritionally depleted by substance abuse. What you may not realize is that alcohol, nicotine, and illicit drugs destroy nutrients, prevent their absorption, and flush them from the body. Cocaine and heroin addictions, in particular, reduce the intake of nutritious foods and cause serious malnutrition, whereas marijuana creates an abnormally large appetite for sweets and snacks, leading to unhealthy weight gain . . . I find malnutrition in every addict I see."

If you're being treated for an addiction or recovering from one, Lawlis and coauthor Greenwood-Robinson recommend that you enhance your recovery by adhering to a diet with five key components:

1. Make sure that protein comprises up to 25 percent of your total daily calorie intake; this ranges from fish to low-fat dairy and legumes.
2. Try to consume foods containing vitamin A in abundance; these range from fish to carrots and sweet potatoes.
3. Include foods that are high in B vitamins; these include whole grains, vegetables, and legumes.
4. Vitamin C foods should be heavily consumed; that means citrus fruits, green and red peppers, collard greens, broccoli, brussels sprouts, cabbage, spinach, artichoke, strawberries, etc.
5. Eat raw fruits and vegetables as much as possible, especially the dark-green leafy veggies like broccoli, kale, and spinach; also try juicing them, which is a fast and effective way to infuse your body with nutrients.

Here are a few representative studies showing a link between nutrition, mind health, behavior, substance abuse, and impulse control:

"Findings support the position that nutrition education is an essential component of substance-abuse treatment programs and can enhance substance-abuse treatment outcomes. Dietitians should promote and encourage the inclusion of nutrition education into substance-abuse treatment programs." *(Source: "Nutrition education is positively associated with substance abuse treatment program outcomes." Louise P. Grant et al.* J Am Diet Assoc. *2004 Apr;104(4):604–10.)*

"Poor nutritional habits in children that lead to low concentrations of water-soluble vitamins in blood impair brain function and subsequently cause violence and other serious antisocial behavior. Correction of nutrient intakes, either through a well-balanced diet or low-dose vitamin-mineral supplementation, corrects the low concentrations of vitamins in blood, improves brain function, and subsequently lowers institutional violence and antisocial behavior by almost half." *(Source: "The effect of vitamin-mineral supplementation on juvenile delinquency among American schoolchildren: A randomized, double-blind placebo-controlled trial." Schoenthaler SJ and Bier ID.* J Altern Complement Med. *2000 Feb;6(1):7–17.)*

"Driving under the influence (DUI) offenders with either alcohol- or cocaine-related problems were studied. The neuronutrients SAAVE and Tropamine significantly reduced relapse rates and enhanced recovery in these DUI outpatient offenders over a 10-week period. Follow-up on both the SAAVE and Tropamine groups after 10 months revealed a 73 percent and 53 percent overall recovery rate, respectively." *(Source: "Neurodynamics of relapse prevention: A neuronutrient approach to outpatient DUI offenders." Brown RJ., Blum K., and Tachtenberg, and MC.* J Psychoactive Drugs. *1990 Apr–Jun; 22(2):173–87.)*

N-acetyl-cysteine (NAC) is an amino acid critical to brain health because it is needed to produce the neurotransmitter glutamate in the reward center of the brain, which is often altered by substance abuse and other compulsions. Several studies have found NAC supplementation can help in the treatment of cocaine and heroin dependence, and even in treating pathological gambling.

Previous studies had found NAC administration inhibits the desire for cocaine in addicts and in animals. A 2008 follow-up study at the University of South Carolina using lab animals found that "Daily NAC inhibits heroin-induced reinstatement and produces an enduring reduction in cue- and heroin-induced drug seeking for over one month after the last injection of NAC." *(Source: "N-acetylcysteine reduces extinction responding and induces enduring reductions in cue- and heroin-induced drug-seeking." Zhou W and Kalivas PW.* Biol Psychiatry. *2008 Feb 1;63(3):338–40. doi: 10.1016. Epub 2007 August 24.)*

Cocaine impairs the brain's ability to develop adaptive behaviors using brain plasticity. In this 2009 study, NAC treatments induced "metaplasticity that inhibits further induction of synaptic plasticity, and this impairment can be reversed by NAC, a drug that also prevents relapse." *(Source: "N–Acetylcysteine reverses cocaine-induced metaplasticity." Khaled Moussawi et al.* Nat Neurosci. *2009 Feb;12(2):182–9.)*

At the University of Minnesota School of Medicine, researchers put 27 pathological gamblers through an eight-week trial of NAC supplementation. Compared to the placebo group, those in the NAC group greatly reduced their scores on an obsessive-compulsive scale. "The efficacy of NAC lends support to the hypothesis that pharmacological manipulation of the glutamate system might target core symptoms of reward-seeking addictive behaviors such as gambling." *(Source: "N-acetyl cysteine, a glutamate-modulating agent, in the treatment of pathological gambling: a pilot study." Jon E. Grant et al.* Biol Psychiatry. *2007 Sep 15;62(6):652–7.)*

Exercise is also about strengthening your brain

Today I do Bikram yoga instead of pounding my knees in the gym. I decided to do something that's more benign, but I'm still going to do it every day. It takes an hour and a half a day. It keeps me healthy and helps me deal with the constant chatter that is always present in the recovering addict's brain.

If you can begin an exercise regimen sooner in your recovery—it could be running, walking, going to the gym, or doing yoga—it will absolutely help you get through the difficult times because of what exercise does for us in terms of the endorphins making us feel good, helping us sleep, all of those kinds of things.

Yoga has been a huge part of my recovery from day one. I've morphed from somebody who ran every single day, five or six miles, to someone, as I've gotten older, who does yoga. Going to yoga every day, no matter whether I felt like it or not, helped me with all of the physical and mental aspects of recovery because it changes the levels of dopamine and serotonin in your brain to minimize any tendency you have toward depression.

Yoga actively reduces stress. That's now a well-established fact of medical science. A July 2011 study in the *Journal of Pain Research* showed how women who engaged in the Hatha form of yoga experienced a level of relaxation that decreased activity of the sympathetic nervous system, which lowers heart rate and increases breath volume. That in turn regulates levels of cortisol, the hormone produced by the body in response to stress. Since stress is one of the primary triggers for cravings associated with toxic compulsions, anything that naturally reduces stress levels also helps to alleviate dependency and relapse.

"Exercise can activate the pleasure circuit" of your brain, wrote Johns Hopkins University School of Medicine neuroscience professor and editor-in-chief of *The Journal of Neurophysiology* David Linden in his book *The Compass of Pleasure.* Aside from the well-documented positive effects of sustained exercise on physical health, exercise is also associated "with long-term improvements in mental function and is the single best thing one can do to slow the cognitive decline that accompanies normal aging. Exercise has a dramatic antidepressive effect. It blunts the brain's response to physical and emotional stress. A regular exercise program produces a large number of changes in the brain, including the new growth and branching of small blood vessels, and increases in the geometric complexity of some neuronal dendrites."

More study support for this idea came in the *Journal of Applied Physiology* (April 28, 2011), with the finding that "aerobic and resistance training are important for maintaining cognitive and brain health in old age." This is also true for children. Research has found that "3 months of aerobic exercise training improved prefrontally mediated executive function abilities in 7- to 11-year-old overweight children."

University of Florida psychiatrist Mark Gold further noted that exercise can actually reverse certain types of brain damage caused by substance abuse. "If you look at the changes in the brain caused by drugs, challenging the survival of some of the neurons and connections, exercise is the best neurogenic treatment we have. It changes brain structure and prompts the growth of new nerve cells and blood vessels."

Studies on exercise for alcohol, drugs, gambling, and smoking

One of the early studies showing the benefits of exercise in diminishing a compulsion—in this case, heavy alcohol use—occurred in 1986 when 60 male students between the ages of 21 and 30, all classified as heavy social drinkers, were randomly assigned to either an exercise group or a control group. The exercise group engaged in a regular running routine. Their alcohol consumption was assessed over a 16-week period. "The results showed that subjects in the exercise condition significantly reduced their alcohol consumption compared to the no-treatment control condition," the study authors concluded. *(Source: "Lifestyle modification with heavy alcohol drinkers: Effects of aerobic exercise and meditation." Timothy J. Murphy et al. Addict Behav. 1986;11(2):175–86.)*

Aerobic exercise as an adjunctive treatment for drug dependence was the focus of a 2010 study of 16 drug-dependent people who participated in a 12-week moderate-intensity aerobic exercise program. Those who attended 75 percent of the exercise sessions "had significantly better substance-use outcomes than those who did not." Exercise participants in general demonstrated a "significant increase" in days abstinent from both alcohol and drug use at the end of treatment. *(Source: "Pilot study of aerobic exercise as an adjunctive treatment for drug dependence." Richard A. Brown et al.* Ment Health Phys Act. *2010 Jun 1;3(1):27–34.)*

In 2009 Brazilian researchers put a group of pathological gamblers through a four-week exercise program that involved 45-minute sessions of stretching and running. This followed their participation in 12 to 15 cognitive behavioral therapy group sessions. The exercise group was evaluated using a 10-item gambling scale both at the beginning of the exercise program and at the end. All patients showed an improvement in their gambling behavior scores to within the range of complete remission after completing the exercise program. *(Source: "Physical exercise for pathological gamblers." Daniela L. Angelo et al.* Rev Bras Psiquiatr. *2009 Mar;31(1):76.)*

Reducing the cravings associated with a smoking cessation program was the goal of a 2011 study at Brown University that used moderately intense aerobic exercise. Sixty previously low-active but healthy female smokers went through an eight-week program that included three sessions a week of exercises, along with smoking cessation counseling and the nicotine patch. Cigarette cravings were assessed throughout the program. "Results suggest that aerobic exercise has potential as a smoking cessation treatment, but that it must be engaged in frequently and consistently over time in order to derive benefits." *(Source: "Acute effects of moderate intensity aerobic exercise on affective withdrawal symptoms and cravings among women smokers." David M. Williams et al.* Addict Behav. *2011 Aug;36(8):894–7.)*

(Note: As with nutrition, you should consider consulting a medical professional first, as various forms of exercise may be risky for individuals with certain medical conditions.)

Tool 6—Body Work

Years ago I did Reichian therapy. It's based on the belief that your emotional history is stored in your body. You talk about things, about your childhood, and when something comes up, the therapist pushes his fingers into different parts of your muscles. You may scream or hit a pillow or something, and that's how you release the pain of the memory.

If you can afford to do that kind of work, it goes a long way toward dealing with the underlying causes and conditions of one's addiction. You can really fast track by doing this kind of psychological work. It's like a depth charge. It can bring clarity and movement to deep emotional issues that otherwise might take years to understand. The therapy moves you dramatically right away, but then, of course, the rubber band of habituation pulls back over time, only it never pulls you back to where you were before.

As the name implies, "body work" concerns ways to manipulate your body to help relieve the cravings and other symptoms associated with a toxic compulsion. If you've ever had therapeutic massage, you can relate. You know it relieves stress, and if you simply allow yourself to experience the ensuing relaxation, your mind is no longer dwelling on any compulsive thoughts.

You probably have heard of acupuncture, but not somatics, which I describe below. Though some people might say that acupuncture isn't body work, it certainly looks that way to me. It simply involves a manipulation of the body using needles rather than hands. There have been a lot of scientific studies examining what acupuncture can and can't do for you. Not so with somatics, which is a relatively new player in the toxic compulsions treatment field.

Some needles may help you recover

Chinese medicine texts describe acupuncture as the stimulation with tiny needles of an energy called qi (pronounced "chee") into areas of the human body known as meridians, vein-like pathways under the skin's surface connected to different body organs.

All of this may sound a bit strange to many Westerners; however, acupuncture has been shown to treat arthritis, nausea, and chronic pain, apparently by releasing the body's beta-endorphins. After a 1989 study published in the British journal *The Lancet* showed acupuncture to be effective in treating alcoholism and its relapses, treatment specialists and drug and alcohol treatment centers in the United States and Europe began to take notice of its potential to treat all types of chemical dependency.

Dr. Kenneth Carter is both a psychiatrist and an acupuncturist at the University of North Carolina–Chapel Hill Medical School Psychiatry Emergency Services, as well as immediate past president of the National Acupuncture Detoxification Association, who specializes in treating symptoms associated with substance abuse; he also teaches medical personnel how to use acupuncture. He described some of its benefits:

"The beautiful part about acupuncture is that it can be used across the spectrum from acute distress, acute illness, to a wellness soul. I use it as an adjunct therapy, not as a replacement therapy. You can do it in your own home.

"Home use of acupuncture to treat drug abuse originated in the Bronx, New York (The Lincoln Recovery Center was an outgrowth), at a time when many people could hardly afford to pay a doctor and there were long waiting lists for drug treatment. It was started by community people concerned about heroin. They brought it into existence in spite of opposition from the mainstream medical system.

"It's so simple and easy. Your grandmother should be able do it for little Johnny who started smoking weed or drinking and is too embarrassed to go see a psychiatrist. It only involves doing five acupuncture points in the ear. A pack of acupuncture needles might cost a dollar for 10 needles.

"First thing I would suggest is to visit our Web site, www.extra-detox.com. There is a lot of very easy-to-read material to guide you. We have a list of registered trainers. We have a training resource manual. And when someone has been a practitioner for up to two years, they're qualified to become a trainer.

"How does such a simple tool work across so many different substances, from drugs to alcohol? It seems to have a general balancing effect on the body. The ears are the only place on the body to access cranial nerves without surgery. The lower half of the ear connects to the vagus nerve. Acupuncture really works to reduce cravings. I don't know of a tool that is more useful across the whole spectrum from acute to long-term recovery."

Lincoln Recovery Center has become a worldwide pilot program in auricular acupuncture for the detoxification and treatment of drug-addicted persons. It has used acupuncture as the primary method of treatment for drug addicted persons and its acupuncture model is used by at least 1,000 programs worldwide. It has trained more than 3,500 alcohol- and substance-abuse counselors in the New York City area in the use of acupuncture.

Here's how the clinic describes its use of the procedure to relieve substance cravings and withdrawal symptoms: "Auricular acupuncture patients receive five thin needles (0.25-mm dia., 15mm long) that are inserted into the appropriate area of the ear cartilage ridge, located next to the outer rim of both ears. Ear points used for detoxification are labeled 'Shen men,' 'Kidney,' 'Liver,' 'Sympathetic,' and 'Lung' in acupuncture texts. The patient is instructed to relax for 45 minutes with needles in place. The needles are then removed. Only sterile needles are used since strict antisepsis is necessary to avoid infections. Before needle insertion, the auricular points are cleaned with 75 percent alcohol." For more information, go to http://sad-lincoln.org.

Mixed study results on acupuncture's effects

A review of medical science studies examining whether acupuncture is effective to help quit smoking, drugs, and alcohol, reveals a variety of results and starkly contrasting opinions about its usefulness.

Let's start with several of the negative result studies:

"The results are consistent with the findings of other studies that failed to find any effect of acupuncture in the treatment of drug dependence. The failure to find any clinical gains from the adjunctive use of auricular acupuncture during detoxification from opiates raises concerns about the widespread acceptance of this intervention." *(Source: "Auricular acupuncture as an adjunct to opiate detoxification treatment: Effects on withdrawal symptoms." Jennifer Bearn et al.* J Subst Abuse Treat. *2009 Apr;36(3):345–9.)*

"The results of the included studies were equivocal, and the poor methodological quality and the limited number of the trials do not allow any conclusion about the efficacy of acupuncture for treatment of alcohol dependence." *(Source: "Acupuncture for alcohol dependence: a systematic review." Cho SH and Whang WW.* Alcohol Clin Exp Res. *2009 Aug;33(8):1305–13.)*

"The NADA (National Acupuncture Detoxification Association) protocol was not more effective than sham or treatment-setting control in reducing anxiety. The widespread acceptance of auricular acupuncture in the treatment of addiction remains controversial." *(Source: "Determining the efficacy of auricular acupuncture for reducing anxiety in patients withdrawing from psychoactive drugs." Shaun Black et al.* J Subst Abuse Treat. *2011 Oct;41(3):279–87.)*

Positive result studies are more numerous. Here are a few:

"Acupuncture can lessen heroin cue-induced activation degree of the brain areas involving psychological craving, suggesting that acupuncture is able to suppress the heroin addiction patients' drug abuse craving." *(Source: "Effect of acupuncture on heroin cue-induced functional magnetic resonance images in heroin-addicted human subjects." Xiao-ge Song et al. Acupunct Res. 2011 Apr;36(2):121–7. www.ncbi.nlm.nih. gov/pubmed/21717780.)*

"The authors think that acupuncture application provides the patients with deterioration in the taste of smoking, decrease in desire of smoking, and the obstruction of psychological symptoms that appear as a result of smoking cessation. Because of these effects it is presumed that acupuncture may be used as an important method for smoking cessation treatment." *(Source: "Smoking cessation after acupuncture treatment." Cabioglu MT, Ergene N, and Tan U. Int J Neurosci. 2007 May;117(5):571–8.)*

"These results provide evidence that acupuncture may be effective for inhibiting the behavioral effects of cocaine by possible modulation of the central dopaminergic system." *(Source: "Acupuncture attenuates cocaine-induced expression of behavioral sensitization in rats: Possible involvement of the dopaminergic system in the ventral tegmental area." Lee B, Han SM, and Shim I. Neurosci Lett. 2009 Jan 9;449(2):128–32.)*

"Over the last three decades there has been an increasing interest in acupuncture treatment of substance abuse around the world. The recent advance in this field was made by Dr. Han of the Peking University, Beijing, who characterized a protocol (2005) using electrical stimulation of identified frequencies on body points to ameliorate heroin withdrawal signs and prevent relapse of heroin use." *(Source: "Acupuncture for the treatment of drug addiction." Cai-Lian Cui et al. Neurochem Res. 2008 Oct;33(10):2013–22.)*

"We determined that acupuncture detoxification programs are a useful component of a substance abuse treatment system." *(Source: "The value of acupuncture detoxification programs in a substance abuse treatment system." Michael Shwartz et al. J Subst Abuse Treat. 1999 Dec;17(4):305–12.)*

What are we to make of these conflicting study results? A common sense observation is that acupuncture has different effects on different people. Whether it's partially a placebo effect or entirely a manipulation of "energy" centers of the body thereby easing substance withdrawal, it's a technique that may benefit you, particularly if alcohol, drugs, or cigarettes are involved. Just don't have high expectations, and don't be disappointed if the results fail to meet your needs.

Other forms of body work

Somatics is a type of body manipulation and deep massage that's designed to release trauma, especially childhood traumas. The Reichian therapy treatment I mentioned earlier might fall under this category.

Somatic Experiencing was developed by Dr. Peter A. Levine, a stress and trauma expert who wrote *Waking the Tiger: Healing Trauma,* which provides many useful exercises based on his medical practice—exercises that have been designed to help resolve shock trauma (the experience of life-threatening events, such as in war) and developmental trauma (experiencing cruelty and neglect in childhood.)

"I believe that people, in community with family and friends, have a remarkable ability to bring about their own healing," wrote Dr. Levine. "Body sensation, rather than intense emotion, is the key to healing trauma . . . . Of all the maladies that attack the human organism, trauma may ultimately be one that is recognized as beneficial. I say this because in the healing of trauma, a transformation takes place—one that can improve the quality of life."

Self-medicating with substance abuse is one of the means that Levine first identified two decades ago "by which traumatized people attempt to stabilize or suppress symptoms" associated with the trauma they experienced. Find out more about Somatic Experiencing, including lists of practitioners of this technique in your area, by going to www.traumahealing.com.

A second pioneer in the field of body-based therapies is somatic psychologist Pat Ogden, PhD, founder and director of the Sensorimotor Psychotherapy Institute and coauthor of *Trauma and the Body.* Written primarily for clinicians and psychotherapists, this scholarly book explains how using body sensation and movement can help heal the wounds of trauma, and though she doesn't specifically address the relationship of trauma to toxic compulsions, her work makes clear that trauma treatment should involve both the body and mind.

Christine Caldwell, PhD, founder and chairperson of the Somatic Counseling Psychology Department at Naropa University in Boulder, Colorado, has developed innovations in the field of body-centered psychotherapy. She calls her work the Moving Cycle. This system goes beyond the limitations of therapy and emphasizes lifelong personal and social evolution through trusting and following body states. She has authored two books: *Getting Our Bodies Back* and *Getting in Touch.* She offers trainings in somatic psychotherapy (Moving Cycle) with a specialization in addictions. For more information, visit www.themov-ingcycle.com.

Try a "vision quest" using sensory deprivation

From Frank Lawlis, PhD, director of Psychological Services, Origins Recovery Center, South Padre Island, Texas, and author of Retraining Your Brain: As the individual begins to detoxify, his or her brain starts to heal itself. It usually takes two years for the addict's brain to heal enough to make responsible decisions; however, that is longer than we have in most rehab situations. Also, there is usually some need or fear that propels us to go for drugs, and that has not gone away. In the grown-up world there are distractions, many distractions, that take us away from what we need to be focusing on. This is why we have a place to go with *no* distractions so you can begin to hear your voice inside, the one that looks out for you and gives you wise counsel.

At Origins Recovery Center in South Padre Island, Texas, we have built such a place. It is called an SDC, which stands for Sensory Deprivation Chamber, built with the express purpose of keeping the world out, including light, smell, sound, and touch. This will be a major vehicle for knowing yourself and especially forgiving yourself as you begin to separate your true self from the ghosts that have haunted you since you were born, giving you the opportunity to confront them in a totally safe environment. Here is where you can find and understand your power. This is the place for you to go and release the monkey on your back, see it, label it, and control it.

We are all born and raised with one part of our self looking in to understand what we need and who we are, while another part of our self is looking out, listening to what the outer world thinks of us, what the expectations are, and how to survive. Too often we forget the first part and try to make our inner world fit our outer world. This is the reason for the Sensory Deprivation Chamber.

An SDC is simply a device designed to eliminate all the external sensory perception of a person in order that they may look within. It is lightproof, soundproof and free of distracting touch. The intention of the SDC is to help you look within yourself and get to know who you are, what thoughts are prevalent, and possibly learn to free yourself of unwanted stressors in the mind through deep relaxation.

By eliminating the outer world for an hour, you can have the opportunity to feel your inner self. You may feel yourself expand beyond your skin boundaries because your energies are very big. You may feel your inner self speak to you internally. Or you may hear your outer self trying to get your attention. The sounds of a busy mind will eventually subside and you will begin to discriminate as to what is your real voice and what are only memories of the outer world demands, such as family names or labels.

So as you enter the SDC, relax with your breath. Let go of all your fears. You will *not* be locked in, so if you start getting panicked, merely push the door open. You can also be heard through an embedded microphone where medical professionals will be monitoring and listening. Remember, the SDC is only empty darkness and that this may be the first time you have experienced the freedom to get to know yourself and the genuine sense of connection with who you have become. This is not problem-solving time, just an opportunity to observe how you think and seek your internal truth.

Tool 7—Journaling

It may not seem relevant at first, or even logical, but regularly writing down your thoughts and feelings can play a significant, positive role in early recovery. I've looked at my journals again and they do validate what you experience on the road to recovery.

Journaling keeps an addict's mind focused on what's real. That's a huge benefit for those of us prone to getting stuck in magical or delusional thinking.

During the process of releasing something from your mind through computer keys or a pen on paper, you get to read it and see your improvement, or your temporary insanity. Sometimes you read it and go, "What am I thinking?!" It gives you a different perspective—a more therapeutic perspective—on what you're thinking and what you're experiencing.

Writing it down can be enormously helpful in working through things. It can be enormously helpful if you have resentment against somebody. Instead of yelling or screaming or getting into a fight, which could put you in such disarray that you run back to whatever behavior you need to stay away from, you can journal it and release the anger that way—a useful technique to circumvent triggers that could cause a relapse to self-destructive behaviors.

You can journal about anything. It could be cravings, what you're feeling, your fears—anything. You write down anything you want; there's no right or wrong here. It's about getting what's in your head out of your head and relieving the pressure these stagnant thoughts can generate. It makes the thoughts more manageable, not as overwhelming.

Journaling also enables you to visualize what you want your life to be like. The pros and cons of everything in terms of relationships become clearer. For example, if you're thinking "I've got to get out of this marriage," and this thought is occurring just 35 days into some kind of recovery, you can journal to see if what you're thinking is real or just a fear that will resolve itself over time.

The thing to keep in mind is that people enslaved by their compulsions believe their feelings. They feel them so strongly. Journaling provides a counterbalance in black and white, whether it's a negative feeling or a positive feeling. Writing is cathartic. Your feelings become concrete. It's hard to write down something that's insane—and a lot of times we addicts can be insane in our thoughts. But in the act of translating our thoughts into the written word, something transformative happens; something that is reality-based occurs. With journaling, you don't just hear a bunch of internal voices screaming and yelling all the crazy shit that enslaves you. Journaling is like calling a committee into session that you can objectively listen to. You realize that you aren't your thoughts.

You can write down your questions. What do you want in your life? What does this behavior mean to you? Does it mean freedom or slavery? Does it mean happiness? Does it mean a new Ferrari? What does recovery really mean to you? The act of just putting it down and getting it out diminishes the negativity of the thoughts, and re-reading what you wrote later can give you a different sense of your reality.

Think of journaling as a really cool tool with two edges. One is the active edge of writing what you're feeling in the moment; the second is the passive edge of reading what you had previously written in the moment. Each serves a beneficial function.

Journaling provides a safety check and reality check on your thoughts, especially the toxic ones. Otherwise, your thoughts will convince you of anything to get back to what the cravings tell you to do. The disease of addiction is cunning, baffling, and powerful. It will use whatever it can to get you to do whatever it wants, and your thoughts are its greatest weapon.

Quite a few of the treatment specialists I interviewed for this book mentioned the benefits of journaling. Prof. Howard Shaffer, for one, said: "People need journals so that they can keep track every day of both their emotional states and their behavioral states. This enables people in recovery to chart and see their improvement."

Scientific data begins to support journaling benefits

Regularly writing down your thoughts and feelings, journaling, is labeled by scientific researchers as "written emotional expression," a technique that has been shown in countless studies to be of use in soothing chronic pain, lowering blood pressure, reducing stress and anxiety, lifting depression, healing post-traumatic stress disorders, and boosting the immune system.

Somehow, written emotional expression seems to unknot and release the chronic cramp of negative emotions that can cause and complicate disease, including the disease of compulsive behaviors. Though few studies have looked at the benefits of journaling on toxic compulsions, the evidence thus far is quite promising.

What may have been the first study examination of the effects of written emotional expression on recovery from drug dependence—in this case, cocaine—came in 2010 from researchers at the Department of Veterans Affairs Medical Center in Kansas City, Missouri. Subjects in this controlled trial experiment were receiving intensive treatment for cocaine dependence in a residential-unit setting. The findings were remarkable: "Treatment [with written emotional expression] produced changes in blood pressure and mood during writing sessions, possibly because of its ability to stimulate active coping behavior. At an initial follow-up visit, patients that had received written emotional expression reported lower values for craving intensity and were less likely to self-report use of cocaine. These results may indicate a therapeutic effect of written emotional expression during recovery from cocaine dependence." *(Source: "The value of acupuncture detoxification programs in a substance abuse treatment system." Michael Shwartz et al. J Subst Abuse Treat. 1999 Dec;17(4):305–12.)*

(Important note to readers: If you want to expand and deepen the integration of the Seven Self-Care Tools into your recovery life and become empowered to take more effective action, then go beyond just reading about the tools in this section of the book and access the extensive support resources for these tools, assembled at www.recover2live.com.)

XI

A Guide to Working 12-Step Programs

W hat I am about to describe for you is based on personal observation, my reading of the study literature, and interviews and conversations I've had with people familiar with how 12-Step programs function and what makes them effective for many people.

The key piece that determines effectiveness is the connection that people have with each other in the program. The nature of relationships is so much more profound in recovery because of the intense experiences we've had and the ability people develop to reveal themselves.

I've seen studies by Dr. Scott Tonigan and others that asked, "What is the most significant piece of the program that gets people sober?" This research confirmed what many of us always suspected: The connections you develop with other people and being part of a group—a group in which you're accepted and able to be completely honest about what you're doing in your life—play the key roles in success.

If you've danced with the 800-pound gorilla of addiction for enough years, you already know what works for you, no matter what a study says. So this is deeply personal for many of you. I've used science and the evidence-based approach to treatment in this book, but you've got to see what works for you on your own, and that means trying on a 12-Step program for size.

It's really simple—a 12-Step program won't hurt you, and it will probably do you some good. Before the advent of the first 12-Step program in 1935, there weren't a lot of options for people with addictive illnesses. They ended up dead, in jail, or in mental institutions. Today we are fortunate to have a proven, free option available whenever and wherever we need it.

There are no real do's and don'ts for membership in a 12-Step program. The only requirement for membership is the desire to stop doing what is hurting you, whether that activity involves drugs, alcohol, food, gambling, hoarding, sex and porn, or smoking. You don't need to have stopped and you don't need to have any money to walk into a meeting.

So that's the first thing. It's absolutely free. Nobody asks you to sign anything. Nobody will tell you to do anything. There are only suggestions, many of which you will find to be valuable. Nobody will make you speak. Nobody will force you to believe in God, any kind of God. You don't have to work the steps. You don't have to do anything. You can go there and sit in the back and you can listen. Nobody will tell you to leave. No matter what you do or say—in fact, you could raise your hand and say, "I think this is all a bunch of bullshit," and everybody will say, "Keep coming back," because it's the most forgiving, loving place.

Each group is autonomous, so each group is different in some way. So much about a meeting has to do with the personalities who are in the room at any given time. It also takes a while to understand the vocabulary being used and what it really means.

When you walk into a meeting, you're not walking into a strange or foreign place, although your anxiety and fear may make it seem that way. You're walking into a room of people who live in your community. Many of them will be your peers, your contemporaries, people fighting the same battles you are, people you can relate to. So keep all of that in mind as your illness tries to protect itself by coming up with a bunch of reasons why you shouldn't go or shouldn't stay in that room.

A good rule of thumb is to try six different meetings in a two-week period. The good thing about 12-Steps is that you're probably going to find a meeting close to you wherever you happen to be. These are your neighbors. If you are in a big city, you're going to find thousands of groups. So that's a huge benefit of 12-Steps: They're easy to access; they're everywhere in the world.

You can take what you like from 12-Step programs and leave the rest. You don't have to buy the whole menu. You can take it a la carte. You can go, "Look, this works for me. I love showing up here. I love listening to stories." When I got sober, a good meeting was a good war story. I loved hearing people talk about shooting dope and throwing up on their sneakers and all that kind of stuff, and I would leave going, "God, I'm glad I'm not doing that anymore." But today, I want to hear about how you live life and how you overcome the craziness of being an addict. I want to hear about learning to live life on life's terms.

12-Step programs exist everywhere in the world and they are composed of people from all walks of life. You can go there just to socialize and simply to confirm that there are other people in the same boat as you. Yes, you can even forget the steps, forget getting a sponsor. But if you really want to work the program, it works and will enhance your recovery.

There are a series of steps you can work with your sponsor; they're not mandatory, but you can if you want. If you try to do the program piecemeal and it isn't effective for you, it's not that the steps and the program failed to work, it's that you chose not to work the program. Really work it and then tell me you failed. That's the genius of it. You don't have to do anything you don't want to do. And these people in the meetings will still love you and tell you to keep coming back.

If you're looking for a reason not to attend 12-Step meetings, you're going to find it. Addicts are notorious for having contempt before investigation. Some people express contempt for 12-Step fellowships based on hearsay, which they accept because it panders to their fears, despite never having personally investigated the claims being made.

For every two people who walk into a 12-Step meeting for the first time, one of them will never go back and often will give one or more rationalizations, such as an aversion to the mention of God, a fear that it's a cult, and all the other myths that go around. Most of the nonsense is like the disease itself. There's a lot of misinformation, a lot of ignorance, a lot of fear.

Disadvantages to 12-Step Programs

So what turns people off 12-Step programs? Let's go through the reasons one by one.

"I don't like groups. I don't like revealing myself in groups."

That's a legitimate fear and I understand that. But this group is unlike any group you've ever seen before. You could be there for a long time before you ever open your mouth and no one will judge you.

There is something contagious about the group dynamic that melts away a lot of those attitudes that people walk in with, if they stay long enough. People who don't stay are people who really don't want to overcome their compulsion. You can find a lot of reasons you don't want to stay, so you really have to be honest with yourself on some level and say, "Am I really done using?"

People in the program say, "Listen, do it for 90 days and your misery is refundable." We don't care, just try it for 90 days, and then you can go back to doing what you were before the 90 days.

This is one of the things that the first 12-Step program originators intuitively knew many years ago. They said 90 days of sobriety is a really big deal in Alcoholics Anonymous. They just seemed to know that something happens in that period of time to really change you. It happens in your brain. Science studies have shown that it takes about 90 days before an alcoholic's brain returns to a base level. That's one reason why spending just 28 days in rehab is ridiculous. It takes 90 days minimum for a person who meets the dependency criteria to really get back to base level where they can actually start to hear things and their cravings diminish to a point where they're actually closer to normal.

Drug addicts and alcoholics are very secretive. So are many people with a gambling or sex compulsion disorder. You have to ask yourself whether being afraid of groups or revealing yourself in public is really who you are, or whether that's a defense mechanism that you've developed over time to protect your disease. I would argue that many of us developed it over time to protect our illness.

Remember that sharing your experience, your struggles, and your strength with somebody else in the program isn't being done in the hope that it will somehow help others, although it might. Sharing honestly and openly in the group is based on the knowledge that the act of doing it, of expressing yourself honestly and openly, will free *you* from the pathology of doing what doesn't work for you over and over again.

As Dr. Robert DuPont explained to me, "The only qualification for membership is a public announcement of your imperfection. 'Hi, I'm Bob. I am an alcoholic and a drug addict.' In those meetings your ego stays outside. Everyone is equal and imperfect. Meetings promote humility and honesty, the twin antidotes to the basic character flaws that lead to and that result from an addiction."

"I've heard that 12-Step programs are Christian in nature and religion isn't my thing."

If there is any religious connotation to draw, think of it as ecumenical. A variety of religious traditions can embrace and relate to the 12 Steps. For example, several books about working the 12 Steps from a Buddhist perspective have been written. In his *One Breath at a Time: Buddhism and the Twelve Steps*, practicing Buddhist Kevin Griffin wrote: "What makes Buddhism and the 12 Steps so compatible? The Buddha said that the cause of suffering is desire, and the 12 Steps try to heal people from desire gone mad: addiction. This connection is the gateway into integrating the two systems. Both ask you to look at the painful realities of life, to understand them, and to use this understanding as the foundation for developing peace, wisdom, faith, and compassion."

Nobody who says the Lord's Prayer in a 12-Step meeting, at least insofar as I'm aware, is thinking of it as necessarily a Christian prayer. But if you went to a meeting and you didn't know, you might think, "Oh, these guys are all Christians." I know there are meetings that are all about Jesus. I've been to those meetings. That's not a 12-Step program, but those kinds of aberrations exist. The fact is, though, if you have a problem with God, whatever that means to you, you're going to need to get beyond that to feel comfortable in 12-Step meetings.

A wise man once said to me, "You could prove to me that God doesn't exist, but I would still believe because belief works for me." If the God thing doesn't work for you, and if you can't find a God of your own understanding, it's going to be very hard for you to access 12-Step programs. Not impossible, just difficult.

People often get lost in feeling the need to define it. They have to say what it is. I don't care. And no addict should care. Nobody who gets any relief from the toxic compulsions that ruin their lives will give a crap where the relief comes from so long as it works.

When they wrote the reference to God in 12-Steps they said, "God as you understand God." I never thought about God until I got sober. And I was like, "I don't have a God." And people said to me, "Well God, G-O-D, Group of Drunks." Call it electricity, nature, anything bigger than yourself. It's a God of your own understanding. I no longer have a Catholic God. So I developed my own idea of God and my own understanding without being religious about it.

There are plenty of atheists in 12-Step programs. Self-professed atheist Marya Hornbacher wrote a book about her healing experience in AA titled *Waiting: A Nonbeliever's Higher Power*, in which she said, "I do believe I'd be dead without the help of the people and the structure of the steps in AA." She recovered without embracing the spiritual component of the program. As she wrote in a column for the CNN Web site: "If you are of an atheistic or strongly agnostic mindset, chances are you'll walk into a meeting, see the steps hanging on the wall [six of which refer to God, a Higher Power, or He] and want to scream, laugh, or walk back out. But this shouldn't be a deal breaker . . . it's perfectly possible to sober up, sans belief in God . . . I believe that the most important spiritual principle of AA is humility. The recognition that we are flawed, that we can and must change, and that our purpose, not only in sobriety but in life, is to be of service to others."

"I heard that if you join a 12-Step program you give up your power to a cult group."

"The most common reason we hear at the Chopra Center for why people do not resonate with AA is its emphasis on personal powerlessness," observed Dr. Deepak Chopra and Dr. David Simon in their book *Freedom from Addiction*. "Most secular and religious philosophies highlight the principle that we are responsible for our choices in life. The first step in 12-Step programs requires an admission of powerlessness that some people are not able or willing to embrace. The implication that people with bad habits must consider themselves lifelong victims of an incurable condition is, for some, untenable. For those who believe free will is a distinguishing feature of human beings, admitting that one has lost free will stops the recovery process before it begins."

This is irony in the idea that you are powerless in the face of your addiction. Willpower is like a muscle you flex, and it can grow stronger the more you learn to use it. This concept of feeling powerless, especially in the beginning of 12-Step involvement, doesn't obliterate you or your free will; it's actually going to increase your power over time. It's like the idea of humility being much more powerful than arrogance. You come to understand that your faith is more powerful than the sense of powerlessness you might feel. Recovery as a process is about empowerment.

Then there is the myth that it's a cult. That somehow somebody's going to make you drink the Kool-Aid. 12-Step programs are the most democratic of groups, so much so that it's almost anarchy. When I wrote my book *Moments of Clarity*, I tried to find out who I could talk to in AA about what anonymity means. There wasn't anybody. There wasn't any minister of information or a marketing department or a president. It's run by the inmates and it works magically.

Believe me, AA and the other 12-Step groups are not a cult on any level. There are no leaders, and the groups have no opinion on any outside issues. They don't get involved in any other thing. Every group is autonomous; there's no central hierarchy. Unlike a real cult, which is hard for someone to get out of once they join, people come and go voluntarily in 12-Step programs every single day.

The program of Alcoholics Anonymous isn't the steps of Alcoholics Anonymous. It can be summed up basically as: "Clean house, serve others, and trust something bigger than you." It's all wrapped up in unity and service. It's a profound template for living that has nothing to do with cult-like programming.

"I've heard that I must have a sponsor who tells me what I can and can't do in my life."

Anyone who ever heard or believed this one was probably playing that game where you whisper a secret around a table. By the time the information gets to the last person in the circle, it's so warped as to be laughable.

A sponsor in a 12-Step program isn't somebody who tells you what to do. That isn't the role a sponsor is supposed to play. What they are supposed to do is to share their experience, strength, and hope with you in terms of working the program and living life on life's terms in recovery. The sponsor is a lifeline, somebody you can talk to openly and honestly and who will listen without judgment.

They call people who sponsor other people pigeons because the pigeons shit all over them. The idea is in order to keep this recovery thing, you have to give it away. That's another part of the genius and power of this program. It reminds you where you were when you see somebody who is just coming in because they're closer to the illness than you. The gift is that when I'm listening to your problems, I'm not thinking about my own.

A good standard to use in a 12-Step program is to look around and see who has what you want. If you want to know how to have a good relationship, don't seek relationship advice from somebody who's been divorced four times. Talk to somebody who has a good marriage and knows what it takes to have a good marriage. Talk to somebody who *has* a job about getting a job and holding a job. Talk to somebody who knows how to manage their money if you have money issues. If you want to know how to work the program, talk to somebody who has worked the program, who has gone through the steps.

It's really about empathy. It's about human connection and about being there for another human being. The steps are important in terms of changing who you are, but that takes some work and time and not everybody does it to completion. Also, doing AA or another 12-Step program isn't necessarily a bridge back to life, but a tunnel to other 12-Step programs.

It's the only organization where the person with the least amount of time in the group, who knows the least walking in, becomes the most important person in the room.

Something else you should know about is the safety factor. You can rest assured that if you go to a 12-Step meeting and you share with everyone in the room, everything said there is supposed to be held safe and sacred. These rooms are meant to be safe rooms where people can trust that what they reveal will be held in confidence. This is the intention and for the most part, this is the reality.

Also keep in mind that 12-Step programs are based on attraction, not promotion. These groups don't try to coerce or recruit people. There is a level of honesty and simplicity in their messaging. A person walking into that room for the first time is going to hear their own internal bias no matter what the true principles and message of 12-Steps happen to be. The critical thing is to try to keep an open mind for as long as possible so you can really hear what's going on.

One more thing I should emphasize: Whatever behaviors you have developed that are hurtful to you have been years and years in the making. You can't change them by just taking a long walk in the woods. The idea of immediate gratification, the "just give me a pill and make it go away" reasoning so prevalent in our culture, doesn't work or apply to this illness. If you can't get your mind around the idea of this being a complicated illness and that the process of recovery will be long and treacherous, then put this book down right now. Seriously! You aren't ready to have your denial pierced.

Give 12-Steps a shot. It won't hurt. Try six different 12-Step meetings in six days. Someone in AA once told me you need to shop around for the AA group that's right for you, just like when you were drinking you tried different bars before you found your "home bar." I thought that was a great analogy.

Ideally, you'll do 90 meetings in 90 days to feel the most dramatic impact. But at least try six different groups, because you've got to find a group of people that you feel like you can engage with. If you really want to change your life for the better, this is a good beginning.

Experts Share What Makes 12-Steps Effective

Every expert I interviewed for this book found something worthwhile in 12-Step programs and each had a slightly different perspective to share.

Get support from recovery winners

From Dr. Drew Pinsky, addiction medicine specialist and clinical professor of psychiatry, University of Southern California School of Medicine: Go to a meeting, raise your hand, and say, "I need help." That's the first thing. What you will find in almost every meeting in every city are people who know who the doctors are that can help you. So ask for help and see what people know. There's a lot of information at 12-Step meetings. People who have really long-term recovery are a core group. They hang with each other. They share deep experiences together. Over time, they trust each other. So it's not just about the 12-Step meeting. It's about the core group of support from peers who are recovery winners. Establishing healthy relationships with people is the job of recovering. The 12-Step program is a guided experience in learning to trust and developing intimate relationships where you are open and honest.

12-Steps offer you their collective wisdom

From Dr. Robert DuPont, President of the Institute for Behavior and Health Inc, first director of the National Institute on Drug Abuse, second White House Drug Chief, and clinical professor of psychiatry at Georgetown Medical School: I'm proud to be an American because of Alcoholics Anonymous. This great gift to the world is American in its origins and global in its remarkable mission. AA is a modern miracle that is repeated daily in every community in our country and increasingly all over the world. There's more honesty in an AA meeting than in any psychiatrist's office, including mine. The wisdom in the 12-Step fellowships is the wisdom of a collective experience that has been distilled over decades in ways that are completely unique. Bill Wilson discovered that the only way he could stay sober was to help another alcoholic. Where else have you ever heard anything like that? When I say that to my medical colleagues, they think I've been possessed. I've seen the miracle of these fellowships over and over again in my family, in my neighborhood, and in my psychiatric practice. One of my medical colleagues who is an AA member called AA a God-aid program rather than a self-help or a mutual-aid program. The reason is that your recovery depends on something bigger than you. The Higher Power of AA does not have to be God or anything else that is specific. It just can't be *you*. Recovery requires the power of something bigger than you. It can be the Higher Power of your group, or of mankind. One of my patients told me that his Higher Power, at the beginning, was his parole officer.

"We" means not recovering alone

From Dr. Sarz Maxwell, medical director, Chicago Recovery Alliance: 12-Step programs give people community. They give people spirituality. People get connection. These are all endorphin-releasing activities. All you need to know is that the first word of the 12 Steps is "we." It's "we," not "I." Most people I ask, "What's the first word of the 12 Steps?" say, "I." No. You're still in your disease when you say that. You need to learn the first word and that's your first step to getting better. "We" means you can't do this alone.

You get as much support as you give

From Marianne Williamson, the author of many books including A Return to Love: Reflections on the Principles of "A Course in Miracles": One of the shadow sides of the addicted mind is to think that their suffering is special. With the 12-Step meetings it's reasonable to assume that no matter where you are in life, if you look to the left and you look to the right, the person next to you has probably suffered as much as you have. It's not just that you're sitting in a room with other people. It's that you care about them. It's that you realized you're not just there to get support; you're also there to give support. And so the only way to remove ourselves from the sense of isolation is by helping someone who is standing in front of us feel less isolated.

Find the 12-Step group that best fits you

From Dr. Jeffrey Roth, addiction psychiatrist, author, editor of Journal of Groups in Addiction Recovery, *and medical director, Working Sobriety Chicago*: Let's look at what kinds of feelings are stirred up by letting go of the compulsion. What kinds of feelings are stirred up by joining a community of people who actually love you? What does it stir up in terms of steps four through twelve in terms of what you didn't get when you were growing up, because, typically, about a year into sobriety, that's when the shit hits the fan. And some people start realizing, "Wait a second, all these people who I'm sitting with are being honest with me, and why didn't I have this when I was growing up?" And they usually can't admit that, and that's when they start getting depressed in their first year of sobriety. And that's when having a sponsor becomes an incredibly important issue.

If you're committed to continuing to drink and you're going to go to AA, I need to warn you that going to AA may produce one of two things. One, it may destroy your enjoyment of alcohol. If it doesn't destroy your joy for drinking and you continue to go to AA and you continue to drink, you may start going crazy because you're going to be in an environment where you're attaching to a mission which you're not part of. I recommend that unless you're willing to get psychotic, don't go long-term to AA if you're going to continue to drink.

No AA group is exactly the same. There are AA groups that are run like a hippie kind of group. And there are AA groups that run like paramilitary organizations. So to say to somebody "AA doesn't work," have you looked for the AA meeting that would be useful for you? Some people need the paramilitary organization, and some people are so allergic to the paramilitary organization that they think, "That's AA, so I'm never going to go back there again."

Fellowships have something to teach each other

From Dr. Patrick Carnes, psychologist, author, and former clinical director of sexual disorders services, The Meadows, Arizona: The real test is not which 12-Step meeting you go to, it's where the best meetings are. In a city like Philadelphia, or even in West Palm Beach, Florida, you can catch a

Sexaholics Anonymous meeting Tuesday night and a Sex Addicts Anonymous meeting on Saturday morning, and a lot of people go to both. Go to the meetings that help you, and they each have their different twist on things.

It was unfortunate in a way for the sex-addiction community that three of the fellowships started within weeks of each other in the summer of 1977. They all have their big boat and the culture was ready. But the truth is, we're wasting money and time, because if you combined at least three to four of those fellowships, we would be dollars ahead in terms of outreach and doing things that we really need to be doing. All of the fellowships have something to teach one another. Choosing among them can be confusing for a new addict coming in. There is a dialogue between the fellowships about that, and I think eventually some of them will consolidate. RCA (Recovering Couples Anonymous) is a different deal. It's something that everybody can go to and should. Sex addicts are changing AA, because they're forcing AA people to start talking about sex. And we're starting to look at matters of food and nicotine and those things that are addiction interactions.

XII

Having a Life Worth Living— the Art of Recovery

Part of me suspects that I'm a loser, and the other part of me thinks I'm God Almighty.
   —John Lennon

People often say that this or that person has not yet found himself. But the self is not something that one finds. It is something that one creates.
   —Thomas Szasz

What Is Recovery . . . What Does It Look Like?

My own journey into recovery was about authenticity. When I got clean and sober I had no idea that the greatest gift would be finding (or creating) my authentic self. It was a very painful, arduous, inconsistent pathway, and I made a lot of wrong moves on the way. But I'm a totally different person at 25 years in recovery than I was at 15 years of recovery.

I thought getting into a recovery was going to be boring, and I'd never be as dynamic again. Yet I do more in a day today than I did in a month when I was using. So it's about perspective, and it takes a long time to change one's perspective. You need to have experience; it doesn't happen overnight, and addicts have to understand this is a process. There aren't any quick fixes.

To maintain a life worth living, I want to identify some of the things people have said that can be helpful to building self-esteem and making yourself happy. Happiness studies around the world have found that money has little to do with it. It's about relationships, about community, about finding a purpose in your life, finding a hobby, having healthy fun.

You could say, "That's what I want my life to be about," but maybe you find yourself falling back into thinking patterns and behaviors that are from the toxic past. You have to understand a couple of things. One is that drugs and other compulsions were not the problem— they were seen as the *solution* to the problem. The real problem existed probably from very early in your life.

Many experts remarked to me that a person's emotional development sort of stops at the age when that person got dependent on a substance or behavior. Often this occurs in early adolescence, so when they come into recovery at age 30, or whenever, they remain emotionally stuck at the age they got hooked. This phenomenon carries huge consequences for how they are going to function in early recovery.

You need to work through the anger, the resentment that you have with your parents, and all that childhood material. It takes time. You can short-circuit that time expenditure by going to specialized therapy programs. They can be expensive, but you can do two years or five years of therapy in just four days doing some types of psychodrama exercises. It's cathartic and meaningful in terms of changing some of the issues or putting them to rest.

Another important piece is life skills, the art of learning how to really engage life. If you've been screwing around with substances or process addictions, you missed the boat on a lot of things that you need to know in terms of getting a life worth living.

Experts I spoke with said community was probably the most important recovery factor, along with family relationships. Those were always at the top of the list. Getting a job, managing your money, taking care of your health, relationships, these are skill sets you need to function well. If you don't get that, you're going to function like an addict. What we're talking about is enabling people to go into real life, mainstream life, and to function effectively.

Getting a job is important. Self-support from your own contributions is important. Decent relationships with the people in your life are important. Your health is important. However, in terms of a deeper understanding of the journey, there is a spiritual dimension that a lot of people come to when they go down this road.

You owe it to yourself to give yourself the opportunity for a different vision and a different experience of your life, but that takes a little time. You've got to give it 90 days to even start seeing and feeling a difference. It takes 90 days for new dendrites in the brain to form, and that gets back to activities and behaviors that use the plasticity of our brain to literally transform ourselves.

One question that I asked a lot of experts was, "What is the one thing people need to have within themselves to be successful in treatment?" The quality picked more than anything else was *the desire to want to get better*. I know that I did two things right. First, I didn't die from this illness, and second, I always had the desire to get better. You need to have that desire to hold on to a part of your life that is the healthy part, and you need to be aware of what stands in the way and with that recognition, learn how to remove the barriers.

In research compiled by Alexandre Laudet, director of the Center for Study of Addictions and Recovery, National Development and Research Institutes Inc, it's clear that when you give up a crutch, whether it's a substance or a behavior, you will get a better, healthier crutch in recovery that will help you to stand up taller than you ever thought possible. That's what you gain by giving up the compulsion. The taller you stand, the less likely you are to uncontrollably crave that toxic crutch again. Dr. Laudet phrased it this way: "The more your life improves in recovery and the more satisfied you are with your life, the more likely you are to maintain healthy habits. It's a vicious cycle in a good way: don't use, improve—that sustains not using, and you improve even more."

Workaholism Can Hinder Long-Term Recovery

Everybody I know in recovery struggles with workaholism, which basically means, "I'd rather be working on my computer than sitting with my kids, getting to know what my kids are doing." Nearly everybody I know in recovery is running fast, working hard, and they will do it sometimes at the expense of their own health and recovery. So they work and they work and they stop going to meetings, and eventually, they may engage in toxic behaviors again.

One of the keys to recovery is finding the capacity to relax. Workaholics find it difficult to relax, at least in the typical way that we define relaxation. For a workaholic, relaxation is doing more work, less strenuously, or not as fast, but it's still the same sort of distraction from the compulsion. It's a strategy, too, filling up life with work in the hope they won't be thinking about their compulsion.

Clinical psychologist Barbara Killinger, author of *Workaholics: The Respectable Addicts*, offers this perspective on how that condition relates to the Seven Toxic Compulsions:

"A workaholic is a person who gradually has become emotionally crippled and addicted to control and power. And they're caught in a compulsive drive to gain approval and success. The addiction in this case is to power and control, but the obsession is work and having a success persona that broadcasts that I am a successful person. So they become very driven, and the obsessive thinking takes over.

"These people have become addicted to the adrenaline high; they cannot *not work*; they get anxious. And so the work doesn't cover it anymore. It's a great downward progression because they're predictable and very down. And so that's when they tend to start drinking too much; they get into smoking, drugs, and all these other things.

"A workaholic cannot *not work* without getting highly anxious, so they are caught on the gerbil wheel and get more and more driven. They aren't emotionally able to be present with people. They start to get very angry and righteous when they can't be as fast as they want to. They talk fast, they eat fast—they are just very, very driven. That's one of the things that I say to people when they're first working with me. 'Could you please slow down? Walk more slowly, talk more slowly.' When you watch a workaholic walking along, they're charging along, and underneath that arrogance is insecurity and self-doubt, but it's largely unconscious until things in their life start to fall apart.

"I had a client who was going out to play golf. I said, 'Would you try something for me this weekend? Could you go out and play golf tomorrow without keeping score?' And he looked at me stunned and said, 'What would be the point?'

"They're not experiencing things because they're all up in their heads. So, if they work from their neck up, they're completely out of touch with their bodies, they're not getting the signals that the body is sending telling them how they're feeling or that they're depressed or anxious. They're repressing so much. The breakdown used to take 20 or 25 years; now it's about five. It's incredible how fast this has escalated. This is what technology is doing for workaholism. Some clients have been worried they were going to have a heart attack or stroke. Workaholism and the stress associated with it really affects health.

"One of the things they can do is make their home a refuge and not take work home. Ask people not to call you at home. Put a fence around the home so that it is a refuge with the rest of the family. Don't over schedule. Don't do two things at once. Don't push yourself to be better at everything. You're going to be miserable for a couple of weeks because you're going to get into adrenaline withdrawal (a sign of the adrenaline junkie). You will be very anxious for quite a while. Meditation is a good tool, and so is mindfulness—anything to help them stay present in the moment and get in touch with their feelings.

"Those who get cured, I call them my butterflies. Their whole life gets transformed. Their values change. As their values change they become much kinder people. One of the things that I noticed is that people's faces change. A workaholic is very intense, and you can see it in their face. And what I noticed as they're getting better is that their whole face softens because their values have changed."

Mindful Self-Compassion Helps Solidify Recovery

Combining mindfulness and self-compassion as an intervention program was an innovation of Dr. Kristin Neff, research psychologist and associate professor at the University of Texas at Austin and author of the book *Self-Compassion: Stop Beating Yourself Up and Leave Insecurity Behind*. Dr. Neff explained:

"Having compassion for yourself is no different than having compassion for other people. Self-compassion operates in the parts of the brain that have to do with soothing. It's the same parts of the brain that are activated when the mother comforts a crying child. If you add the self-soothing system of compassion to mindfulness or mindfulness meditation, that little addition is crucial in making a behavioral change last longer. The self-compassion exercises help to release oxytocin. So if you're going to be addicted to chemicals, it's better to be addicted to the natural chemicals of compassion."

Dr. Neff described three elements of self-compassion:

1. Engage in self-kindness. When you experience failure, suffering, or feelings of inadequacy, rather than engage in self-criticism or ignore the pain, it's important to bring warm and understanding thoughts about oneself forward. Be gentle with yourself. You cannot always get exactly what you want.

Accept this reality with kindness and sympathy toward one's circumstance.

2. Recognize shared human experiences. We are interdependent beings. Other people experience what we experience. We don't have to take our failings and life difficulties so seriously. Acknowledge this fact of life with nonjudgmental understanding and compassion for the human condition.

3. Exercise mindfulness to observe negative thoughts and feelings without judgment. By not over-identifying with our thoughts and feelings, we can more readily maintain control over our impulses and not get swept away by reactivity or negativity. You observe thoughts and feelings as they come up, without trying to deny them or suppress them.

Studies have been done examining the psychological effects of self-compassion exercises. Five self-compassion studies were compared in 2007 by Duke University psychologists who concluded, "In general, these studies suggest that self-compassion attenuates people's reactions to negative events in ways that are distinct from and, in some cases, more beneficial than self-esteem." *(Source: "Self-compassion and reactions to unpleasant self-relevant events: The implications of treating oneself kindly." Mark R. Leary et al. J Pers Soc Psychol. 2007 May;92(5):887–904.)*

University of Montana research psychologists examined the relationship between self-compassion and post-traumatic stress symptoms in 210 university students based on Dr. Neff's work. This study concluded: "Individuals high in self-compassion may engage in less avoidance strategies following trauma exposure," which facilitates healing. *(Source: "Self-compassion and PTSD symptom severity." Thompson BL and Waltz J. J Trauma Stress. 2008 Dec;21(6):556–8.)*

You can find out more about Dr. Neff's approach to self-compassion at www.self-compassion.org.

A second pioneer in developing self-compassion approaches to treating toxic compulsions and their underlying disorders is Prof. Paul Gilbert, head of the Mental Health Research Unit at Kingsway Hospital, associated with the University of Derby in Britain. Here is what Prof. Gilbert had to say:

"Substance abusers are trying to regulate their emotions. They are taking substances to make themselves feel less anxious or more activated. Controlling emotions is really a key to a lot of this stuff. What we know is that for mammals, especially humans, we control our emotions through our relationships, primarily. As a child, Mom gives you a cuddle, calms you down, then you feel better. We know that when children don't get that or when their parents, for one reason or another, are struggling to provide this calming, soothing input to the child, the child actually grows up having difficulty regulating their emotions because they don't internalize this loving and caring part you see in a person. And what we know is that there's a system in the brain which is linked to endorphins and oxytocin. It has a calming effect on us. Endorphins, for example, help to deal with pain.

"These chemicals are released, assuming it is a loving and caring relationship. People who come from relatively secure backgrounds will have an internalized memory, which helps them regulate emotion. But those on drugs find it difficult to do that. The drug becomes a substitute emotional regulator. So we have to teach them how to get that soothing system, that endorphin system, going through other means. That's what compassion does; it teaches them how to practice stimulating their affiliative [associating and befriending behaviors] system.

"One thing we focus on with self-compassion is how people are often very self-critical. And when you're self-critical, you're stimulating threat systems in your brain. Self-criticism is often about fantasy. What you fantasize about influences your brain. Fantasies are a very powerful way of influencing physiological systems. So why not use images that actually juice up other systems, such as your affiliative system, to pump up more endorphins? What we teach people is to create their own image idea of compassion. Supposing you wish to imagine a compassionate figure, what kind of figure would that be like? Would it be somebody who has been through what you've been through and really understands your pain and suffering?

"Anybody can love somebody who is smiling and good all the time. That's easy. But compassion comes into its own when it's tough, when it's difficult, when things are bad for you, when you're feeling really bad. So the point is to train your brain.

"You might want to try this little exercise we use. People often say, 'I need to be self-critical because it keeps me on a straight path and if I keep pulling myself down, then I'll make sure I won't be arrogant.' So what I want you to do is just close your eyes and imagine your self-critic. Spend a few minutes and imagine that you can see the self, the part of you that criticizes yourself. And you can see what it's saying to you and you can see the emotions. So give it room to imagine the emotion for the critic. And normally people say, 'Oh, my critic is very angry with me.' And then you say to them, 'Okay. Now look at that critic. Does it really have your best interest at heart? Does it give joy when you do well and you move forward?' They see that it doesn't. So the point is that what we're doing is developing compassion. It's not about whether you deserve it or not; it's what's in your best interest.

"What would help you move forward? What would help you get stronger? What would help you develop courage? Because you really need courage in order to deal with your anxiety to get out of a bad relationship, or whatever. If you have a kind voice in your head that supports you and understands you, you're more likely to have courage than if you have a critical or panicky or anxiety voice. So pay attention to the voice—that will help you. Pay attention to the voice inside of you that will give you the strength to do what you need to do."

Experts on What Recovery Looks and Feels Like

"Let a thousand flowers bloom" might be the best advice here because recovery from a toxic compulsion can take many forms, at least in terms of how it feels inside and looks outside to others. With that in mind, check out what these experts have to say. Like holding a crystal up to the sun and turning it, each one reveals a different pattern of light and color that defines the experience of a person in recovery.

Recovery is another word for freedom

From Gil Gilchrist, chief executive officer, New Beginnings at Waverly: Recovery is a lot like enlightenment—most of the people who have excellent recovery, you wouldn't even know until you spent time with them. They are human beings first and recovering people second. The recovery ideology does not define them, but it's an integral part of their life. Recovery is not a feeling. It is a state of awareness and realization. You realize that you are free. No matter how good or bad things get, the fundamental realization is that you are free

The recovery process enriches you

From Dr. Drew Pinsky, addiction medicine specialist and clinical professor of psychiatry, University of Southern California School of Medicine: Recovery makes the world look flourishing and inspiring. It takes my breath away sometimes when somebody who I thought was going to die comes up to me a year later and says, "Something happened. I had a moment, and thank you for hanging in there with me as much as you did." They have become so rich as a person. And what often comes along with that is the desire to go and help another person get to that place.

Always keep the recovery steps in mind

From Dr. Charles Whitfield, psychotherapist and trauma recovery expert and author of My Recovery: A Personal Plan for Healing: The first step in treatment is to name the trauma. That takes time. No patient will walk in and say, "I have just discovered I was abused as a kid." If someone does say that, it's often a red flag. I'd rather see someone resist or deny than come to a first session to be healed. It's a process. Repeated individual therapy and weekly group therapy that is trauma-focused and relates current life issues to past traumas are effective. There are stages of recovery. Zero is no recovery. Stage one is going to meetings and working the steps, where the problem is stabilized. Two is addressing the childhood and other repeated traumas. That is the longest stage for many people, up to five years working a full recovery program. Three is the spiritual element. The journey to God often starts with a journey away from God. The Higher Power of 12-Step programs is important in bringing about stage three.

Successful recovery involves seeing new meaning in life

From Dr. Thomas McLellan, CEO of the Treatment Research Institute and former deputy director of the White House Office of National Drug Control Policy: I know a lot of people who are recovering from substance-use problems. I don't know anybody who's been able to go back to their old life without changes and remain sober. They need a new life and in that context, they've got to have new meaning from some of the old things they've been doing. I've seen that happen.

But more often they need new things to give meaning to their lives. That can be service to others in the community of AA, for example. It can be volunteering with kids. It could be mentoring somebody on their job. It could be a lot of things, but I think it's, in its healthiest sense, the substitution of something that's socially desirable and useful for something that really gave them trouble.

You can interpret it in the spiritual sense of being closer to God, that's okay with me, that's all right. But you don't have to be spiritual and you can say, "Look, there's another way of getting enjoyment." Some people call it socialization—learning to feel good about accomplishing things that are also good for society and other people.

Something that changed the way I think about such things was said by Bill White of Chestnut Health Systems. He's the first person I've heard say this: "Addiction is one of those diseases where if you recover, you end up better than you ever were before you had the disease." It's because of that kind of thing, that new perspective on your old life; you're valuing things that you didn't value in your prior life. Your order, your balance comes in ways that, frankly, don't come from medications and they don't come from simple abstinence. They come from other kinds of growth, which I think are really the key parts of recovery.

A participant in one of my National Institutes of Health studies, a 42-year-old African-American guy with a 20-plus year history of severe crack addiction, polysubstance use, jail, and everything else that goes with it, defined recovery thus: "My definition of recovery is *life* . . . 'cause I didn't have no life before I got into recovery."

Seven imperatives for healthy recovery

From Dr. Andrea Barthwell, CEO of the North Carolina treatment center Two Dreams Outer Banks: Here are my recommended seven life-enhancement imperatives for moving from dependent use or nondependent use to recovery: abstinence, peer support, professional guidance, medication, nutrition, exercise, and ritual.

Abstinence is acting on the realization that you can't continue doing that substance or activity if you have a problem.

Peer support can be group therapy or a 12-Step program, but it's about coming out of isolation and getting supported by peers who accept your disease but don't support it.

Professional guidance can be one-on-one therapy, a psychologist, a psychiatrist, a counselor, even a minister or a shaman—anyone who can help you to evaluate what your needs are and how to meet them.

Medication is something given as an outside guidance support from a physician.

Nutrition means getting the nutrients you need rather than sugar and things you put into your system as addiction substitutes.

Exercise such as hot yoga or lifting weights or running helps with sleep hygiene, helps bring your endorphins back to normal, and helps to develop the muscles you need for body support.

Ritual is where you do meditation, your journaling, your attendance at 12-Step meetings, sitting in a hot tub for 30 minutes a day—positive habituation rituals to structure your mind and your life in healthy ways.

Recovery is service to something greater

From William White, senior research consultant, Chestnut Health Systems: What I know from watching people in recovery for the past 42 years is that there are degrees and levels of recovery. The kind of recovery I most admire involves a fundamental change in one's identity, interpersonal relationships, and daily lifestyle. Recovery, like the escape from other near-death experiences, provides an opportunity to reorder priorities and live life in a more conscious, intentional way. It is a window of opportunity to find a level of meaning and fulfillment that might not have otherwise been possible. Through that process, everything in one's life is touched. It is for many people, even with all its early struggles, a way to live simply and comfortably within one's own skin and to live in service to something greater than oneself.

People in recovery can be role models

From Dr. Daniel Hall-Flavin, addictions psychiatrist and professor, Mayo Clinic, and former medical director for the National Council on Alcoholism and Drug Dependence: We need to define very clearly what recovery is, because recovery is not only abstinence. Too many people intellectually appreciate that, but it doesn't get translated into their daily lives. And so you've got people who are miserable, people who are angry, people who may not really make it into recovery.

So then the issue is quality of life. Once somebody has been in addiction, abstinence is necessary but not a sufficient condition for recovery. The recovery will mean different things to different people, but it's going to mean forgiveness of yourself, which means really getting to the issue of stigma—being able to get past that particular issue no matter what society may say or not say, being able understand that stigma starts at home with the messages that we've gotten, and being able to examine that.

What are the things that people need to do in terms of improving their lifestyle and filling in the gaps where the alcohol was or where the drugs were? They're not going to be able to do that very well without the family—their family support and family involvement. And oftentimes, those first steps, those first baby steps, are kind of reintegrating yourself into that larger social fabric and with the family.

This is just an old mantra in the field, but the family is the first to be affected and it's the last to recover. So the family will go back oftentimes to what is comfortable. And so you find people suddenly undermining, one way or another, their loved one's recovery, and being miserable at the same time in doing it, and maybe not even being aware of it. So I think it's really important that the family be involved.

I would say my best teachers have been my patients and people who have lived this and who have been successful. The people I admire the most actually are people who are in recovery, because they've had a very difficult journey. When you have to come face to face with yourself and you have to come face to face with your fears and your demons, you're kind of looking at your own humanity and you're looking your own mortality straight in the face. And so I admire those individuals who've been able to really do that, been able to turn their lives around in such a way as to make this addiction and their past history of addiction work *for* them rather than *against* them.

They're not a victim. They're not a prisoner of the past. They're really not able to erase that past, but they're able to actually move ahead. Some days may be great, some days may not, but they're able to move ahead honestly. And to me, that's a great inspiration.

Recovery management helps create stability

From Melody Heaps, founder, Treatment Alternatives for Safe Communities (TASC) and chair of the steering committee for HHS/SAMHSA's Partners for Recovery Initiative: The population we work with in Illinois is in many ways the worst in terms of high criminality, but we are more successful than regular populations in treatment programs because we offer avenues to the supports necessary for recovery, such as finding housing and leads to getting employment. Recovery management is the key to success. It's about navigating the recovery process. "Okay, am I tied into AA or another support group that helps me when I'm feeling nervous or when I think I'm going to go off or whatever?" We watch that. "Do I have a relationship with my family?" If not, why not, what can we do to get you some counseling? Do you have a job or are you going to school? Do you have hope in a future, and how can we plug you in to a resource that will get you there? Do you have a stable place to live? That is critical. That's probably number one. Do you have a stable place to live? Yeah. Where? How? We help plug you into that. The idea of accountability is also critical. So is tough love and being clear with guidelines so we don't go from recovery management to enabling.

Recovery isn't a one-stop-shop process

From Michel Perron, chief executive officer, Canadian Centre on Substance Abuse, and chair of the Vienna Nongovernmental Organization Committee on Drugs associated with the United Nations Office on Drugs and Crime: All too often our field and addicted people are seen as lost causes. We can't do anything to prevent addiction, and treatment is far from a guaranteed success. But that's simply untrue. We know what works and we need to apply it. Someone with an alcohol or drug addiction shouldn't receive any less support, help, and care than someone with diabetes or cancer. When I injured my knee, I didn't go look for a doctor with a bad knee. And yet, that's very much how the field of addiction is viewed. What we need to do is build off the success of 12-Step programs and medical advances and spiritual enlightenment and the many other resources we know contribute to recovery and help. We have to stop looking at this as a one-stop-shop solution.

Having a life purpose is crucial

From Pamela S. Hyde, administrator, Substance Abuse and Mental Health Services Administration: We at SAMHSA have identified some elements of recovery, and here's how we talk about it. We talk about health and that means not only a healthy lifestyle, but a healthy lifestyle free of drugs and alcohol. So health is critical to recovery. A home—and we mean that in the broadest sense. Literally a place to live, but a home that's supportive and provides the kind of environment that people feel good about and feel good with themselves in it. Community, meaning your social supports, who you live with, the kind of community you live in. And then purpose. You've got to have some purpose in life or it's going to be really hard to maintain recovery. For some people, that purpose is work, for some people it's self-employment or art or volunteer work. But there's got to be a purpose in life. For some people, giving back is the thing they say is what made it possible to be in recovery.

Shedding self-centeredness in recovery

From Dr. Robert DuPont, President of the Institute for Behavior and Health Inc, first director of the National Institute on Drug Abuse, second White House Drug Chief, and clinical professor of psychiatry at Georgetown Medical School: Addiction is a cruel, unforgiving and often lethal teacher. The gift of addiction, for those who survive and are willing to work hard enough and long enough to achieve it, is recovery. Abstinence from alcohol and other drug use is necessary for recovery, but recovery is more than that. It is a better way of living and a shared celebration of the small miracle of your own life.

Recovery involves having looked into, if not having been swallowed by, the abyss. Recovery includes a personal awareness of the slavery and the depravity of addiction. Recovery is emancipation from modern chemical slavery. Recovery is the joy that comes from the release from slavery. There is more to recovery. Bill Wilson [cofounder of AA] talked about self-centeredness being at the heart of addiction. At its heart, recovery is escape from the slavery of self-centeredness. That escape, also, is a source of tremendous joy because the person who is thinking about himself or herself is trapped in misery.

Relapse is a natural part of recovery

From R. Gil Kerlikowske, director, Office of National Drug Control Policy: We think that if somebody goes in for 28 days of inpatient drug treatment that once they leave there, they'll never have another problem. We don't look at any other disease that way. We know that cancer can re-occur; we know that the people who have worked hard to lose weight can sometimes gain some of or even all of that weight back. Why don't we think about drug treatment as a part of the recovery *process*, one that also involves relapse at times? We should just understand it and accept it. And remember, when people do relapse in drug treatment, they always relapse to a lesser degree than the original disease they had, and they end up doing less harm to themselves and others, even during that time of relapse. So there's some positive aspect to relapsing that people should see.

You must believe you can change

From Alexandre Laudet, PhD, director, Center for Study of Addictions and Recovery, National Development and Research Institutes Inc.: Regardless of the specific type of behavior you are trying to change, there is no getting around the fact that we as human beings usually do not like change. Change is difficult. You know what you are giving up; you're not sure of what you'll gain in exchange. This goes double when trying to free oneself of toxic compulsions, or of behaviors that have progressed to the pathological/dependent level. By then, these behaviors have probably constituted the bulk of the person's coping repertoire for many years. So in that context, initiating change essentially boils down to asking someone (oneself) to give up the only crutch they have known and relied on for years, be it drink, drug, sex, or hoarding. Go ahead, put the crutch down and let me see you stand up. Yeah, right!

One of the things we've learned in our NIH-funded studies of people at various stages of recovery from drug and/or alcohol problems is that motivation is key. You have to want something pretty bad to put yourself through the recovery obstacle course and not give up after a brief attempt. So what motivates people? One thing you need is something positive, a goal. Some people want their kids to grow up with a healthy parent; some people want a second chance at life, as they put it—they want to become the person they feel they were meant to be before compulsions took over their lives. That pull is much more effective when it comes from within (intrinsic motivation) than when externally applied, as when your boss or wife gives you an ultimatum (extrinsic motivation). You have to want it yourself because if you do it for someone else, the minute you get mad at them or they get mad at you, or the minute the external pressure lessens, you'll go right back to the crutch. So one of the most important elements of recovery initiation is to find a reason to change that makes you want it. You need to believe that what you are going to gain is more valuable in the long run than what you are giving up, because in the short run, you will have doubts. Temptation will rear its little head and you will have doubts: "Why am I doing this?"

Another way we may look at this is as meaning or purpose in life. You need something meaningful to you that will make you strong and help you stand up when the compulsion crutch is gone and you are not yet strong enough to stand on your own. Most people we've interviewed in our studies, those who were doing well in their recovery, which I understand as meaning not only having freed yourself from toxic compulsions but also developed a healthy lifestyle, had found some meaning or purpose to their challenges and to their path. We conducted a study trying to understand the mechanisms that underlie the demonstrated benefits of participating in 12-Step fellowships among people recovering from drug and/or alcohol problems. A number of mechanisms have been identified by colleagues, especially motivation and social support (meaning that the support people get from peers in 12-Step is one of the key ingredients in why 12-Step works). In one study, we looked at having meaning and purpose in life as a potential mediator of 12-Step benefits. We found that greater 12-Step attendance and involvement (e.g., having a sponsor, working the steps, doing service) in the first year of the study were significantly associated with greater levels of life meaning a year later. They also predicted remaining continuously abstinent over the subsequent year, and the same patterns occurred in the following year. What's more, the association between 12-Step attendance/involvement and subsequent patterns of continuous abstinence from drugs and alcohol was partially mediated by how much meaning and purpose in life people had. Life meaning/purpose is spiritual or religious for some, but not for all. It can be just wanting to raise your kids to give them a better life than you had, making your parents or wife proud, giving back to society, feeling good about yourself, helping other people with similar problems.

Once you are committed to change, you need to believe. Believe not only that change is attainable but that *you* can do it. And that's one of the reasons why 12-Step meetings are useful, especially early on: You sit there and hear people whose experiences are not that different from yours and there they are today—they changed! You want what they have, as the expression goes.

Assuming you are motivated to change and you believe you can make the change, as you start freeing yourself from the grips of compulsion, you start experiencing the miracle of recovery. It's deceptively simple yet critical, and it needs to be emphasized that when people start the process—as you begin accumulating some time free of your compulsion, even as you reduce giving in at the beginning if you cannot fully stop "cold turkey"—you start feeling more free. You start having the energy or time or money to do things you haven't done in a long time because all your energy/time/money was consumed by feeding your compulsion. As recovery progresses, your quality of life satisfaction increases significantly and progressively, especially in the first couple of years. And stress decreases in the opposite direction. That's critical because stress is very often, if not always, implicated in returning to a compulsion or addiction, especially early on, when people haven't yet developed mechanisms to deal with everyday stress.

We did a couple of studies to examine the role of quality of life satisfaction among people in recovery from drugs and/or alcohol problems. What we found is that controlling for how long people had used and how severely addicted they had been in the past, their quality of life satisfaction level predicted whether people were staying in recovery or went back to active use. We also found that when people leave drug treatment (a very vulnerable time for most), there is a strong association between how satisfied they are with their life at the time and how strongly motivated they are to stay clean and sober. That's important because motivation, as I mentioned earlier, is one of the strongest predictors of human behavior. So people who start the change process, regardless of what behavior(s) they are dealing with, any of the seven compulsions really, need to know that it gets better and that improvement is very instrumental to helping you stay on the new healthy lifestyle course you have embarked on. I think that's what they mean in the 12-Step promises where it says: 'If we are painstaking about this phase of our development, we will be amazed before we are halfway through. We are going to know a new freedom and a new happiness.'"

Recovery should be a spiritual quest

From Marianne Williamson, author of many inspirational books, including The Gift of Change: Spiritual Guidance for Living Your Best Life: The Western mind, the American mind particularly, loves the to-do list. They love the silver-bullet theory of making everything all right, just tell me what to do. And that's true if you are dealing with addiction, but also with any level of serious compulsion. What becomes clear is that a deeper inquiry into the nature of human existence is why we're here. How do we realign with that understanding, how do we make it practical, how do we make it operational, what does that mean for our lives and why are we on a mission, how can we carry out whatever mission our soul has here? Any conversation less significant than that is ultimately a conversation that does not allow a person to find genuine sobriety or the deeper purpose of recovery.

I have talked to people in prison. I have talked to people who are disadvantaged. And sometimes it's the people who had suffered the most and then been most cast out by society who are the most receptive to a deeper conversation. And interestingly enough, it is the people who have suffered at the deepest level who know intuitively that a superficial conversation will not be enough to address the deeper source of their despair. It's when the level of real "Oh my God, this really isn't working" fear sets in that people are most ready for a deeper conversation. They need to get very serious with the cultivation of a spiritual practice.

With someone who's a drug addict or someone who's an alcoholic or food addict, they understand that the addiction doesn't just want to inconvenience you, the addiction wants you dead. Once you realize that you are addicted, and you want recovery rather than being at the mercy of false appetites that are increasingly destructive, then that means this is the day your spiritual quest begins.

You lost your job. You lost your money. You lost your wife. You lost your kids. You lost your health. Life itself tends to say to the person, "Are you ready yet?" And when it's not quite loud enough, the universe itself has a way of saying, "Excuse me, are you ready yet?" The line in the *Course in Miracles* says, "It is not up to you what you learn. It is merely up to you whether you learn for joy or through pain."

A New Recovery Movement Is Needed

In my interview with Dr. Patrick Carnes, he told me something about the present state of the recovery movement that needs to be widely shared: "I see that we're making progress. But the reality is we have massive education to go, to teach people about how addiction works and why, how the 12 Steps work, and why therapy works, and how they all work together in extraordinary ways, if we just can get out of the way to make that happen. We [the treatment industry] are a part of the problem because no disease entity ever got what it needed until the people with the problems stood up and said, 'You've got to do something.'"

There is also the attendant problem of what Dr. Carnes calls "convenient recovery," which he defines this way: "Convenient recovery is where you take all that you've got, but if it [the recovery process] asks you to spread the word and to stand up in a community where people are going to judge you, we won't do that. When family members don't stand up and they don't do their therapy and they don't do their part and don't listen, they're part of the problem."

Consider this book to be one of my ways to stand up and shout, "We've got to do something! And we've got to start right now!"

What I've attempted to do with this book is give people the best information available on the planet about these diseases and to provide a new perspective on treatment and recovery. "There are hundreds of competing treatments for addiction," said Dr. Robert DuPont. "None has worked for everyone and none has failed to work for everyone. Some paths to lasting recovery have been successful over long periods for millions of addicted people, while others are less tested. In your struggle to get well, it is important to remember that the core problem of addiction is not getting clean and sober, it is *staying* clean and sober, not for a month or a year or even for five years, but for your lifetime."

People with this illness do recover, but the longer you have it, the more deeply you're in it, the harder the recovery process becomes. That also holds true for the loved ones who are, knowingly or not, accessories to the illness. There are also lots of people who don't meet the dependency criteria but who also need specialized help. This book was written with all of you in mind.

Dr. Christopher Emerson points out that "because dependency is so complex—it's multidimensional, multifactorial, multi-*everything*—we need a more comprehensive way of thinking about it and working with it. I'm always asking myself, 'How do I make a space for something transformative to happen with my patients?' Sometimes it comes out of saying very little, just being a quiet, consistent presence. But many times, it's also in the acknowledgment of my own struggles with drugs, alcohol, and compulsivity."

As a community we need to demand a recovery that we can believe in and one that we deserve. Those already in 12-Step programs understand the power we have as a group, yet they have a very strong orientation to keeping that anonymous, which I agree with as a spiritual principle and to protect the 12-Step organizations and their traditions. However, there are people in those church basements who are yearning for more, who want to do more service, who want to get out into the world and make a difference, and they should feel empowered to do that. If you've danced with the 800-pound gorilla of addiction and you've lived to tell your story, you have a lot to give the world in terms of your perspective and your spiritual fortitude, and God knows, we need spiritual fortitude in the world today.

We have a long road ahead to obliterate the stigma, the shame, and the sort of carnival nature of public discussion surrounding this disease. What the media has made interesting about this illness is the train wreck, the horror. We have to offer more than the horror of our past. We need to offer the triumphs of our present and the hope of our future.

It's a paradigm shift that I am proposing, and it has to come from us. We need to know that we're worth something, and not just in terms of having overcome our illness. Do you think a cancer patient defines their whole life in terms of being in remission from cancer? No. It's just a part of their life. It's a bump in the road. By contrast, we tend to make the addiction illness our whole life, and that's part of the tradition in 12-Step programs. It doesn't have to be that way. You can make that your choice, but you're not condemned to playing that role. You can be in recovery and still become president of the United States of America, as George W. Bush proved.

Just to be clear, I think the 12-Step programs and their traditions should stay in place and should be left alone. I'm just talking about the people who want to do more and are capable of doing more.

Two things we need to do are build an economy and create an advocacy movement. I'm just starting to see where people believe that they're worth enough to create their own businesses in recovery. They don't have to hide anymore. They can hire people in recovery, and everybody that works for that business is in recovery. They want to live in sober communities. We are taxpayers. We win Academy Awards. We have families. We have power. We have a lot to give to society.

Obliterating stigma and shame means millions of people coming out and saying, "We are the real face of addiction." It's not just guys with needles hanging out of their arms on the south side of some city, or alcoholics in dirty raincoats—it's everybody. It's housewives, artists, teachers, children. It's Wall Street guys. It's people in government. This illness affects everybody, and we must recognize this reality and come to terms with it.

We can give people who are in recovery and people who are in the helping professions and who are in the families of addicts the ability to come out and be a part of a movement that states: "We have a community. We have an economy. We have business. We have grassroots. We have power. We vote. We have the ability to get things done and make changes when we need to." We can change the perceptions around this illness. We can change society's commitment to this illness in terms of resources being made available. And most important, we can change things in terms of how addicts feel about themselves and help them see that they deserve recovery.

Treatment centers don't like to talk about a continuum of care, which isn't the conventional and predominant model that we currently have. What we have is like 28 days of treatment, or at most, 90 days. Come and spend $65,000, $75,000, and then go back to your community. And the relapse rates are 80 percent. They've got your 75 grand and then you've got to go back. That clearly doesn't work. Rehab shouldn't be a revolving door, because you're not doing anybody a favor if you keep going in and out. We've got to treat people for long periods of time and, as we learned in this book, outpatient can be as effective as inpatient care, and a brief intervention early in the process is just as effective as going inpatient down the road.

If you don't want to go to 12-Steps, you don't like 12-Steps for whatever reason, then maybe you're not ready for that kind of recovery. Some people will never get ready on those terms, so they need alternatives. Treatment and recovery can happen in a lot of different ways, and we see that reflected in the breadth of ideas presented in this book.

To further promote treatment and recovery options, I am launching **The Global Recovery Initiative** and a Web site, **www.Recover2Live .com**, to bring people together around a lifestyle, not just as a lifestyle of going to meetings, but of really disseminating the information that people need to have a good life in society, in real society, not in a shadow society of people ashamed of their illness. Both initiatives are about disseminating information and giving people tools to enable them to have a full and productive life. We would not tolerate that state of affairs for people affected by diabetes, heart disease, or cancer, and we must never stop our efforts until addiction is treated with the same level of resources, and recovery from addiction becomes celebrated with the same openness.

Why a Global Recovery Initiative

From Dr. Kevin A. Sabet, assistant professor at the University of Florida School of Medicine, policy consultant, columnist, researcher, and former senior advisor to three U.S. presidential administrations: People in recovery have enormous potential to change public policy and erase the stigma associated with addiction and recovery. If only they would move beyond telling their stories—and instead arm themselves with evidence-based, scientific arguments that go beyond anecdote in order to shape responsible public policies—we would live in a very different world.

From Paul N. Samuels, director/president, the Legal Action Center: People with addictions can recover and have a meaningful life in the community—if they get the help they need. Individuals in recovery often suffer discrimination as they seek employment, insurance, and other necessities of life. This failure to integrate addiction prevention, treatment, and recovery effectively into our nation's health care structure has cost us *over 100,000 lives* and *more than a third of a trillion dollars annually*, harming families and communities across the country.

The Global Recovery Initiative

The Global Recovery Initiative (GRI) is a collaborative organization that harnesses the power of people in recovery for policy change. Its mandate focuses on three major areas of public policy:

Build off of the major success we in the addiction recovery community are still celebrating—integrating Addiction Services into primary health care under the Affordable Care Act. As Paul Samuels stated above, not integrating these services into our nation's health care structure has cost us over 100,000 lives and more than a third of a trillion dollars annually. But now we have a commitment from Congress and the president that this will change. GRI and our partners are going to make sure they live up to that promise.

Eliminate barriers to recovery that exist today in the law by getting rid of outdated, discriminatory policies. Several laws were passed in an era with different drug threats (like crack) that today either have shown no evidence of deterrence or simply do not reflect what we have learned about addiction as a disease in the past 10 years. It does not make sense to forbid someone with a 10-year-old drug conviction who has paid his or her debt to society and is now in recovery from obtaining student loans, employment, housing, or the right to vote. People just starting on their road to recovery should not be subject to employment discrimination or get their Social Security disability benefits taken away. And clearly, it does not make sense to incarcerate someone for $30,000 a year and then, as soon as they are let back into society, simply abandon them and not provide them with job training and other skills to succeed.

Advocate for proven, comprehensive strategies that get people into recovery faster and help them stay there. Programs like Project HOPE and drug courts that use a carrot and stick method to change behavior and keep people off of drugs must be expanded. Just because science has told us that addiction is a disease, it doesn't take away responsibility from the user. We as a society need to assist in creating environments where that responsibility is fully realized.

Recover to Live

I was promised a life beyond my wildest dreams in recovery, and it's happened for me. I understand my circumstances. I was really lucky. But I know many people who have found the same thing even when coming from more ordinary circumstances. You've got to change who you are, and not just your spirituality. You have to change your ability to work. You must change your ability to have relationships. You have to change your capacity for healthy living.

We don't come to recovery with all of that. We need to learn it, and sometimes that information isn't available in 12-Step programs. Recover2Live is all about anchoring yourself in a recovery that's expansive in all aspects of your life—your work, your health, your relationships, your home, your spirituality.

Dr. Nora Volkow told me that we spend a lot of money on prevention and a lot of money on treatment. We know a lot about those things and do them pretty well. Yet we spend no money on recovery, and we don't know much of anything about recovery. But it's time we did. The more we know about recovery the better chance we have of getting people into recovery sooner and keeping them there longer.

There is at least one hopeful sign on the horizon for a widening of our scientific understanding of the factors that make for a successful recovery. The world's first systematic registry of addiction recovery was launched in October 2011 by Virginia Tech in Blacksburg, Virginia. It's called the National Quit & Recovery Registry (www. quitandrecovery.org). This site collects the experiences and recovery strategies of those involved with alcohol, drugs, overeating, gambling, and excessive sexual activity. "No one has ever systematically looked at people in long-term recovery for clues about beating addiction," said Warren Bickel, director of the Advanced Recovery Research Center of Virginia Tech's Carilion Research Institute. "We're trying to understand the addictive brain by shining a spotlight on the recovery process. We can learn what methods these recovery heroes used to quit their addiction and what strategies they use to remain in recovery when faced with challenging circumstances. We can learn about their decision-making skills. And, with neuro-imaging techniques, we can learn how their success impacts their brain function."

What I want to do in Recover2Live is to give people a destination to learn what is possible in their life and how to enhance every aspect of their life. When I got sober, people told me I could have a life beyond my wildest dreams. They didn't say, "You're going to spend the rest of your life in a basement talking about what using was like and just feeling kind of grateful that you're not doing that anymore, one day at a time."

For those of you with a dependency on a substance or process, recovery is a lifelong process. But for those of you who have a nondependent use disorder, Dr. Tom McLellan and other experts I spoke with assured me that you can be cured of this. You do not have the genetic component of this disease.

You may ask, "How do I know which one I have?" You'll know it if you can't stop and you keep going back. This is tricky territory, but our 30-day challenges in Part One can help. You can ask, "Well, is there a gene that I have that tells me I'm one or the other?" No, we don't know that for sure yet. So everybody has to assume that this is a chronic condition they're going to have to maintain for the rest of their life.

There shouldn't be any shame attached to the realization that recovery can be a lifetime process, just as there should no longer be any shame attached to going public about this illness. Bill Wilson, the cofounder of Alcoholics Anonymous, testified in front of a Senate subcommittee in the 1950s that included an alcoholic senator named Harold Hughes from the state of Iowa. Sen. Hughes was a public servant and a sober individual who did enormous good in furthering public policy concerning how society treated alcoholism. In his testimony before that subcommittee, Bill Wilson stated that members of AA could and should speak publicly about recovery because they know about recovery. It was his view that those in AA shouldn't discuss publicly their membership in AA, but they should talk about their recovery from alcoholism.

Today within the treatment industry, perceptions about the necessity and usefulness of anonymity are beginning to change. As Michael S. Early, chief clinical officer of Caron and former manager of continuum services for the Hazelden Foundation, said, "We have remained anonymous for so long because of 12-Step traditions, and that anonymity has been misunderstood. As an individual with the disease of alcoholism, I believe it's time to come forward publicly and talk about it. Whatever one might think about the celebrity rehab sort of shows on television, they are helping to dispel public attitudes of stigma and shame when we see these well-known people go public with their struggles against this disease of addiction."

During the final weekend of work on this book, my collaborator, Randall Fitzgerald, attended a memorial service for a 55-year-old construction company owner in Clearlake, California, who had been killed in a motor home fire. Randall observed something remarkable that occurred during this service, a phenomenon that gives me hope that the stigma of public shaming can finally be overcome as members of 12-Step fellowships speak out in public.

"About 200 people were crowded into a small United Methodist church," said Fitzgerald, "and the service to memorialize Jim began with the minister leading everyone in saying the Serenity Prayer: 'God grant me the serenity to accept the things I cannot change; courage to change the things I can; and wisdom to know the difference.' These words were familiar to me because I knew that decades earlier this prayer had been adopted by Alcoholics Anonymous and most other 12-Step programs as an unofficial cornerstone of inspirational sayings and spiritual tools.

"When the time came for mourners to share memories of Jim and comment on his life, it became even clearer this wouldn't be any ordinary memorial service. A full minute of awkward silence passed as the minister brandished a wireless microphone, waiting for someone to take it and speak. It was as if everyone held their breath to see who would summon the courage to be first. Finally, a boyish-looking middle-aged man in the front pew stood up and turned to face the rest of us. 'Hi, I'm Rob and I'm an alcoholic,' said this former coworker of Jim's. 'Hi, Rob,' several dozen mourners replied in unison. As the man explained how Jim had saved his life by offering him support in the local AA fellowship and then by giving him a construction job, I studied the faces of other mourners around me, and it was clear from the puzzled expressions that many people didn't know that Jim was a recovering alcoholic, or that he had met his fiancée in the program.

"Another awkward silence ensued until another person stood and said what was on many people's minds: 'Now that anonymity has been dispensed with today, I feel like I can say, 'Hi, I'm Bill and I'm an addict.' 'Hi, Bill,' came the sing-song response, this time spoken by even more people in the room. The taboo of maintaining anonymity about 12-Step program membership, the reluctance about speaking out honestly while surrounded by 'normies,' as nonalcoholics and nondruggies are called, had been broken. It was like a dam breach and resulted, almost with a collective sigh of relief, in a torrent of emotional testimonials that kept flowing. One by one, other members of the local AA and Narcotics Anonymous fellowships stood, identified themselves, and spoke about Jim's own battles with the disease of dependency and how he had helped them as a friend and sponsor to stay clean and sober.

"People laughed and cried, spoke with gritty unflinching honesty, and everyone present, normies and all, felt drawn together without shame or judgment. It was really a quite extraordinary scene of shared feeling. The minister was moved to remark that love and acceptance had enveloped the room to embrace everyone. I walked out of that service sensing what was possible for the broader recovery movement and society as a whole. This day wasn't a fluke or just an overwrought aberration generated by a sad occasion. This was a level of maturity that could be replicated in room after room, planet-wide."

Randall Fitzgerald's experience is instructive. One reason why 12-Step programs have been so successful is because they really are a recipe for living that can be beneficial for anyone. We can have a program for living, and we can have a program for recovery to secure a life beyond our wildest dreams. We need it. We deserve it. And we're capable of securing it for ourselves.

It isn't just the 12-Step programs that get the job done, of course. For example, the highly regarded Faces and Voices of Recovery (www.facesandvoicesofrecovery.org) helps those in recovery deal with society and the stigma of dependence. For example, Faces recommends those in recovery introduce themselves something like this: "Hi, I'm _____ and I'm a person in long-term recovery. For me, that means it's been _____ years since I used/had _____."
It's not the simple 12-Step greeting but it more than gets the job done. It takes you out of the shadows.

If you've danced with this illness for a decade or however many years, with this gorilla of addiction punching you in the face the entire time, and you've lived to tell your story, you're already one willful, committed human being. That recognition alone should be reason enough to start believing in yourself and your potential again.

You can help me shape what this new recovery paradigm will look like in the Global Recovery Initiative and its partner, Recover2Live (www.recover2live.com). On this Web site you will find accessible self-help tools for treatment and recovery, along with curriculums to deal with second-stage recovery issues. There will be a community of people connected through this site dedicated to making our lives more worth living.

Whether you are in recovery or not, whether you are in a helping profession or not, whatever your station in life happens to be, I would be honored if you would join me in helping establish this new movement. Together we can undertake the challenge of not only bringing long-term recovery to more people, but also delivering the promise of a richer, more fulfilling life.

My uncle, President John F. Kennedy, said that the true measure of a nation is its success in fulfilling the promise of a better life for each of its members. Let this be our measure, too. Our goal should be nothing less than to fulfill the promise of a better life through treatment, care, and eventual recovery for the millions of people struggling with the various forms of addiction around the world.

APPENDIX ONE

Drug-Use Treatment and Health Facts

If you feel concerned about any particular drug or group of drugs, the following information should help you determine the extent of the health risks that might be involved with its use, and whether dependency might result from chronic use.

Amphetamines

Many people got introduced to "speed" doing all-night study cram sessions for a school exam; or while working as long-distance truck drivers or night security guards; or in the military while undergoing intense training and combat missions in the field.

Former White House drug official Dr. Andrea Barthwell explained how some of the clients she has treated began using amphetamines: "Some people are seeking a chemical solution to something because their baseline mood is low. They've heard from their peers that a particular drug lifts you up, and they use it because they want to be lifted up. I've had people describe the first time they used an amphetamine. The edges on everything in the world seemed crisper and they liked the way that felt. So they had been kind of walking around in a fog, and their experience of the world was sharpened, heightened, by the drug's effects. They felt friendlier. They were walking across campus and speaking to people that they wouldn't normally speak to because the drug had brought them out. And they like being brought out into the sunlight where the edges of things were sharper."

What most people don't realize is that amphetamine isn't a single drug but an entire class of chemical stimulants that include amphetamine, methamphetamine (which is more powerful than amphetamine), and MDMA (ecstasy) with its hallucinogenic properties.

Though amphetamine derivatives can be found in nature stored in the leaves of khat and ephedra plants, what we know in Western cultures to be amphetamine is a much stronger synthetic chemical concoction originally developed for the symptomatic treatment of colds. Abuse of it was noted as far back as the 1930s. Exposure to the drug expanded dramatically during World War II, when amphetamines were used on the battlefield to keep soldiers alert.

After prolonged use, according to the National Institute on Drug Abuse, amphetamines can induce strong dependency. Its impact on the central nervous system can create anxiety, psychosis, and both tactile and visual hallucinations. Hypertension can result from amphetamine use and toxicity, along with heart arrhythmia and stroke. High doses also produce neurotoxic symptoms in the brain.

Withdrawal from amphetamine use can generate depression and fatigue. To treat amphetamine dependence, experts generally use the same approach as they do with cocaine withdrawal and treatment. The following drugs are among those that have been used to reduce withdrawal symptoms and cravings: the antidepressant bupropion; the antipsychotic risperidone; and the inhibitors rivastigmine and lobeline.

Barbiturates

Although not used nearly as much or as widely as several decades ago, barbiturates are still around and still being abused as sedatives. The high addiction potential of these prescribed nervous system depressants and sleep aids convinced medical prescribers to limit or discontinue patient use.

Reports from the National Institute on Drug Abuse (NIDA) indicate that the two prescription barbiturates now being most abused in the United States are mephobarbital (Mebaral) and pentobarbital (Nembutal), both sedative hypnotics. (Seconal might be a third.) Physicians and psychiatrists now commonly prescribe a class of drugs that include Valium in place of the previously prescribed barbiturates.

The biggest problem with barbiturates, aside from their high dependency rates, is what happens when they get mixed up in the body with alcohol consumption: Overdose followed by coma and death can be the result. The death of actress Marilyn Monroe was blamed on mixing alcohol and prescription drugs.

Women are particularly vulnerable to prescription drug abuse. NIDA director Dr. Nora Volkow explained why: "Prescription drug abuse must be carefully tracked among women because of their combined vulnerabilities. First, women are more likely than men to suffer from depression, anxiety, trauma, and victimization, all of which frequently appear with substance abuse in the form of comorbidities. Second, girls and women report using drugs to cope with stressful situations in their lives. Third, studies suggest that women are significantly more likely than men to be prescribed an abusable drug, particularly in the form of narcotics and anti-anxiety medications."

Treatments for prescription drug dependence are generally the same as those for dependence on stimulant and opiate drugs. Among specific interventions found to be effective is cognitive behavioral therapy (CBT), discussed in detail in Part Two of this book, which emphasizes the modification of a user's thinking and behavior, while increasing coping skills.

Cocaine

Once it's extracted from the leaves of coca plants in South America, this white powder is either snorted or, in its crystal (compressed powder) form, called crack, smoked. It can also be injected with heroin as a "speedball" to produce the highest blood levels of the drug in the shortest period of time, a dangerous combination that resulted in the overdose deaths of numerous celebrities, including the comedians John Belushi and Chris Farley. United Nations drug-use assessments have placed Spain, followed by the United States, as the countries with the highest rates of cocaine usage.

Smoking or vaporizing cocaine, either by freebasing or in a crack pipe ("crack" refers to the crackling sound it makes when heated), produces the most severe dependence in the shortest amount of time. This central nervous system stimulant is thought to be highly addictive because of the way it affects the brain's reward pathways. British medical journal *The Lancet* ranked it the second-most dependence-producing illicit drug (behind heroin) among the 20 most commonly consumed drugs. Up to 6 percent of cocaine users become dependent within their first year of use.

Estimates are that women may be three times more likely to become addicted to cocaine than men during the early onset of use. Both men and women who started using the drug at the age of 12 or 13 are four times as likely to develop dependency than people who start using after age 18. *(Source: "Risk of becoming cocaine dependent: epidemiological estimates for the United States, 2000–2001." O'Brien MS and Anthony JC. Neuropsychopharmacology. 2005 May;30(5):1006–18.)*

Prolonged cocaine use can cause cardiovascular and brain damage, mood swings, paranoia, insomnia, cognitive impairments, and drastic changes in personality that can lead to aggressive or compulsive behaviors. Overdoses of cocaine (other than from speedballs) can result in hypertensive strokes or heartbeat abnormalities. The typical type of withdrawal produced by cocaine dependence after people stop using is called "hyperdepression," which is a symptom of recovering from hyperstimulation of the central nervous.

Cocaine dependence can literally shrink the size of your brain. That was the finding by a team of University of Minnesota researchers who used diffusion tensor brain imaging on 21 men and women with average age of 42 years and who had been using cocaine for an average of 18.9 years, and then compared their brain images with those of 21 noncocaine users. "The data suggested that duration of use was associated with decreased gray and white matter volumes," the researchers concluded. *(Source: "Brain macrostructural and microstructural abnormalities in cocaine dependence." Kelvin O. Lim et al. Drug Alcohol Depend. 2008 Jan 1;92(1–3):164–72.)*

Researchers at Wake Forest University School of Medicine analyzed the brains of monkeys addicted to cocaine and detected changes in the activity of various proteins in the brain, thereby providing a biological explanation for why cocaine dependence is so difficult to treat. "The changes we identified are profound and affect the structure, metabolism, and signaling of neurons," commented the study's lead author, Dr. Nilesh Tannu. "It is unlikely that these types of changes are easily reversible after drug use is discontinued, which may explain why relapse occurs." *(Posted online May 27, 2008, Molecular Psychiatry.)*

Is cocaine dependence related to pathological gambling? That may sound like a brain teaser, but there really is evidence that both cocaine use and compulsive gambling involve stimulation of the same neurotransmitter reward centers of the brain, resulting in the release of similar brain chemicals.

In 2011 Swiss medical researchers conducted an experiment in which they attempted to break the cycle of cocaine dependence by having users spend time playing blackjack and other casino games of chance coupled with intensive psychotherapy. They found this combination of treatments produced lower relapse rates and decreased cocaine usage more than psychotherapy alone.

Cocaine and gambling are both powerful brain stimulants. The study evidence is compelling for demonstrating a connection between the brains of cokeheads and compulsive gamblers. Here are three more examples of such studies:

Prefrontal cortical brain abnormalities, based on magnetic resonance imaging (MRI), show similarities between pathological gamblers and other impaired impulse-control disorders such as cocaine dependence. People in remission from cocaine or alcohol abuse have a brain predilection to develope pathological gambling, which "highlights the importance of considering co-occurring substance-use disorders when investigating pathological gambling." *(Source: "Reduced genual corpus callosal white matter integrity in pathological gambling and its relationship to alcohol abuse or dependence." Sarah W. Yip et al. World J Biol Psychiatry. 2011 May 5.)*

Using data from three clinical trials, University of Connecticut researchers examined the effectiveness of offering cash prizes (known as prize-based contingency management) to cocaine dependent persons to entice them to quit using. Prizes produced better cocaine cessation outcomes overall. This was true for both substance abusers who did or didn't gamble recreationally. *(Source: "Prize-based contingency management is efficacious in cocaine-abusing patients with and without recent gambling participation." Petry NM and Alessi SM. J Subst Abuse Treat. 2010 Oct;39(3):282–8.)*

Cocaine-abusing outpatients in Connecticut, 120 of them in all, were randomly assigned to one of three 12-week programs: standard treatment, standard treatment with cash prizes of $80 for remaining abstinent, or standard treatment with "reinforcement" cash prizes of $240 for remaining abstinent. Patients in the $240 prize level achieved more abstinence than patients in the other categories, demonstrating that "beneficial effects may be magnitude-dependent [size of the prize] in more severe patients." *(Source: "Prize reinforcement contingency management for treating cocaine users: How low can we go, and with whom?" Nancy M. Petry et al. Addiction. 2004 Mar;99(3):349–60.)*

Ecstasy

This recreational "club" drug, made popular at raves, is both an amphetamine-derived substance (MDMA is the active ingredient) and classified as a mild hallucinogen for its ability to induce dreamy, sensory-heightened states of awareness. Its users and advocates usually choose to believe that the drug poses little or no risk to health.

Reality and medical science tell a very different story. Let's start with brain damage and the risk of developing Alzheimer's disease.

Dutch researchers writing in the April 2011 edition of the *Journal of Neurology, Neurosurgery and Psychiatry* described how they used MRI scans to study the brains of men in their 20s who, over the previous six-and-a-half years, had taken an average of 281 ecstasy tablets, or about one tablet every eight days. Compared to a control group, these ecstasy users had a hippocampus—the part of the brain controlling memory—10.5 percent smaller and 5 percent less overall gray matter than the normal brains. "Hippocampal atrophy is a hallmark for disease of progressive cognitive impairment in older patients, such as Alzheimer's disease," reported the research team.

There are dozens of other studies showing health consequences—and even deaths—from ecstasy use. For example, some animal studies have found that MDMA can kill brain cells in the serotonin system. It's also clear that MDMA elevates body temperature and causes dehydration, conditions that are further exacerbated by the tendency of some users to dance until physically exhausted in the hot confines of group raves.

I'll summarize the findings of just a few of the more recent studies to illustrate the range of health problems associated with ecstasy use that should concern us.

Sudden death: Using ecstasy is "associated with causing death by a number of mechanisms, including hyperpyrexia, cardiac arrhythmia, water intoxication, and liver failure," according to this Canadian study. Seventy-seven deaths "where MDMA was detected in body fluids/organs were reviewed" and there was "a considerable overlap between the concentration of MDMA seen in deaths from direct MDMA toxicity and deaths associated with trauma." (*Source: "Ecstasy associated deaths: what is fatal concentration? Analysis of a case series." Milroy CM. Forensic Sci Med Pathol. 2011 Sep;7(3):248–52. Epub 2011 Jan 25.*)

Death from polydrug use: Australian forensic experts examined 106 fatalities in which MDMA was involved. Nearly half of these deaths in Australia involved ecstasy users who were also simultaneously using other drugs, such as pharmaceuticals, especially antidepressants. Potential drug interactions "between MDMA and pharmaceutical preparations that may result in lethal toxicity" are more common than previously thought. (*Source: "Deaths involving MDMA and the concomitant use of pharmaceutical drugs." Jennifer L. Pilgrim et al.* J Anal Toxicol. *2011 May;35(4):219–26.*)

Heart and adrenal gland alterations: Loud noises such as the music volume typical at raves are magnified by ecstasy use, resulting in heart arrhythmia and hypertension. Alteration of adrenal gland function also occurs. "The convergence of the effects of prolonged loud noise exposure and the consumption of MDMA might explain the sudden fatal events that happen in recreational situations," wrote the seven Italian researchers. (*Source: "MDMA (ecstasy) enhances loud noise-induced morphofunctional alterations in heart and adrenal gland." Federica Fulceri et al.* Microsc Res Tech. *2011 Sept;74(9):874–87. doi: 10.1002/ jemt.20971. Epub 2010 Dec 16.*)

Memory impairment: British scientists tested MDMA, a known neurotoxin in animals, among groups of ecstasy users and a control group of nonecstasy users to determine the impact of use on memory performance. Those who used ecstasy, especially in a polydrug way (use in connection with marijuana or other illicit substances) performed worse in word-recognition tasks. "Our results suggest that ecstasy users, who also use a wide range of other drugs, show a durable abnormality . . . thought to be associated with recollection," the research team concluded. (*Source: "Event related potential (ERP) evidence for selective impairment of verbal recollection in abstinent recreational methylenedioxymethamphetamine ("Ecstasy")/polydrug users." Adrian P. Burgess et al.* Psychopharmacology. *2011 Aug;216(4):545–56. Epub 2011 Mar 10.*)

In a second study of memory, mood, and cognition in former ecstasy users, this one conducted in Germany, the research team found that "ex-ecstasy users'" verbal memory showed no sign of improvement even after over 2.5 years of abstinence and thus may represent persistent functional consequences of MDMA neurotoxicity." (*Source: "Mood, cognition and serotonin transporter availability in current and former ecstasy (MDMA) users: the longitudinal perspective." Rainer Thomasius et al.* J Psychopharmacol. *2006 Mar;20(2):211–25.*)

Heroin

Heroin, along with morphine and codeine, are drugs derived from opium, which is produced by poppies. These are natural pain relievers, but they also produce a "high" accompanying their pain-reducing action on the body.

Heroin can be snorted, but many users choose intravenous injection because the "rush" is faster and more powerful.

Detoxification, going "cold turkey," by itself rarely produces long-term recovery from heroin dependence. Relapse often follows the 28-day rehabs that have been the treatment norm. Detoxes need to be combined with abstinence-oriented treatment programs and, if necessary, substitution of other medications for heroin.

Methadone Maintenance Treatment is a replacement therapy—the usual first line of intervention—used to reduce cravings for heroin, block the euphoric effects of opiates, and reduce the risk of the user's transmitting infectious diseases such as hepatitis and HIV spread by heroin intravenous injection. Though methadone is a synthetic opioid created in a laboratory, it's considered medically safe, in contrast to heroin. (*Source: "Methadone maintenance treatment (MMT): A review of historical and clinical issues." Herman Joseph et al.* Mt. Sinai Journal Medicine. *2000 Oct–Nov;67(5–6):347–64.*)

Why is methadone effective in heroin treatment? "It reduces the craving for heroin, it "stabilizes" the neurotransmitter dysregulation in the brain associated with heroin craving, and it gets the person out of the crime-related activities associated with the acquisition of heroin," according to Carlton Erickson, director of UT Austin's Addiction Science and Research and Education Center and distinguished professor of pharmacy/toxicology. "It doesn't just replace one addiction for another," he says. "Methadone saves lives."

Added Dr. Michael M. Miller, past president of the American Society of Addiction Medicine: "Methadone doesn't substitute one addiction for another. Methadone substitutes one physical codependence for another. When you use methadone in the way it's intended, which is a daily maintenance dose, you treat an addiction. Do you develop tolerance to methadone? Sure. Do you have withdrawal? Yes, if you stop taking it. But that's just two of the seven physical dependence criteria. With methadone you don't have the other criteria for dependence like you do with heroin, such as loss of control or preoccupation with its use and procuring it. Am I going to defend methadone as the perfect medication? No. But it saves lives because people on methadone maintenance have vastly reduced risks of hepatitis and HIV because they're not using injection drugs. Methadone substitution for heroin also has significant effects on criminal justice expenditures and it has significant public health benefits."

The latest treatment for opioid dependence is buprenorphine (brand name Suboxone or the injectable Buprenex), another powerful pain reliever that reduces the cravings for heroin. This medication is considered to have less abuse potential than methadone because it's more difficult to get "high" off it with increasing doses. Unlike methadone, buprenorphine has an opioid "antagonist" effect (i.e., it also blocks opiate receptors and thus works against the opioid effect). It is usually more humane because using it is less demanding than methadone clinics, while being equally or often more effective.

An overdose on heroin can produce respiratory depression resulting in death. Withdrawal from a central nervous system depressant such as heroin stimulates physical hyperexcitability, and this withdrawal and its physical symptoms can occur to varying degrees of severity whether the user has been dependent on the drug or not. Physical symptoms associated with heroin withdrawal include tremors, sweating, cramps, flu-like symptoms, and weakness, as well as psychological symptoms, including anxiety, insomnia, malaise, and depression.

Relatively recent medical studies have discovered other health consequences from heroin use not normally covered by drug education programs:

Neurocognitive effects: In 2007 Harvard Medical School researchers conducted a study on heroin's brain effects and concluded, "Findings to date suggest that the use of opiates has both acute and long-term effects on cognitive performance. Neuropsychological data indicates deficits in attention, concentration, recall, visuospatial skills and psychomotor speed with both acute and chronic opioid use. The long-term effects of opiate use appear to have the greatest impact on executive functions, including the ability to shift cognitive set and inhibit inappropriate response tendencies." (*Source: "Neuropsychological consequences of opiate use." Staci A. Gruber et al.* Neuropsychol Rev. *2007 Sep;17(3):299–315.*)

Oral health: In 2011 Boston University School of Medicine researchers examined 563 substance-dependent persons to determine the condition of their teeth, gums, and overall oral health. "Opioid use was significantly related to a worse overall oral health rating" compared to the other substances abused, the research team concluded. (*Source: "Oral health of substance-dependent individuals: Impact of specific substances." Meredith M. D'Amore et al.* J Subst Abuse Treat. *2011 Sep;41(2):179–85. doi: 10.1016/j.jsat.2011.02.005. Epub 2011 Apr 6.*)

From Dr. Sarz Maxwell, medical director, Chicago Recovery Alliance:
My particular interest is opiate addiction, and I believe that opiate

addiction is a little different from all of the others because my theory of opiate addiction is that it is very neurochemical. People become addicted to opiates because something causes a decrease in the endorphins in the brain.

I don't define addiction by whether or not someone is using a drug. I define it by whether the drug is making their life go to hell. Heroin isn't the problem. The problem is the craziness, the crime, the dirty needles that go with heroin use.

It's like any other disease—if someone has really bad genetics for high blood pressure, they may be able to ward that off by good exercise, good diet, whatever. On the other hand, if someone has good genetics for high blood pressure, they may still have the disease if they become a couch potato. We don't know a lot about the genetics of opiate addiction specifically, but I believe that genetics plays a strong role as with other chronic diseases, like heart disease, like diabetes. We're all born with a set threshold for diseases, and for some people that threshold is so low they get the disease when they're a healthy young child. For other people the threshold is higher, and they only get the disease when they're under stress or obese. Most people are born with a threshold high enough that we never get diabetes our whole lives, no matter how we abuse our bodies.

We're all born with a threshold, and environmental things and behavioral things can lower that threshold, like what happens to our guys when we send them overseas. A lot of our guys in Vietnam were addicted to heroin. It was cheap, it was available, and jungle warfare is way up there on the stress monitors. And when they came back, that's why Nixon set up the "Drug Czar," not to help the addicts, but because they suddenly realized we've got all these addicts, they're going to be coming back, and oops, we taught them how to use automatic weapons. So they set up the Drug Czar in order to protect Americans from the addicts. But what happened is when these guys came back, 80 percent of them, once they were out of the jungle, dropped the heroin, went through a few weeks of hell, and went on about their lives. Only a small percent of them are either dead or still using now.

Opiate addiction is different from all of the others. The only treatment that statistically is helpful for opiate addiction is replacement therapy. Detox alone doesn't work for someone who is addicted to heroin. The only treatment that works is substitution treatment with either methadone or Suboxone. Relapse rates without substitution treatment are 90 to 95 percent. Detox is a procedure, not a treatment. Detox is just a procedure that precedes treatment.

Inhalants

These "huffable" (breathable) substances are mostly pure toxic chemicals such as toluene, contained in consumer products like correction fluid, solvents, marker pens, or air fresheners. Their fumes or vapors are inhaled through the nose and mouth for cheap and quick highs, which is a practice largely embraced by children and teenagers.

Inhalants create more and faster-acting negative effects on the human body than any other category of abused drugs. Inhalants are nothing less than chemical poisons. Aside from causing death in some instances, they produce irregular heartbeats, breathing stoppage, and kidney, liver, and brain damage.

"These chemicals are so dangerous that we don't even know if they're 'addicting' since people rarely use them long enough to develop dependence," noted Prof. Carlton Erickson, director of the Addiction Science Research and Education Center and distinguished professor of pharmacy/toxicology at UT Austin.

Toluene, a chemical present in many inhalants, resembles the effects of amphetamine on the human body. "[Research] results indicate that toluene and amphetamine share, to some extent, similar subjective effects, which may reflect a common neurochemical action," said Dr. Minda Lynch of NIDA's (National Institute on Drug Abuse) Division of Basic Neuroscience and Behavioral Research. The finding is worrisome because, in animals, exposure to one stimulant often enhances the response to another stimulant experienced subsequently. "Young people who abuse inhalants may increase their risk for later drug abuse," observed Dr. Lynch.

Ketamine

Sometimes called Special K or vitamin K, this "club drug" is a "dissociative anesthetic," which, along with PCP, is often used by veterinarians as an anesthetic in animals. It's said to produce hallucinations and a dreamy state in humans that takes away pain like other forms of anesthesia but leaves the user in a wakeful state.

The drug was developed by a pharmaceutical company in 1962 to provide an alternative to PCP, with fewer side effects, because PCP had proven to be a neurotoxin. Despite ketamine's ability to cause sensory distortions, it has proven effective in medical studies for the treatment of regional pain syndrome and some forms of depression.

Evgeny Krupitsky, chief of the Laboratory of Clinical Psychopharmacology of Addictions at St. Petersburg State Pavlov Medical University, has used ketamine as part of his treatment program (along with psychotherapy and group therapy) for alcohol dependence. In a controlled study he conducted using this approach, 60 of the 86 participating alcoholics remained sober through one year of the treatment program. He has also used the same program effectively to treat heroin dependence. (*Source: "Ketamine psychedelic therapy (KPT): A review of the results of ten years of research." Krupitsky EM and Grinenko AY.* J Psychoactive Drugs. *1997 Apr–Jun;29(2):165–83.*)

Though a therapeutic potential use for ketamine certainly exists, abuse of the drug, including high doses and chronic use, produces a range of unhealthy side effects and medical conditions. Short-term side effects may include confusion, slurred speech, heart rate fluctuations, hypertension, nausea, respiratory depression, and loss of motor coordination.

In 2009, a major study of ketamine use found that the heaviest users showed the greatest abnormalities in several measures of memory function, though the damage might have been reversible once a cessation of abuse occurred. (*Source: "Consequences of chronic ketamine self-administration upon neurocognitive function and psychological wellbeing: A 1-year longitudinal study." Celia J. A. Morgan et al.* Addiction. *2010 Jan;105(1):121. doi: 10.1111/j.1360-0443.2009.02761.x.*)

In an experiment with 20 volunteers from a prison population in Michigan, the drug was administered and the subjects were monitored with electroencephalographic machines and medical testing. Although no evidence of liver toxicity was obtained, there were "hypertension, tachycardia, and psychic changes" that were "an undesirable characteristic of the drug." (*Source: "Taming the ketamine tiger." Domino EF.* Anesthesiology. *2010 Sep;113(3):678–84.*)

Finally, there is evidence of urinary tract disease with extended ketamine use. Researchers in Britain found that ketamine inflamed and scarred the bladder lining in some subjects, leading to bleeding, pain on urination, urine leakage, and eventually, kidney damage. (*Source: "Urinary tract disease associated with chronic ketamine use." Angela M. Cottrell et al.* Br Med J. *2008 May 3;336(7651):973. doi: 10.1136/bmj.39562.711713.80.*)

LSD (lysergic acid diethylamide)

There seems to be no level of use among "acidheads" that can produce the type of dependence we see with other drugs, according to most treatment and research experts, and that may be because LSD doesn't initiate strong enough effects in the medial forebrain bundle, which is thought to be the "dependence area" of the human brain.

"LSD is not considered an addictive drug since it does not produce compulsive drug-seeking behavior," said the National Institute on Drug Abuse in a fact sheet posted on its Web site.

Nor is there any compelling evidence to indicate that LSD is lethal or toxic to any body organs. People who die while on an LSD hallucinatory "trip" generally do so as a result of accidents caused by sensory distortions, though there is also some evidence that "bad trips" producing severe anxiety and depression can trigger suicide attempts.

Next to inhalants, LSD is probably the most potent drug ever produced by either nature or a chemical laboratory. Only millionths of a gram of the drug are necessary for hallucinations to be generated in the human brain. It was discovered in 1938 when it was first synthesized from lysergic acid found in a fungus called ergot, which grows on grain crops.

Each time a person takes a dose of this drug—either in tablet, capsule, or liquid form—its effects diminish, a process of quick adaptation that may result in increasing dosages in attempts to replicate previously intense effects. Those effects typically last up to 12 hours.

LSD produces its hallucinations, according to one theory, by causing a malfunction in the base of the brain's filtering mechanism thereby allowing a flood of stimuli to enter and overwhelm the conscious cortex, according to the UT Austin Addiction Science Research and Education Center.

As for treatment options, those listed by the National Institute on Drug Abuse (NIDA InfoFacts: Hallucinogens) center on relieving physical and mental symptoms of bad trips. "Treatment is usually supportive: provision of a quiet room with little sensory stimulation. Occasionally, benzodiazepines are used to control extreme agitation or seizures."

Marijuana (and hashish)

You have probably heard this statement spoken and repeated as if it were an article of faith: "Marijuana is a benign substance." Many people really want to believe that cannabis is completely harmless to the health of users. "Safer than alcohol," is the oft-repeated refrain. But what does the medical evidence tell us?

We do know that "medicinal marijuana" has some documented benefits, such as relief of nausea and vomiting, treatment of glaucoma, premenstrual syndrome, and gastrointestinal illness, along with stimulation of hunger in chemotherapy and AIDS patients. (*Source: "Cannabinoids in medicine: A review of their therapeutic potential." Ben Amar M. J Ethnopharmacol. 2006 Apr 29;105(1–2):1–25.*)

But what else has medical science found about one of the world's most popular drugs? Studies over the past couple of years have turned the cultural belief about cannabis being harmless into a myth, although few of the estimated 94 million people in the United States who have "tried" pot may want to accept this bad news. Some of the most revealing findings about cannabis have been generated by research teams led by Staci A. Gruber, PhD, an assistant professor of psychiatry at Harvard Medical School.

For example, in a 2010 study of 33 chronic marijuana users and 26 nonusing control subjects, Gruber and three research associates found that users who had started smoking marijuana before the age of 16 made twice as many mistakes on cognitive tests, including in their ability to plan and engage in abstract thinking, as did persons who started smoking after age 16. All chronic users demonstrated trouble in maintaining mental focus and following a simple set of rules. Functional MRI scans were performed as the subjects did the battery of cognitive tests, and the findings suggest that neural changes in the brain had occurred in those with early onset of cannabis use.

"Marijuana isn't really a benign substance," Gruber commented at the annual meeting of the Society for Neuroscience. "It has a direct effect on executive function. The earlier you begin using it, and the more you use of it, the more significant that effect."

In other words, the younger you start using cannabis, and the more often you use it after you start using, the dumber you will become and the less control you will be able to exercise over your actions. Daily use can also increase levels of anxiety and depression in some smokers, triggering more severe psychological disorders later in life.

Dr. Andrea Barthwell shared this observation about pot: "Saying marijuana is safer than alcohol is like saying that a bomb is safer than a missile. They're both dangerous. Use starts off as a matter of will. You can choose not to use. But once that switch is flipped, you lose control. And then you just can't say no."

Numerous medical studies over the past few years have uncovered evidence that cannabis use can result in addiction, impulsive behaviors, learning difficulties, impaired decision-making, cardiovascular disease, bipolar disorder, and schizophrenia. Want some evidence? Check out this scientific data.

Addiction: "The psychoactive compounds contained in cannabis induce their pharmacological effects by the activation of at least two different receptors, CB1 and CB2 cannabinoid receptors [in the brain]. Multiple studies have demonstrated the specific involvement of CB1 cannabinoid receptors in the addictive properties of cannabinoids. Several neurotransmitter systems involved in the addictive effects of other prototypical drugs of abuse, such as the dopaminergic and the opioid system, are also involved in cannabis addiction." (*Source: "Neurochemical basis of cannabis addiction." Rafael Maldonado et al.* Neuroscience. *2011 May 5;181:1–17*)

Impulsive behavior: "Significant alterations [occur] in frontal white matter tracts [of the brain] associated with measures of impulsivity in chronic marijuana smokers. Early marijuana use may result in reduced [coherence] . . . which may be associated with increased impulsivity and ultimately contribute to . . . the inability to discontinue use." (*Source: "Why so impulsive? White matter alterations are associated with impulsivity in chronic marijuana smokers." Staci A. Gruber et al.* Exp Clin Psychopharmacol. *2011 Jun;19(3):231–42. Epub 2011 Apr 11.*)

Learning difficulties: "Cannabis use has been shown to impair cognitive functions on a number of levels—from basic motor coordination to more complex executive function tasks, such as the ability to plan, organize, solve problems, make decisions, remember, and control emotions and behavior. Individuals with cannabis-related impairment in executive functions have been found to have trouble learning and applying the skill required for successful recovery, putting them at increased risk for relapse to cannabis use." (*Source: "An evidence based review of acute and long-term effects of cannabis use on executive cognitive functions." Rebecca D. Crean et al.* J Addict Med. *2011 Mar 1;5(1):1–8.*)

Impaired decision-making: "More than 94 million Americans have tried marijuana, and it remains the most widely used illicit drug in the nation. Investigations of the cognitive effects of marijuana report alterations in brain function during tasks requiring executive control, including inhibition and decision-making. Studies using PET and

FMRI have demonstrated changes within the [brain's] anterior cingulated and amygdala regions in marijuana smokers. Smokers demonstrated a relative decrease in both anterior cingulated and amygdalar activity. Marijuana smokers process emotional information differently from those who do not smoke, which may result in negative consequences." (*Source: "Altered affective response in marijuana smokers: An FMRI study." Staci A. Gruber et al.* Drug Alcohol Depend. *2009 Nov 1;105(1–2):139–53.*)

Cardiovascular disease: "Epidemiological research during the past 10 years suggests that regular use of cannabis during adolescence and into adulthood can have adverse effects. The most probable adverse effects include a dependence syndrome, increased risk of motor vehicle crashes, impaired respiratory function, cardiovascular disease, and adverse effects of regular use on adolescent psychosocial development and mental health." (*Source: "Adverse health effects of nonmedical cannabis use." Hall W and Degenhardt L.* Lancet. *2009 Oct 17;374(9698):1383–91.*)

Bipolar disorder: "We investigated a naturalistic sample of 151 patients with bipolar I and II disorder receiving psychiatric treatment. Excessive cannabis use was associated with an earlier onset [of bipolar disorder] . . . lifetime use of cannabis predicted an earlier onset . . . cannabis use may trigger bipolar disorder in vulnerable individuals." (*Source: "Excessive cannabis use is associated with earlier age at onset in bipolar disorder." Trine V. Lagerberg et al.* Eur Arch Psychiatry Clin Neurosci. *2011 Jan 26;261(6):397–405. doi: 10.1007/s00406-011-0188-4.*)

Schizophrenia: "Despite the widely held belief that [marijuana] is a safe drug, its long-term use has potentially harmful consequences. The research on the impact of its use has largely been epidemiological in nature and has consistently found that cannabis use is associated with schizophrenia outcomes later in life. Evidence from both epidemiological and animal studies indicates that cannabis use during adolescence carries particular risk." (*Source: "Cannabis use in young people: The risk for schizophrenia." Paola Casadio P. Et. al.* Neurosci Biobehav Rev. *2011 August; 35(8):1779–87. doi: 10.1016/j.neubiorev.2011.04.007. Epub 2011 Apr 16.*)

Methamphetamine

Of all the drugs discussed in this book, meth is simultaneously one of the most synthetic, one of the easiest to make, and potentially one of the most dangerous. There is nothing natural about meth or the ingredients—such as pseudoephedrine—used to manufacture this synthetic central nervous system stimulant.

It's also relatively easy to spot the physical and behavioral symptoms of a meth user—a "crankhead" or "tweaker," as they've come to be labeled. They often undergo rapid and drastic weight gain, which they ascribe to "a new diet program" or a "thyroid problem." They develop gum disease and often lose all of their teeth at an early age. Their physical movements become jerky and exaggerated; their speech is rapid and excited; and they exhibit restlessness, anxiety, irritability, paranoia, and decreased attention span. They may also engage in repetitive or delusional projects they never seem to complete.

Many experts believe that meth is just as dependence-producing as cocaine. It's also one of the few drugs—along with alcohol, ecstasy, and inhalants—documented to be a brain cell killer, one reason why habitual meth users demonstrate lower IQs during cognitive testing, even years after quitting the drug.

It's the one drug that seems to result in the most life problems. Sudden surges of uncontrollable violence make it, more than any other drug, the one possessing the most potential for crimes against people and property. Because the drug heightens sensitivity to sound, for example, a crying baby can send chronic meth users into a fury. Beginning in the early 1990s, Los Angeles County was one of the first areas of the nation to experience a brutally grim pattern of infant deaths caused by parents or guardians high on meth, people who simply lost their tempers when the babies cried too much.

"Meth is scarier than crack cocaine because violence is a direct effect of its use," observed Prof. Ronald K. Siegel, psychiatrist and research professor, Department of Psychiatry and Biobehavioral Sciences, UCLA School of Medicine. He described how meth creates a "fire in the brain," a storm of intense neurochemical activity from the simultaneous release of three types of neurotransmitters. He likens it to what would occur if all of the spark plugs in your car fired off in powerful but erratic bursts, causing your car engine to go haywire.

Some studies with animals have produced findings that show how meth use by pregnant women could harm the neurodevelopment of their fetuses. Other studies demonstrated how meth use can permanently damage brain cells. One of the first research studies on meth's effects, conducted on monkeys in 1977 by Wayne State University psychiatry professor Charles R. Schuster and colleagues, found that levels of dopamine and serotonin in the monkey brains had been reduced by about 50 percent up to six months after exposure. Similar studies using rats showed that after just four days of high doses, both dopamine and serotonin were reduced significantly. That gives you a glimpse of what's happening in your own brain if you use meth.

How difficult is it to treat meth dependency?

From Clelland "Gil" Gilchrist, chief executive officer, New Beginnings: The hallmark symptom for people who have gone from recreational use of methamphetamine to an addictive illness is "preoccupation." It begins to crowd out competing thoughts in the mind for all other activities—in the case of meth addiction, preoccupation even crowds out biological drives for survival. People don't eat, they don't sleep, they let their children be taken, they don't receive medical care, they commit desperate and violent crimes, because they can only think about one thing—methamphetamine. People who have never used drugs before can play with meth and become instantly addicted.

We do mass treatment here. I've been here since 1984, and we started tracking stimulants like meth in 1985. What we've noticed with meth addicts is even after they get sober, for at least a year after they quit, they're not as smart as they were before they started using it. They also have a hard time working at a job for the first year. They just can't seem to get it together.

Meth is really just longer lasting speed. Whether a person shoots it, snorts it, or takes it in capsule form, it's all bad. It's just instant bad. For everybody, meth addiction can be almost instant. You're going to lose your job real soon. But usually people don't start out using meth. You do some other drugs and then find your way to meth. Wives might do it because their husbands bring it home, and the wife is getting a little overweight, so she starts losing weight and their sex life improves, at least initially. All of that energy they feel from using it soon gets devoted to just getting more and more until they're just obsessed with it. Using it quickly turns on both of them and they lose their jobs, lose their house, get divorced; and they lose their teeth and their health. They stop functioning effectively. It turns into a nightmare real fast. We've seen that pattern a lot.

We have found out that meth is the most difficult drug to treat. Meth addicts are the most difficult group to treat. So how do we treat them? It doesn't matter whether they snort it or shoot it, the detox and the treatment will be the same. Heroin may be the hardest drug of all to detox from, but meth is second, right behind it. First of all, we have to convince the meth user they have a disease just like everybody else with a drug problem. But we also tell them meth has affected them differently and affected their body differently, so they need other information.

Our meth treatment program is six weeks. We also started a clearinghouse so that people come in for pretreatment. If they can get two to four weeks of just being here in a supervised living situation before they actually start treatment, it helps clear their heads a little bit, which is why we call it a clearinghouse. For the detox we use neurontin, an antiseizure medication, which helps them to deal with the cravings.

Then they go into aftercare. We like to push people towards AA because it serves a very valuable function in recovery. We want them to go to as many meetings as possible. They have a sponsor, and they work the steps to get that spiritual experience. We have a large alumni group from our program, and so we can set the clients up with sponsors. I've asked guys who relapsed and have been to multiple treatments what happened that worked this time, and none of them know. They say, "I just got it this time." It could be some kind or physiological change in their brain, or it could be spiritual. The ones that make it seem to have a spiritual awakening.

OxyContin

Sometimes referred to as "hillbilly heroin" because its abuse was first documented in the Appalachia mountains, OxyContin is an opioid drug, the sustained release form of oxycodone, a powerful painkiller. Recreational users crush the tablets to destroy the release formulation and then snort or inject it for a rapid high, with effects that last for about 12 hours.

Oxycodone's chemical name comes from codeine because their chemical structures are similar. Though OxyContin as a brand name was only introduced to the U.S. market in 1996, it quickly became the biggest-selling, non-generic "narcotic" painkiller; more than 80 percent of total world consumption of oxycodone occurs in the United States. That raises an interesting question. Are U.S. citizens in more pain than all of the rest of the world's population combined? (*Source: International Narcotics Control Board (2008)*, Narcotic Drugs: Estimated

World Requirements for 2009; Statistics for 2007. *New York: United Nations Publication, 2009 February, www.incb.org/pdf/technical-reports/narcotic-drugs/2008/narcotics_drugs_2008.pdf.*)

Oxycodone also appears in the painkillers Percocet and Percodan, among other brand names. By some estimates, oxycodone is twice as potent as morphine when it is taken orally.

In 2006 testimony before a U.S. House of Representatives subcommittee, National Institute on Drug Abuse director Nora Volkow described how OxyContin had originally been marketed as having a low potential for abuse because it was formulated to ensure a slow and gradual release of the drug. But, she said, "Abusers quickly learned that the pills could be crushed and their contents injected or snorted, releasing the entire dosage at once. What abusers do not realize is the great risk of overdose and other devastating consequences that may result from this practice. Now widespread in its abuse, OxyContin is the only commonly prescribed opioid analgesic that comes with a 'black box' warning."

In late 2011 the U.S. Centers for Disease Control and Prevention released statistics showing that OxyContin and Vicodin contributed to the deaths of nearly 15,000 people in the United States in 2008, more than three times the overdose death total from less than a decade earlier.

There's no doubt that OxyContin, with its content of oxycodone, produces dependence in many people who use it over any extended period of time. It's considered to be as equally dependence-producing as heroin, cocaine powder, or crack cocaine. The number of infants being born addicted to painkillers as a result of their mothers being addicted resembles the "crack baby" epidemic of decades before. At least 653 babies were born addicted in Florida alone during 2010, based on statistics compiled by state health officials.

Dr. Volkow's agency posts these health effects of OxyContin on its Web site: "Can produce drowsiness, constipation and, depending on amount taken, can depress breathing. [It] slows down brain function; if combined with other medications that cause drowsiness or with alcohol, heart rate and respiration can slow down dangerously. Taken repeatedly or in high doses, [it] can cause anxiety, paranoia, dangerously high body temperatures, irregular heartbeat, or seizures."

As with other opiates, withdrawal symptoms from OxyContin can include anxiety, flu-like conditions, fever, nausea, insomnia, muscle pain and weakness. If a pregnant woman uses OxyContin during her pregnancy, her child can be born with withdrawal symptoms similar to what the mother herself would experience if coming off the drug. (*Source: "OxyContin and neonatal abstinence syndrome." Rao R and Desai NS. J Perinatol. 2002 Jun;22(4):324–5.*)

Peyote and psilocybin

Though peyote comes from buttons on the crown of cactus with an active hallucinogen ingredient of mescaline, and psilocybin comes from certain types of mushrooms containing the active hallucinogen ingredient of psilocin, these two hallucinogenic compounds do have some things in common.

Both can be found growing in Mexico and parts of the Southwestern United States; both have a long history of medicinal and religious ritualistic use by tribal societies; and both have similar psychoactive effects on users, characterized by strong visual and auditory perception distortions and introspective thinking. Both are generally consumed orally. Peyote's effects can last up to 12 hours, depending on the dose, and psilocybin mushrooms exert effects for up to 6 hours, though psilocybin's effects sometimes resemble LSD effects more intensely than peyote.

Here is how the National Institute on Drug Abuse describes the health implications for both drugs:

Peyote: Effects include "increased body temperature and heart rate, uncoordinated movements, profound sweating, and flushing. The active ingredient mescaline has also been associated, in at least one report, to fetal abnormalities. The long-term residual psychological and cognitive effects of mescaline remain poorly understood. A recent study found no evidence of psychological or cognitive deficits among Native Americans that use peyote regularly in a religious setting."

Psilocybin: "It can produce muscle relaxation or weakness, uncoordinated movements, excessive pupil dilation, nausea, vomiting, and drowsiness. Panic reactions and psychosis may occur. Long-term effects such as flashbacks, risk of psychiatric illness, and impaired memory have been described in case reports. Individuals who abuse psilocybin mushrooms also risk poisoning if one of many existing varieties of poisonous mushrooms is incorrectly identified as a psilocybin mushroom."

PCP (phencyclidine)

Developed in the 1950s by a pharmaceutical company as an intravenous dissociative anesthetic, it's no longer clinically used because of its many documented serious neurotoxic effects on health. Patients often became agitated, delusional, and irrational after ingesting it.

Clandestine labs still produce PCP (also called "angel dust") as a crystalline powder that's normally snorted, smoked, or orally ingested. Smokers often sprinkle it on marijuana. Its effects, which include a numbing effect on the mind and exaggerated feelings of strength and power, last for up to six hours.

The National Institute on Drug Abuse lists PCP as dependency-forming because "its repeated abuse can lead to craving and compulsive PCP-seeking behavior, despite severe adverse consequences."

Those health consequences from PCP use are documented on the institute's Web site and include: symptoms that mimic schizophrenia, such as paranoia, delusions, and disordered thinking; sharp elevations in anxiety symptoms during and after use, creating suicidal thoughts; memory loss occurs over time with use, along with depression and speech and thought impairments, which can persist a year or longer after cessation of PCP use.

(Important note to readers: The National Institute on Drug Abuse prepared detailed fact sheets about specific drugs exclusively for our Recover to Live project. Those fact sheets are at our Web site, www.Recover2Live.com.)

APPENDIX TWO

A Resource Guide to Recovery

Trying to navigate the wide range of resources available for treatment and recovery from a toxic compulsion can be a daunting task, especially if you are currently struggling to calm the confusion and desperation accompanying a dependency condition.

The following information about hotlines, treatment centers, therapists, addiction specialists, 12-Step programs, and other resources are organized by state or country to give you faster access. You will also find other useful information on the Recover2Live.com Web site.

If You Are Seeking Quick Help—Hotlines to Call

Alcohol and Drugs

Al-Anon/Alateen, 800-356-9996/800-352-9996
Al-Anon Family Groups Inc., 800-344-2666
Alcoholics Anonymous World Services, 212-870-3400
Alcohol and Drug Referral Hotline, 800-252-6465
Note: Alcoholics Anonymous (AA) local chapter information and phone numbers can be obtained by calling the Alcohol and Drug Referral Hotline.
Cocaine Addiction, 800-559-9503
Covenant House Hotline, 800-999-9999
Grief Recovery Helpline, 800-445-4808
Military Helpline, www.MilitaryHelpline.org; 888-457-4838
Narcotics Anonymous, 818-773-9999

National Association for Children of Alcoholics, 714-499-3889

National Clearinghouse for Alcohol and Drug Information (NCADI), www.ncadi.samhsa.gov; 800-729-6686 (English and Español), 800-487-4889 (TDD)

National Council on Alcoholism and Drug Dependence Hope Line, 800-475-HOPE (4673)

National Domestic Violence Hotline, 800-799-SAFE (7233) and 800-787-3224 (TTY)

National Drug and Alcohol Treatment Referral Service, 800-622-4357

National Institute on Drug Abuse—Drug and Treatment Information, 800-662-4357

National Youth Crisis Hotline, 800-442-HOPE (4673)

Oregon Partnership, regional calls to the National Suicide Prevention Helpline, 800-273-TALK (8255) or 800-SUICIDE (784-2433). Substance Abuse Helpline is available 24/7 at 800-923-4327.

Parent Hotline, 800-840-6537

PRIDE Drug Information Line, 800-677-7433

Recovery Options, 800-662-2873

Relapse Prevention Hotline, 800-RELAPSE (735-2773)

Suicide Prevention, www.suicide.org; (800) 273-TALK (8255), (800)-SUICIDE (784-2433)

Eating Disorders

National Association of Anorexia Nervosa and Associated Disorders, 847-831-3438, 708-831-3438

National Eating Disorders Association Helpline, 800-931-2237

Gambling Compulsion

California Office on Problem Gambling, 800-GAMBLER (426-2537)

Gambling Problems—Arnie and Sheila Wexler Associates, 888-LAST-BET (527-8238)

National Council on Problem Gambling Hotline, 800-522-4700

Hoarding

Hoarder Help Hotline, 888-226-0030
National Institute of Mental Health Depression and Panic
, Disorder, 800-421-4211

Nicotine Dependence

Smoking Quitline, 877-44U-QUIT (448-7848)

Sex Compulsions

Sex Addiction Hotline, 800-551-9888

Treatment for the Seven Toxic Compulsions

This is a partial listing of the available treatment centers and organizations. For best results, consult the clearinghouse links providing the names of treatment centers for the various states, especially if your state isn't listed below. Also be aware that many, though not all, of these treatment centers address multiple compulsions, so you will need to inquire whether the center specializes in your particular compulsion.

Faces and Voices of Recovery

Founded in St. Paul, Minnesota, in 2001, this important online community organization (www.facesandvoicesofrecovery.org) seeks to mobilize and organize the recovery community. Its crucial and ever-growing Guide to Mutual Aid Resources can be found at www.facesandvoicesofrecovery.org/resources/support/index.html. It is a one-stop resource for people in or seeking recovery from addiction, their families and friends, and for addiction-treatment service providers and other allied service professionals.

Treatment Facilities Listed by State

(Check clearinghouse listings above if your state isn't listed below.)

♦ *Alabama*
Alethia House, www.specialkindofcaring.org; 205-324-6502
The Shoulder, www.theshoulder.org

Wade Freedom House, www.wadefreedomhouse.com;
256-435-5010

◆ *Alaska*
All Forms of Addiction: Akeela, www.Akeela.org;
907-565-1200
For Teens: Tanana Chiefs, www.tananachiefs.org;
907-455-4725

◆ *Arizona*
Cottonwood Tucson, www.cottonwooddetucson.com;
800-877-4520
For Men: Prescott House, 866-425-4673
For Teens and Kids: The New Foundation, 480-945-3302
For Women: Pia's Place, 928-445-5081
Sierra Tucson, www.sierratucson.com; 800-842-4487 (in the
UK 0800 891166)
The Meadows, www.themeadows.com; 866-926-7161

◆ *Arkansas*
For Men (ages 14–24; all forms of addiction): www.capstone
treatmentcenter.com; 866-729-4479

◆ *California*
Alta Mira, www.altamirarecovery.com; 877-304-1198
Betty Ford Center, www.bettyfordcenter.org; 800-434-7365
Bridges to Recovery, www.bridgestorecovery.com/specialties.
html; 877-386-3398
Creative Care, www.creativecareinc.com; 800-832-3280
Duffy's Rehab, www.duffysrehab.com; 888-717-9724
Foundations Recovery Network, www.foundationsrecoveryne
work.com; 877-714-1318
Harm Reduction Therapy, harmreductiontherapy.org
High End Profound Private Treatment, www.pftreatment.com;
877-492-1697
Hilltop Recovery Services (Lake County), www.hilltoprecovery
.com; 707-987-9972
Hope by the Sea, www.hopebythesea.com; 866-930-4673
Janus of Santa Cruz, www.janussc.org; 866-526-8772 or
831-462-1060

La Ventana, www.laventanatreatment.com; 888-246-5320 or
   800-560-8518
Living Sober, www.livingsober.com; 866-430-9748
Men Only Luxury, www.soberlanding.com; 877-235-6134
Miramar, www.miramarlagunabeach.com; 866-382-5442
Morning Side Recovery, www.morningsiderecovery.com;
   866-413-4794
New Dawn Recovery (eating disorders), www.newdawnrecovery.com;
   415-331-1383
New Method Wellness, newmethodwellness.com;
   866-951-1824
Ocean Hills Recovery, www.oceanhillsrecovery.com; 888-214-4192
Phoenix House, www.phoenixhouse.org; 800-378-4435
Practical Recovery, www.practicalrecovery.com; 800-977-6110
Promises, www.promises.com; 866-441-6686
Serenity Malibu, www.serenitymalibu.com; 888-886-6495
The Hills Center, www.thehillscenter.com; 800-705-1909
The Nelson Center for Emotional Healing, www.thenelsoncenter
   .com; 800-609-4061
Summit Malibu, www.summitmalibu.com; 888-777-9672
Women Only Luxury, www.roserehab.com; 888-471-0435

◆ *Colorado*
Arapahoe House, www.arapahoehouse.org; 303-657-3700
For Children: www.bettyfordcenter.org; 800-434-7365
Harmony Foundation, www.harmonyfoundationinc.com;
   866-686-7867
Jaywalker Lodge, www.jaywalkerlodge.com; 866-529-9255

◆ *Connecticut*
Connecticut Clearing House, www.ctclearinghouse.org
Driver Intervention Phoenix House, www.phoenixhouse.org;
   800-378-4435
Mountainside, www.mountainside.com; 800-762-5433

◆ *District of Columbia*
Caron Washington, D.C., www.caron.org/caron-washington
   -dc.html; 610-223-4989
Clean and Sober Streets, http://cleanandsoberstreets.org;
   202-783-7343

◆ *Florida*

The Ambrosia Treatment Centers, www.ambrosiatreatment
center.com; 866-577-6868

Caron Renaissance, www.caronrenaissance.org; 561-241-7977

Hanley Center, www.hanleycenter.org; 866-4HANLEY
(442-6535)

Hazelden, www.hazelden.org; 800-257-7810

Phoenix House, www.phoenixhouse.org; 800-378-4435

The Refuge, www.therefuge-ahealingplace.com; 866-473-3843

Transformations Treatment Center, www.transformationtreatment.com;
866-211-5538

◆ *Georgia*

Foundations Recovery Network, www.foundationsrecoverynet
work.com; 877-714-1318

Willingway Hospital, www.willingway.com; 800-242-9455

◆ *Hawaii*

Hawaii Island Recovery, www.hawaiiislandrecovery.com; 866-
515-5032 or 808-345-0868

◆ *Idaho*

For Teens (ages 11–17): SUWS Wilderness Programs, www
.suws.com; 888-879-7897

◆ *Illinois*

Adventist Institute for Behavioral Medicine, www
.keepingyouwell.com; 630-545-6160

Chestnut Health Systems, Bloomington, www.chestnut.org;
309-827-6026

For Adults: all forms of addiction, Hazelden, www.hazelden
.org; 800-257-7810

For Women (ages 12+): Timberline Knolls, www.timber
lineknolls.com; 877-596-9772

Omni Youth Services, Buffalo Grove, www.omniyouth.org;
847-353-1500 or 847-353-1500

Rosecrance Health Network, Rockford, http://rosecrance.org;
888-928-5278

♦ *Kansas*
   Valley Hope, www.valleyhope.org; 800-544-5101

♦ *Maine*
   Phoenix House, www.phoenixhouse.org; 800-378-4435

♦ *Massachusetts*
   Caron Boston, www.caron.org/caron-boston.html;
      781-878-7111
   Phoenix House, www.phoenixhouse.org; 800-378-4435
   Stanley Street Treatment and Resources, www.sstar.org

♦ *Michigan*
   Dawn Farm, www.dawnfarm.org; 734-485-8725 or
      734-669-8265
   Enter Health Ranch, www.enterhealth.com; 800-388-4601

♦ *Minnesota*
   Adults and Teens: Hazelden, www.hazelden.org; 800-257-7810
   Meridian Behavioral Health, www.meridianprograms.com
      /alliance.asp; 877-367-1715
   New Beginnings at Waverly, www.newbeginningsatwaverly
      .com; 800-487-8758

♦ *Mississippi*
   Pine Grove Behavioral Health and Addiction Services, www
      .pinegrovetreatment.com; 888-574-4673

♦ *Missouri*
   Valley Hope, www.valleyhope.org; 800-544-5101

♦ *New Hampshire*
   Phoenix House, www.phoenixhouse.org; 800-378-4435

♦ *New Mexico*
   Life Healing Center, www.life-healing.com; 866-806-7214

♦ *New York*
   Caron New York City, www.caron.org/caron-new-york-city
      .html; 800-854-6023

Core Company and Loft 107, www.corecompanynyc.com;
866-818-8283
Hazelden, www.hazelden.org; 800-257-7810
Phoenix House, www.phoenixhouse.org; 800-378-4435

◆ *North Carolina*
For Young Adults (ages 18–28): Four Circles,
www.fourcirclesrecovery.com; 877-893-2221
Two Dreams Outer Banks, www.twodreamsouterbanks.com;
877-355-DREAM (3732)

◆ *Ohio*
Cornerstone of Recovery, cornerstoneofrecoveryohio.com;
866-359-8551

◆ *Oregon*
For Adults: (all forms of addiction): Hazelden, www.hazelden.
org; 800-257-7810

◆ *Pennsylvania*
Caron, www.caron.org; 800-854-6023
Caron Philadelphia, www.caron.org/caron-philadelphia.html;
610-743-6565
Keystone Center, www.keystonecenterecu.net; 610-876-8448 or
800-733-6840

◆ *Rhode Island*
Phoenix House, www.phoenixhouse.org; 800-378-4435
Stanley Street Treatment and Resources, www.sstar.org;
800-747-6237

◆ *Tennessee*
Foundations Recovery Network, www.foundationsrecovery
network.com; 877-714-1318
Onsite Therapeutic Workshops, www.onsiteworkshops.com;
800-341-7432
Recovery Ranch (all forms of addiction),
www.recoveryranch.com; 866-381-8447

◆ *Texas*
Burning Tree, www.burningtree.com; 866-287-2877
Caron Renaissance, www.carontexas.org; 800-241-0352 or
214-491-3600
For Children: The Betty Ford Center, www.bettyfordcenter.org;
800-434-7365
Hazel Street, www.hazelstreet.com; 903-791-0385
Menninger Clinic, www.menningerclinic.com; 713-275-5000
Phoenix House, www.phoenixhouse.org; 800-378-4435
Spirit Lodge, www.spiritlodge.com; 830-798-2222
Valley Hope, www.valleyhope.org; 800-544-5101

◆ *Utah*
Cirque Lodge, www.cirquelodge.com; 877-997-3422
Sober Living: Project Recovery, www.projectrecovery.com;
877-299-9947

◆ *Vermont*
Maple Leaf Farm, www.mapleleaf.org; 802-899-2911
Phoenix House, www.phoenixhouse.org; 800-378-4435
Spring Lake Ranch, www.springlakeranch.org; 802-492-3322
Vermont Association of Addiction Treatment Programs, www
.vtaddictionservices.org

◆ *Virginia*
Phoenix House, www.phoenixhouse.org; 800-378-4435

◆ *Washington*
Washington State Department of Health, doh.wa.gov/tobacco
/quit/quitline.htm

◆ *Wisconsin*
Herrington Recovery Center, www.rogershospital.org/residen
tial-center/herrington-recovery-center; 800-767-4411

Treatment Facilities Worldwide

+ *Africa*
  Support for Addictions Prevention and Treatment in Africa
    (SAPTA), www.sapta.or.ke/

+ *Asia*
  Breathing Space, http://breathingspacethailand.com

+ *Australia*
  Australian National Council on Drugs (ANCD), www.ancd
    .org.au; 02 6166 9600
  South Pacific Private, www.southpacificprivate.com.au;
    0412 643 505

+ *Bermuda*
  Caron Renaissance, www.caronbermuda.org; 441-236-0823

+ *Canada*
  Canadian Drug Rehab Centres, www.canadiandrugrehabcen
    tres.com
  Centre for Addiction and Mental Health, www.camh.net;
    416 535 8501 or 866 797 0000

+ *Italy*
  San Patrignano, www.sanpatrignano.org; 39 0541 362111

+ *New Zealand*
  Drug and Alcohol Helpline, www.alcoholdrughelp.org.nz;
    0800 787 797

+ *United Kingdom*
  Health Care UK, www.privatehealth.co.uk/hospitaltreatment
    /find-a-treatment/psychiatric/alcohol-addiction
  South London and Maudsley Hospital, www.slam.nhs.uk

+ *Virgin Islands*
  Inspirations, www.inspirationsyouth.com

Find a Therapist for the Seven Toxic Compulsions

The following list is representative and not a complete one. For best results, consult one of the databases for therapists in your area who specialize in the toxic compulsions that concern you.

Overall Databases

NetworkTherapy.com: (therapists, a full library of articles listed by condition, easily searchable links to hotlines, books, support groups), www.networktherapy.com

Psychology Today, http://therapists.psychologytoday.com/rms

Therapy Tribe, www.therapytribe.com

Theravive, www.theravive.com

Practitioner Databases

Academy of Cognitive Therapy Referrals, www.academyofct.org

American Association of Sexuality Educators, Counselors and Therapists, www.aasect.org

Anxiety Disorders Association of America Referrals, https://community.adaa.org/eweb

Association for Behavioral and Cognitive Referrals, www.abct.org

Behavioral Tech, LLC, http://behavioraltech.org/resources/tools_consumers.cfm

Eating Disorder Referrals, www.edreferral.com

International Institute for Trauma and Abuse Professionals Certified Sex-Addiction Therapists Directory, www.iitap.com/find_csat.cfm; 866-575-6853

International OCD Foundation Hoarding Treatment Providers, www.ocfoundation.org/treatment_providers.aspx

Judith Orloff, MD, www.drjudithorloff.com/resources

Moving Cycle Practitioners, www.themovingcycle.com

Naropa Institute Directory of Naropa-Trained Therapists, www.naropa.edu

National Eating Disorders Treatment Referral Line, 800-931-2237

National List of Interventionists, www.lovefirst.net/intervn.htm; 888-220-4400

Network of Independent Interventionists, http://independentinterventionists.com

Paul J. Gallant, Interventionist, www.paulgallant.com; 800-276-1975

Sensorimotor Psychotherapy National and International Referral to Practitioners, www.sensorimotorpsychotherapy.org /referral.html; 800-860-9258

Somatic Practitioner National and International Database, www.traumahealing.com/somatic-experiencing/practitioner -directory.html

Practitioners with Online Workshops

Kay Sheppard, www.kaysheppard.com; 321-727-8040

Marijuana Anonymous Online Meetings, www.marijuana -anonymous.org

Radiant Recovery, Kathleen Des Maisons, www.radiantrecovery.com

Therapists Worldwide

* *Africa*
Therapist Directory, www.therapistdirectory.co.za/addiction _therapists_south_africa.asp

* *Australia*
Australian National Council on Drugs (ANCD), www.ancd .org.au
Therapy Tribe, www.therapytribe.com

* *Canada*
Barbara Killinger, http://drbarbarakillinger.com; bkillinger@ rogers.com
Centre for Addiction and Mental Health, www.camh.net; 416-535-8501, 866-797-0000
NetworkTherapy.com, www.networktherapy.com
Psychology Today, http://therapists.psychologytoday.com/rms
Therapy Tribe, www.therapytribe.com

* *Europe*
European Association for the Treatment of Addiction, www.eata.org.uk

+ *United Kingdom*

 Mike Delaney, Addictions Specialist, www.mikedelaney.co.uk
  7733 120648

 Psychiatric Clinics, www.whatclinic.com/addiction/worldwide

 Simon Leigh, Addictions Counselor, www.addictiontherapy
  .org.uk; 07973 199926

Therapy Associations

 Academy of Cognitive Therapy Referrals, www.academyofct.org

 American Association of Sexuality Educators, www.aasect.org

 Anxiety Disorders Association of America Referrals, https://
  community.adaa.org/eweb

 Association for Behavioral and Cognitive Referrals, www.abct
  .org

 Dialectical Behavioral Therapy, http://behavioraltech.org

 National Association of Cognitive Behavioral Therapists, www
  .nacbt.org

 International Institute for Trauma & Addiction Professionals,
  Patrick Carnes, www.sexhelp.com

 SMART Recovery, www.smartrecovery.org.

U.S.-Based 12-Step Groups

 12 Steps, www.12step.org

 12 Steps and Buddhism, http://the12stepbuddhist.com

 12 Point Medicine Wheel and Alternative Healing,
  www.addictionalchemy.com

 Alcoholics Anonymous, www.aa.org

 Al-Anon Family Groups, www.al-anon.alateen.org

 Alliance for Eating Disorders, www.allianceforeatingdisorders
  .com

 Anorexics and Bulimics Anonymous, http://aba12steps.org

 Chemically Dependent Anonymous, www.cdaweb.org

 Cocaine Anonymous, www.ca.org

 Co-Dependents Anonymous, www.coda.org

 Eating Addictions Anonymous, www.eatingaddictions
  anonymous.org

 Eating Disorders Anonymous National and International
  Clearinghouse, www.eatingdisordersanonymous.org
  /meetings.html#AL

Overeaters Anonymous, www.oa.org
Gamblers Anonymous, www.gamblersanonymous.org
Gam-Anon, www.gam-anon.org
Hoarders Anonymous, www.hoardersanonymous.org
Children of Hoarders, http://childrenofhoarders.com/wordpress
Marijuana Anonymous, www.marijuana-anonymous.org
Narcotics Anonymous, www.na.org
Nar-Anon Family Groups, www.nar-anon.org
Nicotine Addiction, www.smokefree.gov
Nicotine Anonymous, www.nicotine-anonymous.org
Recovering Couples Anonymous, www.recovering-couples.org
Sex Addicts Anonymous, www.sexaa.org
Sexaholics Anonymous, www.sa.org
White Bison (adapted to indigenous people's culture),
    www.whitebison.org/index.php

National and International Organizations, Groups, and Alliances

Addicted.com, www.addicted.com
Alliance for Addiction Solutions, www.allianceforaddictionso
    lutions.org
Australian National Council on Drugs (ANCD), www.ancd
    .org.au
Brent Shapiro Foundation for Alcohol and Drug Awareness,
    www.brentshapiro.org
Centers for Disease Control and Prevention, www.cdc.gov
    /pwud/addiction.html
Cocaine Anonymous Online Service, www.ca-online.org
Computer Based Community and Free Program, www.beco
    meanex.org
Computer Based Intervention, http://collegedrinkerscheckup.
    com
Family-Based Treatment for Eating Disorders, www.maudsley
    parents.org
Integral Transformative Justice, www.prisondharmanetwork.org
International OCD Foundation, www.ocfoundation.org
Legacy for Longer, Healthier Lives, www.legacyforhealth.org
Mental Health America, www.nmha.org

Messies Anonymous, www.messies.com

Minnesota Recovery Connection, www.minnesotarecovery.org
/index.html

Moderate Drinking, www.moderateddrinking.com

Moderation Group, www.moderation.org

National Alliance on Mental Illness, www.nami.org

National Council on Problem Gambling, www.ncpgambling.org

National Eating Disorders Association, www.nationaleating
disorders.org

National Institute of Mental Health, www.nimh.nih.gov/index
.shtml

National Institute on Drug Abuse, www.nida.nih.gov/infofacts
/marijuana.html

National Institute on Drug Abuse, www.nida.nih.gov
/nidahome.html

Obsessive-Compulsive Disorder International Clearinghouse,
www.geonius.com/ocd/organizations.html

Office of National Drug Control Policy, www.whitehouse.gov
/ondcp

Secular Organizations for Sobriety, http://sossobriety.org

Sex Addicts Anonymous Online and Electronic Meetings,
http://saa-recovery.org

Substance Abuse and Mental Health Services Administration,
www.samhsa.gov

U.S. Department of Veterans Affairs (VA), www.va.gov

United Nations Office on Drugs and Crime, www.unodc.org

Women for Sobriety Inc., www.womenforsobriety.org

Women's Health, www.womenshealth.gov

World Health Organization, www.who.int/topics
/substance_abuse/en

Mindfulness and Alternative/Holistic-Based Therapies

Donald Altman, www.mindfulpractices.com

Kristin Neff, www.self-compassion.org

Mindfulness-based Cognitive Therapy, www.mbct.com

Mindfulness-based Relapse Prevention, www.mindfulrp.com

Movement-based Therapy, www.themovingcycle.com

Reichian Therapy, http://reichianinstitute.org/therapy.htm

Somatic Experiencing Trauma Institute, www.traumahealing
.com

Transcendental Meditation, www.tm.org

Urban Zen, www.urbanzen.org/news/families-transition and
www.urbanzen.org/about/wellbeing

Vipassana Meditation, www.dhamma.org

Books for Further Reading

Addiction and Healing Addiction

Amen, Daniel G., MD, and David E. Smith, MD. *Unchain Your Brain: 10 Steps to Breaking the Addictions That Steal Your Life.* Mindworks Press: June 2010 (www.amenclinics.com).

Bacon, Linda. *Health At Every Size.* Dallas, Texas: BenBella Books, 2010 (www.lindabacon.org).

Carr, David. *The Night of the Gun.* New York: Simon & Schuster, 2009.

Chopra, Dr. Deepak, and Dr. David Simon. *Freedom from Addiction.* Deerfield Beach, FL: HCI Books Inc., 2011 (www.chopra.com/freedomfrom addiction).

DuPont, Robert L. *The Selfish Brain: Learning from Addiction.* Center City, MN: Hazelden, 2000.

Gadhia-Smith, Dr. Anita. *From Addiction to Recovery: A Therapist's Personal Journey.* iuniverse.com

Gant, Dr. Charles, and Greg Lewis, PhD. *End Your Addiction Now.* Garden City Park, NY: Squareone, 2010 (www.charlesgantmd.com).

Jay, Debra. *No More Letting Go: The Spirituality of Taking Action Against Alcoholism and Drug Addiction.* New York: Bantam, 2006.

Khaleghi, Dr. Morteza, and Dr. Karen Khaleghi. *The Anatomy of Addiction.* New York: Macmillan, 2011.

Killinger, Barbara. *Workaholics: The Respectable Addicts.* Buffalo, NY: Key Porter Books, 2004 (http://drbarbarakillinger.com).

Kipper, David, MD, and Steven Whitney. *The Addiction Solution.* Emmaus, PA: Rodale, 2011 (http://davidkippermd.com/treatingaddiction.html).

Urschel, Harold C. III., MD. *Healing the Addicted Brain.* Naperville, IL: Sourcebooks, 2009.

White, William. *Slaying the Dragon: The History of Addiction Treatment and Recovery in America.* Bloomington, IL: Chestnut Health Systems, 1998.

Alcoholism

Hester, Reid K., and William R. Miller. *Handbook of Alcoholism Treatment Approaches: Effective Alternatives.* UK: Allyn & Bacon, 2002.

Hornbacher, Maya. *Waiting: A Non-believer's Higher Power.* 2011, Center City, MN: Hazelden, 2011.

Whitfield, Dr. Charles. *My Recovery: A Personal Plan for Healing.* Deerfield Beach, FL: HCI Books Inc., 2003 (www.cbwhit.com, www.barbarawhitfield.com).

Sexual Compulsivity and Addiction

Anand, Margot, and M.E. Naslednikov. *The Art of Sexual Ecstasy: The Path of Sacred Sexuality for Western Lovers.* New York: Jeremy P. Tarcher, 1989.

Carnes, Patrick, PhD. *Out of the Shadows: Understanding Sexual Addiction.* Center City, MN: Hazelden, 2001 (www.sexhelp.com).

Horvath, Dr. Thomas. *Sex, Drugs, Gambling, and Chocolate.* Manassas Park, VA: Impact Publishers, 1998.

Linden, David J. *The Compass of Pleasure: How Our Brains Make Fatty Foods, Orgasms, Exercise, Marijuana, Generosity, Vodka, and Gambling Feel So Good.* New York: Viking, 2011 (www.compassofpleasure.org).

Nicotine Dependency

Rabinoff, Michael, PhD. *Ending The Tobacco Holocaust.* Fulton, CA: Elite Books, 2007 (www.tobaccobook.com).

Hoarding

Benson, April. *To Buy or Not to Buy: Why We Overshop and How to Stop.* Boston: Trumpeter, 2008 (www.addicted.com).

Bubrick, Jerome, and Fugen Neziroglu, PhD, ABBP, Patricia B. Perkins, JD, Jose Yaryura-Tobias, MD. *Overcoming Obsessive Hoarding: Why You Save and How You Can Stop.* Oakland, CA: New Harbinger, 2004.

Frost, Randy O., PhD, and Gail Steketee, PhD. *Stuff: Compulsive Hoarding and the Meaning of Things.* New York: Mariner Books, 2011.

Tompkins, Michael A., and Tamara L. Hartl. *Digging Out: Helping Your Loved One Manage Clutter, Hoarding, and Compulsive Acquiring.* Oakland, CA: New Harbinger, 2009.

Eating Disorders and Food Addiction

Sheppard, Kay. *From the First Bite: A Complete Guide to Recovery from Food Addiction,* Deerfield Beach, FL: HCI Books Inc., 2000 (www.kaysheppard.com).

Gambling

Petry, Nancy M. *Pathological Gambling.* Washington, DC: American Psychological Association, 2005.

Healing the Body and Mind

Alexander, Dr. Ronald. *Wise Mind, Open Mind: Finding Purpose and Meaning in Times of Crisis, Loss and Change.* Oakland, CA: New Harbinger, 2009 (www.ronaldalexander.com).

Bradshaw, John. *Healing the Shame that Binds You.* Deerfield Beach, FL: HCI Books Inc., 2005 (www.johnbradshaw.com).

Caldwell, Christine. *Getting Our Bodies Back.* Boston: Shambhala, 1996 (www.themovingcycle.com).

——. *Getting in Touch: The Guide to New Body-Centered Therapies.* Wheaton, IL: Quest Books, 1997 (www.themovingcycle.com).

Cass, Dr. Hyla, and Patrick Holford. *Natural Highs.* New York: Avery, 2002 (www.Naturalhighsbook.com).

Knauss, William J., EdD, and Albert Ellis, PhD. *The Cognitive Behavioral Workbook for Depression: A Step-By-Step Program.* Oakland, CA: New Harbinger, 2006.

Lawlis, Dr. Frank, and Dr. Maggie Greenwood-Robinson. *The Brain Power Cookbook.* New York: Plume, 2008.

Lerner, Harriet, PhD. *The Dance of Connection: How to Talk to Someone When You're Mad, Hurt, Scared, Frustrated, Insulted, Betrayed, or Desperate.* New York: William Morrow, 2002 (www.harrietlerner.com).

Levine, Dr. Peter A. *Waking the Tiger: Healing Trauma.* Berkeley, CA: North Atlantic Books, 1997 (www.traumahealing.com/somatic-experiencing/peter-levine.html).

Nataraja, Dr. Shanida. *The Blissful Brain (*www.blissfulbrain.com).

Neff, Kristin. *Self Compassion: Stop Beating Yourself Up and Leave Insecurity Behind.* New York: William Morrow, 2011 (www.self-compassion.org).

Ogden, Pat, PhD, Kekuni Minton, and Clare Pain. *Trauma and the Body.* New York: W.W. Norton & Company, 2006 (www.sensorimotorpsychotherapy.org/faculty.html).

Robbins, Anthony: *Awaken the Giant Within.* New York: Free Press, 1992 (www.tonyrobbins.com).

Roth, Jeffrey D. *Group Psychotherapy and Recovery from Addiction: Carrying the Message.* Binghamton, NY: Routledge, 2004.

Schwartz, Dr. Jeffrey M., and Dr. Rebecca Gladding. *You Are Not Your Brain: The 4-Step Solution for Changing Bad Habits, Ending Unhealthy Thinking, and Taking Control of Your Life.* New York: Penguin Group, 2011.

Stone, Hal, Sidra Stone, and Shakti Gawain. *Embracing Ourselves: The Voice Dialogue Manual.* Novato, CA: New World Library, 1998 (http://delosinc.com).

Buddhist-Centered Approaches, Spiritual Approaches, Mindfulness and Meditation

Altman, Donald. *The Mindfulness Code: Keys for Overcoming Stress, Anxiety, Fear and Unhappiness.* Novato, CA: New World Library, 2010 (www.mindfulpractices.com).

Chodron, Pema. *Start Where You Are: A Guide to Compassionate Living.* Boston: Shambhala, 2004 (http://pemachodronfoundation.org).

———. *Taking the Leap: Freeing Ourselves from Old Habits and Fears.* Boston: Shambhala, 2010.

———. *When Things Fall Apart: Heart Advice for Difficult Times.* Boston: Shambhala, 2002.

Griffin, Kevin Edward. *One Breath at a Time: Buddhism and the Twelve Steps.* Emmaus, PA: Rodale, 2004 (www.kevingriffin.net).

Hanh, Thich Nhat. *Happiness: Essential Mindfulness Practices.* Berkeley, CA: Parallax Press, 2009.

———. *Reconciliation: Healing the Inner Child.* Berkeley, CA: Parallax Press, 2010.

———. *True Love: A Practice for Awakening the Heart.* Boston: Shambhala, 2011.

Kabat-Zinn, Jon. *Wherever You Go There You Are.* New York: Hyperion, 2005 (www.mindfulnesscds.com/index.html and www.umassmed.edu/Content.aspx?id=43102).

Moore, Thomas. *Care of the Soul: A Guide for Cultivating Depth and Sacredness in Everyday Life.* New York: HarperPerennial, 1994 (http://careofthesoul.net).

———. *Dark Nights of the Soul: A Guide to Finding Your Way Through Life's Ordeals.* New York: Gotham, 2005 (http://careofthesoul.net).

Siegel, Dr. Daniel J. *The Mindful Brain: Reflection and Attunement in the Cultivation of Well Being.* New York: W.W. Norton & Company, 2007 (http://drdansiegel.com).

Williamson, Marianne. *A Return to Love: Reflections on the Principles of "A Course in Miracles."* New York: Harper, 1996 (www.marianne.com).

———. *The Gift of Change: Spiritual Guidance for Living Your Best Life.* New York: Harper, 2006.

Intervention

Jay, Debra, and Jeff Jay. *Love First: A Family's Guide to Intervention.* Center City, MN: Hazelden, 2008 (www.lovefirst.net/about.htm).

For Parents

Califano, Joseph A., Jr. *How to Raise a Drug-Free Kid: The Straight Dope for Parents*. New York: Fireside, 2009.

Moe, Jerry. *Understanding Addiction and Recovery Through a Child's Eyes: Hope, Help, and Healing for Families*. Deerfield Beach, FL: HCI Books Inc., 2007.

APPENDIX THREE

Experts Cited in This Book

MILES ADCOX, MS. Chief executive officer, Onsite Workshops.

RONALD ALEXANDER, PHD. Executive director, OpenMind Training Institute, Santa Monica. Psychotherapist MFT, executive, and leadership coach; adjunct teaching faculty, UCLA extension; guest lecturer, David Geffen School of Medicine.

STEVEN ALM. Hawaii state court judge; head of Project Hope in Hawaii; cochair of the Interagency Council on Intermediate Sanctions.

DONALD ALTMAN, MA, LPC. Psychotherapist, author, and faculty member, Interpersonal Neurobiology Program at Portland State University; adjunct professor, Lewis and Clarke College Graduate School of Education and Counseling; vice president, the Center for Mindful Eating.

DANIEL G. AMEN, MD. Child psychiatrist and adult psychiatrist; brain imaging specialist; author.

MARGOT ANAND, MA. Psychologist, Sorbonne; world's leading authority on Tantra; author.

LINDA BACON, PHD. Nutrition professor, City College of San Francisco; associate nutritionist, University of California, Davis.

ANDREA BARTHWELL, MD, FASAM. Chief executive officer, Two Dreams Outer Banks.

APRIL LANE BENSON, PHD. Psychologist and expert on compulsive buying; author.

ROSS BELL. Executive director, New Zealand Drug Foundation.

WARREN BICKEL. Director, Advanced Recovery Research Center of Virginia Tech's Carilion Research Institute.

KELLY D. BROWNELL, PHD. Professor of psychology, epidemiology, and public health director, Rudd Center for Food Policy and Obesity, Yale University.

CHRISTINE CALDWELL, PHD, LPC, ADTR. Founder and chairperson, Somatic Counseling Psychology Department, Naropa University, Boulder, Colorado.

JOSEPH A. CALIFANO JR. Founder and chair, the National Center on Addiction and Substance Abuse at Columbia University (CASA Columbia); member, Institute of Medicine, National Academy of Sciences; 21st U.S. Secretary of Health, Education, and Welfare; special assistant for domestic policy to President Lyndon B. Johnson (1965–1969); author.

PATRICK CARNES, PHD. Psychologist and former clinical director of sexual disorders services, The Meadows, Wickenburg, Arizona; author.

KATHLEEN CARROLL, PHD. Professor, Yale University School of Medicine, Division of Substance Abuse.

KENNETH O. CARTER, MD, MPH., DIPL.AC. Immediate past president, National Acupuncture Detoxification Association; adjunct assistant professor, UNC-Chapel Hill Medical School Psychiatry Emergency Services, Carolinas Medical Center, Charlotte, North Carolina.

HYLA CASS, MD. Assistant clinical professor of psychiatry, UCLA School of Medicine; author.

DEEPAK CHOPRA, MD. Founder, Chopra Center for Well-Being; author.

ARTHUR T. DEAN. Major general, U.S. Army (retired); chairman and chief executive officer, Community Anti-Drug Coalitions of America (CADCA).

PETER DELANEY, PHD, LCSW-C. Director, Center for Behavioral Health Statistics and Quality, Substance Abuse and Mental Health Services Administration (SAMHSA).

KIMBERLY DENNIS, MD. Medical director, Timberline Knolls Residential Treatment Center.

DORA DIXIE, MD. Owner, Day By Day Health Consultants, Chicago, Illinois; medical director, The Women's Treatment Center; regional director, American Society of Addiction Medicine.

ROBERT L. DUPONT, MD. President, Institute for Behavior and Health Inc.; first director of the National Institute on Drug Abuse (NIDA, 1973–78); second White House Drug Chief (1973–77; for Presidents Nixon and Ford); clinical professor of psychiatry, Georgetown Medical School.

MICHAEL S. EARLY, chief clinical officer, Caron, and former manager of continuum services, Hazelden Foundation.

JOYCELYN ELDERS, MD. Fifteenth U.S. Surgeon General; professor emeritus, University of Arkansas Medical School.

CHRISTOPHER EMERSON, PHD. Licensed clinical psychologist specializing in anxiety and depression-related disorders and treating addiction and compulsivity issues; psychodynamic/existential therapist for adult individuals and couples.

CARLTON K. ERICKSON, PHD. Distinguished professor of pharmacology/toxicology; director, Addiction Science Research & Education Center, College of Pharmacy, University of Texas at Austin.

STANLEY EVANS. Medical director and addictions medicine specialist, Caron Renaissance, Florida.

GABRIELE FISCHER, MD. Director, Addiction Clinic, Medical University, University of Vienna.

TIMOTHY W. FONG, MD. Codirector, UCLA Gambling Studies Program; associate professor of psychiatry, Semel Institute for Neuroscience and Human Behavior, UCLA.

PAUL J. GALLANT, MC, LPC, BRI-II. Founder, Gallant & Associates; board-registered interventionist.

CHARLES GANT, MD. Former medical director of Tully Hill Hospital, Syracuse, New York; author.

PETER GAUMOND. Chief, Recovery Branch, Office of National Drug Control Policy, Executive Office of the President

GILBERTO GERRA. Chief of the United Nations Office on Drugs and Crime, Drug Prevention and Health Branch.

NASSIR GHAEMI, MD. Professor of psychiatry, Tufts University School of Medicine; author.

PAUL GILBERT, PHD. Head of Mental Health Research Unit, Kingsway Hospital; professor of clinical psychology, University of Derby, UK; author.

CLELLAND "GIL" GILCHRIST. Chief executive officer, New Beginnings at Waverly.

REBECCA GLADDING, MD. Clinical instructor and attending psychiatrist, UCLA Steward and Lynda Resnick Neuropsychiatric Hospital; author.

SID GOODMAN. Director, Caron Renaissance Treatment Facility, Florida.

TRICIA GREAVES. President, the Nelson Center for Emotional Healing, Brentwood, California, which uses healing principles developed by Roy Nelson.

LISA MERLO GREENE, PHD, MPE. Assistant professor of psychiatry, University of Florida; chief, Undergraduate Education, University of Florida; director, Addiction Medicine Public Health Research Group.

DANIEL K. HALL-FLAVIN, MD. Consultant in addiction and adult psychiatry, Department of Psychiatry and Psychology, Mayo Clinic, Rochester, Minnesota; assistant professor of psychiatry, Mayo Medical School; director, Addiction Psychiatry Fellowship Program, Mayo School of Graduate Medical Education; former medical director, National Council on Alcoholism and Drug Dependence, New York, NY, and Washington, D.C.

ADRON HARRIS, PHD. Director, Waggoner Center for Alcohol and Addiction Research, University of Texas at Austin.

TAMARA L. HARTL, PHD. Psychologist, VA Palo Alto Health Care System; author.

CHERYL HEALTON, PHD. Professor of clinical public health, Mailman School of Public Health of Columbia University; president and chief executive officer, American Legacy Foundation.

MELODY M. HEAPS. Founder, Treatment Alternatives for Safe Communities (TASC); chair of steering committee for HHS/SAMHSA's Partners for Recovery Initiative.

REID K. HESTER, PHD. Director, Research Division of Behavior Therapy Associates, LLP.

RALPH HINGSON, SCD. Director, Division of Epidemiology and Prevention Research, National Institute on Alcohol Abuse and Alcoholism.

NORMAN G. HOFFMANN, PHD. President of Evince Clinical Assessments.

ARTHUR TOM HORVATH, PHD. Psychologist and president, Pyrysys Psychology Group Inc.; president.

DEBRA E. JAY. Interventionist, lecturer, and columnist; author.

JEFF JAY. Professional interventionist and author.

ALEXANDRA KATEHAKIS, MFT, CSAT, CST. Clinical director, Center for Healthy Sex, Los Angeles, California.

MURRAY KELLY. Executive director, the Tobacco Healing Centre, Canada.

R. GIL KERLIKOWSKE. Director, White House Office of National Drug Control Policy.

KAREN KHALEGHI, PHD. Addictions specialist and cofounder of Creative Care in Malibu, California; author.

MORTEZA KHALEGHI, PHD. Addictions specialist and cofounder of Creative Care in Malibu, California; author.

BARBARA KILLINGER, MD. Clinical psychologist in Canada; author.

DAVID KIPPER, MD. Treats addictive disorders and practices internal medicine in Beverly Hills, California; author.

HERBERT D. KLEBER, MD. Director, Division on Substance Abuse, Columbia University College of Physicians and Surgeons; former Deputy Director for Demand Reduction, White House Office of National Drug Control Policy.

EVGENY KRUPITSKY, MD. Chief of the Laboratory of Clinical Psychopharmacology of Addictions at St. Petersburg State Pavlov Medical University, Russia.

MARLA D. KUSHNER, DO, FASAM, FSAHM. Medical director, Mercy-Dunbar and Mercy-Phillips Health Centers; clinical professor, Midwestern University, Downer's Grove, Illinois.

ALEXANDRE LAUDET, PHD. Director, Center for Study of Addictions and Recovery, National Development and Research Institutes Inc (NDRI).

FRANK LAWLIS, PHD. Served on five medical school faculties, including Stanford Medical School; director of Psychological Services, Origins Recovery Center, South Padre Island, Texas; author.

PETER A. LEVINE, PHD. Stress and trauma expert; author.

DAVID J. LINDEN. Professor of neuroscience, Johns Hopkins University School of Medicine; editor-in-chief, *The Journal of Neurophysiology*; author.

MONICA LUPPI. International Outreach and Relations Officer, San Patrignano, Italy.

G. ALAN MARLATT, PHD. Director (deceased), Addictive Behavior Research Center, University of Washington.

SARZ MAXWELL, MD, FASAM. Medical director, Chicago Recovery Alliance.

A. THOMAS MCLELLAN, PHD. Chief executive officer, Treatment Research Institute (TRI); former deputy director, White House Office of National Drug Control Policy.

VLADIMIR MENDELEVICH, MD. Professor, Kazan University; leader in Substitution Therapy in Russia.

MICHAEL M. MILLER, MD, FASAM, FAPA. Medical director, Herrington Recovery Center, Rogers Memorial Hospital, Oconomowoc, Wisconsin.; past president, American Society of Addiction Medicine; associate clinical professor, University of Wisconsin School of Medicine and Public Health.

WILLIAM R. MILLER, PHD. Emeritus distinguished professor of psychology and psychiatry, University of New Mexico.

JERRY MOE. Vice president and national director of Children's Programs, Betty Ford Center; advisory board member, National Association for Children of Alcoholics; author of numerous books about children from addicted families.

VERONICA MONET, ACS. CAM-certified sexologist, American College of Sexologists, sex educator certified through San Francisco Sex Information; anger management specialist certified through Century Anger Management; author.

JON MORGENSTERN, PHD. Vice president and director of Health and Treatment Research and Analysis, the National Center on Addiction and Substance Abuse, Columbia University.

JANE NATHANSON, LCSW, LRC, CRC. Social work, rehabilitation counseling, and consulting, Boston.

KRISTIN NEFF, PHD. Research psychologist and associate professor, University of Texas at Austin; author.

CHARLES P. O'BRIEN, MD, PHD. Professor, Department of Psychiatry, The Charles O'Brien Center for Addiction Treatment, University of Pennsylvania.

PAT OGDEN, PHD. Founder and director, Sensorimotor Psychotherapy Institute; author.

GARY PATRONEK, VMD, PHD. Veterinary medicine/epidemiology; vice president for Animal Welfare, Animal Rescue League of Boston; clinical assistant professor, Cummings School of Veterinary Medicine, Tufts University.

MICHEL PERRON. Chief executive officer, Canadian Centre on Substance Abuse, Ottawa, and chair of the Vienna Nongovernmental Organization Committee on Drugs associated with the United Nations Office on Drugs and Crime.

NANCY M. PETRY, MD. Professor of psychiatry, University of Connecticut Health Center.

BILLY PICK, JD, MSW. Regional advisor, Office of HIV/AIDS, Bureau for Global Health, United States Agency for International Development.

DREW PINSKY, MD. Board-certified internist, addiction medicine specialist, and assistant clinical professor of psychology, USC School of Medicine; host of *Lifechangers with Dr. Drew* on the CW; *DrDrew* on cable TV's HLN; *Celebrity Rehab with Dr. Drew* on VH1; and the nationally syndicated radio program *Loveline*.

VLADIMIR POZNYAK, MD. Coordinator, Management of Substance Abuse, Department of Mental Health and Substance Abuse, World Health Organization.

MICHAEL RABINOFF, DO, PHD. Psychiatrist, UCLA research faculty; author.

RICHARD A. RAWSON, PHD. Professor and associate director, UCLA Integrated Substance Abuse Programs, Semel Institute, Geffen School of Medicine, UCLA.

JURGEN REHM, MD. Director, Social and Epidemiological Research (SER) Department, Centre for Addiction and Mental Health (CAMH), Canada; professor and chair of addiction policy, Dalla Lana School of Public Health, University of Toronto; head of epidemiological research unit, Clinical Psychology and Psychotherapy, Dresden University of Technology, Dresden, Germany.

MITCH ROSENTHAL, MD. Child psychiatrist and addictions expert; founder and executive director, Rosenthal Center for Clinical and Policy Studies.

JEFFREY D. ROTH, MD, FASAM, AGPA. Addiction psychiatrist, author, and medical director, Working Sobriety Chicago; editor, *Journal of Groups in Addiction Recovery*.

KEVIN A. SABET, PHD. Assistant professor, University of Florida School of Medicine; policy consultant, columnist, thefix.com and HuffingtonPost.com; researcher through www.kevinsabet.com; former senior advisor to three U.S. presidential administrations.

RICHARD SAITZ, MD. Professor of medicine and epidemiology director, Clinical Addiction Research and Education (CARE) Unit, Boston University Schools of Medicine and Public Health, Boston Medical Center.

PAUL SAMUELS, JD. Director/president, Legal Action Center; author, advocate, litigator on discrimination issues.

SALLY SATEL, MD. Psychiatrist, Partners in Drug Abuse Rehabilitation and Counseling (PIDARC), Washington, DC; fellow, American Enterprise Institute.

JEFFREY M. SCHWARTZ, MD. Research psychiatrist, UCLA School of Medicine; author.

ALAN SCHORE, PHD. Clinical faculty, Department of Psychiatry and Biobehavioral Sciences, UCLA's David Geffen School of Medicine; editor, *Norton Series on Interpersonal Neurobiology*.

EDWARD C. SENAY, MD. Psychiatrist, Chicago; author.

HOWARD SHAFFER, PHD, CAS. Associate professor of psychology, Harvard Medical School; director, Division on Addictions, The Cambridge Health Alliance.

DANIEL J. SIEGEL, MD. Codirector, UCLA Mindful Awareness Research Center; author.

RONALD K. SIEGEL, MD. Psychiatrist and research professor, Department of Psychiatry and Biobehavioral Sciences, UCLA's Geffen School of Medicine; author.

DAVID SIMON, MD. Cofounder and medical director, Chopra Center; author.

WILLIAM SINKELE, D. MIN. Founder and executive director, Support for Addictions Prevention and Treatment (SAPTA), Nairobi, Kenya.

ANN SMITH, LPC, LMFT. Executive director, Breakthrough at Caron; pioneer of codependency treatment.

DAVID E. SMITH, MD. Chairman of addiction medicine, Newport Academy: medical director, Center Point.

MATTHEW SOUTHWELL. Managing director, Traffasi, UK; founder, UK Harm Reduction Alliance, chairman, National Drug Users Development Agency.

J. RICHARD SPATAFORA, MD, psychiatrist and medical director, National Football League.

GAIL STEKETEE, PHD. Dean and professor, Boston University School of Social Work.

JOSE SZAPOCZNIK, PHD. Professor and chair, University of Miami Miller School of Medicine, Department of Epidemiology and Public Health.

DAVID TEMPLEMAN, CEO. The Alcohol and Other Drugs Council of Australia.

BILL TEUTEBERG. Addictions interventionist, Minnesota.

MICHAEL A. TOMPKINS, PHD. Psychologist and founding partner, San Francisco Bay Area Center for Cognitive Therapy; assistant clinical professor, University of California, Berkeley; author.

KENNETH W. THOMPSON. Medical director and addiction medicine specialist, Caron.

J. SCOTT TONIGAN, PHD. Research professor, Center on Alcoholism, Substance Abuse, and Addictions (CASAA), University of New Mexico; project investigator, HelpingOthersLiveSober.org.

HAROLD C. URSCHEL, MD. Chief of medical strategy, www.EnterHealth.com; CEO, Urschel Recovery Science Institute; author.

ALEJANDRO VASSILAQUI. Executive director, Center of Information and Education for Drug Abuse Prevention (CEDRO), Peru.

NORA D. VOLKOW, MD. Director, National Institute on Drug Abuse.

GINO VUMBACA, BSW, MBA, MAICD. Executive director, Australian National Council on Drugs

LEONARD J. WEISS, MD. Psychiatrist and "addictionologist," Atlanta Behavioral Care.

ROBERT WEISS, LCSW, CSAT-S. Sexual-addiction clinician and expert; director, Sex and Intimacy Disorder Programs, Elements Behavioral Health; author.

ARNIE WEXLER, CCGC. Expert, compulsive gambling; counselor, Arnie and Sheila Wexler Associates; author.

SHEILA WEXLER, LCADC, CCGC. Expert, compulsive gambling; counselor, Arnie and Sheila Wexler Associates; author.

WILLIAM WHITE. Senior research consultant, Chestnut Health Systems.

CHARLES L. WHITFIELD, MD, FASAM. Addiction medicine, wholistic psychiatry and trauma psychology recovery physician. Author of several books on recovery from addictions and mental illness.

JEFFREY WIGAND, PHD. Founder, Smoke-Free Kids Inc.

GEORGE A.H. WILLIAMS. Vice president, Community and Government Affairs, Treatment Alternatives for Safe Communities (TASC), Chicago, Illinois.

MARIANNE WILLIAMSON. Spiritual activist, author, lecturer; founder of The Peace Alliance, a grass-roots effort supporting a United States Department of Peace.

ACKNOWLEDGMENTS

Let me begin with a special thanks to my family and friends who are in recovery, or who care for those of us in recovery. Without their enduring patience, their steadfast example, and their unwavering support throughout my own recovery and during the considerable challenge of creating this book, *Recover to Live* would never have happened.

The scores of experts from around the world who agreed to share their wisdom, their experiences, and their passion give this book its credibility, its strength, and—most important—its potential to truly make a difference. These remarkable men and women, who have dedicated their lives to finding answers to this complicated illness, immediately understood my frustration at the misinformation about addiction and recovery that permeates the media and the Internet. Those experts trusted me enough to allow me to channel my frustration and theirs into a comprehensive resource that may help lift the fog.

Bill Gladstone of Waterside Literary Agency was the architect of the project from the beginning. But many big-name publishers said no to our book because they felt it was too broad, that different addictions and their causes vary widely, that some are substance-based (e.g., alcoholism) and others are process-based (e.g., gambling). We should concentrate on just one, they said, narrow our focus.

We didn't see it that way, of course. We wanted to examine addiction in general—virtually all addictions—because we (and the experts in this book) are convinced it is a brain *disease*, a physical affliction as much as polio or arthritis. We planned to examine the causes, both genetic and environmental, of that disease. So Gladstone went beyond the big publishers and found us the perfect match in Dallas, Texas: BenBella Books and its intrepid leader, Glenn Yeffeth.

BenBella and Yeffeth said yes, and their instincts and trust were proven in August 2011, as we were in the early writing stages of the book. That's when the American Society of Addiction Medicine (ASAM) released a new definition of addiction, asserting in no uncertain terms that it is a chronic brain disorder. Said Dr. Michael Miller, past president of ASAM: "At its core, addiction isn't just a social problem or a moral problem or a criminal problem. It's a brain problem whose behaviors manifest in all these other areas."

With brain disease now the official ASAM position, we knew our book was on the right track and would be an important addition to the addiction discussion and its literature. We pushed on with renewed energy.

Randall Fitzgerald is the key component of that "we." Without Randall, who did so much of the research and writing, this book would have taken seven years to complete instead of one. This book is as much Randall's as mine and is better because of his involvement. Thanks to Jhennah Sinclaire who was instrumental in gathering and organizing so much of the detail work, primarily in the resources appendix, as well as to Alexandre Laudet, Andrea Barthwell, and Kevin Sabet for their counsel and expertise in the areas of recovery and public policy.

The entire BenBella team deserves a thank you, of course, especially those in editorial, design and production, and marketing. To name just one, editor Brian Nicol brought years of experience and a stellar talent to these pages and made them better.

A special thanks to Tom McLellan for encouraging me to do this book, for being the first expert interviewed, and for his continuing dedication to bringing knowledge and answers to our field. To my friend Jim Ramstad for being a clarion of courage, reason, and compassion in the advocacy wilderness surrounding this issue. And to my cousin Patrick Kennedy for his friendship, fearlessness, and determination in his own recovery, and for being a champion to those who confront addiction and mental illness.

Finally, a thank you in advance to all of you who will find value in this book for your own recovery or for that of a family member or friend. Keep up the good fight. None of us is alone.

Excerpt From the Author's New Book,
What Addicts Know

INTRODUCTION:
THE "GIFTS" OF ADDICTION

A huge percentage of the recovering drug addicts I know seem to have a few things in common, other than their disease: intelligence, creativity, individualism, humor, and, yes, they all seem to have or have once had enormous amounts of ambition.

> —Kristen Johnston in Guts: *The Endless Follies and Tiny Triumphs of a Giant Disaster*

I've dealt with a wide variety of individuals afflicted with the disease of addiction, and in my estimation they are the most interesting, fascinating, and gifted people I've come across. They are also the most challenging; addicts are deviously manipulative and self-absorbed. Their illness causes suffering and pain for themselves, their loved ones, and the rest of society. Yet from their struggle comes an opportunity for all.

Recovery is about exposing and healing the darker sides of being human. And honing the skills necessary for sustained recovery from addiction reveals a life-enhancing recipe that can benefit everyone. From the darkness come exquisite, profound gifts.

People who get punched in the face by the eight-hundred-pound gorilla of addiction for decades and who live to tell about it are remarkable human beings on many levels. They are not just survivors, they are teachers. And it's time we all paid closer attention to what they have to teach us about human well-being.

"What does the word 'recovery' mean? What do you get back when you recover? It is yourself," Dr. Gabor Maté told me. Maté is the Canadian physician who authored *In the Realm of Hungry Ghosts: Close Encounters with Addiction.* "There is always a loss of self before addiction starts, either from trauma or childhood emotional loss," said

Maté.

> We lose that sense of self in childhood. A child cannot soothe her own pain and an infant cannot soothe his own distress. That movement outside of our self for answers is a very natural human movement. We always think something from the outside is the answer. So we use more substances, try to acquire more things, try to achieve more and more. A lot of people who aren't considered to be addicts have the pattern of addicts. Who in our society isn't cut off from themselves? Who doesn't use behaviors to give temporary relief from stress and then can't give up those behaviors? Addiction, or the capacity to become addicted, is very close to the core of the human experience. An addict's recovery of self is a model for everybody in our culture.

That is what this book is ultimately about. Whether or not you are or have ever been an addict, whether or not you know addicts—in fact, even if you consider yourself hopelessly normal and not prone to any kind of addiction or seriously bad habits—you are still at risk and will benefit from the advice in these pages. Before you snicker with skepticism or indignation, let me tell you why I think this is true.

As a culture we've become addicted not only to gambling, drugs, alcohol, and the other usual suspects, but also to technology, the acquisition of material possessions, and every conceivable promise of instant gratification. *More is better* has become society's mantra. We eat more, spend more, take more risks, and abuse more substances...only to feel more depressed, unsatisfied, discontent, and unhappy. You may know these symptoms firsthand, or recognize them in the lives of the people you care about.

What we are usually left with is the throbbing emptiness that sets in when the fixation on more brings us nothing but more of the same old feelings of want. Consequently, most of us will do or try just about anything to escape the recurrent stress, frustration, discomfort, and boredom. Those are the warning signs on the road leading to the cliff of addiction and social dysfunction.

We've entered an unprecedented period in human history, a period where technology dominates our waking thoughts and actions, and even our dreams. Smart phones, tablets, and computers; social media and the Internet—all have given rise to an entire new category of dependency and addiction. "There's just something about the medium that's addictive," said Stanford University School of Medicine psychiatrist Elias Aboujaoude in a 2012 *Newsweek* interview. "I've seen plenty of patients who have no history of addictive behavior—or substance abuse of any kind—become addicted via the Internet and these other technologies."

Brain scans support the observation that if you are a technology addict, you feel functionally unable to quit. You may not want to believe it, but the brains of technology addicts resemble those of drug and alcohol addicts—their prefrontal cortexes have been fundamentally altered, and abnormal changes are evident in brain areas that govern decision-making, attention, and self-control.[1]

Is Addiction the New Normal?

Once you realize that the brains of technology and other addicts are different from those of non-addicts, you can't rationally continue believing addicts engage in self-destructive behaviors simply because they are weak-willed or morally flawed. Despite the "Just Say No" antidrug sentiments voiced by former First Lady Nancy Reagan in the 1980s, it's not that simple for addicts. They can't just say no, at least not without help. It's clear that as a species we are rewiring our brains, making ourselves vulnerable to addictive behaviors at an ever-faster pace and in an ever-widening range of ways. The repercussions extend to everyone on the planet.

Though we don't have a fix yet on the number of people who meet the criteria for technology addiction, we get a hint of how extensive the problem could be by looking at how many of us already actively wrestle with other toxic compulsions that negatively affect our health and lives. As I pointed out in my previous book *Recover to Live*, the following well-documented statistics for the United States are stark and revealing:

- 17 million alcoholics
- 19.9 million drug abusers
- 4 million with eating disorders
- 10 million problem gamblers
- 12 million with sexual compulsions
- 43 million cigarette smokers

[1] Tony Dokoupil. "Is the Web Driving Us Mad?" *Newsweek.* July 9, 2012.

To complete the picture, we must add in those who also admit to being *in recovery* from an addiction. At least 10 percent of US adults aged eighteen and older are recovering from drug and alcohol abuse, according to the results of an October 2012 survey by The Partnership at Drugfree.org. Add in those folks recovering from sexual compulsions, gambling addiction, smoking, and food-related issues, and we're probably talking about one in five of all adults, maybe even one in four.

Has addiction become the new normal? I don't know, but we do seem to have become a world of addicts. The toxic compulsions affecting so many people in the United States can be found spreading like a metastatic cancer to practically every culture on earth. To repeat, it's not a crisis of moral weakness and lax discipline. It's a brain disease. Medical science has now conclusively proven that.

Having this disease doesn't necessarily mean the end of your quality of life. As the history of drug and alcohol treatment and recovery demonstrates, people can and do recover—and do so magnificently— emerging from the ordeal far stronger and better prepared for life's many and varied challenges. The ways they do this offer a recovery plan for humanity itself, a plan outlined in the ten lessons in these pages.

Take Me to Your Addict

While conducting interviews for *Recover to Live*, several treatment experts emphasized how our culture still tries to overlook addicts' contributions to society and the common good. Stigmatized and marginalized, people in recovery from toxic compulsions are too often defined by their problems and not by their accomplishments, such as mastery of the life skills necessary to remain in recovery—a feat made even more remarkable because it occurs within that *more is better* cultural conditioning and overreliance on brain-altering technologies.

What can any one of us, regardless of culture or upbringing, learn from people in recovery from addiction? This book reveals the often inspiring and amazing gifts that addicts must summon and master to maintain the recovery life. But these gifts are usually overlooked by society because of the stigma still attached to the addiction itself.

If you are a non-addict, or "normie," you may be asking, *Where does addiction lead except to jail, a rehab center or hospital, the gutter, or an early grave, right?* Not so fast. Consider what it takes to be a successful addict. You've got to function halfway decently to keep feeding your addiction. You need to summon the inner resources to survive one of the most punishing and treatment-resistant brain diseases known to man, and you must manage to survive long enough to get into recovery and become a productive citizen again.

Addiction is a full-time job that requires a lot of overtime. You're an addict all day, every day, evenings, weekends, and holidays. If your addiction is to illegal drugs, your job is even harder because you need to stay out of jail so you can continue to feed your addiction. To constantly hunt down the drugs and get the money necessary to purchase the drugs, and to do this without losing your freedom, takes a lot of focus and skill. Believe it or not, these skills can become genuine assets when applied to pursuing a healthy lifestyle.

Even if your addiction is to something legal, such as alcohol or the human need for food or sex, feeding that compulsion requires the skill to prevent the rest of the world from knowing about the world you inhabit. So you hide and cover up, make constant excuses, and manipulate other people. To be a successful addict *you have to work at it like your life depends on it.* And often it does.

People recovering from toxic compulsions confront and surmount enormous traumas and challenges in their lives, much like cancer survivors or disaster survivors. And they have more than just their war stories to give us. They've mastered coping and wellness skills we all can strive to develop for healthier and happier lives of our own.

Moreover, many personality traits of addicts are the very qualities we admire and need in our leaders. This isn't just a random theory or an addict's wishful thinking, nor is it based on simply reviewing the long list of addicts throughout history who have had extraordinary lives and monumental achievements. In fact, a growing body of neuroscience research into the dopamine-using circuitry of the brain supports the contention that there is something special about the addict's mental makeup.

"What we seek in leaders is often the same kind of personality type that is found in addicts, whether they are dependent on gambling, alcohol, sex, or drugs," observed Dr. David J. Linden, a professor of neuroscience at Johns Hopkins University School of Medicine, writing in 2011 for the *New York Times.* "How can this be? We typically see addicts as weak-willed losers, while chief executives and entrepreneurs are the people with discipline and fortitude. To understand this apparent contradiction we need to look under the hood of the brain . . .

the risk-taking, novelty-seeking, and obsessive personality traits often found in addicts can be harnessed to make them very effective in the workplace. For many leaders, it's not the case that they succeed in spite of their addiction; rather, the same brain wiring and chemistry that make them addicts also confer on them behavioral traits that serve them well."

This idea of beneficial traits lurking in what otherwise looks like unbridled misery is gaining a research foothold in other fields of mental disorders. An October 2012 study in the *Journal of Psychiatric Research* found that creativity is "closely entwined with mental illness."[2]

It's never been a secret in the creative professions that, as a group, they are more likely to suffer from the full range of psychiatric disorders, including addiction, compared to people in other less creative professions. Creatives have felt or seen the flameouts firsthand. But what is new is a growing professional psychiatric acceptance that these disorders "should be viewed in a new light and that certain traits might be beneficial or desirable," noted Dr. Simon Kyaga, in an interview with the BBC. He and five Swedish colleagues at the Department of Medical Epidemiology and Biostatistics at the Karolinska Institute of Stockholm surveyed more than 1.1 million people, evaluating their psychiatric diagnoses and occupational data over a forty-year period, and found definite evidence of that link between creativity and mental disorders. "If one takes the view that certain phenomena associated with the patient's illness are beneficial, it opens the way for a new approach to treatment," said Dr. Kyaga. This would be a big step forward from the traditional black-and-white view of these diseases, meaning we can therefore "endeavor to treat the patient by removing everything regarded as morbid."

While we shouldn't romanticize people with mental disorders any more than we should people burdened with toxic compulsions, it's now possible to see the potential benefits of these afflictions without, of course, discounting the obvious liabilities and negative repercussions.

How can we separate the toxic side effects of these disorders and compulsions from the "silver linings"—the artistry, talents, and accomplishments? These are all questions worth asking because the answers, as I hope to show in this book, may ultimately benefit society and humanity as a whole.

---

[2] Simon Kyaga et al. "Mental illness, suicide and creativity: 40-year prospective total population study." *J. Psychiatr Res.* (E-pub) Oct. 9, 2012.

What We All Have to Gain

Who among us hasn't yielded to a temptation or craving that we later regretted? Is there any "normal" person who hasn't experienced a temporary loss of control or recurrent obsessive thoughts, even if it's just a musical jingle you can't get out of your head? How can we release more creativity in ourselves without becoming too much of a risk-taker? What are the most important lessons to be learned from the collective recovery experience, and what role can those in recovery play in moving human consciousness forward?

At surface level the problem facing addicts is usually easy to identify: They can't stop engaging in self-destructive behaviors. For self-described non-addicts who also want to improve their lives, the underlying problem or challenge usually isn't so obvious. Yet in digging deeper, we find important parallels to what the addict faces. It can be the feeling of "stuckness," a refusal to change, denial, dishonesty with self and others, a fear of the unknown, unrealistic expectations, feelings of entitlement, and selfishness. It can be a "quick-fix" tendency to self-medicate with toxic substances or to engage in risky behaviors to relieve boredom or stress. Such feelings and tendencies are, if nothing else, human.

Whether in the throes of a full-blown addiction or not, many of us regularly fail to make a connection between our current behaviors and the future consequences of those behaviors, a classic trait in addiction. As individuals no less than as a culture or even a species, we discount the future at our peril. We live beyond our means. We don't save for tomorrow. We postpone getting into recovery from toxic compulsions. We think that Mother Earth will somehow, someday, clean up the environmental messes we make, just like some among us think that time alone will heal all of the emotional messes they've stirred up in their families and their lives.

"We 'normies' have a lot to learn from the lessons demonstrated every day by the recovery community," explained Brenda Schell, program director at the Missouri Recovery Network, a group that works tirelessly to support people in recovery and educate the public about addiction and recovery issues. She continued:

> People in recovery from addictions have overcome things that, before I took this job, I never imagined people could overcome. I've worked with people who were dirt poor, homeless, or came

out of a prison or a ditch, and then someone, usually someone in recovery, believed in them and they got the help they needed to build a productive life. I am constantly wowed by that. I just don't see that special bond and connectedness within broader society that I see every day among those in the recovery community.

Those in recovery cultivate an attitude of gratitude. We can all benefit from having an attitude of grace about what we have been given. Addicts in recovery have a willingness to pay it forward. They support each other in the recovery community. Society would certainly benefit from that model of behavior. The Twelve Steps of Alcoholics Anonymous doesn't just pertain to alcoholics . . . How we [feel] powerless over a lot of what happens in our lives. How to take an inventory of ourselves. How to admit the exact nature of our wrongs. Being honest with ourselves and others. Being of service to others. Being a messenger of hope…pertains to all of us. These are messages and lessons that need to be carried beyond the recovery community to become a part of our whole culture.

Brenda Schell's remarks underscore why I had to write this book. The skills and techniques that facilitate recovery from an addiction can also provide self-improvement opportunities for anyone, addicted or not. That's what these pages are about.

Shedding Light on Our Darker Nature

Those of us in recovery count our blessings and are grateful. We learn how to want what we have and this helps anchor us in the present time, which is crucial because, as research shows us, a wandering, restless mind is an unhappy mind.

Because you are reading this book, you either sense or have identified a need, an area of improvement you want to focus on. But remember, there is no quick fix, either in this book or in life. I've looked for all of the quick fixes and none of them worked as advertised. So, sorry, the quick fix is a myth.

This book isn't a fad diet, either; it's not some kind of self-help fantasy. But the lessons you will learn here can make life more tolerable. The principles in this book can help you have the fullest possible human experience.

A word of caution: Don't set yourself up for failure by attempting to do all ten lessons simultaneously and incorporate them into your life all at once. Try working on them one at a time. Try to picture the ten lessons as life skills found on a circle. They can be arranged randomly on the circle or in the order I present them. They naturally overlap; life is too messy to ever be compartmentalized. Together, the ten lessons are a process you enter anywhere on the circle, based on mere chance, your own nature and preferences, or your current circumstances. As you get into the process, the order of the lessons that works best for you will become clear.

Think of them as a new lifestyle; changes you will slowly implement for the rest of your time on this planet. This thought can be scary, but just keep reminding yourself, *There are no quick fixes; quick fixes don't exist.*

Consider this book an opportunity to investigate how your life is going. Ask yourself the following questions:

Am I generally content with the way things are?
Are my emotions mostly on an even keel?
Are my personal relationships strong and supportive?
Is there enough joy in my life?

Your answers may lead to the realization that what you need is recovery—a recovery that is unique, personal, and crucial for you. Recovery is about finding something we've lost, and what we have lost is our true self. Alienation from self is a byproduct of this culture of ours and its fixations, and we are all trying to find ourselves—whether we realize it or not. Addicts in recovery have discovered a process for achieving just that.

These pages give you the practical tools mastered and lived every day by those countless people who have successfully stayed in recovery. It may take some time to get off the Ferris wheel of repeating your mistakes over and over, but if you're going to be compulsive about something, you can't do much better than relentlessly pursuing a healthy lifestyle.

So consider this book a gift from the recovery community to all of humanity. Most of society continues to accept us addicts only reluctantly, not yet knowing what we have to give back. But what you now hold in your hands could, hopefully, change all that.

ABOUT THE AUTHOR

Christopher Kennedy Lawford spent twenty years in the film and television industries as an actor, lawyer, executive, and producer. He is the author of three *New York Times* best-selling books, *Recover to Live* (2013), *Symptoms of Withdrawal: A Memoir of Snapshots and Redemption* (2005), and *Moments of Clarity* (2009). He has also published *Healing Hepatitis C* (2009) and *What Addicts Know* (2014).

In recovery for more than twenty-six years from drug addiction, Mr. Lawford campaigns tirelessly on behalf of the recovery community in both the public and private sectors. He currently works with the United Nations, the Canadian Center on Substance Abuse, the White House Office on Drug Control Policy, and the World Health Organization. He also consults with Fortune 500 companies and numerous nonprofit groups, speaking around the world on issues related to addiction, mental health, and hepatitis C.

In 2009, California Gov. Arnold Schwarzenegger appointed Mr. Lawford to the California Public Health Advisory Committee. In 2011, Mr. Lawford was named Goodwill Ambassador for the United Nations Office on Drugs and Crime to promote activities supporting drug treatment, care, and recovery. He also serves as National Advocacy Consultant for Caron Treatment Centers.

Mr. Lawford holds a bachelor of arts from Tufts University, a juris doctor from Boston College Law School, and a masters certification in clinical psychology from Harvard Medical School, where he held an academic appointment as a lecturer in psychiatry. Mr. Lawford has three children and lives in Los Angeles.

INDEX

A

abstinence, 53
  12-Step programs focused on, 242–243
  control *vs.*, 130–131, 247–248
  effects of 90 days of, 276, 287
  in imperatives for recovery, 10, 294
  recovery as more than, 295
  as unrealistic, 104, 171, 173
achievement
  fear of missing out on, 22
  importance in recovery, 293–294
acupuncture, 200–201, 234, 264–267
Adcox, Miles, 211, 213
addictions. *See also* dependencies
  animals developing, 81
  causes of, xxxiv, 47–48, 164, 208, 213, 221
  as choices, 80–81
  co-occurrences of, xxv, xxxix, xlv, 1–3, 17–19, 100–102, 144, 153, 163, 175, 226
  collection of data on experiences and recovery from, 307

  comparisons among, xxvii, 90–93, 127–128
  definitions of, xxii, xxxiv, xliii
  dependency *vs.*, xxiv, xxvii
  development of, xxix, xxxi, 225–226
  as disease, 76–79, 85, 225
  drug use without, 63, 72
  effects of, xxiii–xxv, xxxi, 38, 51–52, 58, 76–77, 227, 230
  families and, 69–70, 212, 224
  as family diseases, xxxvi, 45, 220
  family histories of, 60–61, 74
  food's relation to, 88–89
  genetic susceptibility to, 17, 226–227
  help for, xxxvi, xli–xlii, 47–48, 65–66, 234–235, 254–256
  incarceration and, 51–52, 255–256
  inconvenient truths about, xxxiv
  influences on, 6–7, 256
  myths about, 80–81, 219–220
  obesity and, 88–89
  of parents, 217–218
  prevalence of, xxii–xxiii, 304